Richard Falzmann, Wolfgang Götze, Irmgard Kunzfeld, Rudolf Puryear

Unter Mitarbeit von Anna Vollmer

New College Line

Englisch für die Fachoberschule und Berufsoberschule

1. Auflage, 1. korrigierter Nachdruck

Bestellnummer 11318

Bildungsverlag EINS
a Wolters Kluwer business

Haben Sie Anregungen oder Kritikpunkte zu diesem Buch?
Dann senden Sie eine E-Mail an 11318@bv-1.de
Autoren und Verlag freuen sich auf Ihre Rückmeldung.

www.bildungsverlag1.de

Unter dem Dach des Bildungsverlages EINS sind die Verlage Gehlen, Kieser, Stam, Dähmlow, Dümmler, Wolf, Dürr + Kessler, Konkordia und Fortis zusammengeführt.

Bildungsverlag EINS
Sieglarer Straße 2, 53842 Troisdorf

ISBN 3-427-**11318**-3

Vorwort

NEW COLLEGE LINE wendet sich an Sie: Heranwachsende und junge Erwachsene, die die Fachhochschulreife, die fachgebundene oder die allgemeine Hochschulreife anstreben.

Bei der Erstellung dieses Lehrwerkes haben wir uns von folgenden Gedanken leiten lassen:

- Sie besitzen bereits ein gewisses Maß an Kommunikationsfähigkeit. Sie wissen bereits, dass Ihre mündliche Sprachkompetenz nicht in reiner Sprechfertigkeit enden darf. Sie wollen in allen Bereichen der mündlichen Kommunikation sowohl sachlich als auch sprachlich richtig agieren oder reagieren.

- Sie wollen selbstständig arbeiten lernen oder haben dieses bereits schon praktiziert. Eigenverantwortlichkeit ist für Sie kein Fremdwort mehr.

- Sie kennen schon Projektarbeit und wissen, dass Sie hier Ihre Teamfähigkeit einbringen können. Sie wollen Ihr Problembewusstsein schärfen und problemlösendes Denken üben.

- Sie haben in den vorhergehenden Schuljahren gelernt, dass der Umgang mit einer Fremdsprache Freude bereiten kann und möchten dies vertiefen.

- Sie möchten mehr über die Länder der englischsprachigen Welt erfahren und einen Einblick in die Literatur dieser Kulturen erwerben.

Deshalb ist dieses Buch ...

- aufgeteilt in zwölf Themenbereiche (Units) mit je einem breiten Spektrum aus den Bereichen Literatur, Landeskunde und Lebenskunde.

- aufgebaut nach dem Spiralcurriculum: Alle Texte und Übungen sind einem speziellen Schwierigkeitsgrad zugeordnet.

- aufgebaut nach den Richtlinien zur Weiterentwicklung des modernen Fremdsprachenunterrichts an den Schulen der beruflichen Oberstufe.

- eine Arbeitsgrundlage für die reformierte Form der Fachhochschulreifeprüfung bzw. für die Prüfung zur fachgebundenen oder allgemeinen Hochschulreife: Sie finden viele unterschiedliche Arbeits- und Testformen, die Ihre Lesekompetenz, listening skills und Ihre Kompetenz zur Erstellung eigener Texte festigen bzw. überprüfen sollen. Diese neuen Arbeitsformen werden am Rand mit entsprechenden Icons gekennzeichnet. (Diese Icons werden im Inhaltsverzeichnis erklärt.)

Wir wünschen Ihnen viel Freude und Erfolg!

Contents

MM	*multiple matching*
MC	*multiple choice*
SAQs	*short answer questions*
Med	*mediation*
GapS	*gapped summary*
IG	*information grid*
(lightbulb symbol)	*preparative exercise*

Kennzeichnung/ Empfehlung:

■□□ *11. Klasse*
■■□ *12. Klasse*
■■■ *13. Klasse*

Unit 1: **Travel** 10

■□□	1	Talking about travel	10
■□□		Listening comprehension: Travellers' tales	11
■□□	2	Text: Globetrotting without tears	11
■■□	3	Literature: William Sutcliffe: *Are You Experienced?*	13
■■□	4	Text: Some India travel tips	18
■■□	5	Translation: Eco-tourism	20
■■■	6	Text: How to be a traveller	21
■■■	7	Literature: Tama Janowitz: Sun Poisoning	24
■■■	8	Talkline: Finding accommodation in Dublin	27

Unit 2: **Sports** 29

■□□	1	Talking about sports	29
■□□	2	Text: Some facts about bungee jumping	30
■□□	3	Text: Bungee jumper falls 300 ft to his death	31
■□□	4	Literature: Narinder Dhami: *Bend It Like Beckham*	33
■■□	5	Text: Ten reasons why snowboarding sucks	35
■■□		Listening comprehension: About skaters and snowboarders	38
■■□	6	Text: Snowboarding goes Olympics	39
■■■	7	Text: This sporting lifestyle	40
■■■	8	Translation: Get rid of those national anthems	43
■■■	9	Literature: Aldous Huxley: *Brave New World*	44
■■■	10	Talkline: Famous sportsperson	46

Unit 3: Media and Fine Arts 47

■□□	1	Talking about mass media: Are you a TV addict?	47
■□□	2	What to watch	49
■□□	3	What TV programme?	50
■■□	4	What is DAB Digital Radio?	53
■■□	5	Text: Dizzie Rascal – Prize-winner	57
■■□		Listening comprehension: I've been through madness	59
■■□	6	Text: Newspapers in Great Britain	60
■■□	7	Translation: The prince and the papers	63
■■■	8	Text: One family that forgoes screens of all sizes	64
■■■	9	Literature: Ann Beattie: *Love Always*	66
■■■	10	Text: Spray-can renegades	68
■■□	11	Talkline: Choosing a TV channel	70

Unit 4: Cultural Diversitiy 71

■□□	1	Talking about stereotypes: How tidy can you get?	71
■□□	2	Text: How Singapore deals with litterbugs	71
■□□	3	Text: School regulations in the US	73
■■□	4	Different people have different backgrounds	76
■■□	5	Text: Domestic differences in Britain	77
■■□	6	Text: Race hate in Britain is widespread – just ask my wife	80
■■□		Listening comprehension: The Bradford clashes	82
■■□	7	Translation: Britain's open society	83
■■■	8	Prejudice quiz	84
■■■	9	Literature: Amy Tan: *The Joy Luck Club*	85
■■■	10	Text: Two speeches on race relations in Britain	88
■□□	11	Talkline: What I think	90

Unit 5: The Pressure of Modern Life 92

■□□	1	Talking about crime: Young offenders in Britain	92
■□□	2	Text: A living hell in children's jails	94
■■□	3	Text: Littleton: No place to be different	97
■■□	4	Text: Britain's new epidemic: Binge drinking	100
■■□	5	Literature: Tom Wolfe: *The Bonfire of the Vanities*	103
■■■	6	Robert Crumb: *Whiteman*	105
■■■	7	Text: Road-rage	106
■■■		Listening comprehension: Death on the highway	109
■■□	8	Talkline 1: Those who sleep rough	109
■■□	9	Talkline 2: Young offenders	109

Unit 6: Employment and Economy 110

■□□	1	Talking about jobs and money	110
■□□	2	Text: Working in a summer camp	112
■■□	3	Text: First steps towards a lifetime of debts	116
■□□	4	Two role plays: On the phone/Job interview	118
■■□	5	Class project: Analysing advertisements	120
■■□	6	Literature: Bill Bryson: *Notes From A Big Country*	122
■■■	7	Text: "Shameful" pay makes British women worst off in Europe	124
■■■		Listening comprehension: Girls and IT	127
■■■	8	Literature: Edwin Arlington Robinson: *The Children Of The Night*	128
■■□	9	Talkline: Job applicants	129

Skill Section 130

A Language study and learning skills 130
1. Checking your learning environment 130
2. How to improve your learning environment and your learning habits 130
3. Learning strategies 131
4. Mind maps, clustering and flow charts 135
5. Taking notes 138
6. How to use your dictionary 139
7. Some helpful hints on how to avoid or reduce stress 140

B Writing skills 142
1. Paragraph writing 142
2. Writing a comment or composition 145
3. Dialogue writing 149
4. How to write a summary 152
5. Sentence building 154
6. Avoiding sexist language 155
7. Giving reports and writing papers 157
8. Translating into German 164
9. Describing graphs 168

C Presentation skills 169
1. Impromptu speech 169
2. How to give a presentation 170
3. Designing a handout 173

D Socialising and negotiating skills 174
1. Socialising and small talk 174
2. Telephoning 176
3. Group discussion: Working in a team 181
4. Interpreting 184
5. Dos and Don'ts when dealing with people from English speaking countries 185
6. Benimm-Regeln 187

E Literary skills 189
1. Describing cartoons and pictures 189
2. How to analyse a modern short story 190
3. Analysing a poem 191
4. Writing a poem 192
5. Analysing the elements of humour in a sketch 193

Unit 7: Aspects of Language 196

■□□	1	Talking about accents: Rudolph Dirks: *The Katzenjammer Kids*	197
■□□	2	Some sources of modern English words	197
■■□	3	Literature: George Mikes: *How To Be An Alien*	198
■■□		Listening comprehension: "We don't like your sort here"	200
■■□	4	Text: The text generation	201
■■■	5	Literature: William Shakespeare: *The Tempest*	203
■■■	6	Translation: English as a world language	207
■■■	7	Talkline: Monty Python: *The Dead Parrot*	207

Unit 8: Human Relations 210

■□□	1	Talking about secrets	210
■□□	2	Text: Teenage magazines tell secrets you should never tell	210
■□□	3	Translation: Girlie magazines	212
■■□	4	Text: Mr Huxtable gets real mad	213
■■□	5	Text: Kerry White – Teenage Mother	216
■■□	6	The ideal man	218
■■□		Listening comprehension: Ali Golding, Aboriginal woman activist?	219
■■■	7	Text: A toxin of youth	219
■■■	8	Literature: Ann Beattie: *Where You'll Find Me*	221
■□□	9	Talkline 1: Find someone who ...	225
■■□	10	Talkline 2: Talking about people	226

Unit 9: **Technology** 227

■□□	1	Talking about mobile phones	227
■■□		Listening comprehension: The decline in teenage smoking and the rise of the mobile phone	227
■■□	2	Text: "Walkout" threat over phone mast	228
■■□	3	Text: Scientists caution that their research isn't an "all clear"	229
■■■		Listening comprehension: Call centre	231
■■■	4	Text: Bionic youth	232
■■■	5	Literature: Isaac Asimov: *True Love*	235
■□□	6	Text: Ebay thief reveals tricks of the trade	238
■■■	7	Talkline: Buying equipment for your college	241

Unit 10: **Environment** 242

■□□	1	Talking about environmental issues	242
■□□	2	Text: Snowball Earth	242
■□□		Listening comprehension: Global warming threatens an Alaskan village	245
■□□	3	Text: Car drivers	247
■■□	4	Text: The cadillac that moos	249
■■□		Listening comprehension: Big Mac or big veg?	251
■■□	5	Text: Why do we still let this happen?	252
■■□	6	Literature: Daphne du Maurier: *The Birds*	256
■■■	7	Text: All dried up	259
■■■	8	Translation: As the world gets hotter, will Britain get colder?	262
■■■	9	Talkline: Councillors decide	262

Unit 11: **Politics** 263

■□□	1	Talking about politics	263
■□□	2	Text: The Code of conduct for Members of Parliament	264
■■□	3	Literature: Sue Townsend: *The Queen and I*	266
■■■	4	Translation: Our constitution for Europe	268
■■■	5	Text: "It's time to take the men-only sign off the White House door"	269
■■■		Listening comprehension: Make politics relevant	273
■■■	6	Talkline: UN Security Council	274

Unit 12: **Third World** 276

■□□	1	Talking about childhood in the "Third Word"	276
■□□	2	Text: The killing of a children's rights activist	277
■□□		Listening comprehension 1: Nine stories about child labour	279
■□□		Listening comprehension 2: Move over, you adults	279
■■□	3	Text: Developing countries	280
■■□	4	Text: Some facts on developing countries	281
■■□	5	Literature: Jonathan Lynn and Anthony Jay: *Yes Minister*	282
■■■	6	Text: Bhajis not burgers for India	287
■■□	7	Talkline: Budget Ministry for Economic Cooperation	290

Appendices 291

Talkline 291
Role Cards 312
Ausgewählte Grammatikprobleme 315
- A Eine kleine Zeitreise 315
- B If-Sätze 324
- C Die sehr aktive Rolle des Passivs im Englischen 325
- D Gerund oder Infinitiv – ein wichtiger Unterschied im Englischen 327
- E Ein elegantes Stilmittel: Partizipialkonstruktionen 331
- F Adjektiv oder Adverb – im Englischen sehr wichtig 334
- G Probleme mit bestimmten Artikeln? 336
- H Wie Sie nebenbei Ihre Ansicht einfließen lassen: Modale Hilfsverben 339
- I Erfordert seit langem besondere Aufmerksamkeit: for/since – during/while 340

Vocabulary 342

Unit 1

Travel

1 TALKING ABOUT TRAVEL

Discussing ways of travelling

• by car, with friends • InterRail ticket • coach trip • bicycle tour • backpacking • by plane, staying in a hotel • by car, with your family • camping

1. Which of the things mentioned above have you already done and when? Which of the trips did you like best? Have you done anything completely different?

2. From the ways of travelling mentioned above, pick out the one you'd like to do next. Prepare an impromptu speech (cf. skills) saying why you'd like to do it. Conclude your speech by telling your classmates what you expect from the trip.

Here are some useful words and expressions:

• great thing to do • like • prefer • look forward to (+gerund) • nice • terrific • outstanding • splendid • incredible • interesting • rewarding • challenging • offering insights • it's fun (to) • very relaxing • breathtaking

3. Give an impromptu speech (cf. skills) on this theme:
   I would never like to travel this way (again)!

Here are some useful words and expressions:

• complete failure • didn't /doesn't work at all • heartily dislike(d)/ hate(d) (+gerund) • unbelievable • incredible • disastrous • nerve-racking • tiresome • boring • terrible • I cannot recommend (+gerund) • it's not worth (+gerund) • take this as a warning

Interviewing your partner

Take the following prompts and turn them into a questionnaire. Interview your partner about his or her last holiday trip. Take notes and later report to your classmates what he/she did. Of course you can also add questions of your own or ask for more details.

• destination • sights • means of transport • alone • activities • when? • costs • best thing that happened • worst thing that happened • do it again? • why or why not?

Listening comprehension: Travellers' tales

1. Listen carefully to what happened to David, Polly and James on their backpacking tours and answer the following questions. Try to give as many details as possible:
   a) Which continents did the three backpackers travel to?
   b) Which of the three stories ends most tragically? How did it happen? What was the outcome of the other two incidents? Retell them.
2. Listen again and work in groups: If, after listening to the three stories and learning from them, you were to give guidelines to backpackers, what would they be?

Text

2 Globetrotting without tears

Stories of backpacking nightmares come a dime a dozen – almost every returning traveller has a tale to tell of at least a minor misadventure or a near-miss. It is small wonder, then, that many parents are nervous about their children heading off on long journeys to the corners of the globe. Dreadful things can happen at home, of course, but parental fears are heightened when children are out of touch for long periods and are thousands of miles away.

Early summer is the peak time of the year for backpackers to set off on world tours – about 200,000 are estimated to set off from Britain every year. Many are students with special six-month tickets who must be back for the start of the academic year in October.

So how can they increase their safety while still experiencing the natural thrills of the journey of a life time? How do they satisfy themselves and their parents? Despite all the obvious dangers, confident and trusting young people can be lulled into thinking there is little more to backpacking around the world than trekking around Britain. Take Essie Linton, 18, who is planning a six month tour which includes stops in Thailand, Indonesia, Singapore and Australia: "I've not really thought about looking after myself that much. I'm travelling with two others so I think we can rely on each other to protect ourselves. My biggest concern is losing my flight tickets. It's difficult to know what to expect until you face it. We're definitely going to be cautious, but we don't want to spoil our trip."

To ensure her safety and her parents' peace of mind, however, Essie could do a bit more. Like taking part in a pre-journey personal safety seminar of the *Suzy Lamplugh Trust* to discuss the best way to prepare for trips and how to avoid risks while abroad. The Trust has published a handbook and released a video to accompany its seminars held by 150 trained instructors across the country.

"The key to safe backpacking is to learn how to react to different difficult situations as though it's second nature," says Sarah Simpson, training director, of the backpacking seminars. "It's not simply a matter of memorising a list of certain 'dos' and 'don'ts'. By learning how to act in certain situations almost subconsciously you can avoid possible confrontations from happening at all. For example, by confidently crossing to the other side of the street if you are unsure of someone ahead, you may be avoiding a mugging."

Pippa Faithfull, another course tutor, says: "I was at the Kenyan border and took a photo – before I knew it, guards had surrounded me and pushed a machine gun to my head. I did everything wrong. I totally panicked, which only made them more suspicious; I was lucky I wasn't shoved in a cell for a night. If I had known what I know now, I would have reacted calmly and the situation would probably have been defused with much less fuss."

What you learn in the seminars are relaxation techniques including deep breathing and hand clenching exercises to help see you through nervous moments. One of the most important pieces of advice is to learn to keep cool: hot headed arguments with officials are not recommended.

Travellers in the year between school and university are often in their "difficult" mid-to-late teens, striving for independence and unwilling to listen to advice. Mr Henry Layard, a father of a 19-year-old, who has just set off on a world trip after taking part in the *Suzy Lamplugh* seminar, says: "Teenagers pay more attention to other adults than they do to parents. The seminar made the girls sit up and take notice. Afterwards, they scurried around getting guidebooks, visas and jabs – doing more in a few days than they had in months previously."

Fortunately, the number of backpackers suffering serious problems are few and far between. However, it's important to be as prepared as possible. Backpacking is meant to be fun and it certainly wouldn't be if you ended up getting yourself into trouble of some sort.

Safety tips for backpackers

- Take two photocopies of all documents (passports, medical certificates, traveller's cheque receipts).
- Wear a money belt at all times.
- Carry a personal alarm to "disorientate attackers" in an emergency.
- Phone home regularly (at least once every three weeks).
- Find out about cultures and customs so as not to upset locals.
- Steer clear of drugs and heavy drinking.
- Take a medical kit, including sterile needles and syringes.

(Adapted from **The Independent**, *Section Two, Monday 1 April 1996)*

Activities

SAQs

A Short answer questions

1. Why are parents worried when their children are setting off on backpacking tours? (3 answers)
2. What is typical about Essie Linton's attitude towards backpacking?
3. What precautions has she taken to return home safe and sound?
4. What does the Suzy Lamplugh Trust offer? (2 answers)
5. What you learn in the backpacking seminars that helps you to stay cool in dangerous moments? (3 answers)

Med

B Mediation

Was genau ist „Backpacking"? Skizzieren Sie stichpunktartig auf Deutsch die Information dazu aus dem Text (*wer? – wann? – wohin? – wie?* usw.).

C Comment

Why do you think teenagers prefer attending something like a backpacking seminar rather than listening to their parents' advice? Refer to your own experiences in similar situations.

D Writing

Go through the Safety Tips and contribute your own ideas and examples to say why these measures are useful.

E Words, words, words

Find the expressions in the text that fit the following definitions, then write a sentence with each expression.

a) A very bad dream
b) Shocking
c) To begin
d) To make something useless
e) Away from one's own country
f) To stay away from something
g) A violent attack or robbery out of doors
h) Unnecessary nervous activity
i) To try very hard to achieve something
j) To run around with short quick steps

Literature

■■□ 3 William Sutcliffe: Are you experienced?

Introduction: A gap year in India

The 'gap year' between school and university – an increasingly common phenomenon in Britain – seems today to be taking on the role of a rite of passage into adulthood. For an enterprising 18-year-old looking for something to spice up tomorrow's CV, what could be more attractive than the idea of three months in inexpensive, exotic, fascinating India? Are You Experienced, a book by the young Brit William Sutcliffe (born 1971), is the travel log of Dave's trip to India for his final fling in the year between school and university. His travelling

companion is Liz, his best friend's girlfriend, who is on a search for the 'real' India, as well as her tantric centre. Dave, who wants Liz far more than he actually wants to see India, realises shortly into the trip that he strongly dislikes Liz.
He spends the rest of the book adventuring around India and getting to know his fellow travellers, all of whom are also interested in finding their tantric centres. Dave's explorations include trains, yoga, the East Sweden Women's Hand Ball Team and food poisoning.

Pre-reading activity

What comes to your mind when you think of India? To start you off: Ganges, computer specialists, and?

On our first full day in Delhi we went to the Red Fort, which was enormous and impressive but fundamentally a bit boring. A guy just outside was selling floppy hats with a brim all the way round, wearing a huge pile of them on his head as a crowd-pulling technique. The sight of him made me realize that I felt as if someone had been dropping bricks on my head. I needed one of those hats.
'Hello, friend. You buy hat?'
'How much?'
'Best price.'
'How much?'
'What you like.'
'What I like?'
'You give price.'
'How much are they normally?'
'You give price, friend. Any price – cheap price.'
'Um … fifty rupees?'
This was just under two quid, which seemed reasonable to me, but the instant I said it he plonked a hat on my head and waited for me to pay. I'd

Annotations
rupee (19) – unit of money in India / **two quid** (20) – £ 2

obviously offered far too much, but I didn't really see how I could go about changing my mind, so I gave him the cash.

Liz, pretending that she hadn't seen what happened asked me what I had paid and laughed in my face. I said I didn't care, and thought it was a perfectly fair price for what I had got, since it was a very cool hat.

'Haven't you noticed that every other Westerner in the city is wearing one? You might as well walk around carrying a placard saying 'Tourist'.

I looked around to see if what she had said was true. A group of thirty middle-aged Europeans with a tour guide emerged from the fort. More than half of them were wearing my hat.

'Where's your tour guide, Dave? Aren't you going to join your friends?'

'Look – this isn't a fashion parade, Liz. It feels comfortable, so I'm happy. If you want to get sunstroke just so you don't look like a tourist, that's your problem.

'I am going to buy a hat. I just might not buy it from the first guy I see in front of the biggest tourist spot in the capital city. Personally, I'd rather be just that little bit unobtrusive.'

'Great idea. A hat's really going to do the trick. What else are you going to do? Put shoe polish on your face?'

'Racist.'

I wished I hadn't bought the hat now, but thanks to the argument I'd have to wear it all the time, just to show that she hadn't changed my mind. I did wonder how much everyone else had paid for it though.

Jeremy had told us that the rickshaw to and from the fort shouldn't cost more than ten rupees each way (roughly thirty pence). Our attempts to get this price were met by the rickshaw drivers with derision. Liz managed to respond to their prices with equal, if not greater derision, and I ended up spectating on twenty-minute arguments in both directions. At regular intervals either Liz or the driver marched off in a huff, and when it was Liz's turn, I felt honour-bound to follow her.

Liz managed to get the trip for fifteen going and twenty coming back, both of which she considered to be significant moral victories. Huddled in the back of the noisy, stinking rickshaw, I could tell that she expected some kind of approval for her labours.

'Well done, Liz.'

'Thanks.'

'You saved us at least 15p there. That's almost 8p each.'

'Will you stop acting like such a spoilt Westerner? We're in India, now.'

'So?'

'So you have to haggle. It's part of life.'

'You don't have to. Stump up a few extra pennies, and you don't need to stand in the midday sun screaming your head off like some deranged memsahib.'

'It's not about that, and you know it.'

'What's it about then?'

'Look – if you just take the first price they offer, you look stupid. They laugh at you behind your back.'

'So? Who cares?'

'And if Westerners go around paying double for everything, it gives us a bad reputation. It sets a bad example. It makes us all look spoilt, and far richer than we really are.'

'But we are rich. Ten rupees is nothing. It doesn't matter if we pay double.'

'That's not the point. If we did that, it would completely upset the local economy.'

'Oh, right. I see. It's like the beggars all over again. There I was, thinking you were being tight-fisted, and it turns out you're selflessly doing battle for the good of the local economy.'

'I'm getting very bored of this pseudo-worldly sarcasm, Dave. It's got nothing to do with being tight-fisted. I'm just not going to let those people make me look like an idiot.'

Annotations

unobtrusive (47) – not too obvious, discreet / **in a huff** (65) – verstimmt, eingeschnappt / **huddled** (70) – crowded in a small place / **haggle** (81) – feilschen

'And you looked really sensible giving yourself a haemorrhage over twenty pence.'

'Oh, sod off.'

We were stopped at a junction by a traffic policeman, and a pair of child beggars tapped on the side of the rickshaw, then stuck their heads pleadingly inside. Liz fished around in her money belt for coins, presumably to demonstrate that she wasn't stingy. Both myself and the beggar watched her fiddle with the money belt, which now contained a wad of notes almost half an inch thick. I saw the child's eyes widen with awe.

'I haven't got any coins,' said Liz.

The rickshaw driver revved his engine. Liz flicked through her banknotes, frantically searching for a low denomination.

'Can you give him something?'

'I thought ...'

'DON'T START', she snapped, with impressive venom. Her fuse had obviously been considerably shortened by her arguments with the rickshaw men. And by her lack of a hat.

Just then the driver turned and swore at the beggar in Hindi. The beggar ignored him, sensing that he was close to getting some money.

The driver carried on shouting at the child while I fished in my pocket for a coin. Just as the traffic began to move, I found one and put it in the child's hand as we pulled away. His wrist was knocked by the rickshaw, and I saw the coin fly out.

Spinning round to look out of the back, I saw the child on his knees in the middle of the road, oblivious to the traffic which was hooting and swerving, inches away from smashing into him. As he receded into the distance, I saw the other beggar join the search of the Tarmac, and the beginnings of a scuffle when one of them picked up the coin.

From Are You Experienced? by William Suttcliffe, London: ***Penguin Books**, 1998, pp 65-69*

Annotations
haemorrhage (110) – heavy bleeding, esp. in the brain / **rev** (122) – make an engine run very quickly / **denomination** (124) – unit of money / **Tarmac** (145) – Asphalt

Activities

SAQs

A Text comprehension – short answer questions

1. Why does Dave want to buy a hat?
2. What does the street merchant do in order to attract attention?
3. How much does he want for one hat?
4. Why is Liz basically against Dave wearing that hat?
5. How does Liz treat the rickshaw drivers? (2 answers)
6. How does Dave feel about it?
7. How does Liz justify her attempt to get the lowest possible price for a ride? (4 answers)
8. How does Liz treat the child beggars ?

B More activities

1. Dave's account of his first day in Delhi is made up of three episodes. Find headlines for them.
2. Why can it be rightly said that the child beggars are leading a hard life?
3. Find 5 adjectives to describe Liz's character.
4. Find 5 adjectives to describe Dave's character.

C Words, words, words

In three days time, Liz and Dave are going to fly back to London from Bombay Airport.

In pairs rearrange the words and phrases below in chronological order.

• take off • board the plane • leave the plane • claim baggage • walk through • metal detector • check in • go through customs procedures • wait in the passenger's lounge • land • call airline for flight confirmation • listen to passenger's call • go through passport control (2x) • get on the airport shuttle (2x) • get the boarding pass

D Writing

1. Write Dave's diary entry of the day.
2. Write Liz's diary entry of the day.
3. Write Dave's postcard home.
4. You are working for an alternative travel magazine and have witnessed the rickshaw scene. Write a short article of about 100 words about what you saw. Try to find a good headline! You can also refer to the Indian Travel Tips on page 18.

E Discussion

1. What do you think about Liz's behaviour towards the locals?
2. Could you imagine going to India for a couple of months?
3. Discuss with your partner: If you had the chance to go on a backpacking tour …

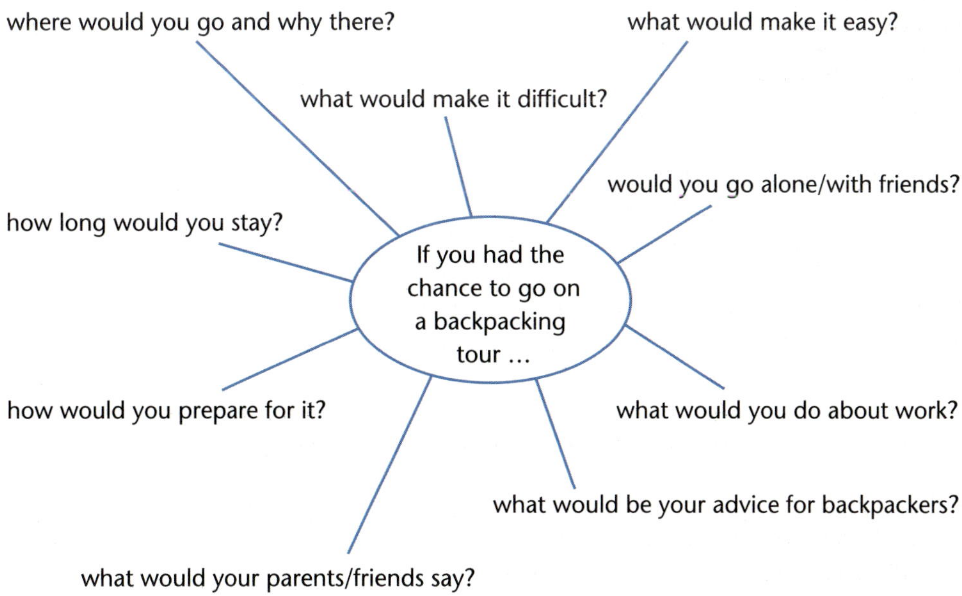

Text

4 Some India Travel Tips

Sentence completion

The following bits and pieces are missing in the text. Match the letters and the numbers. Copy the answers in your notebook.

a) been laid out in the open
b) bills normally include a service
c) by with English in
d) can be fierce
e) can be slow but you will rarely fail
f) cheaper nor easily available is technical
g) hidden underneath
h) prescription from your
i) further precaution bring water purifying
j) hat
k) is fairly low
l) little extra patience
m) negotiate the rate
n) overcharging or cheating
o) pick up additional
p) sandals
q) some places require visitors to observe
r) the same rules of safety
s) their culture, discreet

India has a well established infrastructure for western travellers. You need just a ....*(1)*.... and consideration to have a wonderful experience. The transport and the range of hotels in some ways surpass those you will find at home (except in speed and luxury) and you will comfortably get ....*(2)*.... any established tourist town or city.

What to take

As little as possible, you can buy just about everything when you are out there. Perhaps the only area in which buying in India is neither ....*(3)*.... equipment (i.e. found in camping/trekking shops, although in Nepal, these abound).

What to wear (clothes)

Bare minimum – if you buy out there, you blend in better anyway. During winter months the North and the highlands in the South do get cold at night, but at all other times lightweight cotton is best. Respect ....*(4)*.... clothing for women especially is recommend. For footwear comfortable ....*(5)*.... are all you need.

Email/Internet

Now huge in India, particularly on all well trodden travellers paths. Connection ....*(6)*.... to find a selection of Internet cafes.

General visitors tips

- Avoid drinking water from an unknown source. When in doubt ask for "Bisleri, Kinley, Aqua Fina, Himalaya, etc." mineral water (check the seal). As a ....*(7)*.... tablets.
- As in any location, there are those who steal from others, so follow ....*(8)*.... that you follow travelling anywhere else with respect to using hotel lock boxes, and keeping travel documents safe. Consider using an "interior wallet", e. g. a money or the kind that is either fastened around your neck, or around the calf or ankle. All three kinds are ....*(9)*.... clothing.

- Taxis (cabs) or auto rickshaws (three wheelers) are available from all hotels, and you ....*(10)*.... before starting your journey. Use only authorised, properly identified taxis and buses. Avoid taxis that ....*(11)*.... passengers. Don't accept an offer to share a taxi to your hotel unless you know the individual. In case of complaints against taxi or auto rickshaw for ....*(12)*.... , note down the number of the vehicle and lodge a report with Deputy Commissioner of Police (Traffic).
- There are some areas in India where malaria is still prevalent. Prior to your departure, get a ....*(13)*.... doctor for some anti-malarial tablets.
- Pharmacies or chemists are available in every little town and village and you can buy medication. In case you need to see a doctor for a specific condition, ask for help from your hotel (most have doctors on call) or your tour operator. The cost of visiting a doctor ....*(14)*.... (less than a dollar) compared to western countries.
- Do remember to bring some insect repellent. Mosquitoes in India ....*(15)*.... .
- Avoid foods which have ....*(16)*.... , avoid sweets and candies from local markets. Wash fruits before eating them.
- Do carry sunglasses, sunscreen and a .....*(17)*.... .
- Always respect religious shrines and places of worship, ...*(18)*.... a decent dress code. Take care not to violate any taboos in a mosque or a temple.
- Tipping is a matter of personal discretion. Although ....*(19)*.... charge, it is customary to tip in restaurants and other places that cater to tourists.

Adapted from http://www.thokalath.com/tourism/traveltips.php

Discussion

Choose three tips from the information sheet you consider most important and say why.

Classroom project

Prepare short reports on the following aspects of India. Consult encyclopaedias or explore the Internet.

- geography
- climate
- natural resources
- population
- caste system
- language
- religion
- parliamentary system
- educational system
- art
- modern music
- classical music
- economy and trade
- history
- Mahatma Gandhi
- sari
- food
- and?

5 Eco-tourism

Translation: *The tourism trap: the blight of eco-tourism*

Tourism is by some estimates the world's biggest industry; it's certainly among the fastest-growing, and few believe the events of Sept. 11 will cause anything more than a downward blip on a steep upward curve. In 1950 there were around 25 million international tourist visits. Currently there are around 700 million. By 2020 there will be around 1.6 billion.

As it has grown, so have its destructive effects become manifest, and these are greater than most of us might suspect. Along with television, tourism is one of the most potent agents of globalization – tourists are the shock troops of Western life-styles, distributing social and psychological viruses just as effectively as earlier colonists spread smallpox, measles and TB in their wake. And as with globalization, there are voices urging reform.

Eco-tourism is, supposedly, the antidote to mass tourism – small-scale, locally controlled, environmentally-friendly. Yet eco-tourism represents only 2 to 4 percent of international travel spending. Suppose it grew to the point where it dominated the tourist industry – with hundreds of millions of eco-tourists every year. Could such a large-scale industry be managed in a small-scale way? Can anyone who has flown halfway around the world in a jet powered by subsidized fossil fuel and puffing out greenhouse gases qualify as an eco-tourist – whatever the shape or content of the holiday that awaits them?

***David Nicholson-Lord**, Resurgence June 13, 2002 (adapted)*
http://www.alternet.org/story.html? StoryID=13371

Activities

GapS **A Gapped summary**

Fill in words form the text, one word for each number.

Like no other industry mass tourism promotes ....*(1)*.... . Only ....*(2)*.... is able to work as ....*(3)*.... and on the same scale, spreading Western attitudes and life-styles all over the world. There are ....*(4)*.... that say that eco-tourism might bring a new quality of tourism, one that helps distribute travel spending in a much fairer way as it is ....*(5)*.... ....*(6)*...., one that helps protect the environment e.g. by avoiding ....*(7)*.... ....*(8)*.... . But unfortunately such tourism cannot work on a large scale. ....*(9)*.... eco-tourism makes only a small fraction of the tourism industry, which is still growing faster than ever before in spite of worries in the ....*(10)*.... of the events of "Sept. 11" that the terrorist attacks might seriously affect the tourist boom.

B Translate the text into German.

Text

6 How to be a traveller

Pre-reading activities: Are you a tourist or a traveller?

A Discuss

What do you think is the difference between a traveller and a tourist?
Take the following aspects into consideration:

[• When do they travel? • Length of their journeys? • Where do they go to? • Motives? • Preparations? • What do they bring home?]

B Discuss

Which of the following items rather belong to a package tourist, which to a 'traveller', which probably can be found on both? Give reasons for your choice.

[• binoculars • money belt • mosquito-repellent stick • ADAC tour map • walking boots • book on the history of colonisation • small change • credit card • Swiss Army knife • can opener • diary • sweat-absorbent socks • waterproof camera • suntan oil • sleeping bag • water-purification tablets • inflatable beach ball • bug spray • Dictionary of Pidgin English • two pairs of white sneakers • latest Stephen King novel • water-resistant torch]

C Skim-reading: True or false?

The following text is highly ironical. Read it without looking up the vocabulary you don't know and try to answer the true or false questions. Compare your findings with those of your partner. Do not just say YES or NO, give details from the text to support your choices.

1. Travellers are restless.
2. Travellers are usually more interested in the places they go to than in travelling itself.
3. Travellers mainly travel to be able to tell the people at home about what they have seen.
4. Australians are illiterate.
5. Germans don't go to restaurants when they travel.
6. Travellers go to places tourists usually don't visit.
7. Travellers have a non-materialistic liberal sensibility.
8. Travellers tip generously.
9. True travellers write journals about their trips.
10. Travellers try to avoid dangerous situations.

To be a traveller, as opposed to a tourist, visitor, sightseer or international businessperson, is to understand a fundamental spatial rule in relation to yourself. It is this: you are never anywhere. You are, instead, going to somewhere and coming from somewhere else. A second, related rule is that this place that you are not at, but just so happen to be passing through, is the worst place you've ever been (even worse than the place you've come from, which was really bad) although it will in turn be superseded in badness by the destination to which you're headed. The third and arguably most crucial tenet of travelling is that you hate it; despise every lonely, draining moment of it. Until it's over. Then you love it. Then you adore each revelatory encounter and relish the privilege of being able to witness different cultures first-hand. Most of all, though, you covet that glorious hour when you can share your precious experiences in the form of a photographic slide-show with your friends. You see, travelling is first and foremost a retrospective pastime. With this in mind you can now plan ahead for the optimum travel memories available from exotic lands and far away American Express agencies around the world.

What do you take with you? A change of underwear, a mid-period Graham Greene novel and a Swiss Army knife. Unless you're Australian, that is, in which case you take most things (saucepans, bric-a-brac, two surfboards, a trails bike and a mini-van etc.) but probably leave the Graham Greene.

Or German – drop the surfboards, trails bike and minivan, add a massive rucksack, polar sleeping bag and a few more saucepans and exchange the Greene for Hesse.

Where do you go? Off the beaten track, of course. This is where you can join the multitudinous other travellers who've also left the beaten track and do what travellers like to do most: exchange horror stories about how bad things are wherever you may be.

As a traveller you should display a freedom-loving, ecosensitive, non-materialistic liberal sensibility and travel exclusively in countries whose workforce (and ecology) are under the thumb of ruthless multinational exploitation and subdued by a vicious police-state – they tend to be the cheapest. Travellers understand the value of money. Unlike tourists, they never let themselves be ripped off – this is one of the key principles which sets them apart. So don't take any nonsense from those cunning exploited and subdued Third World workers. Don't pay a single extra rupee for that three mile rickshaw ride. (In fact, it was probably only meant to be a mile but he was trying to stitch you up by pulling you the long way round. Who did he think he was dealing with? A tourist?)

When not making unfavourable comparisons with the last place they passed through or exposing unscrupulous get-rich-quick peasants, travellers write long letters or update their journals in cafes. These are laborious and dull and no one will ever read them (the letters will be thrown away and not even you will look at the journal again) but it's all part of the contemplative nature of a true traveller and, anyway, there's nothing else to do.

No traveller's travels are ever complete without surviving a dangerous situation. Typically, you should be looking to return home with at least one near-death tale to your name. The third-class train journey from Cairo to Luxor used to fulfil this role (second-class, about threepence cheaper, was empty, while you couldn't find a space in the lavatory on the third) but it's all a bit passé. Really, you won't want to settle for less than a hostage scare nowadays. Be careful, though, the last thing you need is actually to be taken captive. It would be desperately unfair on your friends and family. After all, when would they ever get to see your slide show?

*(Adapted from **The Observer LIFE**, January 9, 1994)*

Activities

A Writing a summary

1. Before you do the following task, look up a few words in your dictionary:

[• spatial • related • to supersede • destination • tenet • revelatory • to covet • retrospective • bric-a-brac • ruthless • to subdue • to rip off • cunning • peasant]

2. Now summarise the characteristics and attitudes of a 'typical' traveller.
The following outline and prompts may help you, but try to use your own words.
Try to avoid those highbrow expressions taken from the original text.

Introductory sentence (topic sentence):
... a highly ironic text about the kinds of traveller who think they are better than ...

Main body (keywords from the text):

- *destination* →
- *a retrospective pastime*
- *bric-a-brac*
- *off the beaten track*
- *freedom-loving, ecosensitive, non-materialistic, liberal*
- *money*
- *contemplative nature*
- *near-death tale*

Your version:

- *Travellers don't really like **the places they go to**, they don't even like travelling at all.*
- ...

B Appreciating the writer's tone

MM

1. The ironical touch of the text is being achieved by a number of specific writing techniques:

Exaggeration Stretching the truth	**Irony** Using a word or phrase to mean the exact opposite	**Oxymoron** Two contradictory words used together
Paradox A statement that appears contradictory to common sense	**Satire** Ridiculing or making fun of people's mistakes and weaknesses	**Different levels of language:** Highbrow versus colloquial

2. Match the examples and the writing techniques:

[• fundamental spatial rule • the worst place you've ever been • superseded in badness • you adore each revelatory encounter • precious experiences • far away American • Express agencies • probably leave the Graham Greene • exchange horror stories • "freedom loving" travellers travel in countries with a "vicious police state" • "ecosensitive" travellers travel in countries "whose ecology are under the thumb of multinational exploitation" • "non-materialistic" travellers travel in countries that "tend to be the cheapest" • ripped off • cunningly exploited (and subdued Third World workers) • to stitch you up • get-rich-quick peasants • laborious and dull]

3. Analyse the last passage of the text. Which of the writing techniques from the above grid can you find?

Literature

7 Tama Janowitz: Sun poisoning

Pre-reading activity: Predicting

You're going on a trip to the Caribbean with your boyfriend. What would you expect from a trip to a tropical island in terms of:

[• accommodation • climate • vegetation • service • meals • activities]

You never wanted to take a vacation. Just to stay home requires all of your energy, and when you go away you not only have to do all the normal, exhausting things, you also have to run around getting tickets, contact-lens solution, do the laundry, et cetera. You'd much rather just lie in bed and think about how much fun everyone else is having. But your boy-friend has a show of his paintings and decides you should both get away for a few days.

It takes days of preparation to get ready for your Haitian vacation. You take the big plunge and have your legs waxed. This is one of the most horrifying episodes you will ever undertake. By the time your appointment actually comes, you are prepared for an operation more painful than anything else. You wonder who thought up leg waxing. It involves a tiny woman screaming at you in Spanish while she pours boiling hot wax over your legs and rips out the hairs. You wish women's styles would change and that hairy legs on women would become a new trend. Somebody made a big mistake when they assigned you to a female sex role; you'll never get over feeling like a female impersonator. ...

You are staying on an island about an hour from Port-au Prince. It's curious how, at the travel agent's, the brochure of Haiti showed an island filled with palm trees and natives with excellent dentures; they must have rented palm trees just to shoot the commercials, because there is no vegetation to be seen on the entire place. ...

The only thing on the island is the hotel. You are told at once by the hotel clerk not to drink the water or eat any fresh fruits or vegetables. A surly, superior lackey leads you to your cottage, carrying a thermos of drinkable water. The cottages are A-frame, Swiss chalet type residences; whoever built this hotel saw Heidi and The Sound of Music one too many times. All the buildings are Swiss chalet type. It is as if Walt Disney had a nervous breakdown and got the plans for Bali H'ai and the Swiss Village at Disney World mixed up.

You go in for a dip and when you come out the surly lackey tells you that dinner this evening will be a barbecue by the swimming pool. You can't take a shower because the water Isn't working in your cabin, but you are told this condition is only temporary. ...

After a sleepless night slapping mosquitoes, you get up early and spend the day roasting on the beach. The maitre d' comes over to your lounge chairs and asks if you want one of the two offerings that night for dinner: boeuf bourguignon or churkey. "Jerky?" you say, thinking this is some sort of Haitian dried meat specialty. It turns out the maitre d' doesn't speak any English. You try to ask him, in French, if it would be possible to get a couple of lobsters for dinner. When you finish talking, the maitre d' gives you a puzzled look. "You choose. Boeuf bourguignon or churkey."

You realize what you have in fact said to him was something along the lines of "We are wishing for a need for the lobsters to be prepared for the luncheon event." You are furious with yourself. You have studied French for years – elementary school, high school, college. But apparently none of the lessons have sunk in.

At every meal a three-piece band plays. The band knows two songs. You call this band "The Royal Haitian Zombie Trio." You are sitting on the porch of your alpine hut, while your boyfriend sits under a tree on the beach listening to his Sony Walkman, when the three-piece combo band comes along. They are going from tree to tree, playing the two songs they know – "Yellow Bird" and "Que Sera, Sera" – to each group of sunbathers, for tips. When they arrive at your friend's seat, one starts playing the bongo drums right next to his ear. Your boyfriend can't hear them, he doesn't even turn around. After a minute or so, your boyfriend feels the vibrations from the drum and he turns to look. He points to his ears covered with headphones. You start to laugh. One by one the band stops playing. By now they can hear you laughing, and they slink off. This is the only time during your stay that the band doesn't finish a tune.

The second night your boyfriend tries to figure out some sort of rigging to keep the mosquitoes from biting his ears. Finally he comes up with the idea of wearing your bikini bottom over his head. Just his face sticks out. "They're not going to get me tonight," he says.

It's strange to see a man wearing the bottom half of a bathing suit around his head, but you don't say anything. For a while before you fall asleep you watch the little Watchman TV. Both of you can't imagine traveling anywhere without it. There's only one channel, playing the Jim Jones/Guyana movie massacre dubbed into French. Then an elderly, pudgy singer, who resembles Liberace, sings rock-and-roll songs in French while three girls wearing duck masks dance behind him. "It's funny," your boyfriend says, "I was just thinking that for kids who grow up not speaking any English, American rock – and – roll music must seem really strange. I mean, it can't make any sense to them."

You are pleased that, away from the pressures of New York you and your boyfriend are actually communicating on an intimate level. Now you are glad you have refrained from telling your boyfriend not to wear your bathing suit bottom around his head, even though he is probably stretching it out. ...

*(From: Tama Janowitz, **The slaves of New York**, 1986, excerpts)*

Annotations:
Liberace: *American singer (1919–1987), performed dressed in excentric clothes.*

Activities

A Text comprehension:

Choose one of the following visual prompts and retell the corresponding part of the story.

B Follow up activities

1. Write a phone call between the protagonist and her best friend back home complaining about the situation.
2. Write the boyfriend's letter home telling his best friend that his girlfriend might undergo a little personal crisis and might get a couple of things wrong.
3. The protagonist's diary: Write an entry.
4. Write a postcard home.
5. A phone call: Complain to your local travel agent and ask for a refund.

8 Talkline: Finding accommodation in Dublin

You are planning a school trip for your class. It is the job of your group of four to find accommodation for 30 people (16 males/14 females) for three nights (WED-SAT in July). You have 20 minutes time to come to a conclusion. In the first round each one of you informs the others about "your" quarters, its advantages and disadvantages. During this time nobody is interrupted by questions. Your task is not to read out information but to use this information to explain to the others why your choice might be good. When each member has presented "his" or "her" accommodation, you discuss the pros and cons. It is up to you to decide which criteria are important (price, size of room, facilities, etc.) and which information seems relevant. After 20 minutes your group should have come to a conclusion and decide which accommodation meets your requirements best.

Student A: please, use the information on this page; **student B**: go to page 291; **student C**: go to page 292; **student D**: go to page 294.

Isaac's Hostel

Student A:
2–5 Frenchmans Lane, Dublin 1. **Tel:** +353 1 8556215, **Fax:** +353 1 8556574,
email: hostel@isaacs.ie

Ireland's coolest hostel offering cheap accommodation in Dublin city centre. Vibrant and cosmopolitan, **Isaac's Hostel** is the place to go when you want to meet people, chill out and get lots of great information on what to do in Dublin.

Offering secure and great value accommodation in shared and private rooms, a stay in Isaac's Hostel is one you will never forget.

Once a wine warehouse, this great hostel has been refurbished to a high standard and its location, right in the city centre opposite the bus station and only one minute on foot from the train station makes it the perfect choice when staying in Dublin city.

Facilities

- Open 24 hours
- Backpacker Tour Bookings
- Live Traditional Music
- Barbecue
- Left Luggage & Safe Facilities
- Restaurant
- Self Catering Kitchen
- Bureau de Change
- Secure Keycard System
- Linen
- Internet Facilities
- Ironing Facilities
- Bike Storage

	Jan – Feb	Mar – Oct	Nov – Dec
12 – 16 bed room	€ 10.75	€ 12.50	€ 11.50
6 – 10 bed room	€ 12.50	€ 14.75	€ 12.75
4 – bed room	€ 17.50	€ 20.50	€ 17.95
Twin/Double	€ 26.00	€ 28.75	€ 26.25
Single	€ 29.50	€ 32.50	€ 29.95

Rates do not apply for Bank Holiday or Special Event weekends.

Weekend Supplement
For private rooms 1–4 beds supplement for Friday and Saturday is € 3.00
For 5+ beds supplement is € 2.00 per person

Breakfast
Continental breakfast is € 3.80 and full Irish breakfast is € 5.80.

Making a phone call

After choosing your accommodation you have booked via email. Now you want to change your reservation. Act out the phone call with a partner.

Receptionist	Caller
"Abraham House, Linda O'Reilly. How can I help you?"	Greeting. Say who you are. Say that you have made a reservation and that you would like to change from a dormitory to a 4-bedded room. Give a short explanation why. Try to be polite.
Ask for name, original reservation, dates and number of people.	Answer.
Ask caller to spell his/her name.	Answer.
Ask what day caller will be arriving.	Answer.
Explain that only a four-bed ensuite is available.	Accept. Ask what the extra cost is.
Tell caller about extra cost and say that there is no fee for changing reservations. Confirm reservation: date, number of beds, caller's name.	Thank the receptionist.
React to thanks.	Say goodbye.

Unit 2
Sports

2

■□□ 1 TALKING ABOUT SPORTS

1. Have you ever tried any of the types of sports shown above?

2. Which ones would you never try? Why?

Useful words and expressions

• terrific • gruesome • exhausting • outrageous • life threatening • adrenalin rush

3. Do you associate any kind of subculture with these types of sports?

4. Can you name 10 disciplines of the Summer Olympics?

5. Assign the sports mentioned below to the collective terms above. Work in groups and use a dictionary.

• Track and field athletics (10) • spectator sports (10) • Apparatus gymnastics (7) • trend sports (10)

• Shot-put • rings • hockey • basketball • tennis • pole vault • football • triple jump • relay • decathlon • sprint • long-horse • (throwing the) javelin • baseball • hurdling • assymetric bar • car-racing • beam • paragliding • freeclimbing • long distance running • bungee jumping • parallel bars • marathon • rowing • boxing • skateboarding • inlineskating • cycling • snowboarding • scuba diving • side-horse • parachuting • bar exercises • judo • polo • wind surfing • zorbing

Text

■□□ 2 Some facts about bungee jumping

Pre-reading activities

Imagine you are taking a bungee jump. What would you be afraid of most?

[• the height • the danger of a breaking rope • people watching you]

Ten million make the sporting leap of faith

- Bungee jumping was first seen in Britain when members of the Oxford Dangerous Sports Club leapt from Clifton Suspension Bridge, Bristol, in top hats and tails on April Fool's Day, 1979.
- Participants jump from a high point while attached to a rubber rope, which is intended to halt their fall and bounce them back up.
- The activity was inspired by a South Pacific rite in which islanders threw themselves off bamboo towers with vines around their ankles. It was commercialised by a New Zealander, A. J. Hackett, who established the Kawarau river bridge site near Queenstown in 1988.
- Across the world, more than 10 million people have tried bungee jumping. Out of the 17 known fatalities since 1986, nine were employees at jump sites, according to the North American Bungee Association, the biggest bungee organisation in the world.
- The most popular jump sites include Victoria Falls in Zimbabwe; the Hackett sites in Queenstown, New Zealand; Cairns Rainforest and Kuranda Market in Queensland, Australia; a crane on Long Island, New York; and the Ponssonas Bridge and Le Sautet sites in the French Alps.
- Bungee records: highest jump from a building: 591ft from the Sky Tower, Auckland; highest land-based jump: 1,050ft from Royal Gorge Bridge, Colorado; biggest jump from a helicopter: 3,320ft near Frankfurt.

***The Times**, May 15 2000*

Annotation
fatality (18) – death caused in an accident or in a war

Med

Mediation

Vervollständigen Sie das Exzerpt des obigen Textes. Jede Zahl steht für einen Stichpunkt.

Erster Bungee-Sprung in England am **1** – Bekleidung der Springer damals: **2** und **3** – Südseeinsulaner (Ursprung des Bungee-Springens) verwendeten statt Gummiseilen **4** und sprangen von **5** – Zahl der Todesopfer etwa seit der Kommerzialisierung: **6** – bekannteste Sprunganlage in den USA: **7** – tiefster Sprung von einer Brücke: **8**

Text

■□□ 3 Bungee jumper falls 300ft to his death

A BUNGEE jumper was killed when his rubber rope failed to halt his 300ft fall and he went head-first into a car park. The 22-year-old victim had jumped from a cable car in the Swiss Alps. Several witnesses had to be treated for shock.

Only a couple of months earlier, 21 young people died nearby in Saxetenbach while on a canyoning trip. The group including Britons, Australians, New Zealanders, South Africans and Swiss were swept away by a torrent of black water after a storm.

Bungee jumping is the fastest-growing extreme sport in the world. The activity has claimed 17 lives in the past 14 years. The Royal Society for the Prevention of Accidents has called for tougher regulation in Britain.

The American man went up in the cable car between the Stechelberg and Schilthorn mountains of the Bernese Oberland with a group of six Americans and a Korean. He was the first to jump and instead of bouncing back up he went into freefall.

Shortly before the man's death, two other groups made a 540ft jump. Swiss investigators said that the cord was not damaged or broken and they were looking into whether the organisers had failed to change it for a shorter one after the 540ft jumps.

'It's absolutely incomprehensible,' said Peter Fuez of the Shilthorn-Bahn mountain railway, which runs the cable-car service from the Alpine village of Stechelberg. 'We have been providing transport for bungee jumping since 1994 and more than 30,000 jumps have passed without incident. It was such a horrific sight.'

After the death, the Royal Society for the Prevention of Accidents said that Britons considering booking a bungee jump at home or abroad should take precautions. 'Bungee jumping is a dangerous sport,' a spokeswoman said. 'If something goes wrong, the jumpers will not be left with scratches, they will be dead. People taking part in such extreme activities should be aware of the risks.

'Would-be jumpers should choose the company and jump site carefully before booking. If they feel the information and advice they are given is unsatisfactory, they should not jump.'

However, Graham Goode, who is in charge of safety at the UK Bungee Club, a commercial organiser, said, 'This is not a dangerous sport, particularly when you look at how many horse riders have died recently. There have been no fatalities in Britain from bungee jumping except for a man who had a heart attack during a jump at a pub. The most common problems jumpers experience are rope burns and burst blood vessels in their eyes.'

Jon Nicholls, head of the UK Bungee Club, said, 'The most important thing to remember when booking a jump is to choose a club with the best safety procedures. For example, when the instructor fits your harness it should be checked by a second independent person. There should also be a second back-up connection to your harness in case the first one fails. Bungee jumping is a safe sport if procedures are followed to the letter.'

Adapted from ***The Times****, May 15 2000*

Annotations
torrent (11) – reißender Strom / **incomprehensible** (30) – cannot be understood / **back-up connection** (69) – Sicherungsverbindung

Activities

A Text comprehension

1. What happened to a 22-year-old bungee jumper in the Swiss Alps?
2. What happened only a few months earlier?
3. What might be an explanation for the bungee jumper's freefall to death?

IG

B Short answer questions

After the accident, four people were interviewed. Who are they and what did they say? Copy the grid into your notebook and fill it in. You needn't use complete sentences.

	who?	said what?
Peter Fuez		
a spokeswoman		

C Discussion

Why do extreme sports appeal to so many people?

D Words, words, words

1. Find the nouns in the text that match the explanation:
   a) action taken to prevent dangers
   b) cabin taking passengers up mountains
   c) controlling of an activity, often by laws
   d) people dying in an accident
   e) people trying to find out all the facts about an event
   f) set of straps and ropes holding the bungee jumper
   g) people who see an accident
   h) water rushing rapidly

2. Find the nouns that belong to the following verbs used in the text.
   a) to fail c) to die e) to claim g) to choose
   b) to treat d) to grow f) to provide h) to experience

Literature

■□□ 4 Narinder Dhami: Bend it like Beckham

Pre-reading activities

1. Would you say football players are being idolized too much?
2. What do you think about women's football?
3. Have you seen the movie "Bend it like Beckham" (German title: "Kick it like Beckham")? Tell the class what you know about it.
4. The main character of the following story is Jesminder (Jess) Bhamra, a 17-year-old Indian girl born in England who plays in a women's football team. What do you think the particular difficulties are she has to face being in a football team?

Our breakthrough came in the fifty-sixth minute. I'd left Zoe Turner behind yet again, and was thundering down the touchline towards Millwall's goal. I could see Jules in the penalty area, watching me. I turned smoothly on the ball and crossed it straight towards her.

Jules jumped up, high above all the other players, and headed the ball into the net. We'd equalised!

The other Harriers rushed over to Jules and leapt on her. Jules didn't even look at me so I stayed well away from the celebrations, and applauded politely.

I felt a bit left out, but I reckoned that if I *had* gone over and put my arm round Jules, she'd have punched me on the nose. I was pretty sure that no-one had ever been sent off for attacking one of their own team, but there was always a first time.

Now that Jules had scored, I wanted a goal too. It was getting more difficult for me to dodge Turner because she was becoming frustrated and trying every trick in the book to stop me. She was hassling me again as I ran into the box, keeping an eye on Jules dribbling the ball down the wing. Jules was too far away to take a shot herself, but I was perfectly placed, if I could just get away from my opponent.

The Millwall defenders were expecting a high cross into the box, but Jules outfoxed them. Instead, she hit a waist-high cross straight towards me. I didn't have time to bring the ball down because Turner was so close to me. So I trapped the ball neatly on my thigh, and fired in a volley. The Millwall goalie had no chance, and the crowd went mad as the ball flew into the net.

'YES!' I ran down the pitch, my arms outstretched, wheeling like a plane. The other girls ran after me, whooping and cheering, and we had a massive team hug. Except Jules, who stayed over the other side of the pitch, applauding politely. Just like I'd done when she'd scored.

I was flying now, and nothing and nobody could stop me. Ten minutes later, I picked up the ball from Mel, and dashed forward down the middle of the pitch. I had the goal in my sights again.

Suddenly my stomach lurched as I was yanked roughly backwards. Someone had grabbed hold of my shirt, and they weren't letting go. I staggered and spun round, losing my balance and falling on to the grass. 'What the hell are you playing at?' I yelled at Zoe Turner, as the ref came running over.

Turner glared at me. 'What's the matter, Paki?' she sneered.

I saw all shades of red. I jumped to my feet, boiling with rage, and ran at her. I gave her a hard shove with both my hands, which sent her flying, and she ended up sprawling on the grass. The Millwall team screeched with rage and began yelling at the ref to sort it out.

The ref was blowing his whistle, looking stern, and Mel was in the thick of things, trying to calm me, the ref and everyone else down. But I was too angry to care. I'd been called names before, and I'd always stood up for myself. But somehow I'd never expected it to happen to me *here*. How naive could you get?

The ref was waving Mel, Tina and some of our other players away. 'Number Seven,' he called sternly. 'Come here.'

I walked over to him, still furious and upset. I thought I was just going to get booked – until saw the red card in his hand.

'You're sending me *off*?' I gasped.

The crowd were whistling and shouting. I could even hear a few boos as I trudged off the pitch. Jules was watching me, straight-faced. She didn't look pleased or sympathetic or anything. I didn't dare look at Joe. I just made my way to the changing-room.

'You prat,' I told myself angrily. 'You shouldn't have let her get up your nose. You should just have ignored her. After all, lots of black players in the football league have to put up with that, and worse, every week.' But why did we have to put up with it, I argued silently. It wasn't right. It wasn't fair. And how come I was the one who got sent off? Was shoving someone worse than racist abuse? I didn't think so.

I was showered and changed by the time the match finished. The rest of the Harriers rushed in singing *We Are the Champions*, so I knew we'd won. I was mightily relieved. If they'd lost through being one girl down, I'd have felt horribly guilty.

I got some smiles and sympathetic looks, and Charlie ruffled my hair, but I couldn't say anything. Then I stiffened as Joe walked in.

'Well done,' he yelled over all the excited chatter. 'You were excellent!' Then he spotted me sitting forlornly on the bench, and his face changed. He strode over to me. 'What the hell's wrong with you, Bhamra?' he shouted. I jumped, and everyone else stopped talking to listen. 'I don't want to see anything like that from you again, do you hear me? We're lucky they're not suspending players from this tournament.'

He turned away, dismissing me, and I felt tears pricking at my eyelids. Where did he get off, shouting at me like that? 'Right, we've got QPR in the final,' Joe went on. 'Give yourself three cheers – hip hip ...'

I didn't join in the cheering, I was shaking with anger, as well as from the effort of trying not to cry.

When Joe walked out of the clubhouse, I ran straight after him.

'Why did you yell at me like that?' I demanded aggressively, as I caught up with him. 'You know that ref was out of order!'

'Jess,' Joe said in a much more reasonable voice, 'you could have cost us the tournament.'

'But it wasn't my fault,' I said, my voice quivering. 'You didn't have to shout at me.'

'I'm your coach, Jess,' Joe pointed out. 'I have to treat you the same as everyone else. Look, I saw her foul you. You just overreacted, that's all.'

This time I started to cry. I couldn't help it. 'That's *not* all,' I sobbed. 'She called me a Paki. But I guess you wouldn't understand what that feels like, would you?'

Joe sighed. 'I'm Irish, Jess. Of course I understand what that feels like.'

Now that I'd started crying, I didn't seem to be able to stop. Joe pulled me gently into his arms, and I sobbed against his shoulder. After a moment or two, my arms crept round his waist, and I held him tightly.

'Jesminder!'

I nearly jumped out of my skin. Oh my God, it was Dad.

Narinder Dhami: Bend It Like Beckham. Croydon 2002, p. 118 ff

---

Annotation
QPR (109) = Queens Park Rangers

Activities

SAQs

A Text comprehension – short answer questions

1. How does Jess react when Jules scores and vice versa?
2. Can you think of a reason for their behaviour?
3. What kind of player is Zoe Turner?
4. After being sent off, what are Jess' feelings?
5. How does the audience react when Jess is sent off?
6. How does Joe, the coach, treat Jess after the match?
7. What do you think: Will Jess play in the final? Find hints in the text that tell us what her chances are.

B Words, words, words

1. Use your own words to explain the following expressions and phrases from the text:
   a) "we'd equalized" (8)
   b) She was "trying every trick in the book" (23)
   c) Jess was "wheeling like a plane" (38)
   d) "we had a massive team hug" (40)
   e) "I saw all shades of red" (55)
   f) "racist abuse" (89)
2. Collect all the terms in the text a sports commentator needs to report about a football match.

C Discussion

1. Do you know of any acts of racism in sports? What are the reasons? What can be done against it?
2. What does "fair play" mean to you in football?
3. Why is there so much football hooliganism?
4. Do you think the number of players from foreign countries in professional football teams in your country should be limited?
5. Do you think sport stars earn too much money?

D More activities

Go to www.foxsearchlight.com/benditlikebeckham/ to find out more about the movie.

Text

■■□ 5 Ten reasons why snowboarding sucks

Pre-reading activities

Anticipation

The following ironical text has a few words to say against snowboarding. Here are five things the author mentions: *money – distance – weather – rules – injuries.*
What do you think the author is going to say about them?

MM

Multiple matching

Ten sentences from the following article have been removed. Choose from the sentences **A – L** the one which fits each gap (**1 – 10**). There are two sentences which you do not need to use.

A It would still be called "Snurfing".
B But do you really have to make all those signs and send all those damn ski-patrols after me?
C Ice. Sleet. High Winds. Avalanches. Rain.
D Cable cars suck, too.
E Skiers are usually wealthier, worse dressed, from farther out of town.
F Admittedly, there are respectable, decent people out there who snowboard, but they usually head for the serenity of the backcountry.
G There, I said it. Snowboarding sucks, and I can't stop thinking about it.
H 50 bucks a day for riding little chairlifts is rather criminal.
I You've got to leave everything else behind!
J True, you can't get hit by a car or eaten by a shark while snowboarding, but the nature of the activity makes it all too easy to miss an entire year of riding.
K Just getting to a place where you can snowboard is a task in itself.
L Why can't you just snowboard in your jeans and t-shirt?

"It's summertime up here in the Northern Hemisphere, which means a lot of time to skate and surf, but I only dream about the most decadent of all action sports: snowboarding. So in an effort to get through the summer, I have made a quick list of ten reasons why snowboarding sucks, and why you shouldn't even be thinking about it right now.

1. Money

Snowboarding is too expensive. If you can figure out how to get free lift tickets and equipment and still pay the bills while you snowboard all day, good for you. You probably have rich parents, and because you have rich parents you can ride all day and get good, then you'll get sponsored and get free shit you don't even need. Hooray for you, devil. **(1 ...)**

2. Distance

Do you live at the base of a snowboard mountain? I don't think so. You probably have to drive at least an hour for the closest snowboarding, closer to five if you want decent conditions. **(2 ...)** And then you have to pay for gas, find someone with a big car, try not to crash going through the passes, lose your luggage, get lost, drop your keys in the snow ...

3. Weather

Even if you were dumb enough to want to, you can't even snowboard for half of the year. Nature doesn't suck, but it knows snowboarding does, so it loves to make things harder for you. Remember all those people who took their snowboards out to sand dunes so they could ride in the summer? They were dumb! Go surfing, you morons! Of course, even if you have the right conditions, with low enough temperatures and humidity, you can still have a shitty day snowboarding. **(3 ...)** Weather is just too unpredictable and inconsistent to play an essential role in any respectable activity, so just forget it and give up.

4. Gear

What is this, professional football? Any sport where you have to spend 300 bucks and two hours to get dressed just so you don't get cold and wet, SUCKS. And I'm not even talking about all of the rave/wallet chain/retarded color fashion victims out there, I'm simply concerned about being comfortable and not losing fingers to frostbite. **(4 ...)** Boots, gloves, pants, jackets, hats, goggles: all overpriced necessities for a gigantic waste of human energy.

5. Snowboarders

Yeah, I said it: snowboarding sucks because the people doing it suck. I'm sure you could ride the lift with enough brain-dead, bad-haircutted, MTV baboons in one day that you too would learn to hate snowboarders. **(5 ...)** And if they are on a mountain, they keep their mouths shut so you don't even notice them, unlike the average snowboarding idiot who yells and wears dumb clothes and cuts off little kids and ruins snowboarding for everyone.

6. Non-snowboarders

In close confines, like riding up a lift or being in the same city, the only person worse than a snowboarder is a non-snowboarder. **(6 ...)** Skiers wear boots lined with endangered animal fur, ask stupid questions, drive Saabs etc. Bleaugh!

7. Rules

There are more stupid rules to snowboarding than I had in grade school detention. "Don't go here", "Don't do this", blah blah blah. Yeah, so maybe you are trying to keep me from getting smashed in an avalanche, and maybe you don't want me knocking people unconscious from merging trails. **(7 ...)**

8. Injuries

Hey, I'm no sissy. I can take my slams like a man: bruises, scrapes, cuts, shinners, hippers, even the occasional jammed finger or twisted ankle. But snowboarding usually ends up in season-ending injuries: broken bones, busted knees, compacted spines, snapped necks, death. **(8 ...)**

9. Skateboarding

No, really, snowboarding wouldn't even exist without skateboarding. **(9 ...)** It makes sense; the skateboard industry (and skateboarders) saw an easy, fun new activity and exploited the hell out of it.

10. Fun

OK, here's the point I'm getting at. Snowboarding sucks, for plenty of reasons, but I still keep doing it and so do you. Why? Because it is so much fun. I will put up with overpriced gear, travel for three days, endure sleet and hail, dress up like a fool, deal with stupid people, follow dumb rules and nearly kill myself doing half-ass imitations of skateboard tricks, all because snowboarding is such a ridiculously good time and I love it so much I can't let it go. **(10 ...)**"

(Text adapted from Charles Sashimi: Ten reasons why snowboarding sucks, in: "Charged", http://www.charged.com, July 2004)

Activities

SAQs

A Text comprehension – short answer questions

1. Why, according to the author, is snowboarding so expensive?
2. What recommendations would **you** give to make snowboarding as cheap as possible?
3. The ironical text makes fun of people who snowboard. Make a list of all the (negative) traits of a "typical" snowboarder.
4. Were you surprised at how the article ended?
5. Make a list of all the injuries that snowboarding can involve. Look up the words in a dictionary. There are some very slangy expressions in the text, so you'll have to use your dictionary creatively.

B Text production

1. Summarise each paragraph (1-10) in one sentence of about 15 words.
2. Write a letter to the editor on the question of whether schools should abolish skiing courses in Alpine regions.
3. Write five reasons why you like or dislike cross-country skiing. Do not try to imitate the irony of the above article.
4. Write a little story about the best day you've ever had ...

[• **snowboarding** • **skiing** • **cross-country skiing** • **staying at home and just watching the snow fall on a wonderful winter's day.**]

C Appreciating the writer's tone

> *Slang:* Informal language used between people from the same social group, often not in use for long.

1. Why do you think the author uses a lot of slang here?
2. Go through the text and make a list of all the slang expressions and try to find 'decent' equivalents:
   Example: *Snowboarding sucks = Snowboarding is boring*
3. Think of situations and contexts where you would not recommend using slang.

Listening comprehension: About skaters and snowboarders

What do snowboarders and skaters have in common? In the following story a skater claims that (real) skaters don't like snowboarders. Can you imagine what the reasons are?

Listen to what Susanna has got to say about her skater friends and take notes:

1. How does Susanna characterize skateboarders?
2. What does one of her skater friends say about snowboarders?
3. Why does one of her skater friends compare snowboarders to football players?
4. What does Susanna think about her skater friend's complaints?

Here are some words from the recording you might not know:

[• **geeky = gawky = slim and clumsy** • **7Eleven = an American chain of drugstores, where young people often meet**]

Text

6 Snowboarding goes Olympics

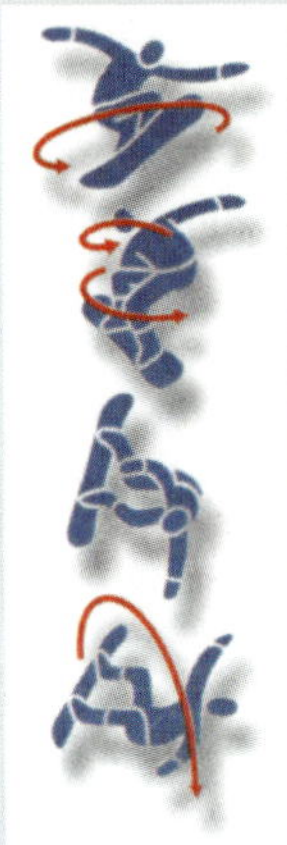

From the moment of their first scra-a-a-ape across the ski slopes, snowboarders were the outlaws of winter sport. Neon punks in baggy pants and jester hats, they hurtled down the mountain, unnerving skiers with their individualistic zigzagging. Most of these 'shredders' were teenage guys who'd crossed over from skateboarding. They approached snow in the same spirit, launching their snowboards off any handy obstacle and catapulting themselves up – way, way up – into the air.

Modern snowboarding got its start in 1965, when Sherman Poppen devised a way for his landbound kids to surf on the snow near their Michigan home. He screwed together a pair of children's skis and invented a primitive, sledgelike device his wife named the Snurfer. It was soon marketed as a $12 toy that caught on, if not quite with Hula-Hoop fervor.

That snowboarders would be sanctioned on the slopes, never mind the Olympic medal podium, was unthinkable just a few years ago. But interest in the sport exploded just as skiing's popularity sagged. Soon it wasn't just adolescent daredevils with their repertoire of don't-try-this-at-home tricks. Women, kids and young professionals began carving powder, too. After the first bruising day or two, snowboarding proved easier to learn than skiing – and surprisingly kinder and gentler on aging knees. Riders relished the simplicity of sailing through the snow on a board, chiseling graceful hip-swiveling turns into the mountain.

Some snowboarding devotees fear that the sport could lose its soul in an Olympic avalanche of commercialism. The nationalistic boosterism of the Games runs counter to the Internet-inspired, no-borders culture of boarding. And like alternative-music fans who live in fear of the day when top-40 radio discovers their favourite band, many boarders simply don't want their sport to hit the mainstream.

Many believe that the Olympics embraced snowboarding only because the administrators saw a marketing opportunity to attract young male viewers to a tired television lineup dominated by little girls on skates. "If anyone says the Olympics isn't about ratings, they're lying," many riders say. And dozens already make six figures hawking clothing and equipment and filming cult action videos. For every rider who denounces Olympic profit-making, there's another with visions of Wheaties boxes dancing in his head.

Adapted from Newsweek February 9, 1998

Annotations
jester hat (4) – Narrenkappe / **landbound** (16) – auf dem Land; nicht am Meer wohnend / **carve powder** (29) – hier: auf die Piste gehen / **nationalistic boosterism** (40) – patriotism / **hit the mainstream** (46) – in der Massenkultur aufgehen

Activities

A Text comprehension

1. Why were snowboarders once regarded as the outlaws of winter sport?
2. How did snowboarding start?
3. Why has snowboarding become attractive for so many people?
4. Why are snowboarding fans not so happy about the fact that their sport is now an Olympic discipline?
5. How have many snowboarding athletes already benefited commercially from the Games?

B Discussion

"It's not nations but talented men and women that compete in the Olympics."
Comment on this statement.

Some useful words

[• national anthem • medal table • flag • flagpole • records • perfection • sweat • preparation • concentration • officials • competition • to compete]

Text

7 This sporting lifestyle

Pre-reading activities: Talking about a cartoon

1. Describe the cartoon in full detail. (See also page 189.)
2. Impromptu speech:
   Do we take sports too seriously? You can make use of the following prompts:

[• football • Olympics • national heroes • fitness cult]

"Please, Mrs. Enright, if I let you pitch-hit for Tommy, all mothers will want to pitch-hit."

None of us can seriously hope to ignore the sports cult that has taken over the world. Political causes are dead, religion on the wane, even getting richer lacks any kind of spiritual depth. But sport and fitness seem, more than ever, to provide an absolute that crosses all cultural boundaries.

Bodily perfection has become the ultimate value. You can argue about whether you want more money, more art or more fun, but everybody, whether they admit it or not, wants a better body.

You can't deny the simple spectacle of somebody running or swimming faster than anybody else. Nor can you deny that those super-cultivated, perfect bodies represent one instantly recognisable, universally acceptable form of human perfection. Indeed, in a confusingly plural world, in which all values are relativised, they begin to represent the only such form. In every other field of human activity, excuses can be made. You don't get on in your career because you have been unfairly treated, or your genius is not recognised because the system is against you. Losing athletes may attempt similar excuses; but, in reality, the other guy is simply going faster, higher or longer. This is too clear a judgement to be relativised by anything.

This is why many athletes are tempted into chemically driving the body to even greater heights. However, doping drags the whole thing back down to the old excuse-laden, relativised marketplace. We don't like sporting drugs because we can't see them. Some hidden cocktail is driving these limbs, not simply determination and fitness. Sport is reduced to a technological arms race like any other. Winning becomes ambiguous, as in Formula One motor racing – is it the driver or the car we applaud? Drugging an athlete makes him into a vehicle, a dualism of chemicals and body, when what we really want from sport is the simple, visible spectacle of human beings stretched to their physical limits.

And we seem to want it now more than ever. The worship of the idea of fitness has become big business. Health, physical and spiritual, became identified with specific rituals – the gym, the jog – and with specific clothes that were worn even when not exercising – the training shoe, the tracksuit. Even pop stars behaving badly, like angry Brit poppers or American gangsta rappers, have helped to sell sportswear, turning it into an essential teen accessory.

Whole nations, which usually compete over conflicting views of economics or ideology, feel obliged to confront each other bodily. Those Chinese gymnasts are expressions not just of individual excellence, but also of the conviction of the ancient imperial Middle Kingdom that it alone possesses the key to all human perfection.

In America sport is even more intensely cherished. Athletes have become superrich gods. In the movies the best thing that can happen to an American dad is that his underachieving son can make a heroic catch in baseball. And the supreme image of familial stability is the basketball net in the yard.

On the other hand, however, there is the world of American high school game. This world – simple, innocent, direct – is now being carefully resurrected by Americans anxious to recapture the older, gentler America that preceded Vietnam and urban decay. They want sport to exist as a reinforcement of small town values, peace and security; they want it to be part of, not the whole of, a culture.

(Adapted from: This sporting lifestyle, The Independent 25 July, 1996)

Activities

A Text comprehension

1. Comment on the author's statement that *"political causes are dead, religion (is) on the wane, (and) even getting richer lacks any kind of spiritual depth."* (line 2)
2. What, according to the author, is the difference between competing in sports and competing in other fields of human activity?
3. Why, according to the text, do many athletes turn to doping? What other reasons do **you** think there are?
4. What does the author mean when he compares chemically drugged athletes to Formula-One motor racing?
5. Why, according to the text, can it be rightly said that the idea of fitness has become big business? Find more aspects to underline this idea. Make use of the following prompts:

[• **super contracts** • **lucrative prizes** • **TV- coverage** • **advertising** • **merchandising**]

6. What role do sports play in the way nations see themselves?
7. What trend does the author see in the world of the American high school game?
8. What image of America do you think the author has in mind when he speaks of *"... the older, gentler America that preceded Vietnam and urban decay?"* (line 76)

B Appreciating the writer's tone: Emphasis

Emphasis: Force or stress given to words to show importance.

In this text the author puts a lot of **emphasis** on what he says. He does so by using words that have a kind of **absolute** meaning, as in line 5:
*"... sport and fitness seem to provide an **absolute** that crosses all cultural boundaries."*
Find more examples from the text: ***too clear*** (line 28), ...

The same effect – emphasis – is achieved by inversion in lines 28:
"This is too clear a judgement to be relativised by anything."
The regular word order is:
"This is a judgement that is too clear to be relativised by anything."

Build sentences from the following prompts by using inversion:

1.	*story*	*long*	*to tell in a few minutes*
2.	*matter*	*delicate*	*to investigate in public*
3.	*problem*	*difficult*	*to solve in a minute*
4.	*friend*	*good*	*to ever forget*
5.	*situation*	*obvious*	*to deny*
6.	*temptation*	*big*	*not to consider the athletes*

Translation: *Get rid of those national anthems*

A ritual is performed before the start of each Six Nations' rugby match, namely the playing of national anthems or, at least, songs of a national character. For some, they offer a heart-swelling moment; for others, me among them, they are stomach-turning.

This is not just because the rugby teams of all participating nations contain people born and brought up in New Zealand, Australia, South Africa, Algeria and Argentina, making nonsense of the idea of a 'national team'. It is worse than that – it is the connection of innocent national ardour in sporting events with the ugly cancer of nationalism.

The central weakness of nationalism is the emptiness of the concept of a 'nation'. Consider the English and the Americans: they are the most mongrel of 'nations'; the idea of an English ethnicity is absurd, that of an American one bizarre.

The biggest mistake is to confuse culture and nationality. There is no country in the world which is not home to several co-existing cultures. Cultural heritage is not the same thing as national identity; Europe has a culture which its many peoples share, in art, music, dance, institutions, related languages and religions, and its bonds are stronger and deeper than the historical accident of where the current boundaries of Europe's states have been left by war and the greed of past kings and emperors.

Sport should be something that draws people together rather than dividing them. Instead of national songs, rugby matches should begin with a single anthem, in which all can participate for the joy of the game, and in which the prowess and honour of a team on the pitch, not a 'nation' it is supposed gladiatorially to represent, is alone what matters.

A. C. Grayling
The Observer Sunday February 10, 2002 (adapted)
http://www.observer.co.uk/comment/story/0,6903,647869,00.html

Literature

9 Aldous Huxley: Brave New World (1932)

Brave New World (1932), an ironic vision of a future utopia 600 years from now, established Huxley's fame. In his novel, Huxley anticipates a world order based on the cloning and manipulation of human life. There are dominant – and unique – 'alphas' down to inferior 'epsilons', groups of up to 96 genetically identical human beings labouring in the factories. Soma, a state controlled drug, keeps everybody happy.
In the following excerpt students are guided through The 'Central London Hatchery and Conditioning Center', where human beings are 'bred' in bottles and brought up.

(Illustration: Chinese Propaganda Poster from the era of Mao Zedong; Süddeutsche Zeitung, Juli 2004)

"Outside in the garden, it was playtime. Naked in the warm June sunshine, six or seven hundred little boys were running with shrill yells over the lawns, or playing ballgames, or squatting silently in twos or threes among the flowering shrubs. The roses were in bloom, two nightingales soliloquized in the boskage, a cuckoo was just going out of tune among the lime trees. The air was drowsy with the murmur of bees and helicopters.

The director and his students stood for a short time watching a game of Centrifugal Bumble-puppy. Twenty children were grouped in a circle round a chrome steel tower. A ball thrown up so as to land on the platform at the top of the tower rolled down into the interior, fell on a rapidly revolving disk, was hurled through one of the numerous apertures pierced in the cylindrical casing, and had to be caught.

'Strange' mused the Director, as they turned away, 'strange to think that even in our Ford's day most games were played without more apparatus than a ball or two and a few sticks and perhaps a bit of netting. Imagine the folly of allowing people to play elaborate games which do nothing whatever to increase consumption. It's madness. Nowadays the Controllers won't approve of any new game unless it can be shown that it requires at least as much apparatus as the most complicated of existing games.' He interrupted himself. 'That's a charming little group,' he said, pointing."

Annotations
to soliloquize (6) – to sing a solo / **boskage** (7) – shrubs / **apertures** (17) – openings

Activities

A Text comprehension

1. Read the first passage (lines 1–9) and say which things in the scene seem to be normal, which unusual.
2. Read the second passage (lines 10–18) and decide which of the following adjectives best describe the ball game:

[• organic • technical • difficult • funny • easy • futuristic • simple • challenging]

3. Look at the following three details from the third passage (lines 19–31) and try to say what kind of society Huxley describes in his novel:

[• the Director • in our Ford's day • the Controllers]

4. Find the word in the third passage that sums up the key principle the society Huxely describes is based upon.
5. What happened to sports in the Brave New World?

B Extension

In groups decide which of the following sports would have a very good image in the Brave New World – offering enough 'apparatus'– and which would be forbidden.
Rank them in a list and give reasons.

[• mountain biking • rafting • yoga • soccer • American football • working out in a fitness centre • judo • skateboarding • Chinese shadowboxing • Formula-One motor racing • running]

Will football radio kill the video star?

Radio, not video, could be the best way to decide if the ball crosses the goalline. Inspired by Geoff Hurst's famous goal in the 1966 World Cup final, a German company has developed technology that tracks the ball and instantly tells the referee if the goal is scored. A tiny radio chip sewn into the ball transmits 2,000 signals a second to a network of aerials hidden in the floodlight or under the stadium roof.

Oliver Braun of Cairos Technologies, which devised the technology, says this allows a computer to pinpoint the ball's position to within 1.5 centimetres anywhere on the pitch. The technology also works in 3D so it can detect when the ball crosses the line in the air. The system does away with one of the strongest arguments against using video evidence – the time taken for referees to stop the game and make up their minds. When the computerised system registers a goal, it immediately sends a message to a vibrating sleeve worn by the referee.

Braun says: "No one has to sit and watch and push a button if it's a goal or not. The information is beamed only to the ref, not to the fans or media. It's still the decision of the ref but he is more sure the decison is correct."

Similar chips in shin-guards can track the players and help judge everything from offsides and if the wall is far enough away at freekicks to whether the goalkeeper moved off his line before a penalty.

The system is undergoing final testing at the Fraunhofer Institut at Nuremberg. Braun says it will be ready in time for the start of next season. The idea came from one of our shareholders who is a crazy football fan and was always angry about how you guys won the World Cup in '66."

Cairos could install the system at top football clubs for free and sell the information gathered to the media and fans as virtual replays. "A fan could download a game and watch it on his PlayStation, but choose the angle of the camera or watch it from the perspective of the favourite player." Several Premiership teams have expressed interest in using the data to coach players. The FA's spokesman Andrin Cooper said the International Football Association Board, the body responsible for the laws of the game, would discuss the technology...

Fifa's president Sepp Blatter has long opposed the use of video replays but, as well as ensuring the flow of the game is unaffected, radio technology would alleviate several other problems that video technology could cause.

One of the most appealing aspects of the radio technology is that the presence of players surrounding the ball, and the angle of view, would not affect the outcome of a decision unlike in video technology.

(adapted from: Guardian Newspapers, March 2005)

GapS **Gapped summary**

A German company has invented a ball which *...(1)...* tells the referee that a goal was scored. On the *...(2)...* the ball is constantly tracked by an internal chip that *...(3)...* its data immediately to a number of invisible *...(4)...* . A spokesperson of the German firm says that the system is able to *...(5)...* the ball even in midair. The advantage over a video replay is the immediacy of the new technology. As soon as the computer *...(6)...* a goal, it exclusively informs the referee by producing vibrations on his *...(7)...* . It is still up to the ref to make up his mind, but he can be quite sure that his *...(8)...* is closer to the truth.
Some famous football teams are interested in the system and even a high-ranking official of the Fifa is convinced that the new technology can *...(9)... ...(10)...* disadvantages of video replays.

■■■ 10 Talkline: Famous sportsperson

Your local town council is considering naming a new street after a famous sportsperson. Your college has been asked to make suggestions. Your task is not to read out the facts to your class mates. (**Student A**: use the information on page 297; **student B**: go to page 298; **student C**: go to page 299; **student D**: go to page 299.)

Unit 3

Media and Fine Arts

3

■□□ 1 TALKING ABOUT MASS MEDIA: ARE YOU A TV ADDICT?

Addicts always think they could give up if they really wanted, but when it comes to the crunch, they can't. Find out how far down the path to total telly addiction you are.

1. On an evening in, how often do you turn the TV on?
a) Always or nearly always b) Frequently
c) Occasionally d) Rarely

2. How many hours of TV do you watch each week?
a) 0–10 b) 11–20 c) 21–0 d) Over 30

3. Do you consider what's on TV before you go out?
a) Always or nearly always b) Frequently
c) Occasionally d) Never or rarely

4. Is there more than one programme you can't miss?
a) Yes b) No

5. What are you most likely to do when watching TV?
a) Concentrate on the screen with just an occasional chat
b) Keep half an eye on the screen while doing something else
c) Watch intently when a programme interests you, but otherwise wander off to do something else

6. Do you turn the TV on ...
a) when you come home and off when you go to bed?
b) just for a particular programme
c) When you can't think of anything else to do?

7. How do you decide what to watch?
a) Buy a TV magazine and plan ahead?
b) Read the daily paper to plan your evening's viewing
c) Read the paper in the evening to see what's on?
d) Just turn on and flick between channels?

8. On pain of death, you can't watch TV for a month. How do you feel?
a) Taken aback – you're not quite sure what you'll do instead
b) Appalled
c) Intrigued – you start to think of what you might do instead
d) Unconcerned. You don't watch it much anyway

Scoring
1a - 4, 1b - 3, 1c - 1, 1d - 1; 2a - 1, 2b - 2, 2c - 3, 2d - 4; 3a - 4, 3b - 3, 3c - 2, 3d - 1; 4a - 3, 4b - 1; 5a - 4, 5b - 3, 5c - 1, 5d - 2; 6a - 4, 6b - 1, 6c - 2, 6d - 2; 7a - 4, 7b - 3, 7c - 1, 7d - 2; 8a - 4, 8b - 3, 8c - 2, 8d - 1

Results
8–12: Virtue itself – your telly is kept firmly in its place. You see what you want when you want, but there are so many other things you like to do that there is just no time to watch any more.
3–18: You have a comfortable relation-ship with your TV. You keep up with what's on, but don't let it dominate your life. Keep it that way.
19–26: This is getting serious. Did you realize hust how much of an addict you've become? If you're trying to laugh it off, we dare you to put yourself to the test with our Off With The Telly Week.
27–31: You are a confirmed addict. Heaven help you if the TV set breaks down!

(By Gill Hudson, in Company, February 1988)

2 What to watch

Have a look at this cartoon:

What do the parents expect?
What do the kids want to watch?
Comment on the difference.

Activities

A Viewing habits

1. What kinds of programmes do you like to watch?
2. Have you changed your viewing habits since your childhood?
3. Do you think that kids are offered enough 'good' programmes nowadays? Discuss your opinion in class.
4. Why are TV cartoons so popular? Think of one you know, then write down every aspect that comes to mind and compare your notes with those of your classmates.
5. Do you know how many cartoons are offered on TV? Have a guess and try to find out the number by checking a TV magazine.

B Paragraph writing

1. How do you and your family avoid discussions about what to watch on TV? Collect as many suggestions as possible – work in groups. Select the three suggestions that you think are the most important. Arrange them in order of importance and write a short paragraph about each.
2. Many parents punish their children by turning off the television. Write a short paragraph pointing out that you feel that this is an unjustified measure.

3 What TV programme?

BBC1

6.00 BBC News
PM With George Alagiah and Sophie Raworth. Including a weather summary. (S) (W) www.bbc.co.uk/news *354*

6.30 Regional news magazine Details on Monday (S) (W) *606*
Followed by **Weather** with Helen Willetts. (S) (W)

7.00 Airport
Preparations for a historic visit are hampered by the wind.
Producer Suni Aden; Series producer David Russell (R) (S) (W) *9441*

7.30 EastEnders
Den and Phil swap home truths. Shirley gets her own back.

Den Watts	**Leslie Grantham**	Yolande Duke	**Angela Wynter**
Lisa Fowler	**Lucy Benjamin**	Paul Trueman	**Gary Beadle**
Phil Mitchell	**Steve McFadden**	Janine Butcher	**Charlie Brooks**
Sharon Watts	**Letitia Dean**	Barry Evans	**Shaun Williamson**
Dennis Rickman	**Nigel Harman**	Ian Beale	**Adam Woodyatt**
Vicki Fowler	**Scarlett Johnson**	Gus Smith	**Mohammed George**
Billy Mitchell	**Perry Fenwick**	Asif Malik	**Ashvin Luximon**
Little Mo Mitchell	**Kacey Ainsworth**	Martin Fowler	**James Alexandrou**
Shirley Benson	**Robyn Moore**	Garry Hobbs	**Ricky Groves**
Pauline Fowler	**Wendy Richard**	Kelly Taylor	**Brooke Kinsella**
Dot Cotton	**June Brown**	Kate Mitchell	**Jill Halfpenny**
Patrick Trueman	**Rudolph Walker**	Minty Peterson	**Cliff Parisi**

Written by Carey Andrews; This week's episodes produced and directed by Nicholas Prosser Repeated at 10pm on BBC3 (S) (W) *118*
Like *EastEnders* on your mobile? Visit www.radiotimes.com

8.00 Garden SOS
Barrie, the leader of Raffles Community Centre in Carlisle, presides over a lot of good work, but not in the garden. The team have just three days to sort it out – a tall order given the scale of the project. Plus, in this last of the series, vote once more for one of the three most popular losing appeals.
Series producer Adrian MacFarlane; Executive producer Jane Lomas (S) (W)*5489*
BOOKLET: £3.95 (inc p&p). Send cheque, payable to the BBC, to: Garden SOS, PO Box 7000, Manchester M60 3HE, or order online at www.bbc.co.uk/beyond

8.30 Bargain Hunt
Trying to conjure up some success today are two teams of amateur magicians who are in Kedleston, Derbyshire, seeking antique bargains. With David Dickinson.
Director Martin O'Collins; Series producer Linda Cleeve (S) (W) *4996*
TAKE PART: visit www.bbc.co.uk/antiques or call 0900 180 0300 (cost 60p)

9.00 Canterbury Tales
CHOICE *The Pardoner's Tale.* In the town of Rochester the local community launch a search for a missing teenager. But then three unemployed wastrels attempt to cash in.

Arty	**Jonny Lee Miller**	Viv Healey	**Tonya Kerins**
Kitty Norman	**Samantha Whittaker**	Amy Healey	**Jade Williams**
Baz	**Ben Bennett**	Chloe Healey	**Jaymie Pennington**
Colin	**William Beck**	Arty's mother	**Vivienne Ritchie**
Mr Norman	**Robert East**	Arty's father	**Richard Hope**
Mrs Norman	**Jill Baker**	Old man	**Rob Brown**
Mandy Briggs	**Melissa Lloyd**	Mrs Preston	**Maxine Evans**
Ian Healey	**Ian Burfield**	Uncle Ronald	**Jack Chissick**

Written by Tony Grounds; Producer Kate Bartlett
Director Andy De Emmony (S) (W) www.bbc.co.uk/canterburytales *4606*

10.00 BBC News With Huw Edwards. **10.25 Regional News**
Followed by **Weather** with Helen Willets. (S) (W) *652793*

10.35 Question Time
Conservative Party chairman Theresa May is among the panellists taking part in this week's topical debate from Morecambe, Lancashire. Chaired by David Dimbleby.
Executive producer George Carey; Series editor Nick Pisani (S) (W) *275793*
CONTACT DETAILS: phone 0901 111 4411 (calls charged at 25p) or email via the programme's website: www.bbc.co.uk/questiontime

BBC2

6.00 The Simpsons
PM *Bart the Murderer.* Mixing with mobsters could spell disaster for Bart. (R) (S) *429373*

6.20 The Fresh Prince of Bel-Air
The Butler Did It. Will rents the house out to a production company that's shooting a music video. (R) (S) *430489*

6.45 Snooker
Round-three coverage of the LG Cup continues at the Guild Hall. Introduced by Hazel Irvine, with Steve Davis and John Parrott. Commentary comes from Clive Everton, Dennis Taylor, Willie Thorne and John Virgo.
(S) (W) www.bbc.co.uk/snooker *799915*

7.30 Essential Poems for Britain
CHOICE In celebration of National Poetry Day, a distinguished line-up of actors – including Timothy West, John Hurt, Sheila Hancock and John Thomson – read an eclectic selection of well-loved verse. Philip Larkin's *An Arundel Tomb* and Robert Browning's *Home Thoughts from Abroad* are just two of the poems that variously sum up the essential Britishness in us all. Presented by Daisy Goodwin. Including the results of the first BBC national poetry competition.
Director/Producer Sally George (S) (W) *460*
Ian McMillan – Poetry of Britain: a Peregrination is on Radio 4 at 8pm
RT SHOP: *Nation's Favourite Poems* boxed set, £27; *Nation's Favourite Poems of Celebration,* £5.99; *Nation's Favourite Poems of Childhood,* £5.99; *Nation's Favourite Poems of Desire,* £6.99; *Nation's Favourite Poems of Remembrance,* £6.99; *Nation's Favourite Poems of Journeys,* £5.99; *Nation's Favourite Poems,* £9.99. To order any book call 0870 770 7979 (national rate)
Daisy Goodwin on National Poetry Day: page 27

8.00 Time Commanders
It's 48 BC, and mighty Julius Caesar marshals his army in the civil war for control of the Roman state. Tonight's team of modern-day commanders attempt to defeat the military genius, thus saving the Republic. Hosted by Eddie Mair.
Series producer Ludo Graham
Executive producers Cassian Harrison and Adam Macdonald (S) (W) *5712*

9.00 Seven Wonders of the Industrial World
Drama-documentary, focusing on great visionaries whose technological achievements shaped the modern world. *The Panama Canal.* French engineer Ferdinand de Lesseps's grand scheme was to build a canal across Panama that would link the Atlantic and Pacific Oceans. Work started in 1880, but, rocked by financial scandal, the plan was not completed until 20 years after de Lessep's death in 1894.

Monsieur de Lesseps	**John Walters**	Dingler	**Stephen Mangan**
Goethals	**Angus MacInnes**	Bunau Varilla	**Daniel Coonan**
Gorgas	**Robert Jezek**	Madame de Lesseps	**Cora Branley**
Stevens	**Jeff Harding**	Marie Gorgas	**Tara Hugo**

Written by Rachel Wright; Producer Philip Smith
Series producer Deborah Cadbury (S) (W) *646426*
BBC EDUCATION: for information on special events, and to claim a free poster, phone 0870 902 0777 (calls are charged at the national rate)

9.50 Industrial Nation
Adam Hart-Davis meets fans with a passion for reconstructing the heritage of the industrial revolution in the third of four editions. Hart-Davis presents *Science Shack* at 12.30am.
Series producer Archie Barron; Executive producer Stephen Haggard (S) (W)*462489*

10.00 QI
Gyles Brandreth, Rob Brydon, Alan Davies and Rich Hall guest on the comedy quiz show. Hosted by Stephen Fry. The next edition follows on BBC4 at 10.30pm.
Director Ian Lorimer; Producer John Lloyd (S) (W) *58118*

10.30 Newsnight Presented by Gavin Esler. (S) (W) *561002*

Source: Radio Times, p. 136, August 2005

ITV1 London

6.00 Regional news magazine Details on Monday (S) *422*
PM Followed by **Regional Weather**

6.30 ITV Evening News With Mark Austin and Mary Nightingale. **Weather** with Martyn Davies. (S) *642*

7.00 Emmerdale
Andy has a surprise visitor, while Debbie struggles to deal with her warring parents. Zoe decides to move back home.
Today's episode written by Chris Thompson For cast see Tuesday
Repeated tomorrow at 9.55am on ITV2 (S) (W) *1809*

7.30 Friday Night Fight Club
Documentary illustrating a typical weekend for Southend emergency services dealing with teenage binge drinkers who cause problems in the seafront town.
Director Neil Rawles (W) *286*

8.00 The Bill
On her first day, new PC Yvonne Hemmingway proves that she's no pushover when she deals with a girl gang. Jack Meadows tries to extract information over lunch with Sally Johnson. Des quizzes Sheelagh about the baby.

PC Yvonne Hemmingway	**Michele Austin**	Beth Tyler	**Seroca Davis**
		PC Honey Harman	**Kim Tiddy**
PC Nick Klein	**Rene Zagger**	PC Tony Stamp	**Graham Cole**
PC Kerry Young	**Beth Cordingly**	Josie Pike	**Alix Wilton-Regan**
Annabelle Jameson	**Amanda Drew**	Margaret Flint	**Yvonne O'Grady**
Warren Jameson	**Ken Bradshaw**	PC Cathy Bradford	**Connie Hyde**
Carly Flint	**Ophelia Lovibond**	Max Wyatt	**David Cardy**

Written by Maxwell Young; Producer Tom Cotter
Director Sue Tully (S) (W) www.thebill.com *9538*

9.00 Sweet Medicine
The Sweet boys get involved in an alcohol-induced prank at a farmhouse they presume deserted. The reclusive owner (played by guest star Peter Vaughan) has them arrested for trespassing. Nick tries to get the charges dropped but the man wants something in return that could jeopardise Nick's career.

Georgina Sweet	**Patricia Hodge**	Zoe	**Sarah Churm**
Nick Sweet	**Jason Merrells**	Faye	**Ashley Jensen**
Deb Sweet	**Gillian Kearney**	Mr Barber	**Peter Vaughan**
Geoff Sweet	**Oliver Chris**	Rev Simon Roberts	**Derren Litten**
Eddie Sweet	**Oliver Milburn**	Sheena	**Jo-Anne Knowles**
Muriel Parsons	**Annie Hulley**	Glen	**Ian Keith**

Written by Nick Collins; Producer Claire Phillips; Director David Holroyd (S) *2002*

10.00 ITV News at Ten With Trevor McDonald. Including **Regional News; Weather** with Martyn Davies. (S) *45644*

10.30 Killers on Camera
Final episode in the real-life crime documentary series that uses previously unseen interview footage to follow every twist and turn of recent murder cases.
Director/Producer Paul Griffin (S) (W) *69644*

11.30 Anne Summers Uncovered
In a penultimate tour of the lingerie super-chain, the shop girls learn to pole dance, a couple make their own saucy movie and a party planner holds a fashion show.
Director/Producer Lorraine O'Keeffe (S) (W) *106644*
Followed by **Regional Weather**

12.05 LXG – Behind the Fantasy A behind-the-scenes tour in AM the company of Sean Connery as he talks about his new film, *The League of Extraordinary Gentlemen.* *4049316*

Channel 4

6.00 PM **The Salon**
Juicy gossip and chat from the hair-and-beauty haven.
Repeated at 8pm on E4 *The Salon: After Hours* is at 11.05pm (S) *444*

6.30 Hollyoaks
Debbie is furious to learn about Steph and Dan's kiss.

Scott Anderson	**Daniel Hyde**	Robbie Flynn	**Andrew Newton**
Izzy Cornwell	**Elize du Toit**	Becca Hayton	**Ali Bastian**
Ben Davies	**Marcus Patric**	Abby Davies	**Helen Noble**
Debbie Dean	**Jodi Albert**	Lee Hunter	**Alex Carter**
Steph Dean	**Carley Stenson**	Tony Hutchinson	**Nick Pickard**

Episode written by Tara Byrne More cast on Monday
Repeated at 11.55pm on E4 (S) (W) *644*

7.00 Channel 4 News
With Jon Snow and Samira Ahmed. **Weather** (S) *674267*

7.55 Building of the Year
Anderson House in London features in the final short film focusing on RIBA Stirling Prize contenders. The result is announced next Sunday at 8pm. (S) *574977*

8.00 Tales from River Cottage
Hugh Fearnley-Whittingstall recalls his self-sufficient days in rural Dorset. This week, entertaining – at River Cottage and at the homes of others – from a posh dinner at the manor house to a riotous evening at the local Cider Shed.
Series producers Richard Ellingham and Jane Stephenson (S) *8199*

8.30 French Leave
The series charting the relocation of John Burton Race and his family to a remote farmhouse in France continues. The chef decides that the only thing missing from his life is a goat, but his wife Kim is not pleased by the idea.
Director/Producer Jim Funnell Repeated next Saturday (S) *7606*
RT SHOP: a book accompanying the series is available for £18.00, including p&p: call 0870 770 7979 (national rate), Monday to Friday 8.30am to 6pm

9.00 Cutting Edge: Child Sex Trade
CHOICE
Liviu Tiparita returns to his homeland of Romania to investigate reports of an increase in the trafficking of children into the sex trade in this disturbing documentary. There he meets street children, some as young as 11, who are being preyed on by paedophiles from Western Europe.
Director Liviu Tiparita; Executive producer David Henshaw (S) *4204*

10.00 Russell Crowe's Greatest Fights
CCTV footage captures the tempestuous antipodean actor in action as he plays out his tough-guy roles off screen. Despite his reputation as a brawling hothead, has recent marriage and imminent fatherhood cooled his temper?
Producer Emma Hawley; Executive producer Bill Jones (S) *5901719*

11.05 The Salon: After Hours
A revealing late-night visit to the London beauty parlour, featuring previously unseen footage. *233002*

Five

6.00 PM **Home and Away**
Dylan has betrayed his mother.
Repeated tomorrow at 12.30pm (S) *3416828*

6.30 Family Affairs
Gary tells Myra about his finances.

Pete Callan	**David Easter**
Chrissy Costello	**Kazia Pelka**
Gary Costello	**Gary Webster**
Melanie Costello	**Rebecca Hunter**
Chloe Costello	**Leah Coombes**
Myra Costello	**Kate Williams**
Yasmin Matthews	**Ebony Thomas**
Doug McKenzie	**Gareth Hale**
Marc McKenzie	**Michael Wildman**

Today's and tomorrow's episode written by Dare Aiyegbayo More cast on Wednesday
Repeated tomorrow at 1pm (S) *3490880*

7.00 Five News
With Charlie Stayt. (S) *1367996*
Followed by **Weather**

7.30 Great Artists 2 with Tim Marlow
Stubbs. Considered by many to be the greatest painter of horses in the history of art, the 18th-century Liverpool-born George Stubbs is often underrated due to his reputation as a genre artist.
Director Andrew Hutton; Producer Phil Grabsky (S) *3496064*

8.00 House Doctor
Ann Maurice is in Sandhurst, Berkshire, to help a woman sell her outdated home, which also has an "unfinished" feel.
Series producer Isabelle Gunner (S) *1376644*

8.30 Help Me Rhonda
Adam Williams has the skills to be a radio producer but lacks confidence. Rhonda Britten steps in to give advice.
Series producer Claire Masters (S) *1355151*

9.00 Lock Up ★★
Tough prison drama. Convict Frank Leone only bucked the prison system once. That rebellious act is severely punished when he is at the mercy of a sadistic warden. **Review page 57.**

Frank Leone	**Sylvester Stallone**
Warden Drumgoole	**Donald Sutherland**
Meissner	**John Amos**
Dallas	**Tom Sizemore**
Eclipse	**Frank McRae**

Director John Flynn (1989, 18) (S) *32628644*

CBBC

Freeview 30, **Sky** 616, **cable**

7.00am Animadness **7.30** Xchange **8.00** All or Nothing **8.25** Newsround **8.30** Blue Peter **8.55** Newsround **9.00–12.55pm** *Class TV:* Tales from Europe: double bill **9.30** Look and Read **9.50** Words and Pictures Plus **10.10** Zig Zag **10.30** Let's Write a Story **10.50** Tales from Europe: double bill **11.20** Look and Read **11.40** Words and Pictures Plus **12 noon** Zig Zag **12.20pm** Let's Write a Story **12.40** English Express **12.55** Newsround **1.00** Xchange **1.30** ChuckleVision **2.30** Animadness **3.30** The Story of Tracy Beaker **4.00** All or Nothing **4.25** Newsround Showbiz **4.30** Stitch Up **5.30** Xchange **6.00** Hollywood 7 **6.30** UGetMe **6.40–7.00pm** The Nelly Nut Show

Sky One

Sky 106, **cable**

6.00am Star Trek: Deep Space Nine (S) **7.00** Zoids **7.30** Transformers: Armada **8.00** Gamezville (W) **9.00** Beverly Hills 90210 **10.00** Buffy the Vampire Slayer (S) **11.00** Angel (S) **12 noon** The X Files (S) **1.00pm** Pop Years: 1981 (W) **2.00** Temptation Island **3.00** Beverly Hills 90210 **4.00** Gamezville (W) **5.00** Star Trek: the Next Generation (S)

6.00pm Buffy the Vampire Slayer Xander gets a job as a bartender. (S) *71052*

7.00 The Simpsons Lisa befriends a once-famous saxophone player, and Bart is rushed into hospital. (S) *8731*

7.30 Lisa and Bart's ice hockey teams meet in a bitter penalty shoot out. (S) *1170*

UK Gold

Sky 109, **cable**

6.00am As Time Goes By (S) **6.30** The Flying Doctors **7.20** Neighbours **7.50** Doctors (S) **8.25** EastEnders (S) **9.00** The Bill (S) **10.00** Lovejoy (S) **11.00** Holby City (S) **12 noon** Thomas and Sarah (S) **1.00pm** Weakest Link (S) **2.00** As Time Goes By (S) **2.40** EastEnders (S) **3.20** Doctors (S) **4.00** The Bill (S) **5.00** Lovejoy (S)

6.00pm Doctor Who *The Underworld* (part 2). The Doctor discovers a computer has imposed a despotic rule on the planet. *5289557*

7.00 Are You Being Served? The staff are asked to take a ten per cent pay cut. (S) *3955539*

UK History

Freeview 12, **Sky** 582, **cable**

7.00am Wernher von Braun: From the Nazis to Nasa **8.00** I, Caesar **9.00** The Boer War – the First Media War **9.57** Scenic Days Out: Duxford **10.00** Cold War (S) **11.00** Battle Front: How Weather Shapes War **12 noon** The Fifty Years War: Israel and the Arabs (S) **1.00pm** Wernher von Braun: From the Nazis to Nasa **2.00** I, Caesar **3.00** The Boer War – the First Media War **4.00** Cold War (S) **5.00** Battle Front: How Weather Shapes War

6.00pm The Fifty Years War: Israel and the Arabs The Yom Kippur War. (S) *35489183*

7.00 Wernher von Braun: From the Nazis to Nasa A profile of the designer of *Apollo 11.* *62779002*

7.57 Scenic Days Out Powis Castle. *242837489*

8.00 I, Caesar Hadrian. *62755422*

9.00 The Boer War – the First Media War The role of the media in the Boer War. *62775286*

Source: Radio Times, p. 136, August 2005

Discovery

6.00pm 1940s House The Hymers reflect on their stay. *5287199*
7.00 Time Team A cliff-top mound in the Shetland Islands. *1354606*
8.00 He's Gotta Have It John Thompson gets a gadget. *2462373*
8.30 Extraordinary People A girl with accelerated ageing. *2441880*
9.00 The FBI Files A land developer suspected of kidnapping. *1383118*
10.00 Murder Trail *1353977*
11.00 Forensic Detectives *3008967*
12 midnight Sex Sense **12.30am** Trauma **1.00** Amazing Medical Stories **2.00** Operation **3.00** As 9pm **4.00** As 8.30pm **4.30** As 8pm **5.00–6.00am** Ultimate Ten

CBeebies

Freeview 31, **Sky** 617, **cable**

6.00am Teletubbies **6.25** Bits and Bobs **6.45** Come Outside **7.00** Tweenies **7.20** The Story Makers **7.40** Fimbles **8.00** Tikkabilla **8.30** Bob the Builder **8.40** Spot's Musical Adventures **8.50** Boo! **9.00** Balamory **9.25** SMarteenies **9.40** Tweenies **10.00** Teletubbies **10.25** Bits and Bobs **10.45** Come Outside **11.00** Tweenies **11.20** The Story Makers **11.40** Fimbles **12 noon** Tikkabilla **12.30pm** Bob the Builder **12.40** Spot's Musical

BBC3

Freeview 7, **Sky** 115, **cable**

7.00pm The 7 o'Clock News on BBC3 (W) *8737489*
7.15 The Best of Fame Academy Choice moments from the competition. (W) *4846460*
8.00 Liquid News (W) Then **Celebdaq Daily Update** *9763712*
8.30 EastEnders Revealed Veteran cast member Todd Carty talks about life as Barrow boy Mark Fowler. (S) (W) *9782847*
9.00 The Third Degree: Stars, Stripes and Human Rights Comedian Barry Weintraub tours the USA, uncovering, in the "world's greatest democracy", a plethora of human rights abuses, from the frivolous to the deadly serious. (S) (W) *9627267*
9.30 Art and the City On a visit to New York roving art lover James Gooding meets sculptor Rachel Feinstein, painter Erik Parker and conceptual artist DJ Spooky. (S) (W) *8936731*
10.00 EastEnders Shown at 7.30pm on BBC1. (S) (W) *6623151*
10.30 Two Pints of Lager and a Packet of Crisps The girls go shopping for Janet's wedding dress. (S) (W) *6649199*
11.00 New Tycoons *Winning Business*. Brighton's young entrepreneurs seek novel ways to secure new clients. (S) (W) *9622712*
11.30 As 7.15pm. *5348847*
12.15am as 8pm **12.45** Stupid Punts (S) (W) **1.15** as 11pm **1.45** CCTV (W) **2.15** Changemakers (W) **2.45** as 7.15pm **3.30–4.00am** as 8pm

BBC4

Freeview 10, **Sky** 116, **cable**

7.00pm Business Confessions The secrets of inventor Trevor Bayliss. (W) *6475793*
7.10 Art Crime How did a Rubens painting vanish at the end of the war? (S) (W) *5714286*
8.00 BBC4 News and Weather www.bbc.co.uk/bbcfour *1893354*
8.30 The Big Read: Battle of the Books *The Wind in the Willows* takes on *Swallows and Amazons*. (S) (W) *1612489*
9.00 Kathleen Ferrier – an Ordinary Diva Janet Baker is among those celebrating the late contralto. (S) (W) *8670557*
10.00 Art Safari A look at the art world's court jester, sculptor Maurizio Cattelan. (S) (W) *8879151*
10.30 QI Alan Davies, Jo Brand, Howard Goodall and Danny Baker on angels, alsatians and more. (S) (W) *8895199*
11.00 The Mark Steel Lectures Lord Byron is the first subject in the new series. (S) (W) *8933731*
11.30 What If . . . Clinton and Lewinsky Suppose Bill had never met Monica. With Clive Anderson. (S) (W) *8770880*
12 midnight Profile JG Ballard talks to Tom Sutcliffe about his life and works. (S) *7035774*
12.40am As 8.30pm. *8492300*
1.10 The Big Read: Battle of the Books *Harry Potter v Alice in Wonderland*. (W) *7213213*
1.40–2.30am As 7.10pm. With sign language. (S) *3790774*

UK Horizons

6.00pm Secrets of World War II The Norsk Hydro factory. *7403489*
7.00 Robot Wars Further mechanical carnage. (S) *6880489*
8.00 Cops Arresting action. *5675002*
8.30 Airport A "fear-of-flying" course is arranged for staff. *5661809*
9.00 Forensic Files Profiling a man's deteriorating health. *2978644*
9.30 Examining the death of a female prison guard. *7475606*
10.00 Crash Looking at research into safer motoring. (S) *6872460*
11.00 444 Days to Freedom: The Inside Story The Iranian hostage crisis of 1979. *7158460*
11.55 Dishing the Dirt: Smashing the System Protests. *9523199*

History

6.00pm Unsung Heroes Swede Momsen, inventor of the submarine escape chamber. *5503083*
7.00 The Greek Gods *1899460*
8.00 Battle Stations The Dakota and the D-Day landings. *1875880*
9.00 Hell in the Pacific The savage action before the atom bomb ended the Second World War. *1895644*
10.00 Cold Case Files A killer trapped by bite marks *1898731*
11.00 The Hunt for Jack the Ripper The quest to identify the notorious serial killer. *1874170*

Sky Movies Max 3

Sky 310, **cable**

7.00am Death of a Doxy: a Nero Wolfe Mystery See 2pm.
8.45 A Little Romance ★★★ See 3.45pm. **10.40 Young Einstein** ★★★ See 5.40pm.
12.20pm Staying Alive ★★ See 7.20pm. **2.00 Death of a Doxy: a Nero Wolfe Mystery** Detective drama *1976460* **3.45 A Little Romance** ★★★ Romantic comedy. Laurence Olivier, Diane Lane (George Roy Hill, 1979, PG) *3038977* **5.40 Young Einstein** ★★★ Comedy. (Yahoo Serious, 1988, PG) *34508731*

7.20pm Staying Alive ★★ John Travolta reprises his Tony Manero role from *Saturday Night Fever* in this vastly inferior sequel. Bizarrely, Sylvester Stallone directs. (1983, PG) *80083064*

9.00 Thir13en Ghosts ★★ A man discovers that the house he has inherited is part the gateway to hell in this fright-less horror remake. Tony Shalhoub (Steve Beck, 2001, 15) *64674625*

10.35 Stephen King's The Night Flier ★★★ A sleazy reporter and his young rival pursue a mysterious killer in this atmospheric horror thriller. Miguel Ferrer (Mark Pavia, 1997, 18) *19243286*

Biography

Sky 563, **cable**

8.00am Carrie Fisher **9.00** Great Crimes **9.30** J Edgar Hoover **10.30** Kim Cattrall **11.00** George Lucas **1.00pm** Carrie Fisher **2.00** Great Crimes **2.30** J Edgar Hoover **3.30** Kim Cattrall **4.00** Harrison Ford **5.00** Samuel L Jackson **6.00** The Lost Generation **8.00** David Lynch **9.00 CHOICE:** Michael Moore **9.30** Stanley Donen **10.30** Henry Hill **11.30** Great Crimes and Trials **12 midnight** David Lynch **1.00–2.00am** Stanley Donen

Paramount

6.00pm Frasier: Kenny's divorce is finalised **6.30** Roseanne: Darlene is leaving for college **7.00** MASH: double bill. Hawkeye makes a will, then promotion places are up for grabs **8.00** Spin City: Caitlin finds love with an older man. The mayor is depressed **8.30** Ink: Mike stands in for a talk-show host on live TV **9.00** Bill Plympton's Shorts **9.05** Becker: John reluctantly embraces the festive spirit for a poor child **9.35** Frasier **10.05** Bill Plympton's Shorts **10.10** Sex and the City **10.45** Saturday Night Live **11.45** The New Statesman

Source: Radio Times, p. 136, August 2005

IG

Information grid

1. Draw a table like the following and find examples of each category if possible

News and current affairs	Light entertain-ment	Documentaries	Feature film	Education	Crime

2. Where is the shortest "news-free" zone you can find?
3. Find a programme that deals with the background of the Iran crisis of 1979.

■■□ 4 What is DAB Digital Radio?

DAB digital radio is not satellite radio. DAB digital radio is not internet radio. DAB digital radio is a new way of broadcasting radio via a network of terrestrial transmitters. It provides listeners with more choice, better sound quality and more information. DAB digital radio is like analogue radio, only better.

More Choice

Listeners in most major towns and cities in the UK can receive between 30 and 50 radio stations with a digital radio, in many cases that's more than double what's available on analogue. And it's not just more of the same – the content within that choice of stations is unique and exciting, delivering station formats that just don't exist on analogue. The FM spectrum is so clogged right now that there's no room for new stations that would expand listeners' choice with, for example, soul music, or country music, or big band swing, or any of the other 100+ brands that are available uniquely to DAB.

Because digital radio uses the spectrum more efficiently than analogue, it is possible to broadcast more channels using the same frequency, making room for broadcasters to expand their station portfolios.

Less Noise

DAB digital radio delivers improved sound quality. The technology allows the receiver to lock on to the strongest signal it can find and ignore everything else. This eliminates the hiss, crackle and fade so familiar on analogue radio.

With DAB digital radio there are no frequencies to remember and sets are tuned by station name. National stations stay put, so there's no retuning on the move.

More Information

Each DAB broadcaster (multiplex operator) has 20% of its capacity reserved for data services. Digital radio receivers have a screen on which stations can transmit information via Dynamic Label Segments (DLS). Some stations already transmit the latest news, trav-

el, and weather, what's on now and next, website addresses and phone numbers. Tomorrow's radios will offer much more sophisticated data. The potential for advertisers to use the DLS facility on DAB for targeted advertising is an exciting prospect, and in the future, advertisers can use DAB to deliver web-type commercials.
http://www.drbd.org/whats.php

Activities

Text comprehension

1. How many radio programmes can be received in most large British places?
2. What advantage does digital radio have when you drive a long distance?
3. How would you characterise the following programmes?

BBC Radio 1

News and **Newsbeat** as Monday except no news at 7.30pm and 12 midnight
7.00 AM **Sara Cox**
10.00 Jo Whiley
1.00 PM **Mark Radcliffe**
3.00 Chris Moyles
6.00 The Essential Selection with Pete Tong The latest dance-floor music.
9.00 Westwood – the Radio 1 Rap Show
11.00 Fergie Hard house.
1.00 Fabio and Grooverider AM The latest drum 'n' bass.
3.00 Bobby Friction and Nihal Presents Asian sounds.
5.00 The Blue Room Chris Coco and Rob Da Bank with ambient tracks.
Radio 1: Get in touch by phone on 0870 010 0100 or text 81199. Calls charged at national rates. Write to Radio 1, BBC, London W1N 4DJ www.bbc.co.uk/radio1

BBC Radio 2

News, weather, travel as Monday except no news at 8.00pm and 9.00
6.00 Sarah Kennedy AM At **6.15 Pause for Thought** with Nick Baines.
7.30 Wake Up to Wogan At **9.15 Pause for Thought** with David Cooper.
9.30 Ken Bruce
12.00 Jeremy Vine
2.00 PM **Mark Goodier**
5.00 Stuart Maconie
7.00 Real Songs: The Diane Warren Story Robin Gibb profiles the songwriting giant. 6: This final edition looks at Warren's attempts to move away from power ballads, and considers the future for her music.
7.30 Friday Night Is Music Night Ken Bruce presents music linked with Nelson Riddle, performed by Catherine Porter and Graham Bickley with the BBC Concert Orchestra conducted by Martin Koch.

BBC Radio 3

News, weather as Monday
7.00 Morning on 3
AM With Penny Gore. Music includes:
7.00–8.00: Gershwin *Overture: Let 'Em Eat Cake* Buffalo Philharmonic Orchestra, conductor Michael Tilson Thomas **Schubert** *Klavierstück in E flat, D946 No 1* Mitsuko Uchida (piano)
8.00–9.00: Part *Nunc Dimittis* Polyphony, Christopher Bowers-Broadbent (organ), conductor Stephen Layton **Strauss** *Ist ein Traum (Der Rosenkavalier)* Soloists, Dresden Staatskapelle, conductor Bernard Haitink
9.00–10.00: Listeners may choose a Mozart piano concerto from the recordings by Mitsuko Uchida and the English Chamber Orchestra conducted by Jeffrey Tate
10.00 CD Masters
With Rob Cowan.
Glinka *Jota Aragonesa* Suisse Romande Orchestra, conductor Ernest Ansermet
10.11 Schubert *Grande Marche in G minor, D819 No 2* Artur and Karl Ulrich Schnabel (piano)
10.16 Harris *Symphony No 3* Dallas Symphony Orchestra, conductor Eduardo Mata
10.35 Lehar *Von Apfelblüten einen Kranz; Dein Ist Mein Ganzes Herz (Das Land des Lächelns)* Richard Tauber (tenor), Berlin State Opera Orchestra conducted by the Composer
10.42 Beethoven *Piano Concerto No 3 in C minor, Op 37* Artur Schnabel, Philharmonia, conductor Issay Dobrowen
11.22 William Schuman *Symphony No 3* New York Philharmonic Orchestra, conductor Leonard Bernstein
12.00 Composer of the Week: Verdi
Donald Macleod introduces Verdi's last two operas, both inspired by Shakespeare – the tragic *Otello* and the quicksilver brilliance and wit of *Falstaff*.
Otello, Act 1 Scene 3; Act 2 Scene 5
Otello **Placido Domingo (tenor)**
Desdemona **Cheryl Studer (soprano)**
Iago **Sergei Leiferkus (baritone)**
Bastille Opera Orchestra, conductor Myung-Whun Chung
Falstaff, Act 3 Part 2 (end)
Fenton **Daniil Shtoda (tenor)**
Nannetta **Dorothea Roschmann (soprano)**
Alice **Adrianne Pieczonka (soprano)**
Mistress Quickly **Larissa Diadkova (mezzo)**
Meg **Stella Doufexis (contralto)**
Falstaff **Bryn Terfel (baritone)**
Bardolph **Antony Mee (tenor)**
Pistol **Anatoli Kotscherga (baritone)**
Ford **Thomas Hampson (baritone)**
Dr Caius **Enrico Facini (tenor)**
Berlin Radio Choir, Berlin Philharmonic Orchestra, conductor Claudio Abbado
Repeated Thursday 12 midnight

4.00 Jazz Legends
Mose Allison
Julian Joseph talks to Mose Allison, the revered singer, songwriter and pianist from Tippo, Mississippi.
5.00 In Tune
Sean Rafferty presents a selection of music, with arts news and interviews.
7.45 Performance on 3
Ulster Orchestra
LIVE
Freddy Kempf (piano), conductor Nicolae Moldoveanu
Live from the Ulster Hall, Belfast, a concert given by the Ulster Orchestra featuring the music of two Ulster composers and two classics of the symphonic repertoire. Presented by John Toal.
Handel, arr Hamilton Harty *Music for the Royal Fireworks*
Tchaikovsky *Piano Concerto No 1 in B flat minor*
8.35 Twenty Minutes: Belfast Beat
Belfast poet Frank Ormsby investigates the work of John Hewitt, Roy McFadden and Robert Greacen – Belfast poets who first came to prominence in the 1940s and who eloquently bridged the gap between Yeats and Heaney.
8.55 Philip Hammond . . . *the Starry Dynamo in the Machinery of Night* . . .
Nielsen *Symphony No 2 (The Four Temperaments)*
9.45 Night Waves
Thirty years after Henry Kissinger won the Nobel Peace Prize and Tom Lehrer famously declared "satire is dead", Susan Hitch and guests consider whether satire has ever done more than make us laugh.
10.15 Mixing It
Mark Russell and Robert Sandall present an eclectic mix of musical styles, including an interview with Brian Eno about his latest projects, which include an album of bell music inspired by his work on the *Clock of the Long Now*, a clock that will mark time for ten thousand years.

BBC 7

www.bbc.co.uk/bbc7

SATURDAY
7.00am The Little Toe Radio Show: kids' stories **8.00 CHOICE** The Comedy Controller: Helen Lederer chooses comedy favourites: Life with Lederer – the Party, Life with Lederer – the Cruise, Jeremy Hardy Speaks to the Nation, Arthur Smith Sings Leonard Cohen, Hearing with Hegley, Ross Noble Goes Global – Ireland **11.00** The Barchester Chronicles (14/20)
12 noon Just a Minute: 1978 panel game **12.30pm** Jeeves and the Feudal Spirit: comedy **1.00** The Night of the Hunter: thriller (1/2) **2.00** Garrison Keillor's Radio Show **3.00** The Little Toe Radio Show **4.00** Big Toe Radio Show
6.00 The Seventh Dimension: Frankenstein (2/2) **7.00** Just a Minute **7.30** Jeeves and the Feudal Spirit **8.00** Garrison Keillor's Radio Show **9.00 CHOICE** The Comedy Controller: see 8am
12 midnight The Seventh Dimension: Frankenstein (2/2) **1.00am** The Barchester Chronicles (14/20) **2.00** The Night of the Hunter (1/2)

SUNDAY
7.00am The Little Toe Radio Show **8.00** Tess of the d'Urbevilles: Thomas Hardy drama (1/4) **9.00** A Room with a View (3/4) **10.00** The Woman in White: Victorian thriller (1/4) **11.00** The Barchester Chronicles (15/20)
12 noon Beyond Our Ken: 1960 comedy **12.30pm** Take It from Here: 1958 comedy **1.00** Body of Glass: drama set in 2059 **2.30** The Betty Witherspoon Show: 1974 comedy **3.00** The Little Toe Radio Show **4.00** The Big Toe Radio Show
6.00 The Seventh Dimension: Journey into Space – The Red Planet: 50s sci-fi (6/20) **6.30** Fear on Four: Dark Feathers **7.00** Beyond Our Ken **7.30** Take It from Here **8.00** Flywheel, Shyster and Flywheel: comedy **8.30** The Betty Witherspoon Show **9.00** Tess of the d'Urbevilles (1/4) **10.00** A Room with a View, by EM Forster (3/4) **11.00** The Woman in White: thriller (1/4)
12 midnight The Seventh Dimension: Journey into Space – The Red Planet (6/20) **12.30am** Fear on Four: Dark Feathers **1.00** The Barchester Chronicles (15/20) **2.00** Body of Glass: drama set in 2059

MONDAY–FRIDAY
7.00am The Little Toe Radio Show **8.00 Mon** In Conversation with . . . Mel and Sue **Tue** How Tickled Am I: Ted Ray; **Wed** Parson and Naylor's Pull-out Sections; **Thu** A Swift Laugh **Fri** The Jason Explanation **8.30** Comedy: **Mon** Whose Line Is It Anyway?; **Tue** Room 101; **Wed** In the Chair; **Thu** Delve Special **Fri** Dead Ringers **9.00** Letters from a Diplomat: Douglas Hurd reflects on his career (1–5/5) **9.15** As It Is in Heaven: love story set in Ireland and in Venice (1–5/5) **9.30** King Street Junior: comedy drama **10.00 Mon–Wed** The Marseilles Trilogy (1–3/3) **Thu–Fri** Villette, by Charlotte Brontë, with Joseph Fiennes and Catherine McCormack (1–2/3) **11.00** Maigret: French detective **11.45** Life with Lederer: Helen Lederer comedy
12 noon Comedy: **Mon** I'm Sorry I Haven't a Clue; **Tue** The News Quiz; **Wed** The Write Stuff; **Thu** Just a Minute; **Fri** My Music **12.30pm** Comedy: **Mon** The Goon Show; **Tue** Hancock's Half-Hour; **Wed** Round the Horne; **Thu** The Navy Lark; **Fri** I'm Sorry I'll Read That Again **1.00** Bolt: thriller (1–5/5) **1.30 Mon–Wed** The Blackburn Files; **Thu–Fri** Secret Agent X9: spy drama (1–2/4) **2.00** Comedy: **Mon** The Sunday Format; **Tue** The Masterson Inheritance; **Wed** The Skivers; **Thu** Dial M for Pizza; **Fri** Life, Death and Sex with Mike and Sue **2.30** Classic Comedy: **Mon** Dad's Army; **Tue** It Sticks Out Half a Mile; **Wed** The Men from the Ministry; **Thu** After Henry; **Fri** To the Manor Born **3.00** The Little Toe Radio Show **4.00** The Big Toe Radio Show

Oneword

www.oneword.co.uk

SATURDAY
6.00am Children: The Merman **7.15** The Curious Incident of the Dog in the Night-Time **9.45** Footnotes **10.30** Planet Politics **11.00** My East End, written by and read by Gilda O'Neill
12.15pm Colony, by Rob Grant **1.30** Fever Pitch, by Nick Hornby **3.00** The Adventure of the Lion's Mane and Other Stories **4.30** Farewell to Fairacre
6.00 Vintage Radio: Midnight, with Claudette Colbert **7.00** Port Authority: drama **8.00** Between the Lines: Paul Blezard talks to Amanda Craig **8.30** Boston Blackie **9.00** Sleeping Cruelty **10.00** A Man Lay Dead, followed by The Tesseract **11.30** Vintage Radio: Gunsmoke
12 midnight Frankenstein, followed by Anna Karenina **5.00am** Midnight: classic 30s comedy with Claudette Colbert **5.45** Poetry

SUNDAY
6.00am Children: The Merman, followed by Frank and the Chamber of Fear **7.15** Tulip Touch, read by Rula Lenska **9.45** Famous Women: Florence Nightingale **11.00** My East End
12.15pm Colony, by Rob Grant **1.30** Fever Pitch (3/4) **3.00** The Adventure of the Lion's Mane and Other Stories (3/3) **4.30** Farewell to Fairacre
6.00 Kerry Shale's Listy Show **6.30** Planet Politics: with Iain Dale **7.00** Port Authority: drama (2/2) **8.00** Paul Blezard talks to Adam Williams **8.30** Vintage Radio: The Time Machine **9.00** Sleeping Cruelty, by Lynda La Plante **10.00** The Tesseract, by Alex Garland **11.30** Vintage Radio: Gunsmoke
12 midnight Anna Karenina, followed by Lord Arthur Saville's Crime **5.00am** Midnight: 30s comedy with Claudette Colbert **5.45** Poetry

MONDAY–FRIDAY
6:00am Mon Farewell to Fairacre (3/3), followed by The Soldier's Return (1/3); **Tue** The Soldier's Return (2/3); **Wed** The Soldier's Return (3/3), followed by An Equal Music, by Vikram Seth (1/15); **Fri** An Equal Music (2/15) **7.30** Frank and the Chamber of Fear (2–6/8) **8.00 Mon–Wed** A Guilty Thing Surprised (1–3/4); **Thu** A Guilty Thing Surprised (4/4), followed by The Tree of Hands (1/4); **Fri** The Tree of Hands (2/4) **9.00 Mon** Colony, by Rob Grant (8/8); **Tue–Fri** The European, by Jonathan Booth (1–4/23) **9.30 Mon–Wed** Lord Arthur Saville's Crime (2–4/5); **Thu** Lord Arthur Saville's Crime (5/5), followed by Sir Harry Hotspur of Humblethwaite (1/6); **Fri** Sir Harry Hotspur of Humblethwaite (2/6) **11.30 Mon** Farewell to Fairacre (3/3), followed by The Soldier's Return (1/3); **Tue** The Soldier's Return (2/3); **Wed** The Soldier's Return (3/3), followed by An Equal Music, by Vikram Seth (1/15); **Fri** An Equal Music (2/15)
1.00pm Mon Fever Pitch (4/4), followed by Grace Notes (1/9); **Tue–Fri** Grace Notes (2–5/9) **2.00** Between the Lines: Paul Blezard talks to a different author daily **2.30 Mon–Tue** My East End (14–15/15); **Wed–Fri** Marie Antoinette, by Antonia Fraser and read by Lindsay Duncan (1–3/17) **3.00 Mon–Wed** A Guilty Thing Surprised (1–3/4); **Thu** A Guilty Thing Surprised (4/4), followed by The Tree of Hands (1/4); **Fri** The Tree of Hands by Ruth Rendell (2/4) **4.00** Children: Frank and the Chamber of Fear (2–6/8) **4.30 Mon** Tulip Touch (4/5); **Tue** Tulip Touch (5/5), followed by The Seeing Stone(1/6) **Wed–Fri** The Seeing Stone(2–4/6) **5.30** The Story of the WI Calendar Girls (1–5/5) **5.45** Hamlet, performed by a cast featuring Anton Lesser (1–5/17)

BBC 6 Music

www.bbc.co.uk/6music

SATURDAY
6.00am Janice Long **8.00** Jayne Middlemiss: music news **9.00** Roundtable: with Andrew Collins **10.00** Clare McDonnell
1.00pm Steve Lamacq **4.00** Tracey MacLeod **5.00** Brinsley Forde: rocksteady, ska, dub and reggae
6.00 Craig Charles: funk **9.00** Bruce Dickinson: rock
12 midnight 6 Mix: dance music from the past 30 years **2.00am** Gary Burton: contemporary hits

SUNDAY
7.00am Janice Long **9.00** Tracey MacLeod: My Life in CD **10.00** Stuart Maconie
1.00pm Chris Hawkins **4.00** Bob Harris
7.00 6 Mix **9.00** Bruce Dickinson Freak Zone
12 midnight Gary Burton: contemporary hits

MONDAY–FRIDAY
7.00am Phill Jupitus **10.00** Gideon Coe
1.00pm Liz Kershaw **4.00** Tony Wilson: sitting in for Andrew Collins: including at **6.00 Fri** Roundtable, repeated Saturday 9am
7.00 Mon–Thu Tom Robinson with special guests, exclusive sessions and documentaries. **10.00–12 midnight Mon–Thu** Janice Long **7.00 Fri** Jayne Middlemiss **8.00 Fri** Craig Charles: funk **11.00– 12 midnight Fri** Brinsley Forde: ska, dancehall and reggae
12 midnight Mon–Thu Chris Hawkins; **Fri** Gary Burton with contemporary tracks

BBC World Service

6.00am World Today **7.00** World Today **8.00** World News **8.05** Outlook **8.45** Off the Shelf: A Man of Mystery **9.00** News **9.05** Sports International: Basketball **9.30** John Peel **10.00** News **10.05** Science in Action **10.30** Westway **10.45** What's the Problem? **11.00** World Briefing **11.30** World Business Report **11.45** Football Extra **12.00** News **12.05pm** Outlook **12.45** Off the Shelf **1.00** Newshour **2.00** News **2.05** Sports International **2.30** John Peel **3.00** News **3.05** Science in Action **3.30** Westway **3.45** What's the Problem? **4.00** World Briefing **4.30** British News **4.45** Analysis **5.00** Europe Today **6.00** Newshour **7.00** News **7.05** Sports International **7.30** John Peel **8.00** News **8.05** Science in Action **8.30** Westway **8.45** What's the Problem? **9.00** Newshour **10.00** World Briefing **10.20** British News **10.30** World Business Report **10.45** Off the Shelf **11.00** World Today **11.30** Analysis **11.45** Sports **12.00** News **12.05am** Outlook **12.45** Off the Shelf **1.00** News **1.05** Sports International: Basketball **1.30** John Peel **2.00** World News **2.05** Science in Action **2.30** Westway **2.45** What's the Problem? **3.00** World Today **3.30** World Business Report **3.45** Analysis **4.00** News **4.05** Pick of the World **4.45** Write On **5.00** World Briefing **5.30** Reporting Religion

Classic FM

5.00 AM **Easier Breakfast** With Jamie Crick.
7.00 Simon Bates
11.00 Most Wanted With Jane Jones.
12.00 Lunchtime Requests With Jane Jones.
2.00 PM **Relaxing Classics** With Nick Bailey.
4.00 Drivetime With Mark Forrest.
6.30 Classic Newsnight
John Brunning's guest is Mark Elder, music director of the Hallé Orchestra.
7.00 Smooth Classics With John Brunning.
9.00 Evening Concert
Verdi *Anvil Chorus (Il Trovatore)* Milan La Scala Chorus and Orchestra/Abbado **Lambert** *Ballet: Mr Bear Squash-You-All-Flat* Nigel Hawthorne (narrator), Nash Ensemble/Friend **Verdi** *Messa da Requiem* Soloists, Monteverdi Choir, Orchestre Révolutionnaire et Romantique/Gardiner
11.00 Late Night Lisa With Lisa Duncombe.
2.00 AM **Chiller Cabinet** Laid-back classics.
4.00 Jonathan Ray

BBC Radio 4

News, weather and **shipping forecasts** as Tuesday, except news at 11.00am (*FM only*)

5.35 AM **World News**

5.43 Prayer for the Day With Canon Ralph Godsall.
Producer Mark O'Brien

5.45 Farming Today With Miriam O'Reilly.
Producer Sarah Swadling

6.00 Today With Martha Doyle and John Humphrys.
6.25, 7.25, 8.25 Sports News
6.45 Yesterday in Parliament With Mark D'Arcy.
Editor Peter Knowles
7.48 Thought for the Day
With the Rt Rev Richard Harries.
8.51 *LW only* **Yesterday in Parliament**

9.00 Desert Island Discs
Sue Lawley's castaway is Nigella Lawson.
Producer Leanne Buckle Shortened repeat from Sunday at 11.15am

9.45 *FM only* **Book of the Week: Ricky**
Ricky Tomlinson reads the last extract from his autobiography. 5: Tomlinson finds success playing Bobby Grant in *Brookside*, only to lose everything and start again. For details see Monday Repeated at 12.30am

9.45 *LW only* **Act of Worship**
Presented by the Rev Ernest Rea.

10.00 Woman's Hour *FM only from around 10.38am*
Presented by Martha Kearney.
10.38 *LW only* **Our Kath** Part 10.
10.45 *FM only* **Our Kath** Part 10.
Drama repeated at 7.45pm

10.53–11.59 *LW only* **A Service of Remembrance for Iraq 2003**
Her Majesty the Queen and members of the royal family join politicians, representatives of the armed forces and their familes at a Service of Remembrance for Iraq from St Paul's Cathedral in London. Nicholas Witchell introduces the service, which is led by the Dean, the Very Rev John Moses. The sermon is given by the Archbishop of Canterbury, Dr Rowan Williams.
Producer Mark O'Brien

11.00 *FM only* **Romantics and Revolutionaries**
CHOICE
Shelley, Wordsworth and Thackeray visited Ireland at times of political turmoil. Pete McCarthy talks to Irish experts about these writers' views of Ireland and reflects on Anglo-Irish stereotypes today.
Producer Anke Lueddecke

11.30 *FM only* **Two Doors Down**
Comedy drama by Annie McCartney. 4: *And It Was All Yellow*. Rory and Evie have a joint birthday party.

Sally	**Frances Tomelty**	Trevor	**Gerard McSorley**
Fintan	**Gerard Murphy**	Edith	**Roma Tomelty**
Victor	**Alan McKee**	Saffron	**Ali White**
Clare	**Marcella Riordan**	Anna	**Hannah R Gordon**
Evie	**Katy Gleadhill**	Simon	**Lloyd Houston**
Rory	**Richard Clements**	Layla	**Eadaoin Hegarty**
Tony	**Robert Patterson**		

Producer/director Tanya Nash

3.45 Behind the Taverna
5: Brett Westwood follows the tourist buses up Tenerife's famous volcano. For details see Monday (R)

4.00 Law in Action
Another edition of the series in which Marcel Berlins unpicks the complexities of the law.
Producer Charles Sigler Editor Nicola Meyrick

4.30 The Message
Jenni Murray and guests discuss media trends
Producer Cecile Wright

5.00 PM With Razia Iqbal and Eddie Mair. Editor Peter Rippon

6.00 Six o'Clock News

6.30 The Now Show
New series Starring Steve Punt and Hugh Dennis in the satirical sketch show. With Mitch Benn, Marcus Brigstocke, Laura Shavin and Jon Holmes.
Producer Adam Bromley Repeated on Saturday at 12.30pm
BBC RADIO COLLECTION: Four episodes from the first series are available on audio cassette or CD from good retail outlets or from www.bbcshop.com Call 01225 443400

7.00 The Archers Lynda tries to drum up support.

Phil	**Norman Painting**	Kathy	**Hedli Niklaus**
Jill	**Patricia Greene**	Joe	**Edward Kelsey**
Alistair	**Michael Lumsden**	Eddie	**Trevor Harrison**
Shula	**Judy Bennett**	Neil	**Brian Hewlett**
David	**Timothy Bentinck**	Susan	**Charlotte Martin**
Ruth	**Felicity Finch**	Caroline	**Sara Coward**
Nigel	**Graham Seed**	Lynda	**Carole Boyd**
Elizabeth	**Alison Dowling**	Usha	**Souad Faress**
Tony	**Colin Skipp**	Bert	**Eric Allan**
Brian	**Charles Collingwood**	Oliver	**Michael Cochrane**
Jennifer	**Angela Piper**	Alan	**John Telfer**
Adam	**Andrew Wincott**	Amy	**Natalia Keery-Fisher**
Alice	**Hollie Chapman**	Legal adviser	**Susan Jeffrey**
George	**Graham Roberts**	Clive	**Alex Jones**
Christine	**Lesley Saweard**		

Written by Tim Stimpson Director Kate Oates
Editor Vanessa Whitburn
ARCHERS ADDICTS FAN CLUB: send an SAE to PO Box 1951, Moseley, Birmingham B13 9DD

7.15 Front Row
Francine Stock presents the arts magazine, with news, views and interviews. Producer Kirsty Pope

7.45 Our Kath
By Claire Luckham. 10: In the last instalment, Kathleen is in and out of hospital after collapsing on stage at Covent Garden.

Kathleen	**Becky Hindley**	Sir John Barbirolli	**John Carlisle**
Winifred	**Shirley Dixon**	Benjamin Britten	**Nicholas Boulton**
Bernie	**Susan Curnow**	Bruno Walter	**Robert Rietti**

For details see Monday Repeated from 10.45am

8.00 Any Questions
Jonathan Dimbleby chairs the discussion as an audience at Wareham, Dorset, puts questions to a panel that includes the shadow Chancellor of the Exchequer Michael Howard and the American lawyer and Republican Colleen Graffy.
Producer Anne Peacock Repeated on Saturday at 1.15pm

BBC Radio 5 Live

News, sport, travel and **entertainment news** as Monday

5.00 AM **Morning Reports**

5.30 Wake Up to Money
Guy Ruddle and Mickey Clark present a roundup of financial stories and features.
5 Live Sports Extra *Digital only*
5.55–7.05pm Grand Prix Qualifier
Live commentary on the first qualifying session for the Japanese Grand Prix,

6.00 Breakfast
With Nicky Campbell and Victoria Derbyshire.

9.00 Julian Worricker

11.00 Sport on 5: Rugby World Cup
Australia begin their defence of the Webb Ellis trophy with a match against Argentina. John Inverdale presents the opening game of the Rugby World Cup live from Sydney, with commentary from Ian Robertson and Alastair Hignell and expert summaries from former Wallaby Mark Ella.

1.30 PM **Simon Mayo**

4.00 Drive With Peter Allen and Aasmah Mir.

7.00 Sport on 5
Jonathan Pearce and Susan Bookbinder host a special preview of the upcoming international football matches, including Turkey v England in Istanbul. Plus the latest news from the Rugby World Cup, and at **9.00** second-half commentary on the Super League final eliminator game.
9.30–10.00 5 Live Formula One
Jonathan Legard and guests look ahead to the Japanese Grand Prix, the last of the season.

10.00 Brian Hayes

1.00 AM **Up All Night** With Dotun Adebayo.

Radio 5 Live: Get in touch by phone with on-air calls for free on 0500 909693 or on 0870 010 0500 for all other calls and faxes. TEXT: 85058 www.bbc.co.uk/fivelive

MC

Multiple choice

Which sentence describes best what is said in the text "What is DAB Digital Radio"? (1 answer)

1.

A	In many regions you can listen to more than 100 different sorts of music on FM.
B	In some regions DAB offers a choice of dozens of programmes, which was not possible on analogue FM.
C	Radio stations with more than 100 different sorts of music have clogged the FM band so much that there is no room for new stations.
D	There are more stations on DAB, because digital radio uses more frequencies.

2. Which statements on the radio programme listings are correct (more than one correct solution possible)?

A	Radio 3 is a channel with an emphasis on culture and classical music.
B	The typical listener of Radio 2 is younger than the one of Radio 1.
C	On BBC 7 you can listen to a comedy programme every day of the week.
D	The listing for Oneword contains a Shakespeare play every day of the week.

E	BBC 6 music is a special channel for techno fans.
F	BBC World Service seems to have a programme with book reviews.
G	Classic FM gives you a chance to listen to a complete opera for most of the day.
H	Radio 4 has a religious programme that is broadcast both on FM and on LW.
I	Radio 5 live is a pop music programme.

Presentation

Find more information in the Internet. Work in a group and use the material you find there to give a presentation to your class. Explain how DAB works, what the advantages over FM are and compare the British situation to the German one. Make sure your presentation can also be understood by less technically minded people.

Text

■■□ 5 Dizzee Rascal – Prize-winner

Pre-reading activities

Create acrostics for **MUSIC, PROTEST,** and **PRIZE.**

1. Scan both texts for the names of all musicians mentioned.
2. Group work – Do a research on them: find out what they have in common and where they differ.

Rapper wins Mercury prize

Dizzee Rascal stuns expectations to carry off £ 20,000 prize and create a tradition in wake of Ms Dynamite's triumph last year Britain's hidden army of urban teenagers making music in their tower block bedrooms edged closer to the mainstream last night when an 19-year-old rapper from Bow, east London, won the £ 20,000 Mercury music prize. MC Dizzee Rascal, born Dylan Mills, was acknowledged for his debut album Boy In Da Corner, a depressing comment on high-rise Britain. In it, he raps about guns, knives, depression and making 15-year-old girls pregnant – finally admitting, "I am a problem for Anthony Blair".

The Mercury judges, a respectable collection of music insiders and journalists, succeeded in breaking their persistent image of peddling a pompous "Booker prize of music". For the second year running they ignored the sage bet and nominated their second young black urban MC after Ms Dynamite won last year, aged 21. Dizzee Rascal, who is hailed to be the future of both British garage and British hip-hop calls himself a champion of the "Playstation generation". His music is not aspirational but grim. He was excluded from every subject at school until a music teacher took him under her wing.

Dizzee Rascal, the youngest ever Mercury winner, accepted his prize from Ms Dynamite and thanked everyone who had "suffered" for urban British music. He was among those who had suffered, having been repeatedly stabbed this summer while working in the club resorts of Ayia Napa in Cyprus. He refused to comment on the stabbing, saying: "I have been acknowledged now, that's all I care about."

"I come from nothing, man. I come from the underground, from the ground." He added that young, black music from the street needed to be acknowledged in the mainstream, but was so strong it would break through anyway. Breaking the stereotype of the rebellious broken home, Rascal repeatedly thanked his mum, with whom he still lives in a tower block in Bow. In a video he made specially for the Mercury audience, he filmed his east London neighbourhood, panning across to the more affluent Docklands. He said: "That is Canary Wharf. It's in your face. It takes the piss. There are rich people moving in now, people who work in the city. You can tell they are not living the same way as us."

The question remains as to whether the Mercury will be the mixed blessing for Dizzee Rascal that it has been for some other artists. Although Ms Dynamite got a lot of exposure from the prize, her album sales did not increase on the back of it.

Angelique Chrisafis, September 10, 2003 The Guardian

Judges ignore rock to reward rebel MC

There is a kind of dull inevitability about the Mercury Prize. Every year, the same things happen: It is a given that nominees from the genres of folk, jazz and modern classical will be sent home empty-handed; the NME and its readership will work themselves into an indignant fury over the shortlist's exclusion of an obscure indie combo; broadsheets worry over the same list for its inclusion/exclusion of bands that are too famous or too unknown. and bookmakers immediately give the shortest odds to the most commercially successful outfit – despite this never securing winners in the past. The bookies don't appear to have a clue what the Mercury Prize is for. Then again, nobody appears to have a clue what the Mercury Prize ist for. The official line is that it "celebrates the best in British music", but it's doubtful that even the members of the judging panel honestly think that the roll-call of past winners represents the most artistically important British albums of recent years: Blur have never won, no Massive Attack, The Chemical Brothers, Basement Jaxx, Oasis, nor Radiohead.

Some years it appears to reward artistic endeavour. In other years, it seems to favour commercial success.

Occasionally, the Mercury Prize has appeared to be a kind of long-service medal.

This year, however, there can be little argument with the winner. On a shortlist heavy with traditional guitar rock and soul, Dizzee Rascal's debut stood out as the one genuinely innovative album; by contrast, even Radiohead sound oddly familiar and cosy.

Quite aside from its remarkable lyrical content – an unfinchingly grim depiction of East London council estate life, packed with guns, drugs, teenage pregnancy and depression – its music is entirely without precedent: a virtually unheard-of occurrence in current rock and pop. Stammering arhythmic beats, squawking, panicked vocals, screeching electronics: Dylan Mills may have sprung from the same UK garage scene as previous winner Ms. Dynamite, but his individual sound has nothing in common with that of his peers.

Whether the prize will translate into commercial success in an undecided point – the Mercury has an odd habit of killing winners' careers stone dead, and Mills' vision may simply be too bleak and challenging for mass acceptance. Nevertheless, for once, the Mercury panel can congratulate themselves on getting it exactly right.

Alexius Petridis (the Guardian's rock critic), September 10, 2003
The Gardian

Activities

SAQs

Text comprehension – short answer questions

Both texts appeared in the same issue of the Guardian.

1. How did Dizzee Rascal stun all expectations?
2. What sort of music does Dizzee Rascal create?
3. What happened to this musician, when he worked in Cyprus?
4. Where does Dizzee Rascal live?
5. What happens in his neighbourhood right now?
6. Can Dizzee Rascal expect to sell more albums now?
7. What is the official purpose of the Mercury Prize?
8. Why did Dizzee Rascal win? (2 answers)
9. What are the songs about?
10. How is the type of music described?

Listening comprehension: I've been through madness

True-false test

1. Read the statements below before listening to the tape.
2. Decide on as many statements as you can during the first listening. The text will be read out a second time. Work on the rest of the statements while listening.
3. Compare notes with the class.
   a) The tabloids want to talk to Dizzee Rascal because he released another album.
   b) Dizzee Rascal can be compared to the prizewinners before him.
   c) Rascal had always hoped to win the Mercury Prize.
   d) The Mercury Prize is quite popular with musicians like Rascal.
   e) Dizzie's family background left him to lead quite a lonely life.
   f) During the times as a teenager he led a quiet and unspectacular life.
   g) In his surroundings, the only way to earn enough money is to be good at music or sport.
   h) His academic career was quite successful.
   i) Rascal and his music easily fit into the garage scene.
   j) The topics of Rascal's album reflect on the hard life in the council estate he grew up.
   k) Rascal's lifestyle and winning the award are rather mismatched.
   l) Many people outside the world he comes from think Rascal's text are just made up stories.
   m) Rascal is impressed by his new fame.

Text

6 Newspapers in Great Britain

Pre-reading activities

1. In order to stay informed about politics or cultural or sport events when do you usually turn to ...:

[• TV? • a newspaper? • the radio? • the internet?]

2. Make lists on the advantages and disadvantages of these mass media and discuss them in class.
3. On an average day two out of three people read a morning newspaper. Can you explain why they turn to this particular type of mass media?
4. In Britain, people have access to many more national dailies than people in Germany. These national newspapers can be divided into two groups: the quality papers and the popular papers.
   Find out about the differences and report the results to the class.
5. Do you know any other expressions for "quality" and "popular" press?
6. Here are the titles of some national dailies in Great Britain. Find out if they are quality or popular papers:

All newspapers in Britain, daily or Sunday ones, can broadly be divided into the quality press and the popular press. The quality newspapers are also known as "heavies" and they usually deal with home and overseas news, with detailed and extensive coverage of sports and cultural events. Besides they also carry financial reports, travel news and book and film reviews. The popular press or the "populars" are also known as tabloids as they are smaller in size being halfsheet in format. Some people also call them the "gutter press" offering news for the people less interested in daily detailed news reports. They are characterised by large headlines, carry a lot of big photographs, concentrate on the personal aspects of news, with reports of the recent sensational and juicy bits of events, not excluding the Royal family. The language of a tabloid is much more colloquial, if not specific, than that of quality newspapers.

Here is a possibly witty though true classification of English newspapers:
"The Times" is read by the people who run the country;
"The Mirror" is read by the people who think they run the country;
"The Guardian" is read by the people who think about running the country;
"The Mail" is read by wives of the people who run the country;
"The Daily Telegraph" is read by the people who think the country ought to be run as it used to be;
"The Express" is read by the people who think it is still run as it used to be;
"The Sun" is read by the people who don't care who runs the country as long as the naked girl at page three is attractive.

In Britain today there are four nationwide quality papers: "The Times", "The Daily Telegraph", "The Guardian" and "The Independent". "The Daily Mail", "The Daily Mirror", "The Sun", "The Daily Express" and "The Daily Star" are usually considered to be "populars".

"The Times", founded in 1785, is read by the minority of people today. It has a rather small circulation, but its influence is greater than its circulation figures (100,000 copies a day). It is an establishment newspaper, read by lawyers, politicians, and businessmen, by all those who work in the government at large. It is not an organ of the Conservative Party, but still is rather conservative in views it expresses, though it is reliable and unbiased and claims to be politically independent.

"The Daily Telegraph", founded in 1855, is a very conservative paper. However, it has a circulation twice as big as that of "The Times", "The Guardian" or "The Independent". It has a nickname – "The Torygraph" after the nickname "Tory" of the Conservative Party.

"The Guardian" has a slightly bigger circulation than "The Times". It is a liberal newspaper, noted for its lively reporting and campaigning support for "worthy causes" such as education, medical reforms, the problems of aging people and retirees, protection of the environment, etc.

"The Independent" was founded in 1986 and has rapidly acquired a reputation for its excellent news coverage, intelligent reports, informal commentaries, and a good balanced sense of humour. "The Sun", founded in 1964, has a circulation of around four million and outsells all other "populars".

"The Daily Mirror" with a circulation of about three million, was founded in 1903 and has always traditionally supported the Labour Party. Both "The Daily Mail" and "The Daily Express" have circulations of about a million and a half and were founded in 1900 and 1896 respectively. Of the above mentioned newspapers, "The Mail" is the most sophisticated of the others. The populars as a rule, however, express, though they are mass circulation papers, no news. There you will find leading articles about murders, games, bingo and lotteries.

Actually all newspapers in Britain, both the quality and popular ones, have their sister Sunday issues. Thus, "The Sunday Times" leads the field in the Sunday qualities. It has a circulation of over a million.

"The Observer" is the oldest Sunday paper. It was founded in 1791 and today has a circulation of around half a million.

Founded in 1961 "The Sunday Telegraph" has a circulation which has been steadily declining.

The best-selling Sunday popular newspaper is "The News of the World". Its circulation is over five million.

"The Sunday Mirror" offers a lot of photographs and much gossip. Other Sunday mass papers resemble their daily equivalents in style, in coverage and colour.

In general, however, English people themselves, though slightly sniffy and condescending about their "populars", underline that the quality of newspapers in Great Britain of late is much better than 20 years ago. They argue that it is much lower if they take the example of "The Times" newspaper, which was taken over by Rupert Murdoch in the early eighties. He is the owner of News International and is among the people who have control over the press. Rupert Murdoch also owns "The Sun", which is, as it has already been stressed, a very low quality newspaper. To increase readership into "The Times" he gradually increases a lot of techniques in it similar to those he introduced in "The Sun" paper.

Most people in Great Britain perceive the press in Great Britain as objective, since they claim that there is no overt censorship, no overt bias in reporting the news, and that there is a wide choice of newspapers apart from the national dailies.

They say that the British press is also investigative, uncovers scandals in the governments, and if they are not satisfied with what they read in "The Times" and think it is not true, they have the opportunity to go and pick up another newspaper and compare reportings.

By Natalya Predtechenskaya, archive.1.september.ruleng/2002/08/1.htm

True-false test

1. Read the text carefully
2. Decide on the statements of the test. Adjust the statements when necessary.
   Take care: the statements do not appear in the order of the text.
   a) "The Guardian" caters for the interest of those for who think "The Times" is too conservative.
   b) "The Independent" is rather young and therefore has an excellent image.
   c) "The Times" is being changed step by step to increase its circulation.
   d) "The Times" though being one of the oldest papers on the market, is read by only a group of people.
   e) All the populars roughly mirror the same political views.
   f) British people think they won't need a censorship, as the large competition on the market is control enough.
   g) Many papers have Sunday editions.
   h) Most readers of quality papers read the "Daily Telegraph".
   i) The British press can be divided into national and regional papers.
   j) The newspapers use their own type of language each.
   k) The papers can be divided according to the interest of their readers as far as the fate of the nation is concerned.
   l) The populars provide their readership with news about bets, sleazy scandals and popular idols.
   m) The quality of British newspapers has increased in general.

Translation: *The prince and the papers*

After years of media restraint, a palace aide's error of judgment has resulted in a flood of stories about Prince William appearing in the press

Here we go again. Sunday's tabloids overflowed with pictures and stories about Prince William in an uncanny rerun of the media barrage that regularly greeted his late mother. The News of the World and the Mail on Sunday ran paparazzi shots of the prince indulging in horseplay with a girl during a sports day at his Scottish university, St Andrews. The People, citing an unnamed police source, claimed the prince is planning to celebrate his 21st birthday next month by going on a „marathon pub crawl". The Sunday Mirror, quoting anonymous „courtiers", splashed on a story that alleged the prince is planning to spend „a few years living in the States" once he finishes his degree course. A similar tale appeared in the Sunday Express. Those stories followed Saturday's two-page article in the Sun, which suggested – on very little evidence – the prince and a fellow student are enjoying a romance, again illustrated by scandal pictures.

So, after years of press restraint due to an agreement orchestrated by the press complaints commission and St James's Palace, why was Prince William suddenly in the headlines? Wasn't he supposed to be left alone during his undergraduate years? It appears the prince is a victim of an error of judgment by his father's palace aides, who have agreed he will give Glasgow-based tabloid the Daily Record, the first media interview of his life. In view of the ferocious level of competition among tabloids, this ranks as a naive decision. When rival papers realised the Record was about to get an exclusive they would all die for, they complained bitterly to the palace. They argued the deal broke the informal „level playing field" agreement which means no paper is to be treated any differently from any other as long as they continue not to intrude the prince's privacy.

The new dispute has the hallmarks of a more profound problem that echoes the experiences of William's mother, Diana, Princess of Wales. Once he turns 21 and leaves university, the prince will no longer be able to rely on the press's self-denying ordinance. The paparazzi, who have been stalking William for months, have previously had no market for their pictures in Britain. It already looks as if the situation is changing. Are we on our way back to 1997?

Roy Greenslade, May 7 2003, Guardian Newspapers Limited

Text

8 One family that forgoes screens of all sizes

The first thing you notice when you walk into the Rodriguez home is the quiet. It takes a while to figure out what's different. There's a grand piano, a football table, a dog named Rusty, books that fill every crevice, and a well spun globe.

But missing are the wisecracks of Bart Simpson, the thump-thumping of Snoop Dogg, and the shrieks of Mortal Kombat. In this house, Shakespeare and Beethoven rule.

This is the story of one family that said no to the electronic media. To most Americans, it may seem like a radical statement – and experts themselves are divided over whether such a step is wholly beneficial or even attainable.

But in a time of increasing backlash to violent and sexual images aimed at children, the Rodriguezes believe they have made the right decision. The couple's two boys spend less time fighting and more time sharing, less time glued to a monitor and more time glued to a book, says mom Betsy Peck. As a result, she adds, they're learning to entertain themselves, rather than always expecting to be entertained and are developing their sense of curiosity and their imaginations.

Take 12-year-old Geoffrey, a huge Red Sox fan who has never seen the team play on TV. Rather, he listens to games on the radio. "I imagine the games in my head," he says, sprawled over a chair in the family's living room. "I imagine Fenway [Park] and how the players look hitting the ball."

Truth be told, the family does own a TV, but it's kept in the basement. When they watch, it's always as a family – complete with popcorn. They might spend two hours a month in front of the tube – way be low the national average of three hours a day for children.

And there's also a computer, but it's dad's. Sixteen-year-old Daniel gets to use it sparingly for homework. Geoffrey isn't allowed to log on.

Studies of media boycotters like this Massachusetts family are almost nonexistent. But many educators support limits on kids' time in front of a screen. "Children who don't have a large diet of electronic media tend to be more curious, creative, interactive, imaginative, and able to solve a problem", says Diane Lievin, an education professor at Wheelock College in Boston and author of "Remote Control Childhood".

But electronic media can have benefits as well. Banning them from the home is neither easy nor the best solution for every family, experts say. "Television can really be a tool for teaching kids about violence, sex and racism," says P. Miller of Children & the Media in Oakland. "When sensitive scenes appear, parents can use the opportunity to explain why they disapprove. That can happen only when parents watch with their children."

At the Rodriguez household, the limits work because they are consistently enforced – and the boys themselves seem to understand the reasons behind them. Here's how each family member views the electronic embargo.

Betsy Peck, mother of the Rodriguez clan, grew up in a typical 1960s television-watching family. "We ate dinner on TV trays in front of the television set and were only allowed to talk during the commercials," she recounts. "I knew right then I wasn't going to be like that." Before her sons visit the home of a new friend, she explains her rules to the parents. To avoid sticky situations, she encourages the boys to invite friends to their house. She admits that some children are initially bored there. But she's taken care to provide a house full of fun (…)

Tony Rodriguez has been the biggest holdout to an electronics-free family. Indeed, the TV wouldn't be in the house at all if not for him.

Mr. Rodriguez admits he loves watching movies on DVD and enjoys an occasional TV show. He is down to a few programs a week now that he gets the news online. Still, he enforces the limits for the boys. The programs the family watches, chosen carefully, might be the Olympics, the presidential debates, or "Star Trek" re-runs – a big favorite. The shows are always taped without commercials, and the boys are never allowed to turn on the TV just to see what's on.

"My wife and I believe you have to say no – and that it doesn't hurt a child to do so," Rodriguez says. Daniel Rodriguez says he's simply not interested in seeing or listening to most of what's out there in the e-world. An avid musician, he prefers jazz and classical over rap and rock. ("Those don't require any musical talent," he asserts.) And he reads voraciously – magazines like Time, Newsweek, Popular Science, National Geographic and books by the dozens.

Steering clear of TV, popular music, and the Net hasn't made Daniel feel left out. Any reference to pop culture he will have read about. "I can quote lines from movies I haven't even seen."

Moreover, his schedule isn't exactly empty. Currently, he's the pianist for the school musical, "Cabaret". He's playing Quince in the schools' production of "A Midsummer Night's Dream". He spends Saturdays at the Longy School of Music in Cambridge. He's in concert choir, jazz ensemble, and jazz improvisation. He also is in honors and advanced placement courses[1] at school.

Geoffrey, who is emerging as a class leader, seems more aware that he isn't up on[2] popular culture – that he's different from his friends.

His parents believe that's because he's more social than his older brother. But Geoffrey, easygoing and fun, exhibits the same self-discipline as Daniel does. He knows about Diabolo, a video game rated 17 or older, that his friends play. When they discuss a strategy or read the instructions Geoffrey doesn't participate. "I think it's sometimes seen as a negative by his friends," says his dad. "But he has learned how to deal with it."

(adapted from: The Christian Science Monitor, 2000-11-9)

[1] höhere Kurse in bestimmten Fächern / [2] über etw. Bescheid wissen

Activities

A Mediation

Med

1. Geben Sie den Inhalt der Überschrift wieder. (Keine Übersetzung)
2. Stellen Sie in zwei bis drei Sätzen die Besonderheit im Haus der Familie Rodriguez sowie das Verhalten der beiden Söhne dar.
3. Wie ist das Fernsehverhalten der Familie? Verwenden Sie auch Zahlenmaterial.
4. Wie beurteilt Diane Lievin Kinder, die sich kaum mit elektronischen Medien beschäftigen?
5. Welche Gründe werden von Experten für den Fernsehnkonsum angeführt, welche Rolle spielen die Eltern?

SAQs **B Text comprehension – short answer questions**

1. In the text, the TV and computer ban in the Rodriguez family is called ...
2. The Rodriguez boys are allowed to watch few types of taped programs, these are...
3. What are Daniel's preferences concerning his hobbies? Refer to lines 100-106.
4. Give a British synonym for the word schedule (l.112) in this context.
5. What does the word "that" (l. 129) refer to?

Literature

9 Ann Beattie: Love Always

Ann Beattie's novel *Love Always*, written in 1985, depicts the life of Lucy Spenser, who writes a lonely hearts column for a chic counter-culture magazine. Her teenage niece Nicole is the star of America's hottest soap opera, *Passionate Intensity*. In the following excerpt Ann Beattie gives an account of what this show is about.

For the last two years, Nicole Nelson had appeared on *Passionate Intensity* as Stephanie Sykes, an abused child from a broken family, a teenage alcoholic who was being rehabilitated by a woman internist and her husband, Gerald, a wimpy would-be novelist who felt misunderstood not only by his wife but by the world. The woman internist, who secretly subjected herself to experimental surgery to correct sterility, then found out that she could conceive. She faced the dilemma of whether to divorce her husband, who was at last working on his novel, to have a child with her true love, another doctor at the hospital, thereby disrupting the family routine she had established that had put young Stephanie on the road to recovery, or to settle for what she now realized was probably the correct thing: a childless marriage. This was also complicated by the fact that her husband's sister, a volunteer worker at the hospital who had always envied her sister-in-law and who had had a brief affair with the same doctor, was now considering blackmail, wanting to force her sister-in-law into the dull routine of motherhood with the wrong man, so that she could make the handsome doctor who would be left behind fall in love with her again. The further complication was that when his wife's wealthy benefactor died, the wimpy husband had buckled down long enough to put his wife through the last two years of medical school. The day of her graduation, he had had a mental breakdown and, when he was recovering, a brief affair with a woman who worked in the lab. Then he had at last gotten an advance for his book, *Barren*, a fictionalized account of his and his wife's failure to have children. What no one but the doctor/lover knew was that Stephanie Sykes was pregnant and begging the doctor to abort her. What even the doctor did not realize was that his lover's husband's ex-lover, the woman who worked in the lab, had found out that Stephanie was pregnant. She was anti-abortion, and if the doctor performed the surgery, she was going to go to the wimpy novelist and let him know what a farce his happy family life was, in hopes of getting him herself.

*From **Love Always**. Ann Beattie, Penguin Books: Harmondsworth, 1986, pp. 12, 13*

Annotations:
wimpy (6) – schwächlich / **conceive** (10) – become pregnant / **disrupt** (14) – cause disorder / **buckle down** (28) – do something in a determined way

Activities

A Text comprehension – multiple matching

MM

Who are they?

Match the boxes in the graph and the characters. Copy the answers in your notebook

1. Gerald
2. Gerald's sister, a volunteer worker at the hospital
3. Gerald's wife, the woman internist
4. handsome doctor
5. Stephanie, a teenage alcoholic
6. wealthy benefactor
7. woman working in the lab

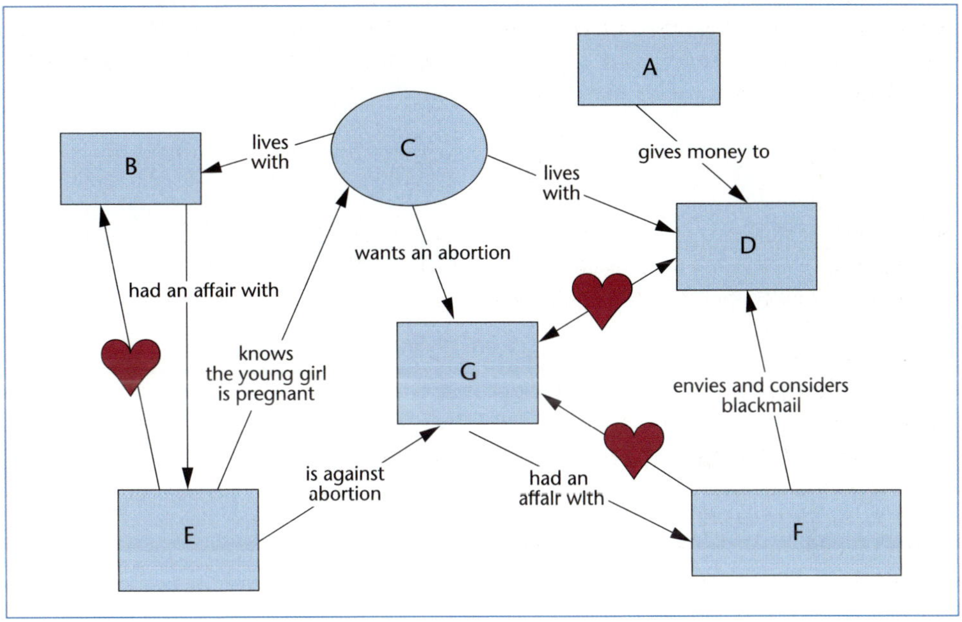

B Creative writing

Create your own TV show: characters, settings, story outline, values you want to convey. Here are some ideas to start you off:

characters	settings	story outline complications	values
student	boarding school and …	student has failed important test and …	honesty and …
his/her mother	… supermarket	… mother wants to marry again	… caring for others
etc	etc	etc	etc

Text

10 Spray-can renegades

Pre-reading activities

1. What is graffiti?
2. Is spraying an act of vandalism or an art form in its own right? Discuss.
3. When did you first see a work of graffiti?
4. Which country do you associate most with the graffiti scene? Could you give reasons?

Picture 1

Picture 2

5. Please have a look at the pictures above.
   a) What is their impression on you?
   b) What – in your opinion – was the intention of the painters?
   c) Can the painters make themselves understood by all groups? Explain, why.

From subway to gallery, from criminal records to record covers. New York's original graffiti provocateurs are still fighting the good fight, minding the gap between Seventies train vandalism and the cultural universalism of Nineties art.

"There was once a time
When the Lexington was a beautiful line
When children of the ghetto expressed
with art, not with crime
But then, as evolution passed
The trains look like rusted trash
Now we wonder if graffiti will ever last???"
(Epitaph, as sprayed on a New York train)

Five years were to elapse before Lee's spray-canned fears were fully realized. By the mid-Eighties the Metropolitan Transport Authority had won the battle for control of New York's subway system. And the graffiti crews – the writers and kings, the taggers and bombers and wild-stylers – had come to the surface, and somehow moved on.

"The mid-Eighties saw what you could call the death of modern-day graffiti art," argues Futura 2000, acknowledged as the founding father of the subway army. "Access to the subway was totally cut off. And then there was no more gallery interest, no more exhibitions.

At the time people were thinking that the scene was going to go on forever, but I remember thinking, it won't last, they're going to kill the golden goose. And it didn't last."

Futura was one of the subway kings way back. He'd amuse you. But most of his adult life has been a battle to survive above the ground, to move upwards, and onwards and outwards. The battle to keep the spray-can spirit of the activists alive. "Recognize where I'm from, but give a chance to explain where I'm going to," he asks.

Where he is going to is London for an exhibition, *Contents Under Pressure*, which is the fruit of a mutual admiration, involving a New York group and long-term English fans. They have developed strong ties, designing sleeve artwork and covers for British DJs. Fraser Cook, organizer of *Contents Under Pressure*, claims that the exhibition responds to an increased enthusiasm in Europe for the whole Graf Art scene. "A lot of the interest has to do with the whole trip hop thing and its packaging. Now a lot of studenty white kids are into Graf Art, which is good. And the thing is that it has been very influential. It is a real art form – in some ways the best new art form."

The clothing, the record covers and the exhibitions are part of the battle – the battle to keep Graf Art alive, above ground, on canvas, permanent, official, in galleries or as commercial art; but anyway far away from its roots as spontaneous and illegal public art, a flash-by logo of the (literal) underground.

Often this has meant looking to Europe and Japan. "The classic subway artists never really got any credit," says Futura. "The support, from the time I got into the 'art world', has been European and through foreign money. It has been simply enormous."

Some even left New York, artist exiles in search of their still unpaid respect. They admit, however, that there is a downside to this European and Japanese attention: the danger is that Graf Art could become an even more debased museum piece. A dying art vegetating on a European life-support machine. A new way of fighting back is taking Graf Art into the Internet. They have their own websites and are enthusiastic advocates of the World Wide Web. "If you think of the Graf movement and its history, you think of the trains – and the trains were definitely about motion. About how many different people get to see your art at any given moment; the Internet lends itself to that. It is the world-wide train."

They see the Net as a potential new subway system: uncontrolled, short-lived and public, a medium for keeping Graf Art alive. For them, there is unlimited power in the Net, and the most exciting thing is the total control that the person has, in terms of broadcasting, producing and publishing the site.

More than anything these artists of subway spraying are sure there is a living, breathing and forward-looking culture around Graf Art and what it can do. "You have kids all over the world who have been inspired and live in this culture that has a fashion, that likes to listen to certain music, that has a look. It is subculture, a growing, developing subculture."

(Adapted from Spray-can renegades by Nick Compton in The Face, May 1997)

Activities

A Working with vocabulary

1. Find your own ways to express the same ideas.
   a) *"A founding father"* (line 25).
   b) *"They're going to kill the golden goose"* (line 31)
   c) Who is meant by *"studenty white kids"*? (line 52)
   d) What is a *"flash-by logo"*? (line 62)
2. Find out the meaning of *'subculture'*. (line 99)
   Give a short description of this special subculture characterized in this text.

B Short answer questions

1. What do graffiti artists try to achieve in New York? (2 answers)
2. What did MTA achieve in the mid-Eighties?
3. How does Futura 2000 see MTA's achievement?
4. How can Futura's life be described?
5. How can the exhibition in London be explained?
6. What sort of people are interested in Graf Art?
7. Where do the artists get their best support?
8. Why is this support dangerous for this type of art?
9. How do Graf Artists fight back?
10. In what way is the new way of showing graffiti similar to the original one?
11. What is typical about the subculture Graf Artists work for?

11 Talkline: Choosing a TV channel

You live in a block of flats with more than 300 people. The house has its own reception equipment. It has been decided that one channel is to be used for receiving one of the following unencrypted[1)] programmes: BBC 1, BBC 2, BBC 3, BBC 4, BBC News 24 and BBC Parliament. Go to http://www.radiotimes.beeb.com/ or to some other page listing TV programmes. Each member of your group chooses one channel he/she supports. With the help of programme listings you describe "your" channel to the rest of the group. After 30 minutes of discussion you should have come to a conclusion which programme should become part of your package.

[1)] Encrypted programmes can only be viewed with a special receiver and a smartcard.

Unit 4

Cultural diversity

4

1 TALKING ABOUT STEREOTYPES: HOW TIDY CAN YOU GET?

Discuss the following British stereotypes about Germans.
To what extent do they apply / do they not apply?

Positive: Germans are considered to be hard-working, organised and tidy.

Less Positive: Germans lack imagination, have no sense of humour and are arrogant.

Text

2 How Singapore deals with litterbugs

Pre-reading activity

1. Are you "tidy" or rather a "messy" person? (What would your mother say?) Discuss.
2. Which of the things mentioned below (a – h) do you find most annoying in public places and why?
3. What can or should be done about it?
4. If you were to find people for the acts of littering or vandalism mentioned below, how high would your fines be? Arrange the following (a – h) according to how serious your fine would be.

[a) chewing gum b) dog dirt c) bottles d) cigarette butts e) graffiti f) matchsticks g) cigarette box wrappers h) drink cans]

A taxi driver in Singapore tells an often-told joke: "Singapore is a fine country. In Singapore, we have fines for everything." The joke is popular because fines are a defining element of life in Singapore. Some of the fines are for offences that international travellers might expect, such as littering or jaywalking. However, the penalties for these crimes and the strictness with which they are enforced may surprise travellers. First-time offenders can be fined S$500 or more.

Other laws are more unique to Singapore. Some examples: it is illegal to use a toilet in Singapore and then not flush it. You will also be given a fine if you are caught spitting. Furthermore the sale, importation and possession of chewing gum is banned and subject to heavy fines. First-time offenders can be fined S$1,000 and repeat-offenders are fined S$2,000 and given corrective work, such as cleaning a public place. The offenders are made to wear bright yellow jackets, and sometimes, media are invited to cover the spectacle.

The community work, involving clearing areas that have litter, may be seen as a preventive measure because of the prospect for offenders to be embarrassed by the punishment. But not all offenders see it that way.

"There is nothing to be embarrassed about," said a 19-year-old Malay woman, when asked if she felt embarrassed to wear a vest which reads on the back "Corrective Work Order". "It's legal work that I am doing," she said with a shrug. She declined to give her name. She was caught littering with her boyfriend, who was serving a CWO on the same day in a nearby residential area.

An elderly Chinese man in CWO vest appeared embarrassed. Wearing a cap, he kept his head low and refused to make any comment.

"It was pure bad luck," said another Chinese girl in her 20s, who claimed she dropped a plastic bag "by accident." "Anyway, it is very embarrassing. I just saw someone I know walk by. I quickly turned my back to him," she said.

Not every litterbug will have to face the Corrective Work Order. That is imposed for repeat-offenders or first-time major offenders. Small litter is considered as cigarette butts, bus tickets, sweet and cigarette box wrappers, carpark coupons and matchsticks. Drink cans and rubbish other than the list of small litter is considered major litter.

The CWO only applies to Singapore residents, so tourists are exempt. Also, no foreigner residing in Singapore has yet served a CWO. For repeat offenders, one other penalty awaits them: a counselling session. For 15 minutes, litterbugs watch a video which will explain how litter can be washed down into our watercourses and cause pollution in the environment. The purpose is to educate them and inform them of the consequences of their action.

*From **University of Northern Illinois** (www.niu.edu/cseas/outreach/singlaw.htm, July 2004) and **Singapore Window** (www.singapore-window.org/sw01/010306nz.htm, July 2004)*

Annotation
S$1 = € 0.62

Activities

SAQs

A Short answer questions

In Singapore, what penalties are there for littering and jaywalking? Copy the grid into your notebook and fill it in. You needn't use complete sentences.

Penalty	Definition
CWO	

B More activities

1. Explain the taxi driver's joke about Singapore.
2. What do you think of the idea of CWO?
3. How, according to the text, do the people sentenced to a CWO react?

C Discussion

1. Where do you find the most litter in your school? Who or what causes it?
2. What is done about litter at your school?
3. How could the amount of littering at your school be reduced?
4. What do you think of a "voluntary cleaning brigade" at your school? How could it be organised?
5. In Joanne K. Rowling's *Harry Potter*, the four different houses at Hogwarts (a boarding school for young magicians) are awarded points or have points taken away for the good or bad performance or behaviour of the members of the house. The house with the highest number of points is given a prize. Could you imagine having a competition like that at your school for the different classes in order to – among other things – reduce littering or acts of vandalism?
   Make a list of the kinds of behaviour you would award or take away points for and how many. Give reasons.

Text

■□□ 3 School regulations in the US

The following is an excerpt from the Student/Parent Handbook 2003/2004 for parents and students at *Hogan High School* in Vallejo, California. Most American Handbooks contain regulations similar to the ones you will find below. Look at the titles first. Are there similar headlines in your school regulations (*Schulordnung*)?

Student/Parent Handbook 2003/2004

Use/Possession of Controlled Substance

Students under the influence of illegal drugs/alcohol will be subject to the following actions:

- They shall be removed from the class or activity where they will be isolated from others.
- The student's parent, guardians or other designated responsible person will be notified and asked to come to the school.
- Law enforcement officials will be contacted and the facts reported to them.
- Consequences: 1st offense: 3 to 5 days suspension/Referred to Student Assistance Program
  2nd offense: 5 days suspension and recommendation for expulsion.

Students in possession of illegal drugs/alcohol will be subject to the following actions:

- The drug(s)/alcohol will be confiscated.
- Parents/Guardians will be asked to come to school.
- The violation will be reported to the police.
- Consequences: 1st offense: 3 to 5 days suspension/Referred to Student Assistance Program
  2nd offense: 5 days suspension and recommendation for expulsion.

Smoking/Use of Tobacco Products

The term "Tobacco Products" includes, but is not limited to, cigarettes, cigars, pipes, chewing tobacco, smokeless tobacco, and snuff. The possession and/or use of tobacco products by students is prohibited by State Law (EC 48900) and Vallejo City Unified School District policy. All students are prohibited possession and/or use of tobacco products during the student day. The student day begins when the student leaves home for school, during lunch, after school, and at school activities.

Searches

A student's attire, personal property, vehicle, or school property including books, desks, and school lockers may be searched by a principal/principal designee when there is reason to suspect a student possesses illegal items or illegally obtained items.

Dress Code

Students shall not be prevented from attending school, a school function, or otherwise be discriminated against, so long as his/her clothing is not of an intimidating or provocative fashion, is not destructive to school property and does not interfere with the educational process.
The administration will take action in instances where individuals do not meet the stated requirements.

- Shirts advertising any controlled substance (alcoholic beverages, marijuana, etc.) or those with obscene, vulgar or threatening or questionable messages on them will not be permitted.
- Skirts must be fingertip length or longer.
- There must not be any exposed undergarments of any kind.
- See through clothing and indecent body exposure is not allowed.
- All students will remove their hats and hoods while inside any building on campus (this includes both gyms and the auditorium).

Used with permission of Hogan High School, Vallejo, California

Activities

A Text comprehension

Compare the Student Handbook with your school regulations.

1. What action is taken at your school if a teacher finds students smoking, drinking beer or taking drugs on a field trip or on the way home? What measures are taken at an American High School if this happens?
2. Are there any clear cut regulations in your school regulations as far as drugs and alcohol are concerned? What are they?
3. If yes, how are these rules enforced?
4. Have there ever been searches of a student's clothing, car, or personal property at your school when there was reason to suspect that he or she possessed illegal items like weapons, alcohol, drugs, etc?
5. Do you think German schools should be stricter in this respect?
6. Is there a dress code at your school?
7. What do you think of a dress code? If you do not like the idea, remember that schools in a way are comparable to places of work. There are rules – formal and informal – in order to prevent people from being distracted or sexually harassed by indecent clothing at their place of work.

B Writing

1. Contact an American High School to set up an e-mail project to discuss differences in school policies with American students.
2. Would stricter smoking/drug/alcohol policies help students to refrain from tobacco/drugs/alcohol abuse?

4 Different people have different backgrounds

Andrew Pang, 25, software developer

I am British. I was born in Hong Kong and my parents are Chinese but I married here and have lived here for eight years.

Dorothy King, 36 solicitor

I call myself Jewish because my religious identity defines me. I was born in Hull and my parents were born in Britain too, but I am Jewish first.

Valery Ashcroft, 22 music graduate

I'm British – if you were born here, you're British, if you weren't, you're not. My dad was born in Jamaica, so what?

Patrick McGuilford, 72, retired

I'm Irish. I'm from County Down, my accent is strong and Irish and there's nothing about me that's British.

Mansour Hussain, 31, van driver

I call myself British because I was born in England, grew up in Scotland and I like Scottish things: I drink Irn Bru and I support Celtic.

Paula Dobson, 16, school pupil

I call myself Scottish because I was born in Glasgow and this is the country that I'm most proud of – Britishness is fine but it's a bit too English.

The Guardian Wednesday October 11, 2000
http://www.guardian.co.uk/britain/article/0,2763,380482,00.html

Activities

Text comprehension

1. According to which categories do the people in the pictures define themselves? To start you off: One category could be called "religion".
2. What do you call yourself? Prepare a short statement.

Text

5 Domestic differences in Britain

Pre-reading activity

MM

Multiple matching

Match the words and the explanations

A divorce	1. moral principles
B cohabitation	2. living together and having a sexual relationship without being married
C couple	3. money you borrow to buy a house
D issue	4. legal ending of a marriage
E mortgage	5. topic of discussion
F ethic	6. two people who have a relationship of some kind

The ethnic group most likely to uphold the "old-fashioned" structure of British family life is that from the Pakistani and Bangladeshi communities. On the other hand, white and particularly Caribbean relationships are increasingly characterised by divorce, cohabitation and single parenthood. While Caribbean lone parents are far more likely to work than their white counterparts, more than half still depend on income support. With half of the British-born Caribbean men and one third of the women who are in relationships having chosen white partners, they are also far more likely to intermarry than any other group.

The majority of Pakistani and Bangladeshi women look after their home and family full-time, although that proportion declines considerably among those with more qualifications. The combination of large families and non-working wives means that half Pakistani and Bangladeshi households have a standard of living below half the national average, even if the father is working.

Case study 1: The married couple

Kashif and Sabeen Ashraf are a model nuclear family: a young, happily married couple with a one-year-old son. Sabeen, from Pakistan, joined Kashif in Oldham after their arranged marriage in 1996, and says she would never have dreamed of living with him out of wedlock.

"You hear of people who've cohabited, but none of my friends have," says Kashif, 32, a careers officer. "It tends to be people in interracial relationships. Maybe a generation down the line it might happen."

He adds: "I think marriage is more binding. And also, once I graduated and got a job, the next thing in life was to have a family to complete the circle. I was born in Oldham and have been to university, but I still chose the traditional route."

He says that divorce is still stigmatised, although he knows a few Asian divorcees.

Sabeen, 25, who runs a boutique, is similarly pragmatic about the rising divorce rate. "Nobody wants to get divorced, but if they're not happy then there's no point living together," she says.

Case study 2: The unmarried couple

Janet McLean and her partner Aled Murphy are a typical example of a modern-day white couple. After two years living together in Fife they say marriage is "not an issue", although they would like to wed if they have children.

The couple see their bond of trust and their practical commitments – a mortgage and joint bank account – as more important than a piece of paper. Forty years ago their families might have disagreed. But what was once condemned as living in sin is now a normal way of life for millions of Britons.

"Nobody in my family is married," says Janet, 27, a research psychologist. "My brother and mum and dad all cohabit with partners, and my dad keeps pointing out to me that it doesn't matter any more because under Scottish law we are more or less man and wife."

Aled, 30, an electronics engineer, agrees that families are now much more understanding: "A lot of people's parents did it themselves in the 60s and 70s, although my mum didn't; I don't think she would have been allowed to."

Case study 3: The single mother

Yasmin Ferguson spent 13 years with her childhood sweetheart, but moved out of their shared house in Bristol after their son was born eight years ago. "I didn't want my son growing up with shouting and I knew it was the fact we were living together that was causing problems," she explains. She continued to see her partner until a year ago.

Yasmin, 29, is a qualified social worker studying for a degree in health and community studies. She believes her self-reliance is partly due to an immigrant work ethic inherited from her parents.

"My mum and dad came over from Jamaica to find a better life for themselves. When we were growing up we were taught we should be independent and self-sufficient," she says. "Women in general tend to be told you have to go out and find prince charming."

None of her seven elder brothers and sisters are married, but she still hopes to find a lifelong partner. "I think that's why I'm single," she says. "I contribute a lot to relationships and I want my expectations to be met. I do hope one day I will meet someone for ever."

*From **The Guardian**, December 18, 2000*

Activities

A Scanning

Scan the text to find out more about ...

1. where the people we are told about in the three case studies live.
2. what their jobs are.

B Text comprehension – short answer questions

SAQs

Case study 1

What is Kashif's and Sabeen's attitude towards

1. marriage?
2. cohabitation?
3. divorce?

Case study 2

What do Janet and Aled say about

1. children?
2. financial matters?
3. cohabitation?

Case study 3

1. Why has Yasmin chosen to be a single parent?
2. What does she say about the values she was brought up with?
3. Why has she stayed single for such a long time?

C Writing

Write a comment on the topic *My Prince Charming* or *The Woman of my dreams.*

D Discussion

Could you imagine staying single? What are the pros and cons of single life?

E Words, words, words

Give the corresponding nouns.

a) to relate	f) to graduate
b) to characterise	g) to complete
c) to marry	h) to divorce
d) to qualify	i) to disagree
e) to wed	j) to cohabit

Text

■■□ 6 Race hate in Britain is widespread – just ask my wife

Pre-reading activity

The following story is about a white journalist married to a black woman. They have two children.

What problems do you think might occur, when coloured people ...

- go shopping?
- have to deal with the police?
- go to a football match?
- are looking for a job?

Liberal white Britons must face facts: despite smug boasts of 'aren't we a nice multicultural, all-get-on-together society', it just isn't so.

As a white Briton married to a black Briton, I have seen at first hand what goes on everyday in homes, offices, schools and on the streets. We have been lucky, and avoided serious racist attacks. We live in a nice, largely middle-class area of London.

Yet those incidents that have happened are enough to make me sometimes feel ashamed to be white. After I first introduced my wife to my family, one relative saw absolutely nothing wrong in telling a 'good one' that involved a black man with 'big rubbery lips'. He still wonders why I haven't spoken to or seen him since.

Shortly after my son was born, our white au pair took him swimming to the local pool in south London. She fled home in tears after two white youths began shouting at her, calling her a 'nigger lover'.

Out shopping at *Marks & Spencer* when my son was eighteen months old, he became fascinated, as kids of that age do, by the shiny rings of the middle-aged white woman standing in the queue behind us. As Joshua's little hands tried to grab the rings, she remarked: 'Starting young, isn't he?' I didn't know whether to cry or just simply tell her to get lost.

When my brother-in-law and his mixed race team went to play a football match in Kent, taking the then eight-year-old Josh for a day out, it descended into a running battle of racist abuse that left my son shaking and asking why white people disliked black people. It is an incident to which he still refers, and to which he still seeks answers.

A couple of months ago, a man rang our doorbell at 4 am. My wife spoke to him through the door, where he tried (but failed) to gain entrance by spinning a story about having run out of cash for his electricity meter and needing our help. The next day, she rang to report the incident to the police. Having not seen the man, she was unable to provide a description. 'Did he sound black or white?' the policeman asked. 'That's an interesting question,' she replied. 'What do I sound like?' 'Well, you sound white,' the policeman replied. It was a week after the new commissioner of the Met had proclaimed the force as on the way to being 'a truly anti-racist police service'.

Twenty-odd years ago, I went to Rock Against Racism concerts and marched in Anti-Nazi League demonstrations hoping for a better future. The future is now, and as my children grow older, I grow increasingly concerned about the prejudices and discrimination they still face only on the basis of their skin colour. My son's experiences out on the streets of London are likely to be little different from his uncle's 20 years ago. The statistics stink. The reality stinks.

My son – who is 12 in July – is more likely to be stopped, searched, arrested, sent to prison, than his 12-year-old white cousin. He's more likely to be attacked on the street because of his skin colour than his cousin. He's more likely to be regarded with suspicion when he walks into a shop. He's less likely to get a bank loan, more likely to be unemployed, less likely to get promotion should he get a job. The list is depressingly endless.

Whites have got to realise there are not just a few bad apples out in society ruining their 'multicultural dream'. The bad apples are in a majority and the so-called multicultural dream is actually a nightmare.

Adapted from The Observer, March 26, 2000

Annotations

smug (2) – assured, self-satisfied / **Marks & Spencer** (23) – chain of department stores in Great Britain / **electricity meter** (43) – some British households have meters that provide electricity or gas when you throw in a coin / **Met** (51) – London Metropolitan Police / **twenty-odd years ago** (54) – about, or a bit more than, twenty years ago

Activities

A Text comprehension – short answer questions

SAQs

Scan the text to find out what happened to Josh when he was ...

1. a baby.
2. eighteen months old.
3. eight years old.

MM

B Text comprehension – multiple matching

In the report we are told about different forms of racism:

a) jokes
b) insults
c) prejudice
d) harassment (attacks)
e) discrimination

What are the examples that are given in the text for each form of racism?

C Writing

While surfing the internet you have come across a discussion platform dealing with everyday racism and asking for contributions on that subject. Write an entry about incidents of everyday racism you have experienced or observed.

D Discussion

Discuss with your partner or group: A multicultural society is a fact, not a dream.

E Words, words, words

1. Explain in your own words what the author means when he says ...
   a) They must face facts (line 1).
   b) ... to get lost (line 30)
   c) The statistics stink (line 63).
   d) ... a few bad apples out in society ... (line 76)
2. Give the opposites.
   a) liberal (line 1)
   b) lucky (line 7)
   c) serious (line 7)
   d) sometimes (line 11)
   e) ashamed (line 12)
   f) shiny (line 25)
   g) mixed (line 31)
   h) increasingly (line 58)
   i) different (line 62)
   j) endless (line 74)

Listening comprehension: The Bradford clashes

From April to July 2001, the northern English towns of Oldham, Burnley and Bradford saw violent confrontations between young Asians and the police, culminating in the clashes of 7–9 July in Bradford in which 200 police officers were injured, cars were set on fire and three police horses were stabbed. Allegedly, the clashes were prompted by racist gangs attacking Asian communities and the failure of the police to provide protection from this threat. In the scale of the damage caused and the shock they delivered to the nation, the 2001 riots were the worst riots in Britain since the Handsworth, Brixton and Tottenham uprisings of 1985.

Listen to six voices commenting on the Bradford clashes.
What are their opinions on the cause of the riots? Choose from the list **A – G**.
Use each letter only once. There is one extra with wrong information.

A Bradford is a peaceful town where Asians and Whites get along very well – the rioters were simply thugs looking for destruction.
B Alcohol was the main reason why the riots started.
C Riots like that are only possible because from childhood on the members of the different ethnic communities don't learn enough about each other.
D The police had to be that strict, otherwise police officers might have got killed.
E The riots were a warning to rightwing extremists not to cause trouble in the Asian communities.
F The riots were the expression of an inadequate policy that promotes segregation.
G The underlying cause of the riots seems to be that there is too much racism in the UK.

FACT BOX

Ethnicity in Bradford
Out of Bradford's population of 460,000, nearly 80,000 are Asian, most of them from the Pakistani part of Kashmir. About 30 per cent of schoolchildren are from the ethnic minorities, with that predicted to rise to 50 per cent by 2010.

Translation: *Britain's open society*

British society in the years to come will be the most open and cosmopolitan in Western Europe. It was not always so; Britain's reputation has long been that of a class-ridden island with bad food and funny ideas about foreigners.

The success of Asian incomers, mostly Indians and Pakistanis will make Britain resemble California. The proportion of Asians attending Britain's universities and colleges will be higher than the proportion of "indigenous" whites; and they will, on average, gain higher grades. The typical young British economist and business-school graduate will soon be Asian. Britain's Afro-Caribbeans used to complain that "there ain't no black in the Union Jack." There is now, at least in sport. England's 1982 World Cup squad contained no blacks. Its 1998 World Cup squad contained four.

Britain's increasingly open society will be open to the outside world. The simple rule that allows any EU citizen to work wherever he wishes is drawing tens of thousands of young continentals to Britain. High unemployment at home in France or Spain and a huge number of job opportunities in England pulls them across the channel. Britain's universities are also now open to EU students: applications which were once only a trickle are now becoming an actual flood.

In any case, the British were never as insular and self-absorbed as they were made out to be. If they had been, English would not be the world language it now is. It would be a strange blend of Anglo-Saxon and Norman French spoken on a small island moored off the north European coast.

*From **The World** in 1999, Economist Publications, London*

8 Prejudice quiz

You will find out how much you know about how prejudice works by doing the following quiz.

1. *Prejudice* refers to ...
   a) positive attitudes of a special kind.
   b) any kind of bias or inclination toward anything or anyone that may be considered inherently irrational.
   c) a usually negative attitude toward the members of some social group.
   d) attitudes of a majority toward a minority.

2. What are stereotypes?
   a) Beliefs and expectations about a particular group.
   b) Negative emotions experienced in the presence of members of a specific group.
   c) Any mental process that is involved in the evaluation of people.
   d) Negative behavioural tendencies with respect to the people who are the object of prejudice.

3. How do most people handle information that is inconsistent with a stereotype they hold?
   a) They assimilate the information, and it changes the stereotype.
   b) They react with a boomerang effect; the stereotype becomes much stronger.
   c) They deny the information or refute it.
   d) They misinterpret the information as supporting their stereotype.

4. According to theories on social learning, negative attitudes toward various social groups are due to ...
   a) sex-role training.
   b) inborn social tendencies.
   c) parents and friends.
   d) the political-economic-social climate.

5. Relative to men, women tend to be ...
   a) more ambitious.
   b) more concerned about money.
   c) less creative.
   d) less confident.

6. What do parents do to their children when they are prejudiced themselves?
   a) Raise their self-esteem and pride in their own group.
   b) Fill them with needless fear, anxiety, and anger.
   c) Make them less prejudiced, because the parents' model will necessarily look bad.
   d) Make them indifferent, as harping on a subject makes the children turn away from it.

7. Why does contact between groups work to reduce prejudice?
   a) Contact may increase the perception of similarity of members belonging to the different group.
   b) "Mere exposure" leads to liking regardless of the circumstance.
   c) Contact promotes the illusion that groups are all alike.
   d) It works, but nobody knows why.

8. If a white person is prejudiced against Blacks, but is placed in a job situation where he/she has to work with Blacks, you would expect him/her to show ...
   a) more prejudice immediately.
   b) more prejudice over time.
   c) less prejudice immediately.
   d) less prejudice over time.

Used with permission of Dr. M. Whatley, Valdosta State University

Activities

Explore the internet to find out about more about the following terms.
- Socialising agencies
- Sherif experiment
- Reinforcement

Literature

9 Amy Tan: The Joy Luck Club

Amy Tan was born in Oakland, California, in 1952, two and a half years after her parents had immigrated to the United States. Amy Tan lives in San Francisco with her husband. *The Joy Luck Club* is her first book. It is the story of a Chinese-American family living in San Francisco. A young Chinese-American woman wants to introduce her American boyfriend to her Chinese mother.

The night of the dinner, I sat in the kitchen watching her cook, waiting for the right moment to tell her about our marriage plans, that we had decided to get married next July, about seven months away. She was chopping eggplant into wedges, chattering at the same time about Auntie Suyuan: "She can only cook looking at a recipe. My instructions are in my fingers. I know what secret ingredients to put in just by using my nose!" And she was slicing with such a ferocity, seemingly inattentive to her sharp cleaver, that I was afraid her fingertips would become one of the ingredients of the red-cooked eggplant and shredded pork dish.

I was hoping she would say something first about Rich. I had seen her expression when she opened the door, her forced smile as she scrutinized him from head to toe, checking her appraisal of him against that already given to her by Auntie Suyuan. I tried to anticipate what criticisms she would have.

Rich was not only *not* Chinese, he was a few years younger than I was. And unfortunately, he looked much younger with his curly red hair, smooth pale skin, and the splash of orange freckles across his nose. He was a bit on the short side, compactly built. In his dark business suits, he looked nice but easily forgettable, like somebody's nephew at a funeral. Which was why I didn't notice him the first year we worked together at the firm. But my mother noticed everything.

"So what do you think of Rich?" I finally asked, holding my breath.

She tossed the eggplant in the hot oil and it made a loud, angry-hissing sound. "So many spots on his face," she said.

I could feel the pinpricks on my back. "They're freckles. Freckles are good luck, you know," I said a bit too heatedly in trying to raise my voice above the din of the kitchen.

"Oh?" she said innocently.

"Yes, the more spots the better. Everybody knows that."

She considered this a moment and then smiled and spoke in Chinese: "Maybe this is true. When you were young, you got the chicken pox. So many spots, you had to stay home for ten days. So lucky, you thought."

I couldn't save Rich in the kitchen. And I couldn't save him later at the dinner table.

He had brought a bottle of French wine, something he did not know my parents could not appreciate. My parents did not even own wine glasses. And then he also made the mistake of drinking not one but two frosted glasses full, while everybody else had a half-inch "just for taste."

When I offered Rich a fork, he insisted on using the slippery ivory chopsticks. He held them splayed like the knock-kneed legs of an ostrich while picking up a large chunk of sauce-coated eggplant. Halfway between his plate and his open mouth, the chunk fell on his crisp white shirt and then slid into his crotch. It took several minutes to get Shoshana to stop shrieking with laughter.

And then he had helped himself to big portions of the shrimp and snow peas not realizing he should have taken only a polite spoonful, until everybody had had a morsel.

He had declined the sauteed new greens, the tender and expensive leaves of bean plants plucked before the sprouts turn into beans. And Shoshana refused to eat them also, pointing to Rich: "He didn't eat them! He didn't eat them!"

He thought he was being polite by refusing seconds, when he should have followed my father's example, who made a big show of taking small portions of seconds, thirds, and even fourths, always saying he could not resist another bite of something or other, and then groaning that he was so full he thought he would burst.

But the worst was when Rich criticized my mother's cooking, and he didn't even know what he had done. As is the Chinese cook's custom, my mother always made disparaging remarks about her own cooking. That night she chose to direct it toward her famous steamed pork and preserved vegetable dish, which she always served with special pride.

"Ai! This dish not salty enough, no flavor," she complained, after tasting a small bite. "It is too bad to eat."

This was our family's cue to eat some and proclaim it the best she had ever made. But before we could do so, Rich said, "You know, all it needs is a little soy sauce." And he proceeded to pour a riverful of the salty black stuff on the platter, right before my mother's horrified eyes.

And even though I was hoping throughout the dinner that my mother would somehow see Rich's kindness, his sense of humor and boyish charm, I knew he had failed miserably in her eyes.

Rich obviously had had a different opinion on how the evening had gone. When we got home that night, after we put Shoshana to bed, he said modestly, "Well. I think we hit it off A-o-kay." He had the look of a dalmatian, panting, loyal, waiting to be petted.

"Uh-hmm," I said. I was putting on an old nightgown, a hint that I was not feeling amorous. I was still shuddering, remembering how Rich had firmly shaken both my parents' hands with that same easy familiarity he used with nervous new clients. "Linda, Tim" he said, "we'll see you again soon, I'm sure." My parents' names are Lindo and Tin Jong, and nobody, except a few older family friends, ever calls them by their first names.

"So what did she say when you told her?" And I knew he was referring to our getting married. I had told Rich earlier that I would tell my mother first and let her break the news to my father.

"I never had a chance," I said, which was true. How could I have told my mother I was getting married, when at every possible moment we were alone, she seemed to remark on how much expensive wine Rich liked to drink, or how pale and ill he looked, or how sad Shoshana seemed to be.

Rich was smiling. "How long does it take to say, Mom, Dad, I'm getting married?"

"You don't understand. You don't understand my mother."

Rich shook his head. "Whew! You can say that again. Her English was so bad. You know, when she was talking about that dead guy showing up on *Dynasty*. I thought she was talking about something that happened in China a long time ago."

From The Joy Luck Club by Amy Tan, New York: Ballantine Books, 1989

Annotations

chop eggplant into wedges (5) – Aubergine in Stückchen schneiden / **cleaver** (11) – Küchenmesser / **pinprick** (37) – Nadelstich / **din** (40) – Lärm / **chicken-pox** (46) – Windpocken / **frosted glass** (55) – Matt-, Milchglas / **splayed** (60) – nach außen gebogen / **knock-kneed** (60) – X-beinig / **ostrich** (60) – Strauß / **crotch** (64) – Schoß / **snow peas** (68) – Zuckererbsen / **morsel** (70) – Stückchen, kleine Portion

Activities

A Text comprehension

1. Rich unknowingly makes a lot of mistakes. What does he do wrong?
2. What could he have done to avoid these mistakes?
3. How do cultural differences affect the couple's relationship?

B Writing

1. Imagine you are Rich's girlfriend. Write down your feelings in your diary. Think of a way to solve this problem you are having with your mother and with Rich.
2. Imagine a friend of yours is going to China. Write down a list of tips on how to behave as a guest in a Chinese family.

Text

10 Two speeches on race relations in Britain

Speech 1: Brittle Britain

Sir Herman Ouseley was formerly executive chairman of the Commission for Racial Equality. This is an extract from a speech given at the University of Salford in June 2001.

Cloze-activity

Complete the words and copy them in your notebook.

"Most British people are fair-minded and tol..1... I am sure my view is sha..2.. by many other people. Today Britain can point to the nine black/Asian MPs (all Labour) and a score of peers from the vis..3.. minorities (though still a long way short of proportionate) as evi..4.. of political success. One could also cite many Asian millio..5... Thus there is an argument for talking up the success story of Britain's approaches to race rel..6...

Leadership and the media play a critical role in chal..7.. racist attitudes and promoting fair practices and behav..8... But on the other hand, they can distort, sensationalise and reinf..9.. negative stereot..10... The recent foot and mouth epidemic, it was suggested in at least one newspaper, may have been due to illegal meat im..11.. by a Chinese restaurant. I heard similar stories about infected meat smug..12.. in from Pakistan and Africa.

Children come out of their formal education beli..13.. black people's link with Britain is recent and they have contri..14.. little to Britain's well-being. But in Roman t..15.., Septimus Severus led a garrison of African soldiers who guarded Hadrian's Wall. Elizabeth I pronouncement about *blackamoors* in London in the 1660s was evid..4.. of a signif..16.. black presence.

During the great wars of the 20th century, Africans were visible alongside thousands of Asian soldiers in Burma and Indian soldiers who sup..17.. the allied forces and many from the Caribbean who supported the British Empire contingents.

How galling there..18.. it was as a black child in Britain to hear people say: 'We didn't win the war for you people to take our jobs and homes.'

How can we build tolerance, acc..19.. and respect without accurate information, kno..20.., understanding, truth and honesty?

While significant sections of the British me..21.. are very fair, some consistently use words such as "swamping", "overrun", "tide", "sea", "army", "waves" and "torr..22.." to demonise incoming refu..23... Opinion polls show overw..24.. resentment and distrust of immigrants and asylum se..25... I wonder where they get their information from?

Only last autumn a sur..26.. showed most people believe there are "too many" immigrants in Britain getting "too much" assi..26... Most believed asylum se..25.. received an average £113 per week. Fact: £36.54. Most believed that on average 26 % belong to et..27.. minorities. The reality is 7 %.

How are we so badly informed? Why are we so ig..28..?"

From http://society.guardian.co.uk/Print/0,3858,42208613,00.html, May 2004

Annotations

brittle (heading) – fragile / **MP** (4) – Member of Parliament / **peer** (5) – here: life peer, title is only granted to himself and is not inherited by his heirs / **to talk sb./sth.up** (9) – to describe sb./sth. in a way that makes them sound better than they really are

Activities

A Text comprehension

1. What shows that race relations in Britain seem to be improving?
2. Sum up what can be said about the role the media play in Britain's race relations.
3. What misconceptions are there about coloured people and immigrants in Britain?
4. How, according to Sir Herman Ouseley, can intolerance between races be abolished?

B Discussion

How would you describe the situation of guest workers, immigrants and asylum seekers in your home country?

Speech 2: Robin Cook – Chicken Tikka Massala

This is an extract from a speech given by then Foreign Secretary Robin Cook to the Social Market Foundation in London in April 2001.

"Today's London is a perfect hub of the globe. It is home to over 30 ethnic communities of at least 10,000 residents each. In this city tonight, over 300 languages will be spoken by families over their evening meal at home.

This pluralism is not a burden we must reluctantly accept. It is an immense asset that contributes to the cultural and economic vitality of our nation.

We must create an open and inclusive society that welcomes incomers for their contribution to our growth and prosperity. Our measures to attract specialists in information technology are a good example.

And it isn't just our economy that has been enriched by the arrival of new communities. Our lifestyles and cultural horizons have also been broadened in the process. This point is perhaps more readily understood by young Britons, who are more open to new influences and more likely to have been educated in a multi-ethnic environment. But it reaches into every aspect of our national life.

Chicken Tikka Massala is now a true British national dish, not only because it is the most popular, but because it is a perfect illustration of the way Britain absorbs and adapts external influences. Chicken Tikka is an Indian dish. The Massala sauce was added to satisfy the desire of British people to have their meat served in gravy. Coming to terms with multiculturalism as a positive force for our economy and society will have significant implications for our understanding of Britishness."

Published in The Guardian, April 19, 2001

Annotations
hub (1) – here: heart / **reluctantly** (7) – unwillingly / **asset** (7) – advantage

Activities

A Scanning

Below are the keywords of Robin Cook's speech. Read the text, then try to repeat in what contexts he uses those words without looking at the text.

- London
- not a burden
- specialists in information technology
- young Britons
- Chicken Tikka Massala

B Writing

1. A British friend of yours has expressed his/her deep concern about the clashes in Bradford and Oldham and asks you to tell him/her about the state of race relations in Germany.
2. Describe your favourite foreign restaurant and foreign dish.
3. Write a guide to the foreign restaurants in your home town. Include information about what is offered and about the prices.
4. Make a list of all the things that you have got in your home that are of foreign origin or originate from a foreign culture.
   To start you off: Your rap CDs, ...

C Discussion

1. In what way do incomers broaden our *lifestyles and cultural horizons* (line 17–18)?
2. Young people are more open to multi-ethnic influences. Do you agree?
3. Multiculturalism – blessing or burden?

■□□ 11 Talkline: What I think

Make notes stating to what degree you agree or disagree with the following statements. Write 1 if you agree strongly, 2 if you agree to a certain extent, 3 if you disagree to a certain extent and 4 if you disagree strongly. Make also short notes on possible reasons.
Then you work in groups of about 4 people. The first student makes a statement, then the others say if they agree or not and give reasons. Then the next student chooses a statement from the list and the others react. Continue until you have dealt with all (or almost all) statements.
Then each group chooses one statement they had differed on and discusses it trying to reach agreement.

Statements:

1. Married couples should stay together.
2. Germans work harder than others.
3. If people are poor it is up to their family and relatives to support them and not the job of the government.
4. Latin Americans are better football players.
5. When we travel to a foreign country we should read books about the country first.
6. Jobs should be given to women only until they represent 50 % of the workforce.
7. We should have friends with different nationalities.
8. A woman's place is in the house.
9. Germans are very popular in other countries.
10. Students ought to spend some time abroad.
11. Immigrants should not be allowed to live all in the same area of a city.
12. We must not look away if somebody is discriminated against.
13. Unmarried couples should not be allowed to live in the same flat.
14. We should introduce school uniforms.
15. We should try to get our cities as clean as Singapore.
16. Single mothers should be given money so that they can stay at home with their children.
17. The American way of life has too much influence on Europe.
18. Minorities should be represented in the police force.
19. Immigrants must be forced to learn the language of the country quickly.
20. When Germans are abroad they often try to tell people how to run their country.

Unit 5

The Pressure of Modern Life

5

1 TALKING ABOUT CRIME: YOUNG OFFENDERS IN BRITAIN

Figure 1: The number of young people per 100,000 of the population found guilty or cautioned, 1999 (indictable offences only)

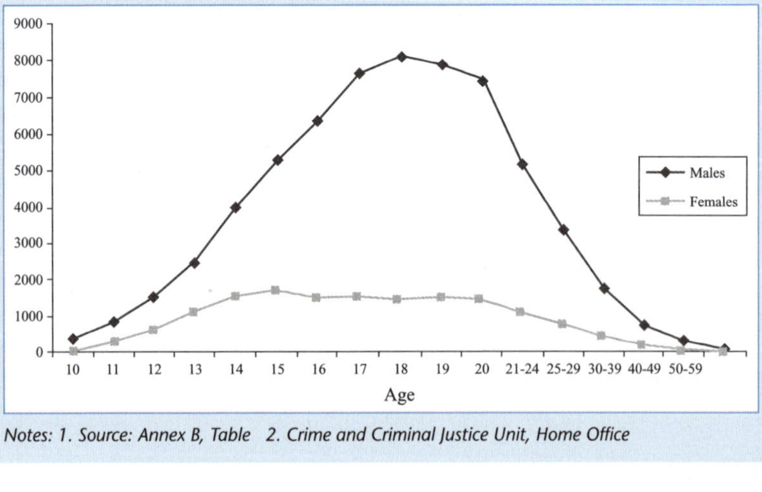

Notes: 1. Source: Annex B, Table 2. Crime and Criminal Justice Unit, Home Office

Figure 2: The offending rate per 100,000 per population for 10–17 years old males and females, 2001–2004

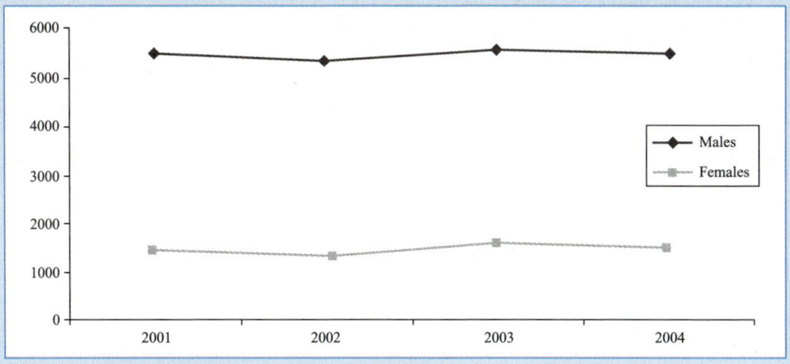

Notes: 1. Source: Annex B, Table 2. Crime and Criminal Justice Unit, Home Office

Figure 3: The type of offences committed by known young offenders (10–17 years olds) in England & Wales, 1999

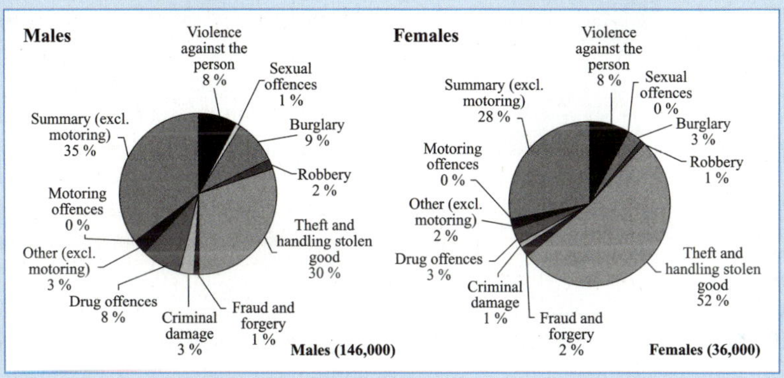

Notes: 1. Source: Annex B, Table 2. Crime and Criminal Justice Unit, Home Office

Annotiation: **Summary (offence)** = A summary offence is a minor criminal offence such as 'assault and battery' (=Körperverletzung) or minor theft.

Interpret the charts (see page 168)

1. Describe figure 1 and figure 2.
   Useful words:

   • steady increase • to reach its peak • to decline, to drop, sharply, constantly • considerably higher • to stagnate • fairly the same level

2. Explore and describe figure 3. Which of the facts presented here did you expect, which are surprising?
3. Discuss: What do you think the reasons are why young people turn to crime?
4. Explore the Internet to find the corresponding figures for your country.

Text

2 A living hell in children's jails

Pre-reading activity

Discuss:

1. Have you ever experienced or witnessed fights among young people and how did you react?
2. What do you think are the reasons for aggressive behaviour in young people?
3. Should young offenders be punished more severely?

A Children's Society report argues that under-18s should not go to prison.

Kevin Henson's troubles began when his mother died of cancer on his 14th birthday. He started drinking heavily, taking speed, bunking off school, associating with a bad crowd of older boys and engaging in petty crime.

In August this year he got into a fight with another boy and was arrested for wounding with intent. Refused bail (despite support from a social worker who had devised a detailed rehabilitation plan), he was remanded to Feltham in West London, where – as is customary in a place which has to control up to 900 teenage boys at once – he was banged up in a cell for 22 hours a day with no access to psychiatric or emotional support. On his ninth lonely night in this, the largest and most notorious youth jail in Europe (a place described as "rotten to the core" by the Chief Inspector of Prisons), he took his life.

Regrettably, his story is unexceptional. Death is becoming a commonplace in Britain's young offender institutions. In 2003 alone there were 12 suicides and an astonishing 994 recorded incidents of "self-harm" among teenagers locked up in England and Wales.

Kevin Henson's story is what lies at the heart of *Tough Justice*, a report published by the Children's Society. What it says is that prison custody should be abolished for all under-18s. According to the society, the youth offender institutions are either destroying the lives of convicted teenagers or turning them into even more hardened criminals. More than that, the Children's Society argues that community-based projects which "address anti-social and offending behaviour constructively" are so much more effective than prisons at stopping re-offending, and so much cheaper. To rehabilitate an offender in the community, for instance, probably costs around £250 a week. Keeping them locked up costs the taxpayer twice that.

And since we set the age of criminal responsibility at ten, lower than any of our neighbours (it is 13 in France, 14 in Germany and 18 in Belgium), we lock up more children, per head of population, than almost any other country in Western Europe. The report calls for the age to be lifted to 14.

But others are less convinced. "Abolishing prison for the under-18s is a totally unrealistic goal, says Lord Warner, chairman of the Youth Justice Board, the body set up last April to oversee every aspect of the youth justice system in England and Wales, from crime prevention to prison conditions. "A significant number of 16 and 17-year-olds are actually quite dangerous to the public," he says. "Some cannot stop offending. They come from too high a level of deprivation, or a history of abuse or, frankly, from criminal families." Undoubtedly, Warner has popular opinion with him. The public has generally been unsympathetic to pleas that children who commit crimes, particularly crimes of violence, should be given a chance to reform and redeem themselves. As a matter of fact, there's a widespread public belief that only harsh punishments can stop an increase in youth crime. What's more, many professionals within the justice system also question whether non-custodial sentences would work for all under-18s. "How could the probation service cope with all those hardened 16-year-olds on the streets?" asks one prison education specialist.

Who is right? How grim do we want the lives of young offenders to be? How much hope do we want to blot out? "The grimmer the better," some will say, with some reason. The milk of human kindness flows slowly from anyone who has been viciously mugged by a gang of 16-year-olds.

But if prison serves only to turn delinquent teenagers into hardened adult criminals, what good is that to anyone? "I cannot accept that people are irredeemable," the Archbishop of Canterbury writes in the Children's Society report. But in the cells of Feltham you won't find many teenagers on the road to redemption. You will find a great many on the road to a living hell. And for a few, like Kevin Henson, the only exit will be through a knotted bed sheet.

Adapted from ***The Times****, November 24, 2003*

Activities

A Text comprehension – short answer questions

SAQs

1. When did Kevin Henson turn to anti-social behaviour?
2. Why was Kevin Henson sent to jail?
3. Why shouldn't he have gone to jail?
4. What were the circumstances he had to suffer while under remand? (2 answers).
5. What did Kevin do on the ninth night in his cell?
6. Why can it be rightly said that what happened to Kevin is not so unusual?

B Mediation

Med

Haftstrafen für Jugendliche unter 18 Jahren abschaffen?
Nennen Sie die Befürworter und Gegner dieser Forderung, die im Text genannt werden, und stellen Sie auf Deutsch stichpunktartig ihre jeweiligen Argumente gegenüber.

C Discuss

1. In Britain, the age of criminal responsibility is set at ten. What does that mean, and where would you set it? Speak with your partner about it.
2. Are there enough positive role models around in society? Who would you consider as a positive role model?

D Writing: A Letter to the Editor

A youth magazine has published an article about young people in jail and has asked its readers for contributions on the question:
"What would you say are the worst things for a young person about having to go to jail?"

FACT BOX

1. Risk factors associated with young offenders

A multitude of factors contribute to youth offending behaviour. Various studies have identified the following key traits:

- Being male
- Coming from a low-income background
- Having parents or siblings who offend
- Experiencing poor parenting and lack of supervision
- Playing truant or being excluded from school
- Low academic performance
- Using drugs and alcohol regularly
- Associating with friends who are in trouble with the police

2. Youth Court Sentencing Framework

There are 4 basic levels of sentencing:

- Discharge (Conditional or Unconditional)
- Fines (commensurate to the offence committed)
- Community Sentences, e. g.
  - Drug treatment and testing
  - Supervision
  - Probation
  - Community Service
  - Curfew
- Custody:
  - Young Offender Institution (aged 15+)
  - Secure Training Order (aged 13–14)
  - Detention and Training Order (10–17)

3. Sentencing statistics: Young offenders under sentence, mid-2003

- The population of young offenders under sentence reached 8,340
- 1,170 young offenders under sentence were aged 17 or under
- There were 317 young females under sentence, a slight rise on the previous year
- 21,000 young offenders were received into Prison Service establishments under sentence in 2003, 1,400 more than the previous year
- 5,900 sentenced offenders aged 17 or under were received in 2003, 300 more than in previous year
- 1,233 sentenced young females were received in 2003, more than double the number in the previous year
- The average length of sentence was 11.4 months for male young offenders and 7.7 months for females
- Average time served for male young offenders was 5.9 months, including remand time, or 4.7 excluding remand time
- In 2003, discharged male young offenders had served an average of 52 % of their sentence, or 41 % excluding remand time.

(Source: Home Office, Research Development Statistics 2003)

4. Prison occupancy

Home Office figures show a rising prison population trend. The numbers sentenced to custody at all courts rose by 8 % between 2002-2003. Projections to the year 2007 show further increases in custody rates.

There was a reduction in the average length of sentences between 2002–2003. Crown Court Sentences to immediate imprisonment for males over 21 were reduced from 24.2 months in 2002 to 23.6 in 2003. For males under 21, average sentence lengths also decreased from 19.4 to 18.4 months.

(Home Office, Prison Population Brief, England and Wales July 2003)

Prison occupancy for young offenders is currently a critical issue.

5. Community Sentencing: Costs

Supervision order (10–17 year olds) £200 per month
Probation order £1710 per order
Community Service £1500 per order
Detention in Young Offenders Institution £26,000 per detention, per annum
Local authority secure accommodation £32,400 per place, per annum
Secure Training Order (12–14 year olds) £126,000 per place, per annum

(Source: DfEE 2003. The Scale & Costs of Underachievement)

Text

3 Littleton: No place to be different

Pre-reading activities

Group discussion:

1. Have you ever witnessed acts of violence at your school or at schools you have previously attended?
2. Mobbing at school – What do you think are the causes and what can be done to prevent it?
3. What are the differences between school shootings in the USA and in Germany?

On 20th April 1999, two students of Columbine High School in Littleton, a peaceful suburb of Denver, Colorado, killed 12 of their schoolmates, one teacher and finally themselves in one of the worst high school massacres that occurred at US schools.

This was revenge, pure and simple – and the signs of its impending arrival were there all along. First, Eric Harris had flicked through Columbine High School's 1998 yearbook, scribbling "save", "dead" and "dying" against the photographs of his schoolmates. Next, he wrote on the internet that anyone who crossed him would die. When a schoolmate collided with him in a corridor one day, Harris told him he would "rip out two of your damn ribs and shove 'em into your f … ing eyeballs". And then, with his friend, Dylan Klebold, he rampaged through the school with a number of semi-automatic weapons and home-made pipe bombs, killing 12 students and one teacher.

The two teenage killers made it abundantly clear who they were after – the 'jocks', the kids in smart suburban clothing and white baseball hats, the school athletes who enjoyed the favour of the school establishment and felt at liberty to sneer at others who, like the two killers, could not or did not want to fit in. Ask Joe Costello. Costello is a 16-year-old punk with spikes in his hair and a large white skull printed on his leather jacket. "Just because I was different, just because I didn't believe in God or dress in Abercrombie & Fitch or play their dumb-ass sports, that gave the jocks an excuse to beat me up, to throw trash and rocks at me when I passed by or call me a shithead," he says. "Sometimes me and others like me who wanted to be different would get attacked but the authorities never did anything because the jocks are the kind of people they like and we are despised."

Talking to kids like Costello, it seems anger against the stifling conformism of suburbia is boiling away just below the surface. Littleton has little public space to speak of, just a large shopping mall whose security guards are forever hovering around the punks and threatening to throw them out. Furthermore, there are no cafés, no alternative bookstores, and just one slightly wacky clothing outlet called Hot Topic. And there's a curfew that keeps young people off the streets after 11 p.m. during the week and midnight on weekends.

According to Costello and his friends, people put all their energy and money into keeping up appearances – a nicely painted porch, a neat garden, the right upscale clothes, the appropriate appearance in church and at community events – and many less well-off residents are quietly ruining themselves in the process. The community is defined by peer groups – a church, a sports team – rather than more general neighborly goodwill. That might explain why Eric Harris could move from upstate New York three years ago as a bright student and keen sportsman, if slightly withdrawn, and gradually descend into destructive madness in a suburban cul-de-sac without anyone noticing. When he and Klebold were put on probation last year for breaking into a van and stealing electrical equipment, they were obliged to attend an anger management course. Surprisingly, their case officer wrote just a few weeks ago that their future was full of promise and potential.

Experts do not have one answer for what is behind the shootings; they have many. Lack of supervision, accessible guns, permissive or absent parents, school officials who fail to act on warning signs, a culture fascinated with violence – all are cited as contributing factors.

"These kids have never learned how to solve problems," said Bill Reisman, a criminologist who has advised officials at several school districts where there were earlier shootings. "They have an instant answer, and that's a gun. Increasingly, the shootings are suicide missions, as seems to have been the case here," he said. "Most of them believe that death is now the solution. And in order to get the maximum amount of attention they do these bizarre, terrible crimes," Mr Reisman said.

Several students said the shooters, identified as Eric Harris and Dylan Klebold, were deeply into death – talking, reading and dreaming about it. Black trench coats are a consistent theme in the Gothic subculture that has attracted many teenagers. Inspired by computer games such as Dungeons and Dragons, Gothic has become a fascination of many American highschoolers, some of whom simply dress and paint their fingernails black. On Web sites featuring poetry called "The Written Work of the Trenchcoat" and in political pamphlets, trench coats serve as a symbol for things from Hitler and the Nazis to mass murder and suicidal fantasies. The day of the shooting was Hitler's birthday.

Violent movies and music can add "fuel to a fire", Mr Reisman says, but, "we can't blame things. People are responsible." Underpinning those problems is a society in which family and community ties are unravelling. "It used to be, when I was a kid, if I did something wrong down the street, before I got home that neighbor would have called my parents," Mr Reisman said. "These days they're afraid they're going to get sued."

After the shooting, searching questions have been raised by political and religious leaders in Denver. Mayor Wellington Webb, a black Democrat, said at a public meeting that parents and teachers had let children down and had to look where they had gone wrong. He also lobbied, with some success, for the National Rifle Association to stay out of Denver rather than hold their annual convention there this week. Law makers in the state assembly also withdrew a trio of bills intended to loosen, rather than tighten, gun restrictions, delivering an unexpected victory to anti-gunners.

In communities like Littleton, the prevailing belief is that guns protect people more than they kill them. Perhaps the biggest test of the coming weeks is whether this attitude, and other deeply cherished notions of the suburban good-life, are open to some radical re-examination and change.

Adapted from The Independent, 25 April 1999 and International Herald Tribune, April 22, 1999

Annotations
dumb-ass (28) – (sl.) really stupid / **cul-de-sac** (62) – Sackgasse / **National Rifle Association** (119) – Vereinigung von Waffenbesitzern in USA

Activities

A Text comprehension – short answer questions

SAQs

1. Why were the "jocks" the teenage killers' main targets? (2 answers)
2. Why is it not so easy for teenagers in Littleton to enjoy their free-time? (3 answers)
3. What have criminologists found out about how kids involved in school shootings deal with problems? (3 answers)
4. How have political and religious leaders in Denver reacted after the tragedy? (3 answers)

B Mediation

Med

1. Erstellen Sie auf Deutsch eine Liste der Gründe, die – laut Text – die Experten hinter den Schießereien an den Schulen sehen.
2. Welche typischen Elemente der Subkultur der „Gothics" werden im Text genannt? Erstellen Sie eine Liste.

C Writing

1. "In our affluent society it seems we've got everything. Except one thing: We don't have enough time for our children."
   Write a letter to the editor in which you say what you think the reasons are.
2. "It's mainly the violence in the media that is to blame for violent teenage behaviour."
   Write a composition in which you comment on this statement.

D Discussion

Discuss the following statements/question with your classmates.

1. Growing up in a small town is the worst thing that can happen to any teenager!
2. Should cameras be installed in schools to prevent violence at school?

E Describing a cartoon (see page 189)

Describe the cartoon.

Useful words:

• Halloween • pumpkin • Trick or Treat • NRA (National Rifle Organisation) • 2nd Amendment (an additional constitutional right in the USA granting 'the people to keep and bear arms') • ammo = ammunation • armor piercing = going through bulletproof vests

Text

4 Britain's new epedemic: Binge drinking

Pre-reading activities

1. What do you drink at parties?
2. Which alcoholic beverages do you prefer?
3. Are there any negative effects connected with alcohol consumption?

Death rates from alcohol-related liver disease rose by nearly half in a decade in the United Kingdom, according to WHO[1] advisers worried by the binge drinking epidemic in parts of Europe. In England and Wales alone, 33,000 people are dying from drink-induced causes, including ill-health, road crashes, violence, alcohol poisoning and other accidents.

The advisers report that as many as one in eight deaths among young men across western Europe is related to drink and condemn the "little bit does you good" health messages of recent years – saying moderate drinking only helped middle-aged and older people if any one at all. Tougher advertising rules and higher taxation may be needed to curb consumption, according to papers prepared for a WHO conference opening in Stockholm today. It is being attended by represetatives from 51 European countries.

These comments reinforce many concerns voiced recently by British doctors worried by a rise in drinking among women, their growing need for hospital treatment for chronic liver disease, and the wider after-work and binge-drinking culture to which young Britons appear increa-singly addicted. Overall consumption in the UK has remained fairly constant – with a 1 % drop in 10 years – compared with many European neighbours and drinking-laws have helped bring significant falls in deaths from road accidents. Deaths from cirrhosis and other liver problems – which caused eight victims per 100,000 in 1998, 47 % more than in 1988 – are still low compared with most countries. But the rate of increase is worrying and only exceeded by former Eastern block states.

In addition, a quarter of all people arrested are drunk and half of all violent crime, two thirds of suicide attempts and 75 % of assaults are committed by people under the influence of alcohol.There is growing concern, too, about drinking among children.

One in seven English boys aged 11, one in four Welsh boys of 13 and around a half of 15-year-old boys in England and Wales drink wine, spirit or beer once a week, putting them among the highest youthful consumers in Europe. "We are receiving signal from all across the region that many young people are turning to alcohol as a drug," says C. Goos a WHO adviser. "There is an increase in high-risk drinking, such as binge-drinking and drunkenness."

Advisers and voluntary organisations are concered at marketing strategies used by such drink giants as Carlsberg and Budweiser during the 1998 World Cup which link drink to sport. G. Edwards, of the Institute of Psychiatry, London, among the authors of the WHO papers, said: "Within stable and saturated markets, the main role of advertisements is to ensure that old consumers are replaced by new ones and that educational messages do not diminish alcohol consumption (…). Through its messages , it maintains the social desirability of drinking, overshadows the risk of alcohol use to individual and public health, and contradicts prevention initiatives. These indirect effects alone are sufficient to justify the need to control the volume and content of alcohol advertising."

He said evidence from countries that ban spirit advertsing suggested they had 16 % lower alcohol consumption than countries with no bans and those with bans on beer and wine ad-

[1] World Health Organisation

vertising had 11 % lower alcohol consumption than those with bans only on spirit advertising.

The Department of Health, which will publish its own plans to tackle alcohol abuse this summer, said: "It is not so much advertising as drinking patterns we want to tackle." This would include new measures to tackle under-age drinking and buying of alcohol.

(adapted from: The Guardian, Feb.19, 2001)

Activities

Gapped summary

Fill in the gaps with words taken from the text.

In a recent report, the World Health Organisation is concerned about the rise of alocohol consumption and qualifies it as an *...(1)...* in certain parts of Western Europe, where more than 10% of all young men die from drink-induced causes.
A similar concern was *...(2)...* by British doctors who have noticed a remarkable rise of drinking women mostly due to the habit of having a drink after work or consuming too much alcohol at parties and in their spare time.
But the most alarming figures document the behaviour of *...(3)...* drinkers from Britain and Wales. Almost 15% of 11-year-old English boys treat themselves to a hard drink once a week. Unfortunately drinking and sport is often linked in advertising by multinational breweries, a psychiatrist and author of the WHO papers said. As markets for alcoholic beverages are *...(4)...* the ads have to appeal to young consumers who will have to replace the older ones. So the role of this kind of advertising is to keep up the *...(5)...* of alcohol in a society. There is *...(6)...* that a total ban of spirit commercials would lead to a considerable drop of consumption. The British Department of Health, however, intends to deal with *...(7)...* *...(8)...*by introducing a different array of measures.

Listening comprehension: The dangers and fascination of Ecstasy

Listen carefully to what a physician and a psychologist say about the dangers and fascination of Ecstasy and answer the questions:

Recording 1: Doctor

1. How many people get killed in Britain a year due to Ecstasy?
2. What dangers involved with the use of Ecstasy does the doctor mention?

Recording 2: Psychologist

1. Why do ravers prefer Ecstasy to alcohol?
2. What do girls find positive about Ecstasy?
3. Why is it so difficult for parents to understand rave and Ecstasy?

Literature

5 Tom Wolfe: The Bonfire of the Vanities

Introduction

Larry Kramer lives with his wife and his child in an uncomfortable three-and-a-half room apartment on the third floor of a townhouse in New York's West Side with three windows overlooking the street. Larry works as an Assistant District Attorney in the Bronx, the northernmost borough of New York City. Parts of the Bronx, especially in the southeast, are characterized by slums and urban decay. When Kramer takes the subway to the Bronx County Building, he always wears a pair of sneakers, carrying his leather shoes with him in a bag. With the sneakers on, Kramer feels much safer on the train.

One thing Kramer had learned within two weeks as an assistant DA in the Bronx was that 95 percent of the defendants who got as far as the indictment stage, perhaps 98 percent, were truly guilty. The caseload was so overwhelming, you didn't waste time trying to bring the marginal cases forward, unless the press was on your back. They hauled in guilt by the ton, those blue-and orange vans out there on Walton Avenue. But the poor bastards behind the wire mesh barely deserved the term criminal, if by criminal you had in mind the romantic notion of someone who has a goal and seeks to achieve it through some desperate way outside the law. No, they were simple-minded incompetents, most of them, and they did unbelievably stupid, vile things. (...)

Herbert 92X's legal name was Herbert Cantrell; 92X was his Muslim name. He was a driver for a liquor distributor. That was one of a number of things that made Kramer believe he wasn't a real Muslim. A real Muslim wouldn't have anything to do with liquor. In any case, one day Herbert's truck was hijacked on Willis Avenue by three Italians from Brooklyn who had done little else for the past decade but hijack trucks for whoever was paying for hijacking trucks. They pulled guns on Herbert, tied him up, gave him a punch in the face, threw him into a dumpster on a side street, and warned him not to move for an hour. Then the three Italians drove the liquor truck to the warehouse of their employer of the moment, a wiseguy liquor distributor who routinely cut costs by hijacking merchandise. They drove up with the hijacked truck, and the loading-dock foreman said, "Holy shit! You guys are in a lotta trouble! That's one a our trucks!"

"Whaddaya mean?"

"That's one a our trucks! I just loaded it two hours ago! You're boosting stuff we just got through boosting! You just worked over one a our guys! You're in a lotta trouble!" So the three Italians jumped into the truck and sped to the dumpster to give Herbert 92X back his truck – but Herbert had managed to get out. They started driving up and down the streets in the truck, looking for him. They finally found him in a bar where he had gone to steady his nerves. This was definitely not the Muslim way. They came walking in to tell him they were sorry and that he could have his truck back, but Herbert thought they were coming after him because he had ignored their warning to stay in the dumpster. So he pulled a .38-caliber revolver out from under his thermal jacket – it had been there all along, but these hard cases had gotten the drop on him and he fired two shots. He missed the three Italians but hit and killed a man named Nestor Cabrillo, who had come in to make a telephone call. The firearm was perhaps a necessary item of defense in what was obviously a hazardous occupation. But he was not licensed to carry it, and Nestor Cabrillo was an upstanding citizen with five children. So Herbert was charged with manslaughter and criminal possession of a weapon, and the case had to be presented, and Kramer was stuck with that task. The case was a study in stupidity, incompetence, and uselessness; in short, a piece a shit. Herbert 92X refused to accept a plea bargain, since he regarded what had happened as an accident. He was only sorry that the .38 had jerked his hand around so.

(Tom Wolfe: From "The Bonfire of the Vanities, 1987")

Annotation
to get the drop on so. (56) – schneller sein als jmd.

Activities

SAQs

A Text comprehension – short answer questions

1. What did assistant District Attorney Kramer learn about crime in the Bronx?
2. Why does Kramer not believe that Herbert 92X is a real Muslim?
3. Who hijacked Herbert's liquor truck and why?
4. How did the gangsters treat Herbert?
5. What did the gangsters find out when they wanted to sell the truck and its load?
6. Where did the gangsters finally find Herbert and how did he react?
7. Why do you think he hadn't made use of his gun earlier, when he was robbed?
8. Why is Herbert charged for manslaughter?
9. Why did he refuse to make a deal with the judge and plead guilty?
10. What shows that he really feels completely innocent?

B More activities

Make a list of all the words in the text that have to do with crime and the law.

C Creative writing

Write a short newspaper article about what happened in the bar:

Father of five killed in Mafia shooting

6 Robert Crumb: Whiteman

Robert Crumb (born 1943) is probably one of the most influential comic strip writers of the second half of the twentieth century, giving the comic strip new impulses and directions both in content and style.

Analysing the comic strip

1. What time of the day is it?
2. How does Whiteman feel in the first picture?
3. What do you think are the reasons for Whiteman's outburst of aggression?
4. Analyse the onomatopoeia in the first three pictures. What do they express?
5. How does Whiteman cope with his aggression? Do you agree?
6. From the information available here, what would you say Whiteman's job is? What's his social background? Where and how does he live? Who are his neighbours? What are his values and beliefs? Describe his family and family life.

Text

7 Road-rage

Pre-reading activities

1. Classroom discussion: Have you ever experienced dangerous situations on the road caused by reckless drivers?
2. What do you think are the reasons why people drive aggressively?

It's a jungle out there. Well, not really: it's worse than a jungle. It's a stretch of roadway anywhere in America, and in place of the hungry tigers and stampeding rhinos and slithery anacondas are your friends, neighbors and co-workers, that nice lady from the church choir and the cheerful kid who bags your food at the local grocery store – even Mom and Dad and Buddy and Sis. They're in a hurry. And you're in their way. So step on it! That light is not going to get any greener! Move it or park it! Tarzan had it easy. Tarzan didn't have to drive to work.

It may be morning in America – crime down, incomes up, inflation nonexistent – but it's high noon on America's streets and highways. This is road recklessness, auto anarchy, an epidemic of careless driving. Incidents of "road-rage" were up 51% in the first half of the decade, according to a report from the AAA (pronounce: triple A) Foundation for Traffic Safety. Road-recklessness has become the car-related sickness of today, a bigger problem at the moment than drunken driving.

Road anarchy manifests itself in small things: the unsignaled lane change by the driver next to you, the guy who tailgates you if you go too slow, and the person ahead who brakes abruptly if you go too fast – each act accented by an obscene gesture or a blast of the horn.

Residents of the late 20th century America are the luckiest human beings in history: the most technologically advanced, the richest, the freest things on two legs the world has ever seen. Then why do we Americans drive like such jerks? The most common answer: What do you mean by 'we'? Of course, you don't drive like a jerk. Very few drivers admit to being an offensive road warrior. There seem to be only three types of people on the road these days: the insane (those who drive faster than you), the moronic (who drive slower than you) and ... you.

Aggressive driving seems to be basically a matter of numbers, as the quantity of cars on the American roads and highways has risen. There are 17 % more cars in America than there were 10 years ago, while the number of drivers is up 10%. More to the point: the number of kilometers driven has increased 35% since 1987, while only 1% more roads have been built. Maybe the congestion is making everyone cranky?

Not only are roads more crowded than ever, but they are crowded with drivers whom science has now discovered to be extremely touchy. Modern life offers plenty of ready-made excuses for bad driving, the most common being: "I'm late."

Driving is a curious combination of public and private acts. A car isolates a driver from the world even as it carries him through it. The sensation of personal power is intoxicating. Sealed in your little cell, you control the climate with the touch of a button, from Arctic tundra to equatorial tropic. The cabin is virtually soundproof. You can't listen to that old Beatles tape at home because your kids will think you're a dweeb, but in the car, the audience roars as you shout "All you need is love!", and God knows you're safe. The safety belt is strapped snugly across your body. Little bells and lights go off if you make a mistake: don't forget to buckle up! Change your oil, you sleepy-head! The illusions – of power, of anonymity, of independence – pile up. You are the master of your domain. Actually driving the car is the last thing you need to worry about. So you can pick your nose and fantasize to your heart's content. Who's to know?

There's a real illusion of anonymity combined with potency because you have a heavy machine you can command. Top it off with the stress of work and people perhaps feeling insecure there, or with troubles at home, and it can make for a dangerous combination.

Road-rage experts have come up with various solutions to the anarchy of our streets and highways. We could legislate it (lower speed limits, build more roads to relieve congestion), adjudicate it (more highway cops, stiffer penalties), regulate it (more elaborate licensing procedures) or educate it away (mandatory driver's education). Others suggest an option perhaps more typical of America circa 1998: therapize it. Road-rage therapists are calling for new driver's education programs from kindergarten on – to teach a spirit of cooperation rather than competition.

Will it work? A better question might be, Do we want it to? Road-rage therapists come perilously close to calling for a transformation of the American character – remaking our highly individualistic country into a large-scale version of a college town where everyone recycles kitty litter, drinks latte and eats whole grains. Is that really what we want? Until we have discussed this question anyone braving the streets and highways of America would be well advised to employ a technique older than therapy: prayer.

(Adapted from: TIME, January 12, 1998)

Activities

A Text comprehension

1. Who, according to the author, is the potential opponent in the car threatening you (not only!) on US roads and highways?
2. What does the author allude to with the following statement?
   It's high noon on America's streets and highways (line 15).
3. What are typical acts of road-rage?

4. What does the author want to express with the phrase *auto anarchy* (line 16)?
5. What's the typical reaction when you ask someone whether they think they drive carefully?
6. Why does driving a car give people the feeling of personal power and safety?
7. The author says that ... *driving is a curious combination of public and private acts,* and then concentrates on depicting the private aspects.
   What would **you** say are the 'public acts' that driving involves?
8. Make a list of the reasons that make people drive aggressively.
9. How do experts suggest solving the problem?
10. Why is the author against the idea of therapy for reckless drivers? Is he serious?

B Appreciating the writer's tone: satire

Satire is writing that ridicules or makes fun of people's mistakes and weaknesses.
It is often used to raise questions about a current trend or political decision.

The text mixes satirical description with information.
1. Which passages focus on information? What's typical here?
2. Which passages are satirical descriptions? What do they describe?

C What can you do to avoid road-rage?

The words in the sentences are in alphabetical order.
Rearrange them to reconstruct the leaflet. (Add commas.)

1. *don't eyes off road take the your*
2. *an aggressive avoid contact driver eye with*
3. *and cool don't provocation react stay to*
4. *away behaving drivers erratically from keep*
5. *do gestures make not obscene*
6. *horn sparingly use your*
7. *(anyway hang horn illegal it's onto the to)*
8. *lanes never signaling switch without*
9. *do not more one parking space take than*
10. *a are disabled disabled don't if in not park space you*
11. *allow car do door hit next not parked the to to you your*
12. *do not tailgate* *
13. *and allow if over pass pull slowly to traffic travel you*
14. *avoid beam headlights high of unnecessary use*
15. *a don't driver in or other pedestrian road stop talk the to with*
16. *cars don't inflict loud music neighboring on*

(Author's note: this is a difficult one!)*

D Other useful attitudes

There are two mistakes in each of the following sentences.
Find them and write the correct versions of the sentences into your notebook.
1. Assume other drivers mistakes are not personnel.
2. Be polite and cortous, even if the other's driver isn't.
3. Avoid all conflict as possible. If another driver challanges you, get out of the way.

E Reduce your stress

Add 'completing sentences' (minor support sentences) to support the following recommendations:

1. Allow plenty of time for the trip (e.g.: plan exactly when to start; stops etc.).
2. Listen to soothing music.
3. Improve the comfort in your vehicle.
4. Understand that you can't control the traffic, only your reaction to it.

F Listening comprehension: Death on the highway

Listen carefully to the recording and find the answers to the following questions:

1. What incidents of road-rage does the speaker mention?
2. Why does he refer to the 1984 Olympics in Los Angeles?
3. What, according to the speaker, are the reasons why people drive aggressively?
4. Who carried out a race on a highway in Ohio?
5. What happened?
6. Why was one driver sent to jail for over a year?

8 Talkline 1: Those who sleep rough

Get into teams of two. **Student A** looks at picture 1 (page 299), **student B** at picture 2 (page 311). First you describe your picture to your partner and vice versa. Then try to find out what the pictures have in common and how they differ.

9 Talkline 2: Young offenders

Your college is trying to fight vandalism and crime by letting other students decide what steps should be taken. You are a member of this "court", and this court is sitting at the moment to reach agreement on punishment for students. Each member of the court presents his/her ideas how to punish each defendant.

1. Alfred (18) has been binge drinking all weekend and keeps falling asleep in class.
2. Sally (19, pregnant) has been caught smoking on the toilet for the third time.
3. Peter (20) is the school bully and has forced another student to give him his new jacket. This is the second time he has bullied someone. He already had to work in a hospital for four weekends.
4. Mick (18) consumed Ecstasy and sold it to fellow-students for one year as has been just found out. He has already stopped consuming and selling drugs for half a year.
5. Prunella (18) has carved obscene graffiti into the door of a female toilet.
6. Paul (17) has deliberately given his classmate Sheila erroneous information about what is relevant for the next class-test to put her at a disadvantage.

Make precise suggestions what exactly the punishment should be. When each member of the court has presented their ideas, the court discusses the ideas and then pronounces their sentence.

Unit 6

Employment and Economy

1 TALKING ABOUT JOBS AND MONEY

1. Have you ever done any of the jobs above? Have you ever worked during your holidays? Tell us about the job you've done.
Say something about …

• how you got the job and how long you did it • the working conditions • the difficulties involved • your colleagues • the qualities one needs to do that job well • something funny that happened when you were doing the job • a problem that was difficult to solve • the money you earned (and what you did with it!)

Useful words and expressions

• waiter/waitress • to serve • to take orders • bill • to make out bills • to do a newspaper round • to work on an assembly line • to work shifts • construction/ building worker • blisters on your hands • to stack shelves • to fix price tags • cashier (BE) • checkout girl/boy (AE) • trolley • private tuition (BE) • private tutoring (AE)

2. Which job would you/wouldn't you like to do during your next vacation or between leaving school and going to university or starting in a permanent job? Explain your reasons.

3. What do you do (or would you do) with your money (and what not)?

[**• invest it in a savings account • buy shares • use it to make your pocket money go a bit further • spend it on expensive projects and items (travels, CD player etc)**]

FACT BOX

Employment of children and young persons in the UK

About half of the country's teenagers under 16 do some paid work each week. The most popular jobs are newspaper rounds and milk deliveries, followed by sales jobs in shops. Under 13-year-olds are not allowed to work at all. (The only exceptions are child performers and 10+ year old children who can help their parents with light farming and horticultural work.)
13-16-year-olds can only work for 2 hours on school days and on Sundays, must not work before 7am or after 7pm and should not work more than one hour in the morning. They must work for the same employer if working both morning and evening. On Saturdays and school holidays, under 15's must not work more than 5 hours daily, over 15's must not work more than 8 hours daily.
Any money they earn is legally theirs, not their parents'. They can be taxed but the restriction on working hours means they are unlikely to earn enough for this to happen.
Prohibited occupations: pubs, clubs, kitchens, fairgrounds and abattoirs.

Adapted from http://www.silenceingthebell.btinternet.co.uk/examsadvice.html, June 2004

Find out about the corresponding regulations in your country!

Text

■□□ 2 Working in a summer camp

Summer camps have a long tradition in the United States and Canada. They promise fun and excitement to children and young people of all ages for about 6 to 8 weeks during the summer holidays. Camp directors often point out that summer camps don't only offer outdoor activities, but also promote cooperation, team spirit and self-esteem.

Summer camps all over the United States and Canada are looking for staff during the summer months. Most camps require 'counselors' to have at least one year of college or similar experience (which is what you can offer as you're attending a vocational college) and also to have a real interest in working with children.

So, what about working in a summer camp for a couple of weeks during your next holidays or after finishing *Fachoberschule* or *Berufsoberschule*?

Activities

A Group discussion

Study the Camp Mohican information sheet on p. 113 for a few minutes before you discuss the following questions with your classmates.

- Would you like to work as a 'cabin counselor' (caring for a group of 5–7 children and living with them in a cabin) or as an activity instructor (or both), and why?
- What type of activity would you like to instruct? (Look at Job description.)
- Is there any kind of activity which you've never done before, but you'd like to try out?
- What region of the United States would you like to go to?
- Look at the options below. What type of camp would you prefer?

• wilderness • private • boy scout • YMCA • religious • non-religious • competetive • non-competitive • serving special groups e.g. the mentally handicapped, underprivileged children, children with impaired hearing and/or speech, children with chronic or terminal illnesses, visually-impaired children • co-ed (co-educational) • boys • girls

Camp Mohican in the Pocona Mountains, Pennsylvania

Job description

We have over 200 positions available for counsellors, supervisors, group leaders and instructors. Activities include: all land sports, all water sports (including jet-skiing, water-skiing, sailing, etc.); an extensive creative arts department including 14 arts and crafts workshops in addition to pottery/ceramics, woodworking, etc.; dance, theater, horseback riding; an extensive outdoor adventure program including rock climbing, mountain cycling, backpacking, river canoe trips; gymnastics, judo and karate; archery, riflery, skateboarding and rollerblading, roller hockey, computers, newspaper production, radio broadcasting, video production, circus arts such as juggling, flying trapeze and lots more.

Positions available

General cabin counsellors, Kitchen staff, Medical staff, Campfire program staff, Group leaders, Certified Lifeguards, Water safety instructors, Van drivers, Head counsellor, Transportation in-charge, Trips supervisor, Pool instructors, Horseback riding instructors, Trapeze professionals, Music program instructors, Performing arts director, Creative arts instructors, Communication arts instructors, Field sports director, Woodshop head instructors, Athletic director, Intercamp games director, Registered nurses, Evening program directors, Attendance supervisors, Office staff, Tennis instructors, Head gymnastics professional, Stable staff.

PO Box 189, Suite CMPG, Gladstone, NJ 07934; United States (Tel.: 908 - 470 - 9317)

What you get

We pay the best salaries to recruit the best staff! Our staff salaries start at $125 per week, including room and board and pay increases based on qualifications and age. All of our counsellors must have completed at least one year of college. Travel allowance is available. Tipping is permitted. Room, board and laundry services are provided. Nights-off and days-off are scheduled throughout the summer. Pre- and post-camp employment is available. All expenses paid for annual 3-day reunion invitation. Top-caliber staff recruited from across the US and Europe provide a stimulating social experience. Work in a non-competitive, supportive camp environment where the emphasis is on fun.

Please note: You must be at least 18 years old and have completed one year in college to be considered for employment with our camp.

Dates of employment: June – September

B Further activities

1. Based on the information sheet on page 113, write a letter to a British penfriend trying to persuade him or her to apply with you. Tell him/her ...
   - which activities appeal to you most,
   - what the pay is,
   - whether you've got spare time,
   - why you think working there could be a good experience.

2. Write a summary of the information sheet in German for your school magazine.

3. Write an **informal letter** to Camp Mohican applying for a job.
   Tell them ...

   - who you are and where you live,
   - your age,
   - which school you are currently attending,
   - what your special interests are,
   - in which areas of activities you think you can contribute,
   - what you expect from the experience.

   Ask them ...

   - whether there is a strict age limit, (If you're too young, tell them that you're planning ahead!)
   - for more detailed information,
   - for an application form.

4. Write an *informal resumé* similar to the one on page 115, which Tanja sent to camp Mohican as an e-mail. Give a few details about yourself and list all your skills and the jobs that you've already had.
   You might refer to ...
   - job experience or job training,
   - any summer holiday jobs that you've had,
   - tutoring and counseling experience in school (e. g. helping children with their homework),
   - voluntary work such as lifeguard, member of a fire brigade, first-aid attendant etc.
   - practical training accompanying *Fachoberschule*,
   - sports activities such as coaching, refereeing

MM

C Multiple matching

Compare Tanja's resumé to the positions available in Camp Mohican. For which jobs could she apply?

Tanja's informal resumé

Author: Tanja
Email: tanja@byxlink.berkeley.edu
Subject: Resumé

I'm a student at the University of California at Berkeley. I love working with kids. I also love nature and the outdoors (I've just finished an ecology/plant biology course), so I would love to be a camp councillor this summer! Here's my job resumé:

Voluntary work
Throughout all four years of High School (Volunteers Club). Everything from serving food for the Big Brother/Big Sister organization to control guard at marathons to helping children with art projects at the Annual Youth Arts Festival in Golden Gate Park.

Badminton team manager
This was in my sophomore year of High School. I was a team player in my junior year.

Guide
I led a group of 16 –19 year-old Austrian boys (I speak German) on a tour of San Francisco (my home city) and Berkeley (my college city) during the Easter vacation in April, 2003.

Journalism: newspaper staff
(Summer of 2000.) We wrote for, edited, and obtained advertisers for our Summer School newspaper.

Drama
(Summer of 2001) I co-directed a sketch put on by the Americans when I went to a summer language camp in Salzburg, Austria. (Each country performed their own sketch.)

Math, Science and German tutoring
At various times during my junior and senior years.

I'm planning on becoming a health worker next year, so I'd like to get First Aid training from the Red Cross this summer. I can do this before camp if it's required.

I hope to hear from you soon.

Tanja

Text

3 First steps towards a lifetime of debts

Pre-reading activities

Work with a partner.

1. Each partner first makes a list of where his/her money goes and then tells his/her partner about it. What have the two lists got in common? What differences are there? Tell the class.
2. Make a list of occasions when you would pay a) cash or b) with a credit card.

1 IT is easy to be the envy of your mates when you are strolling down the high street, credit card in hand, about to buy the latest CDs. But flexing plastic spending power before you have even left school could have drastic consequences, as illustrated by 17-year-old Christopher Hill [name changed] who acquired a credit card and £ 1,000 credit limit.

Although obtaining credit before the age of 18 is illegal, Christopher was sent the credit card after he lied about his age and circumstances on the application form. A year later, on turning 18, he reached his credit limit with his first card, so applied for one from a different institution and was granted a £ 3,500 credit limit. The borrowing facility was easily extended on demand. Worried about his growing debt, he applied for yet another card to consolidate his borrowing. He got a credit limit of £ 6,500. Now a cross-channel ferry steward earning £ 150 a week, whose £ 3,500 of debts force him to live with his parents, he admits that this final offer would have finished him had his mother not intervened and cut up his cards. He says that his friends, who also applied for credit cards while under-age, have far worse debts.

His mother, a teacher, is angry that teenagers find it so easy to borrow such high sums of money. "These companies are creating a nation of parent-dependent adults who will never be able to leave home, pay their rent or buy their own homes because of their debts," she says. Cut-throat competition among lenders and an increase in the number of players in the market has made it easier than ever to obtain credit. Lenders lure borrowers by offering fascinating low initial rates that sometimes come close to 0 percent.

According to figures from the Credit Card Research Group, 24 per cent of all 18 to 21-year-olds have a credit card, compared with the national average of 29 per cent of adults. There are no figures for cards held by under-18s but, as new credit card lenders flood into the market, under-age borrowers are slipping through the safety net of checks. Geeta Varma, one of the councillors with the organisation, believes that part of the problem is a lack of financial education among youngsters. "Many are just not prepared to handle a budget, let alone start to use a credit card wisely," she says.

The law puts the burden on the lender to carry out necessary checks. Some underage borrowers may be able to write off their debts because extending credit to under-18s is an "unenforceable contract" under the Sale of Goods Act. However, Mrs Varma does warn young debtors to seek professional advice. Young people who lied on their application forms could be found guilty of fraud and may end up with a criminal record if the credit card company takes the matter to the police.

Most lenders rely on credit agencies to check the applications. Although lenders are reluctant to give details of how credit checks are conducted, the information on applications is often cross-checked with the electoral roll. Unless there is evidence of bad debt, the inquiries are unlikely to be taken any further, even if under-age teenagers are not normally listed on the electoral roll.

Adapted from ***The Times****, November 4, 2000*

Activities

A Ordering task

Read the text quickly to get the following sentences outlining the text into the correct order.

- A mother helps and worries.
- A teenager trapped in a vicious circle of debts.
- An organisation that tries to help teenagers with credit card debts.
- Measures taken by the card companies before giving anyone a credit card.
- Showing off with your credit card.
- Statistics and facts.
- Why it has become so easy to get credit.

B Text comprehension

1. How did Christopher amass such an enormous amount of debts?
2. Who helped him to stop making more debts?
3. What is Christopher's current employment? Could you imagine doing his job? Give the reasons why you would or would not like this job.
4. Why is it difficult for Christopher to pay back his debts?
5. What, according to Christopher's mother, will be the negative consequences if teenagers borrow such high sums of money?
6. Why has it become so easy for teenagers to get a credit card?

7. According to the Credit Card Research Group, what is the main reason why young people get into debt so easily?
8. When seeking help from organisations like the Credit Card Research Group, what are the chances and dangers?

C Writing

Write a short essay of about 100 words.

1. He/She never paid it back.
2. My parents wouldn't lend me any money although I really needed it.
3. That money was well deserved.

FACT BOX

Kids and money in the US

America faces a financial literacy crisis – especially among young people.

- Teenagers spent $94 billion of their own money in 1998, and influenced an additional $47 billion in family spending.
- Teenagers have few skills to manage their money and 53 % received little or no financial advice from their parents.
- The average college student who takes out student loans graduates with a debt burden of $20,000.
- 64 % of college students have credit cards in their own names and 20 % have four or more cards.
- 28 % of college students with a credit card roll over debt each month.
- A survey of individuals who filed for bankruptcy in 1997 found that 8.7 % of all filings were among young adults aged 18–25.

Source: Facts on Saving and Investing, 1999 Report on Financial Literacy, U.S. Securities and Exchange Commission

MC **Words, words, words**

1. Find the correct explanation.
   a) *flexing plastic spending power* (l. 4) means
      - throwing away your credit card.
      - buying a lot of things and paying with your credit card.
      - having more than one credit card.

   b) *the borrowing facility was easily extended on demand* (l. 16f) means
      - Christopher was readily granted a higher credit limit when he asked for it.
      - Christopher promptly got another card when he applied for one.
      - Christopher was sent the credit card he applied for within a few days.

   c) *cut-throat competition* (l. 33) means
      - credit card companies want to gain maximum profit from their borrowers.
      - credit card companies make attractive offers to borrowers in order to get more customers than their rivals.
      - advertisements for credit cards are so funny that they attract young people.

   d) *fascinating low initial rates that sometimes come close to 0 percent* (l. 37f) means
      - the credit limit you are offered can easily be raised.
      - you can use your new credit card as soon as you get it.
      - during the first weeks or months when you use your new credit card there practically aren't any fees.

   e) It is *an "unenforceable contract" under the Sale of Goods Act* (l. 56) means
      - it is unlawful to give credit to under-18s.
      - underage borrowers who have overspent their budgets need not go to jail.
      - there is a law that says that young debtors must give back their credit cards.

2. Make a spider chart or list chart of all the words in the text that have to do with credit cards.

Two role plays

Role play 1

On the phone

Work in pairs. **Partner A** should refer to the information below and **Partner B** to the information on page 312. Take down all the information. After the call check whether you have taken it down correctly.

Role card A

Your subscription to JoJo, a monthly English music magazine, is running out. Phone the magazine to extend the subscription.

Say who you are and what you want.
You don't know your customer number but are sure they have your address in their computer.
Insist on another 1 year subscription that saves you 25 % off the regular price.
You are moving to another street. The next two issues should be sent to your old address, Aegidienstr. 3. Tell them to send the April issue and all the following to Weißenmüllerstr. 47.
Ask what your customer number is and take it down.
You have a VIMA EUREX EXPRESS credit card:

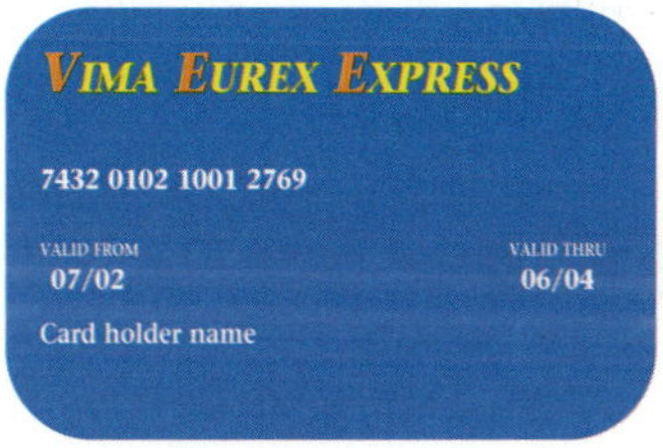

Ask whether it is safe to pay by credit card.
Thank the employee at JoJo.

Useful expressions

- I'd like to ... • Could you please ... • No, thanks ... • That would be nice ...
- Could you repeat that, please? • double 0 [dʌbl əʊ]

Role play 2

Job interview

Work in pairs. **Partner A** should refer to the information below and **partner B** to the information on page 313.

Role card A

Applicant

You want to work for an IT firm during your holidays.

Be prepared to

- say who you are
- speak about what you are doing at the moment and about your qualifications
- speak about your previous job experiences
- say how well you can use a computer
- speak about your interests and hobbies
- speak about your strong points

Useful expressions

[• **to leave school** • **to graduate from school** • **to go to "name of the school"** (No article when you refer to the institution! An article is only used when you refer to the building) • **volunteer work** • **tutoring** • **sports club**]

Class project

■■□ 5 Analysing advertisements

Analyse TV commercials or adverts in the print media for

a) sweets b) alcoholic beverages.

A Find out what patterns of behaviour are being presented.

- When and under what circumstances do the people shown in the TV commercials or the magazine adverts consume the product which is being advertised?
- What quantities do they consume and how? (One at a time? Two? Limitless?)
- How do they get the products they consume? (Do they buy them? Are they given to them? Are they taken from another person?)
- What's their body language? (How do they hold the candy bar, for example?) Does their body language show that they want to impress others? Are there any hidden sexual signals?
- How important does consuming the product seem to be – are other activities interrupted, neglected, turned down?

B Find out which of the following values the commercials and adverts are conveying:

- *Friendship/Having Fun:* People are shown using this product with attractive, fun-loving friends.
  Message: This product will make you popular, especially with the opposite sex, and will help you have a good time or even guarantee that you are successful sexually.

- *Fitness and Health:* Advertisements show people using a product while performing outdoor activities.
  Message: Young, healthy, active people use this product. If you use it, you too can be young and healthy.

- *Taking a Risk:* Advertisements suggest that people who use a certain product aren't afraid to take risks and aren't worried about others' opinions.
  Message: Buying this product shows you are brave and you think for yourself.

Source (B): Suggested by Vickie Holloway, Laura Versaci, Julie James, and outlined in: Lions-Quest: Skills for Adolescence (1992).

C Find out, whether the advertisements use classical formulas, like:
A I D A (<u>A</u>ttention → <u>I</u>nterest → <u>D</u>esire → <u>A</u>ction)

Attention – You must get the viewers', listeners', readers' attention (provocative picture, slogan or headline).
Interest – Appeal to the viewers', listeners', readers' needs (fresh breath, better hair, clean laundry).
Desire – Show them that the product improves their lives, makes them more successful or attractive. Offer them strong guarantees or bonuses.
Action – Ask people to act immediately. Tell the potential customer, "it is easy to order", or, "all you have to do is", or "call this number", "fill this out,"Offer as many payment options as possible, especially credit cards.

Other formulas are:
PPPP: **P**icture, **P**romise, **P**rove, **P**ush
USP: Unique-Selling-Proposition (the advertisement concentrates on one single argument)

Literature

6 Bill Bryson: Notes from a big country

Pre-reading activities

What was your best shopping experience? What was your worst?

Bill Bryson was born in Des Moines, Iowa, in 1951. He settled in England in 1977, and lived with his English wife and four children in North Yorkshire for many years. He and his family recently moved back to America.

Shopping Madness

Apart from working, sleeping, watching TV and accumulating fatty tissue, Americans devote more time to shopping than to any other pastime. Indeed, according to the Travel Industry Association of America, shopping is now the number one holiday activity of Americans. People actually plan their vacations around shopping trips. Hundreds of thousands of people a year travel to Niagara Falls, it transpires, not to see the falls but to wander through its two mega-malls. Soon, if developers in Arizona get their way, holidaymakers will be able to travel to the Grand Canyon and not see it either, for there are plans, if you can believe it, to build a 450,000 square-foot shopping centre by its main entrance. Shopping these days is not so much a business as a science. There is even now an academic discipline called retail anthropology whose proponents can tell you exactly where, how and why people shop the way they do. They know which proportion of customers will turn right upon entering a store (87 per cent) and how long on average those people will browse before wandering out again (2 minutes and 36 seconds). They know the best ways to lure shoppers into the magic, high-margin depths of the shop (an area known in the trade as 'Zone 4') and the layouts, colour schemes and music that will most effectively hypnotize the unassuming browser into becoming a helpless purchaser. They know everything.

So here is my question. Why, then, is it that I cannot go shopping in America without wanting either to burst into tears or kill someone? For all its science, you see, shopping in this country is no longer a fun experience, if it ever was.

A big part of the problem is the stores. They come in three types, all disagreeable. First, there are the stores where you can never find anyone to help you. Then there are the stores where you don't want any help, but you are pestered to the brink of madness by a persistent sales assistant, probably working on commission.

Finally, there are the stores where, when you ask where anything is, the answer is always 'Aisle seven.' I don't know why, but that is what they always tell you.
'Where's women's lingerie?' you ask.
'Aisle seven.'
'Where's pet food?'
'Aisle seven.'
'Where's aisle six?'
'Aisle seven.'

My least favourite of all store types is the one where you can't get rid of the sales assistant. Usually these are department stores at big malls. The sales assistant is always a white-haired lady working in the menswear department.

'Can I help you find anything?' she says.
'No thank you, I'm just browsing,' you tell her.
'OK,' she replies, and gives you a smarmy smile that says: 'I don't really like you; I'm just required to smile at everyone.'

So you wander round the department and at some point you idly finger a sweater. You don't know why because you don't like it, but you touch it anyway. In an instant, the sales assistant is with you.
'That's one of our most popular lines,' she says. 'Would you like to try it on?'
'No, thank you.'
'Go ahead, try it on. It's you.'
'No, I really don't think so.'
'The changing rooms are just there.'
'I really don't want to try it on.'
'What's your size?'
'Please understand, I don't want to try it on. I'm just browsing.'
She gives you another smile – her withdrawing smile – but 30 seconds later she is back, bearing another sweater. 'We have it in peach,' she announces.
'I don't want that sweater. In any colour.'
'How about a nice tie, then?'
'I don't want a tie. I don't want a sweater. I don't want anything. My wife is having her legs waxed and told me to wait for her here. I wish she hadn't, but she did. She could be hours and I still won't want anything, so please don't ask me any more questions. Please.'
'Then how are you off for pants?'

Do you see what I mean? It becomes a choice between tears and manslaughter. The irony is that when you actually require assistance there is never anyone around.

From Notes from a Big Country by Bill Bryson, London: Random House, 1998, pp 300-302 (excerpt)

Annotations
fatty tissue (2) – Fettgewebe / **transpire** (9) – hier: durchsickern / **smarmy** (43) – schleimig

Activities

A Text comprehension

1. What, according to Bill Bryson, is *retail anthropology* (line 18), and what is its paradoxical result?
2. Why did Bill have to wait for his wife?
3. What happened when he was waiting? Use the following prompts to retell what happened.

[• browsing • sweater • peach • tie • pants]

B Understanding satire

1. Bill Bryson's story is a satire. A satire makes fun of people's mistakes and weaknesses, often by exaggerating things a lot. So, what does Bill say about
   a) where Americans preferably go on holiday?
   b) the answer you get when you ask a sales person where to find anything?
   c) the feelings he often has when he is shopping?
2. There are at least two groups of people the text makes fun of – to a degree that's almost unfair (but satire is allowed to do that). Who are they?
3. The headline of the story is ambiguous, i.e. has two meanings. What are they?

Text

7 "Shameful" pay makes British women worst off in Europe

Pre-reading activities

1. Write acrostics on **part-time job (see page 192)**.
2. Read the statistics and answer the questions.
   a) Compare the usual working hours per week for women with dependent children to women without dependent children. Where do you find differences?
   b) Comment on the fact that most men work more than 46 hours per week.
      - What are the consequences for their income?
      - What are the consequences for family life?
   c) In which industries do most women work?
   d) Find reasons why they work there and nowhere else.
   e) What are the consequences for their salaries?

Figure 1: Usual hours worked per week for men and for women with and without children; United Kingdom, spring 2002, not seasonally adjusted

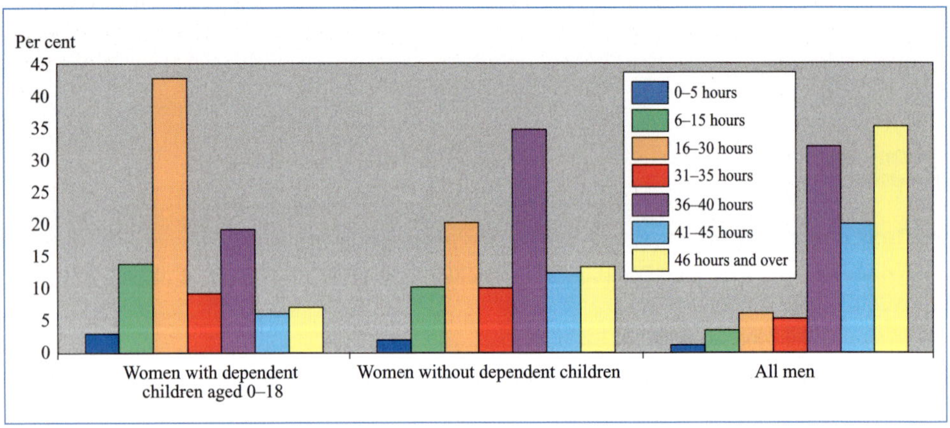

Figure 2: Change in workforce jobs; United Kingdom; March 1997–2002, seasonally adjusted

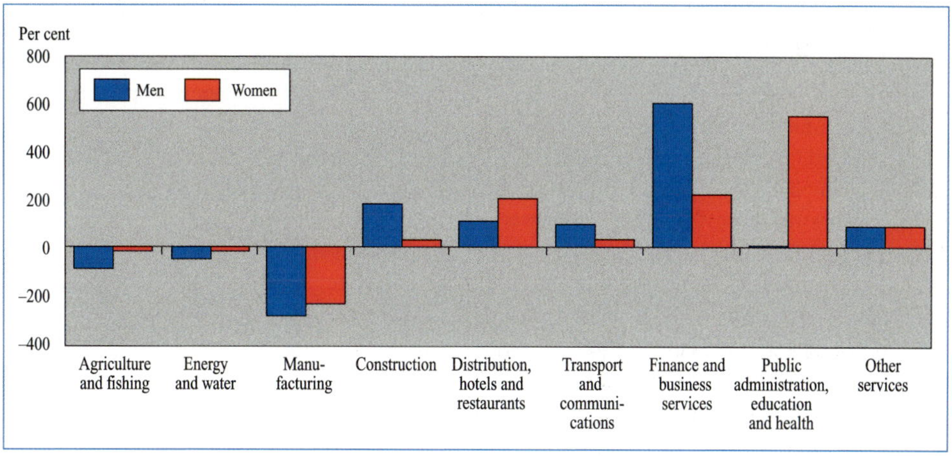

Career choices and lack of childcare facilities keep up persistent gender gap.

One hundred years after the creation of the Suffragette Movement, British women may have the vote but their salaries remain steadfastly below the amount earned by men for the same jobs.

A survey shows that the average British woman's pay packet is less than two-thirds that of the average British man. The disparity is by far the widest in the European Union and shatters claims that gender inequalities in Britain are disappearing.

The survey, based on statistics produced by EU member states, shows that the average British woman is paid 63 per cent that of the average man, compared with an EU average of 82 per cent and a US average of 90 per cent. For British women aged 35 to 49 the figure rises to 69 per cent, compared with an EU average of 82 per cent. For girls aged 14 to 17, the figure is 26 per cent of boys' earnings, compared with an EU average of 35 per cent.

Andrew Russell, an analyst with Datamonitor, which produced the analysis, attributes the pay gap to differences in men's and women's occupational choices.

'The results are more to do with the jobs women take rather than any inherent discrimination,' he said. Women were drawn towards occupations such as social work, nursing and teaching, which traditionally in Britain have low rates of pay compared with countries such as France, Sweden and the Netherlands.

Hopes that conditions will automatically improve may be overly optimistic. 'Looking back to similar data collected in 1997 shows nothing has really changed,' Russell said.

Julie Mellor, chair of the Equal Opportunities Commission, said the UK's poor record in improving childcare facilities was largely to blame: 'Although women are gaining more ed ucational qualifications than ever, they are still concentrated in low-paid, part-time jobs such as cleaning, caring and catering, because these are the only jobs that fit around the limited childcare available.'

'We need a massive increase in childcare and more employers offering part-time work at all levels of the economy. These figures reveal Britain's shameful record on women's pay.'

Research by the Work Foundation also suggests that the pay gap may be perpetuated because employers often rely on previous salary data as an indication of what to offer potential staff. For women, whose existing pay is likely to be much lower than a male counterpart, salary history often keeps them lower down the pay scales.

Datamonitor's findings follow a report by the Chartered Institute of Personnel and Development, which shows that the proportion of women working more than 48 hours a week has risen from 1-in-10 to 1-in-4 in the past five years. In addition, women's average working week has increased by more than 10 per cent since 1998. The average female employee now works almost 34 hours a week - three-and-a-half hours more than five years ago.

A tale of two experiences in the marketplace

The Nurse

Bernadette Murphy, 38, is a community staff nurse from Sutton, in London. 'Nursing is struggling to recruit people now because women's attitudes have changed so much. When I started my training in 1984, women weren't expected to go out and have a career. Today nearly all my friends work. 'It's not surprising that people don't want to come into a profession like nursing when there are so many other more glamorous and better-paid careers out there.'

'It is possible to earn quite a decent living from nursing, but to do so you have to really strive to get up the career ladder. And then that leaves you in a situation whereby you are no longer having that one-on-one contact with the patients, which is probably why you came into the profession in the first place. You get stuck doing administration and mountains of paperwork.'

'I do get annoyed when I think of how much I get paid, when you compare that to some jobs where there is next to no training needed. If you look at labourers on building sites, I think most of them are paid far better than nurses, even though I had to spend three years training and have to keep updating my skills and taking exams every year.'

The Manager

Sonja Owen, 36, is an Asda store manager in St Helens, Merseyside. Asda won a 2002 Castle Award in recognition of its efforts to promote equal pay and opportunity in the workplace.

'Part of the reason I was attracted to joining the Asda group was their culture of treating staff really well. When I joined in 1998 I had a son who was under 12 months, but rather than be put off by that, as some companies might, I think they were actually quite keen, as they could see that I would be committed to them.'

'When I returned from maternity leave after having my second child, I was able to job-share with a colleague. This meant I only had to work three days a week, allowing me more time to spend with my children, which was really important to me. To do this required the company to pay two people for three days' work pro rata, effectively paying 120 per cent of a manager's wage.'

'They were able to "marry me" with another manager in the area, who was also returning after having kids, so between us we were able to manage the store while still making sure we were there for our families. By job-sharing I was also able to maintain my position and not lose any momentum on the career ladder, or lose any of my responsibilities.'

Jamie Doward and Tom Reilly, The Observer, October 12, 2003

Activities

MM

Multiple matching

Match the questions with the answers.

a. What is a plausible reason for the gender gap in income?
b. When will the situation for female employees in Britain change?
c. What does a survey on statistics about incomes by gender show?
d. How can the philosophy of the Asda group be described?
e. Which age group is worst paid if compared by European standards?
f. Why is nursing trying hard to employ new people?

1. Looking after ill people has become hard work and is still lowly paid, women find better jobs nowadays.
2. The employees shold feel at ease in the companies: women are offered several solutions to have kids and careers at the same time.
3. Women in Britain are much worse off than their European counterparts.
4. Women are not offered enough help for looking after their kids, which means they have to accept less lucrative jobs that match with the restricted offers on this sector.
5. Women still earn less in Britain than their male colleagues holding the same positions.
6. It's the female teenagers who roughly earn about a quarter of what their male peers get.
7. If you want to have a successful career in nursing, you will have to reckon with much deskwork and little work with patients.
8. The young British women strive for a high amount of education today. Thus employers think women can look after themselves and don't need any special support.

Listening comprehension: Girls and IT

Pre-listening activities

1. In which of the jobs mentioned below would you expect more men than women and why? What qualities are needed for those jobs?

[• police officer • nurse • doctor • mechanical engineer • teacher • sales assistant in a car firm • architect • cashier • construction worker • kindergarten nurse]

2. In 2000, which country had the highest proportion of women in IT jobs? (IT = Information Technology)

[• Britain • North America • Singapore]

3. Discuss with your partner: What qualities must someone have who works in the IT sector?

Listen to three people talking about girls and IT.

1. Which of the three speakers is
   a) the head of recruitment for an IT firm?
   b) a consultant in an IT firm?
   c) a teacher?

2. Listen again. What do the three speakers say about
   a) what girls wrongly think about IT and jobs in IT?
   b) which qualities are needed if you want to work in the IT sector?
   c) what a job in IT might actually look like?

FACT BOX

Some IT jobs

- Customer Support: installation, trouble shooting, user assistance and training
- Data Management: acquisition, storage and retrieval of data
- Enterprise: policy, strategic, capital and workforce planning
- Information Security: confidentiality and reliability of information systems
- Network Services: network systems and internet/intranet systems
- Project Management: development and management of IT projects
- Software Development: new or existing applications or operating systems software
- Systems Administration: installation, testing, operation and maintenance
- Systems Analysis: planning, analysis and design to meet user needs
- Web Development: all aspects of internal and external Web sites
- Graphic design: production of communication vehicles for all kinds of media

Literature

8 Edwin Arlington Robinson: The children of the night

Pre-reading activities

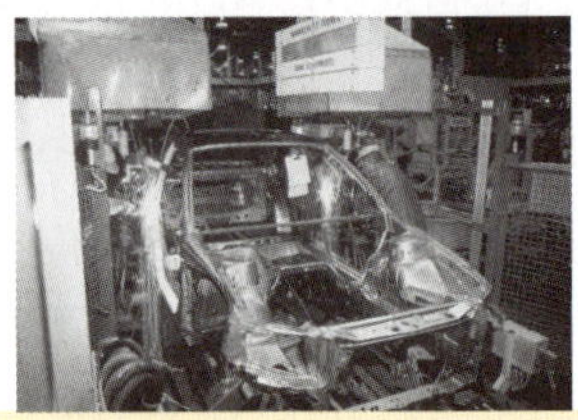

1. With the help of the picture explain the meaning of the term "industrial relationship".
2. How would you paraphrase the expression "them and us"?

Richard Cory

Whenever Richard Cory went down town,
We people on the pavement looked at him:
He was a gentleman from sole to crown,
Clean favored, and imperially slim.

And he was always quietly arrayed,
And he was always human when he talked;
But still he fluttered pulses when he said,
„Good-morning," and he glittered when he
walked.

And he was rich – yes, richer than a king –
And admirably schooled in every grace;
In fine we thought that he was everything
To make us wish that we were in his place.

So on we worked, and waited for the light,
And went without the meat, and cursed the
bread;
And Richard Cory, one calm summer night,
Went home and put a bullet through his head.

Edwin Arlington Robinson, "The Children Of The Night", 1897

Activities (also: see skill "Analysing a poem", page 193)

A Working with the material
1. Make a list of the adjectives that describe Richard Cory.
2. List Richard Cory's actions and the narrators' actions. Compare the lists: look for similarities and differences.
3. Characterise Richard Cory.
4. Describe the connections between Richard Cory and the people: how do they communicate with each other.

B Use your imagination
1. Think up a description of Richard Cory's private life.
2. When and where could the story have happened? Give reasonable suggestions and try to prove them.

C Creative writing
Turn the contents of this poem into a short note for
1. the local newspaper.
2. a tabloid.

■■□ 9 Talkline: Job applicants

You work for a German IT company. Your firm plans to establish a branch in the USA and is looking for an all-rounder who seems to be able to build up this branch. You are a member of the selection committee and you are now in a meeting with the other members in order to select one out of four applicants for an interview.

Task:
Each one of you has read one of the CVs (see pages 300–303) in detail. Initially you introduce and defend "your" applicant. The others will do the same. Then you have a discussion in which you support whoever is worth supporting. You need to come to an agreement and decide who to invite.

Roles: 1 chairman, 3 members of selection committee
Student A: you are the chairman. Your applicant is George Walker, see page 300; **student B**: go to page 301; **student C**: go to page 302; **student D**: go to page 303.

A Language study and learning skills

1. Checking your learning environment

Classroom survey

Make up a questionnaire for your class which includes the following questions. Add other questions that you think are important for successful studying:

- Have you got
  - your own room
  - your own desk
  - your own 'library' (dictionaries, reference books, etc)
- Do you always work in the same room?
- Have you got a computer/internet access?
- If so, do you use the computer as
  - a word processor?
  - a learning aid?
  - just for games, relaxation and amusement?
- Can you recommend any computer programmes?
- When do you do your homework?
  - immediately after school/lunch
  - at a fixed time
  - whenever you feel like it
- Do you need a quiet atmosphere to concentrate on your assignments?
- Do you listen to music while working?
- How often is your TV on while you're working?
  - never
  - sometimes
  - always
- Do you like being distracted from studying by visitors, telephone calls?

2. How to improve your learning environment and your learning habits

Your own study would be ideal, your own desk is necessary

- The table you work at should be big enough to put material you regularly need within reach.
- Make sure that the height of the table and the chair you use correspond to your height. Uncomfortable sitting is tiring and may lead to pains that can keep you from studying.

Avoid acoustic, optical and climatic disturbances

- Make sure that there is no noise when you study. Work at a time when there is least noise or use ear plugs.
- Don't listen to music when solving (mathematical) problems or writing compositions. There's evidence that especially radio programmes or loud rock or techno music hinder problem solving.
- When memorising or repeating something you have to learn, listening to (slow, not too loud) music may be helpful.
- Make sure that there is enough light preferably from the left (for right handers) or from the front.
- Put things that may distract you (e. g. photos) out of sight.
- Make sure that it's not too cold or too warm or dry in your room. See to it that there is enough fresh air but no draught in your room. Bad light and climate are tiring and hinder concentration.

Keep your desk neat and tidy

- Check that you have all the office supplies you need.
- Put the office supplies and reference books you regularly need on your desk or in a nearby shelf within reach.
- File your notes from school regularly and neatly so that you don't have to look for something when you want to start studying. Looking for a pen or certain notes somewhere in the house may distract you and gives you the opportunity to delay studying again.

Time management

- Use a diary: Write down all appointments (class-tests, extracurricular activities, free-time activities) and assignments that have to be finished by a certain date (homework, preparation for a class test or exam) so that you can keep track of all the things that have to be done.
- Decide when and how long you study. Fix times for the preparation of class tests or exams, e. g. every second day half an hour for a class test that is due in two weeks, or once a week one hour for an exam that is due at the end of the term. This makes endless (and highly ineffective) studying sessions one day before the exam unnecessary.
- Set priorities: Short-term assignments for the next day have to be finished whereas long-term assignments e. g. revision etc may be finished on a certain day. Write 'to do lists' and tick or cross out all the assignments that are done.
- Fix times for breaks: 2–5 minutes after 20–30 minutes of studying; 15–20 minutes after 1½–2 hours and 1–1½ hours after 3 hours of studying. This ensures a maximum of concentration.

3. Learning strategies

Learning efficiently means organizing your work and creating an atmosphere of relaxed concentration.

How do you best learn vocabulary?

Here are two useful ways to write down new words:

1. Buy a box of filing cards and keep a record of all the new vocabulary in alphabetical order by writing it down on a filing card – the English word(s) on one side and the corresponding German word(s) on the other. Go through your vocabulary regularly, look at the German word first. If you don't know the English meaning put this card aside and check the next one. At the end of a run-through you will see at a glance all the words you don't know for sure.
2. Draw three columns in a vocabulary book (DIN A5/A4):
   The first column is for the English word, the second, wider one, is for a context, and the third column is for the corresponding German term. When learning or repeating the new words you must cover up the English column and successively uncover it while pronouncing the corresponding English word. The third column will help you to put the new vocabulary in a suitable context, if necessary.

Find out which method of learning new words suits you best, in general you will have to practise a method-mix.

1st method:
Systematic word families
(ideal for entry on file-cards)

Love

*to love – loving –
lovable – beloved –
lover*

2nd method:
Classified word fields:
Choose a generic term (Oberbegriff) and divide it up into various classes.

FOOD					
fruits	meats	fish	vegetables	beverages	other
pear	beef	salmon	potato(es)	beer	chocolate
plum	pork	trout	cabbage	wine	honey
grapes	lamb	bass	spinach	coffee	nuts
cherry	chicken	pike	cauliflower	milk	cheese
apple	venison	sturgeon	peas	tea	eggs

3rd method
Making associations
(Write them down in your vocabulary book)

elephant → trunk
potato → to peel
chips (French fries) → crisps

4th method
Synonyms
(Write them on filing cards using a different colour)

to laze about = to loaf
a lazybone = loafer
filthy = dirty
filth = dirt

5th method
Antonyms (opposites)

to scold ≠ to praise
wealth ≠ poverty
urban ≠ rural
rude ≠ polite

6th method
Explanations
Choose objects that are similar but differ in detail, do the same with more complicated and abstract terms.

What's the difference?

stool

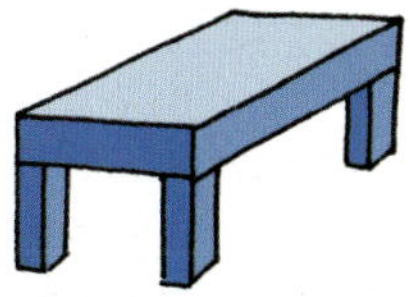

chair

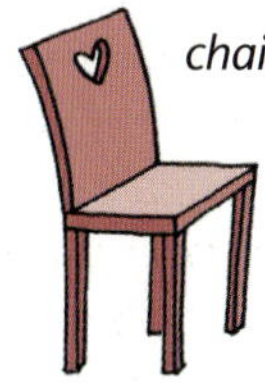

How to learn grammar

If you learn a foreign language or repeat grammar on your own you have to consult a grammar book and/or a textbook. You must be able then to understand and apply rules by a process of deduction.

A teacher can help you to understand certain explanations and to solve problems. If you look up grammar rules, you must be able to understand them.

Learn the basic terminology before starting to learn grammar. For example:

Types of words:
Find examples for each type.

[• verbs • nouns • adjectives • adverbs • prepositions • articles (definite/indefinite) • conjunctions • numerals]

Try to find rules or part of a rule:

[• I walk home. • You walk home. • Sue/Tom walks home. • We walk home. • You walk home. • They walk home.]

But:
He misses the early trains. The early bird catches the worm.

Rule:
In the third person singular, the simple present tense of a full verb always ends in -s or ... (Now finish the rule!)

- Learn the simple rules first. If there is a mnemonic *(Eselsbrücke)* learn it.
  (A German mnemonic is: *He, she, it, das -s muss mit.*)

How to learn more complex grammar rules

- Read the rule carefully, try to understand it.
- Look at the example (in general it's a sentence which optically or graphically emphasizes the new rule).
- Invent other sentences, write them down and apply the rule.
- Check if there are exceptions to the rules.
- Collect other material where you can do exercises.

Example:

SOME and ANY

(+ compounds: *somebody, anybody, something, anything* etc.)

Rule:
Some is used if the idea is restricted in some way, it applies to a part.
Any is used if the idea is unrestricted, it applies to all or none.
The following diagrams can illustrate this rule:

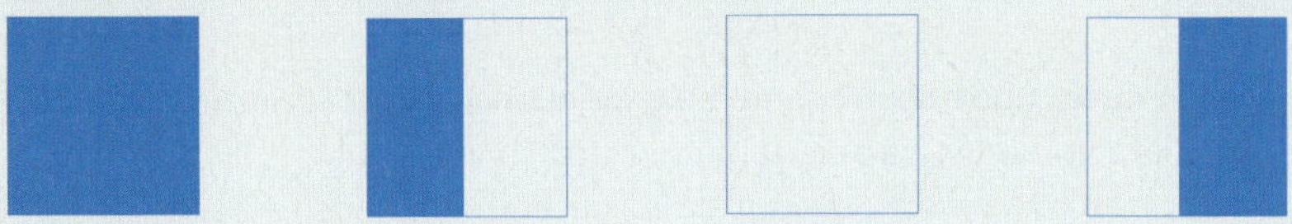

*I like **any** pop music.*	*I like **some** pop music.*	*I don't like **any** pop music.*	*I don't like **some** pop music.*

(The shaded areas represent the pop music liked.)

- ***Find other examples:***

*Do you like **any** drinks?*	*No, I don't like **some** alcoholic drinks.*
*And I don't eat **any** fast food.*	*Well, I don't eat **some** of it.*
*Can you see **anything**?*	*Can you see **something**? (part of...)*
*I can't go **anywhere**.*	*Why, can't you go at least **somewhere**?*

- ***Use patterns to apply and practise rules.***
  For example:
  Sentence structure. The word order in an English sentence is very rigid.
  The basic rule is **Subject** → **Verb** → **Object** for a statement, a negative statement, a question, and a negative question. So even the question or the negative cannot change the word order.

He/She learns a foreign language.	*She **doesn't** learn a foreign language.*
(It)	***Does** he learn a foreign language?*
	***Doesn't** she learn a foreign language?*
I/You/We/They learn a foreign language	*We **don't** learn a foreign language.*
	***Do** we learn a foreign language?*
	***Don't** we learn a foreign language?*

What is introduced to maintain the word order?

Grammar rules are tools for the understanding of a language. By applying these rules you can generate sentences that follow a certain pattern. Repeating patterns is a useful means to learn and memorize typical structures. With structures you can generate sentences.

Other useful tools to learn grammar are various types of exercises:

Fill in the blank with the correct tense:
Yesterday we (go) ... to the seaside and we (take) ... a picnic basket.

Rewrite the sentences using the passive form:
They serve lunch from 6 pm. to 1 am. → Lunch ... ... from 6 p.m. – 1 a.m.
A British advertising company launched this ad. → This ad ... ... by a British ... .
The police arrested two men after a car chase. → Two men ... ... after a car chase.

Complete the sentences with the correct article where necessary:
John loves ... oranges.
... oranges he likes best come from Florida.
Stockton ... High Street is a good example of Georgian architecture.
... High Street in Norwich was lined with flags and bunting in celebration.

Ask your teacher where to find books containing grammar exercises.
Your teacher might also supply you with his grammar worksheets.

4. Mind maps, clustering and flow charts

Mind maps, clusters and flow charts are useful methods of creating and expressing ideas and processing information.

The combination of pictures and words stimulates both halves of your brain, which is essential to support the creative process and to provide deeper and longer-lasting understanding.

Researchers have shown that the two halves of our brain think in quite different ways. You need both ways to be a well-rounded thinker.
In general, the left half is a *splitter*, breaking thoughts into logical parts.
The right half, by contrast, is a *lumper*, composing wholes and grasping them intuitively:

Left Brain
- Thinks **logically**: If *it flops, then we're in trouble, unless we go to plan B.*
- Uses **language**: *apple*
- Bound by rules: **Subject** *must agree with verb in number.*
- Processes items **one by one**: *fries, root beer, hamburger, ...*
- Sees **details**: *brush strokes*

Right brain
- Thinks in **analogies** and **comparisons**: *This is a time bomb.*
- Uses **pictures**:

- Unbounded, **open**: *This essay is powerful, like a bull, a train, a thunderstorm*
- Processes items **all at once**: *supper*
- Sees **overall designs**: *a landscape*

Complete the list with the following items:

Left or right?
• Recognises wholes: forest • Recognises parts: trees • Grasps information: "I've just stepped on a snail." • Grasps emotions: "Ouch" • Perceives words as rhythmic patterns: "How do I love thee? Let me count the ways." • Perceives words as verbal signs: I + Love + You

Discussion
Which of the two halves of the brain do we usually neglect more and why?

Source: Sebranek, Patrick, et al. Write source 2000. Wilmington, Mass: Houghton Mifflin Company, 1995 (adapted)

Mind maps
Mind maps can be very useful to trigger ideas (for compositions, classroom reports, talks, or for your *Fachreferat*).
They also help process information (e.g. word families, vocabulary outlines for all kinds of texts etc.).

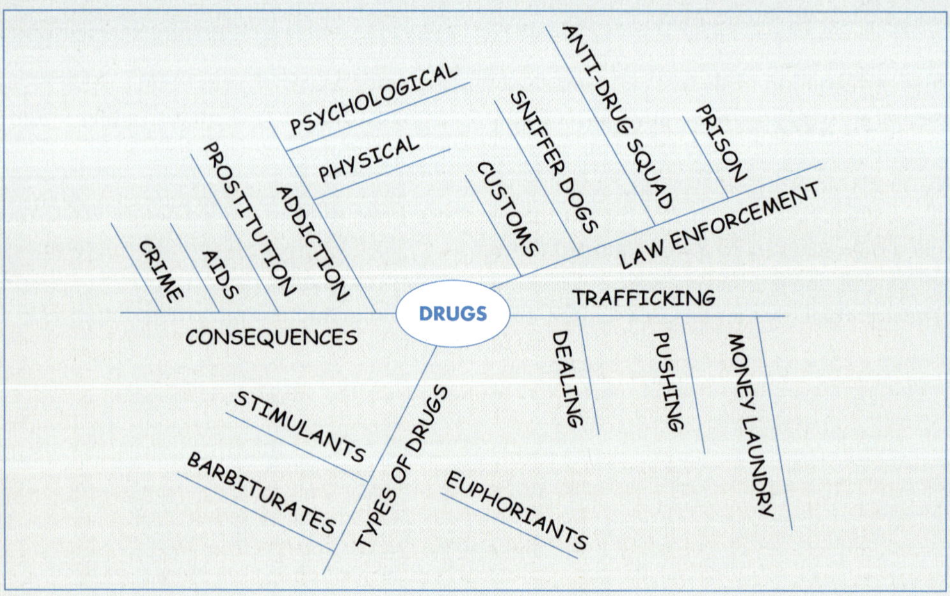

Basic rules for mind mapping

- Reduce your thoughts, ideas or your material to keywords.
- Put the central keyword (topic) into the oval in the centre of the mind map. In the example shown above: **DRUGS**.
- Add branches. Explore the topic by creating headlines, e.g.: **TYPES OF DRUGS, TRAFFICKING** etc.
- Add details (or, if you want to go even deeper, more branches) to the main branches: **STIMULANTS; EUPHORIANTS; BARBITURATES** etc.
- Use only nouns as far as possible.
- Write in capital letters.
- All you need is a pencil, a rubber and a piece of paper, preferably without lines.
- If you reach the end of your sheet, just glue another sheet to it and go on mapping!
- However, although there are no limitations, your mind map should be reasonable in size.
- Add symbols to emphasise keywords: 

HINT:
Mind maps can be done alone, with a partner or in groups.

Clustering

Clustering is more useful if you want to create ideas. Unlike mind maps, which can be quite elaborate and can take some time to develop, it's rather more of a brainstorming activity. You definitely won't need a rubber here.

Clustering is recommended for preparing impromptu speeches, free compositions, sketches or other more literary forms of writing.

Basic rules for clustering:

- Begin a cluster with a nucleus word (topic).
- Record words that come to mind when you think of this word.
- Don't pick and choose, record every word.
- Circle each word and draw a line to the closest related word.

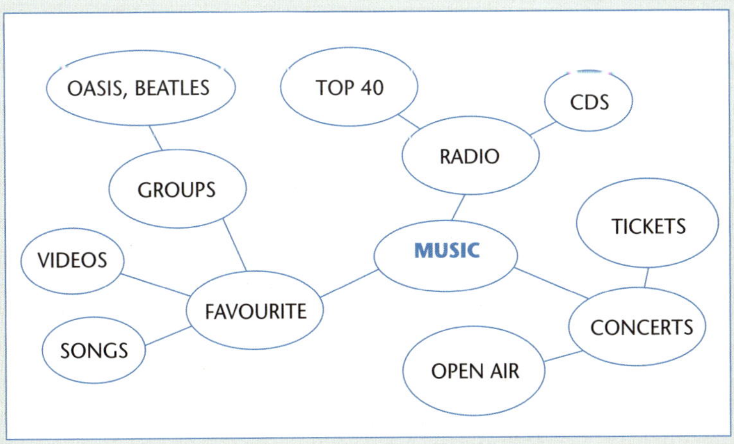

After 3–4 minutes of clustering you will have gathered enough material.
Now choose one of the words or ideas in your cluster that starts your writing off.

Flow charts

Like mind maps and clusters, flowcharts start off with a central keyword.
Arrows or branches indicate how an idea develops or how material is structured. The arrows or branches lead from one point or problem to the next, or, as with our example, from the general to more specific aspects.

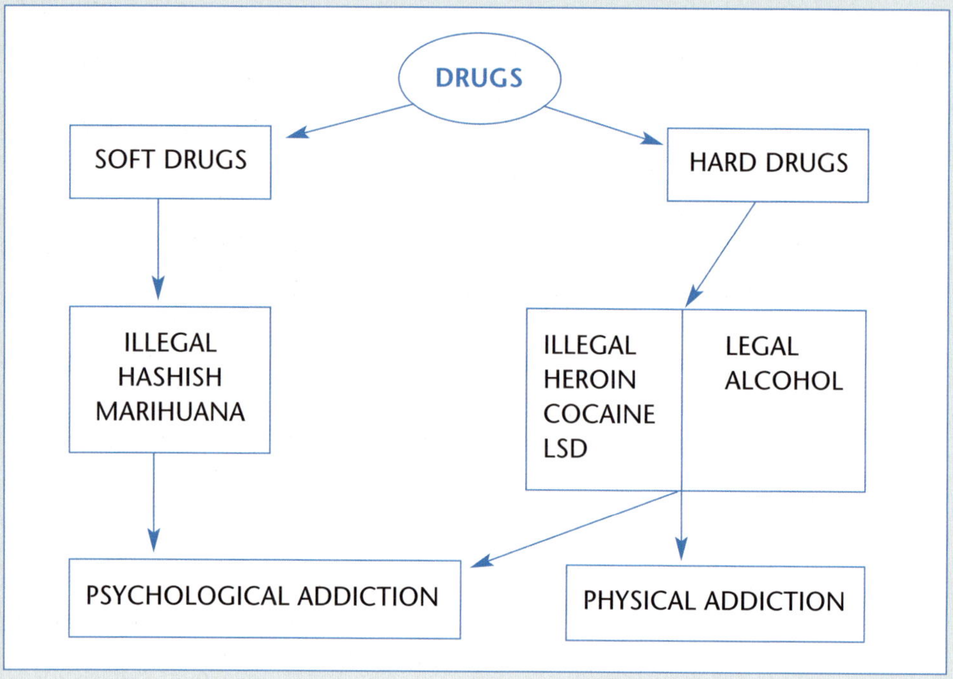

5. Taking notes

Taking notes changes information you have only heard into information you have done something with. This makes it much easier to remember and to use. The basic virtues of taking notes are:

- Be **attentive**. Listen carefully.
- Be **concise**. Taking good notes does not mean writing everything down.
- Be **organised**. Structure your notes.

The following 10 guidelines will help you to improve your note-taking skill.

1. Divide the page that you are going to take notes on into two sections as shown in the example below.

2. Place **the topic of the lesson** here ...

3. Write your notes in ink on this side of the paper.

5. Begin taking notes immediately. Do not wait for the teacher/speaker to say something amazing or earthshaking.

6. Write as concisely as you can. Write your notes in phrases rather than complete sentences. Leave space between different points and ideas.

7. Always copy down what is put on the board or an overhead projector.

8. Draw simple illustrations in your notes whenever it helps make a point clearer.

9. Circle or <u>underline</u> those words or ideas which you will need to ask about later.

... **and the date** ... here

4. Leave space in the margin for revising and adding notes later

10. After having taken down the notes on the left side, you use this side to react to these notes. This could include the following:

– a **comment** on what you think about a particular idea;

– a **reaction** to a particular point you strongly agree or disagree with;

– a **question** – is there anything you have not understood or which needs to be discussed?

! TIP

If you know that there is only little or no time to revise your notes carefully, e. g. after a classroom presentation, just use single words or symbols on the margin to mark where you want to ask a question or make a comment in the following classroom discussion: terrible!, awkward!, fine!, seriously?, !!!, ???, ?!, etc.

6. How to use your dictionary

The right use of an English-English dictionary is one of the most basic skills.
By learning the meanings of unfamiliar expressions you can develop and widen your language competence. A good dictionary will tell you everything about:

[• spelling and pronunciation • language levels • grammar • restricted meanings]

The very **first step** you should take is to realize that your dictionary is a friend and not an enemy. It is a useful tool that will stay by you through thick and thin.

A very useful **second step** is to mark the beginnings of each individual section with the help of tiny file tags. You should also train yourself to focus on the indices at the top and the bottom of the pages as a help in finding the word you are looking for.

The **third step** is learning when to use the dictionary:
When reading or listening to a new text for the first time the dictionary should stay firmly shut. Don't panic because the text contains lots of words and expressions that you don't know. Looking them up at this stage is too time-consuming.

1. While reading a text for the second time, start to work on unknown vocabulary:
   a) Reduce the possibility of several meanings by looking for hints in the context.
   b) Avoid senseless searches by learning common stems and affixes, e. g.:

[• trans *(over to)* • script *(write)* • tion *(common suffix for a noun)* = transcription
il *(prefix meaning non, no)* • liter *(read, write)* • ate *(suffix for an adjective)* = illiterate
pre *(before)* • dict *(say)* • tion = prediction]

When you become familiar with the stems of the expressions, everything else falls into place.

2. When producing your own texts it is advisable to stick to vocabulary you are familiar with. Use your dictionary only when you are unsure about:

[• spelling • language level • structures and the right use of prepositions]

This especially applies to those famous ten last minutes of an examination when you feel you've done enough – use the time you have wisely!

Refer to your dictionary when you don't want to use the same expression for a second or even a third time, because you want your text to be livelier and more colourful. But beware of mistakes involving structure and language levels (restricted meanings, colloquial or formal). Read the entries carefully – including the examples!

7. Some helpful hints on how to avoid or reduce stress

- Always try to do your **best**. Keep in mind that nobody can be perfect.
- Try to avoid negative thoughts (e. g. "that was a stupid thing I did") and replace them with more positive thoughts (e. g. "it's OK to make mistakes").
- Reserve time for fun activities. They are just as important as studying.
- Try to stay physically healthy. Get involved in some sort of physical activity (e. g. jogging, skating, biking, or simply walking, etc.).
- Talk about your stress to friends or family members who are understanding.
- Learn techniques how to relax your mind and your body (e. g. breathing exercises and exercises to reduce muscle tension).
- Try to eat a well-balanced diet and do not skip meals.
- Do not use alcohol or drugs to reduce your stress.

Here are some easy breathing and relaxation exercises that you can do at home or in class.

Breathing exercise

- Sit in your chair or stand comfortably, but erect. Place the palms of your hands against your stomach.
- Breathe in slowly through your nose and allow your stomach to expand forward against your hands. Hold the deep breath for a few seconds.
- Slowly exhale through your mouth, slightly purse your lips together and feel the tension drain away.
- When you have exhaled as much as you can, repeat the technique.

writing
presentation
socialising
literary

Muscle relaxation exercise

This exercise releases the muscles in your back that have been locked into position from sitting for a long time on end.

- Sit toward the front of your chair. Do not lean.
- Move your knees toward the right side of your chair so you are sitting diagonally on your seat.
- Inhale and lift your right arm to the ceiling.
- Exhale and move your right arm to the back of the chair on the opposite side to hold the seat.
- Bring the left hand to your right knee.
- Now do the twist:
  Inhale and lengthen your spine.
  Exhale and press your knees against the left hand. The right hand holds fast. Stay in this position for at least 5 seconds. Breathe in, let tension go (body moves to the left a bit) and lengthen your spine again.

Repeat the twist for 5 to 10 breaths. Return to the centre and breathe a few times. Now repeat the exercise on the opposite side.

Progressive muscle relaxation

Listen to the instructions on CD.

After you've done the exercise, summarise the techniques in German.

language study

writing

presentation

socialising

literary

B Writing skills

1. Paragraph writing

Paragraph writing is the basic skill of unfolding your arguments.
You need it when doing
- commentary questions
- compositions
- letters
- dialogues.

The basic parts of a paragraph

- **The topic sentence**
  The topic sentence refers directly to the topic and makes clear what your point is.
  I really think boxing should be banned.

- **The body of the paragraph, your arguments**
  In a well-written paragraph your arguments are unfolded on two levels:

  Clarifying sentence *(Argument, Begründung)*
  Completing sentence(s) *(Beweis, Erläuterung)*

  Clarifying sentence
  It helps to make the topic clearer by giving an argument.
  Boxing is the only sport where the sole object is to injure the opponent.

  Completing sentence(s)
  It/They add specific details, give reasons, facts, examples, personal experiences etc.
  Think about what a knockout really is: It is a cerebral concussion that knocks the victim senseless!

- **The closing sentence**
  Your closing sentence can be a call to action, a warning, a hint on future developments, a personal statement.
  It's an illusion to think that professional boxing will be banned in the near future as there is simply too much money involved. However, amateur boxing should only be allowed under strict regulation, accompanied by education and research programs with mandatory long-term follow-up of all boxers.

! TIP
Your closing sentence must not be identical with your topic sentence.
Don't write things like:
I hope it has become quite clear now why boxing should be banned.

An example of a paragraph

Study the following comment taken from USA TODAY:

Regulation won't work, ban boxing

by Robert E. McAfee, guest columnist

PORTLAND, Maine – **As a practicing physician, I'm convinced that boxing should be banned.** ← Topic sentence

First, boxing is a very visible example that violence is accepted behavior in our society – outside the ring as well as inside. ← clarifying sentence This sends the wrong message to America's youth, and at a time when so many kinds of violence are on the rise, it is a message we should stop. ← completing sentence (reason)

Second, boxing is the only sport where the sole object is to injure the opponent. ← clarifying sentence Think about what a knockout really is: It is a cerebral concussion that knocks the victim senseless! ← completing sentence (explanation)

Third, medical science can't take someone who has suffered repeated blows to the head and restore that person to normal function. ← clarifying sentence Many physicians, with new methods of brain scanning, have seen an otherwise young and healthy individual sustain serious and permanently disabling injuries due to boxing, sometimes in just one fight. ← completing sentence (facts)

To those who say boxing "gives poor kids an opportunity to get out of the ghetto," I have a better suggestion. Let's take each young person with that precious, undamaged brain and combine some education with that same commitment to excellence he has for boxing. I guarantee that youngster's better success over a lifetime – and perhaps a longer and healthier life, too. ← closing sentences

USA TODAY, April 2004
(212 words)

! TIP
- Now just add an introduction to this, and you get a perfect composition.
- Add a few formalities, and you get a letter to the editor.

Paragraph writing and how to use it (overview)

- **Commentary Questions**

  Topic sentence

  Clarifying sentence
  Completing sentence(s)*

  Closing remark

  or

  Topic sentence

  Clarifying sentence
  Clarifying sentence
  Clarifying sentence

- **Composition** (dialectical order)

  Introduction

  Topic sentence 1

  Clarifying sentence
  Completing sentence(s)*

  On the other hand …
  Topic sentence 2

  Clarifying sentence
  Completing sentence(s)*

  Conclusion

* Repeat the sequence if a greater number of words are required.

language study
writing
presentation
socialising
literary

- **Composition** (listing order)

  Introduction

  Topic sentence

  Clarifying sentence
  Completing sentence(s)

  Clarifying sentence
  Completing sentence(s)

  Clarifying sentence
  Completing sentence(s)*

  Conclusion

- **(Formal) letter**

  Your address Date
  (Recipient's address)
  Salutation

  Introduction

  Topic sentence

  Clarifying sentence
  Completing sentence(s)

  Clarifying sentence
  Completing sentence(s)

  Clarifying sentence
  Completing sentence(s)*

  Conclusion

  Closing

  Signature

  (arguments here: listing order)

- **Dialogue**

  A: Topic sentence
  Clarifying sentence
  Completing sentence(s)

  B: (Notional phrase)
  Topic sentence
  Clarifying sentence
  Completing sentence(s)

  A: (Notional phrase)
  Clarifying sentence
  Completing sentence(s)

  B: (Notional phrase)
  Clarifying sentence
  Completing sentence(s)

  A: *

  A: Closing remark

  and/or

  (B: Closing remark)

* Repeat the sequence if a greater number of words are required.

Some general hints on writing introductions

Do not simply paraphrase the topic. Show that you have understood the topic by

- presenting relevant facts and data.
- referring to something that happened recently.
- telling about a personal experience.
- citing a quotation or a proverb.
- pointing to a historical event.
- giving a definition of the problem (e.g. what are soft drugs, cult novels, etc?).

! TIP
Make your introduction as lively as possible.

2. Writing a comment or a composition

A composition is a form of writing located between a comment (personal point of view) and an essay (rather objective and without any personal judgement). As a comment is not usually expected to be much longer than 200 words, there cannot be a long introduction or lengthy weighing of arguments and counter-arguments. Depending on the topic, a comment can be completely one-sided, i.e. a personal opinion supported by a number of reasons and possibly examples.

Possible steps

Although there are no precise rules, the following steps could be useful:

Step 1 – Ideas

Write your spontaneous ideas on a sheet of paper and then get them ordered in a cluster. This helps you to structure your ideas.

Step 2 – Structure

Once you have more routine in structuring a comment you can try a more "liberal" approach, where each part can have as many sentences as you feel are necessary. But there must still be some structure in the text. A very common one is the following:

- situation
- problem
- solution
- evaluation

Step 3 – Introduction

There must be a *situation* you start from. You can begin with facts everybody knows:

- a look back at history
- a quotation from a famous person
- a surprising statement

Which of the above methods have been combined in the following introduction to a comment on the relationship between Europe and the USA?
We have a firm commitment to NATO, we are a part of NATO. We have a firm commitment to Europe. We are a part of Europe (former US Vice President Dan Quayle).

In a more conventional (or more continental) approach you can start with expressions like

• ... as far as I am aware • as far as I am concerned, In view of ... • ... as far as I know • As far as the debate on ... is concerned

Do not start off by explaining that you know nothing about the topic or by giving a summary of your whole argument. ("In this comment I will show ...")

Step 4 – Main Body
You can either mention a *problem*, suggest a *solution* and then *evaluate* the solution or you can list a number of problems, then suggest solutions, which you then evaluate.

Useful phrases
Structuring your arguments:
First..then.., moreover, additionally, furthermore, due to, first, second, finally, in addition to this

Comparing things
On the one hand, on the other hand, partly, likewise, similarly,

Contrasting arguments:
But, however, yet, although, even if, while

Emphasising your point of view:
In other words, for instance, for example, e.g., that is, i.e., for this reason, again, in fact, really, that is why, without any reasonable doubt, undoubtedly, because of, since, I would like to emphasize that, let me emphasize this

Step 5 – Conclusion
You can conclude by comparing and evaluating the possible solutions, by predicting future developments or by summarizing your arguments. Whichever you choose, make it clear that your text is drawing to its conclusion: don't just write the last argument and then stop.

Useful phrases:
As a result, finally, in conclusion, summing all the facts up, all things considered, all in all, to put it in a nutshell

Write a comment on the following topic (about 200 words):

More and more communities try to encourage young people to get more involved in local politics by setting up youth councils which can influence decision-making. Do you think this is a good idea?

Many cities have set up youth councils. In youth councils, young people can discuss their specific problems and can pass on a sort of "official youth opinion" to the local politicians who then may or may not adopt this suggestion. First of all this may help to solve problems young people have. They might even have their own budget and take their own decisions in running a youth center, for example. This might train their sense of responsibility and their ability to influence democratic decisions. The training effect could be more important than the real influence they would have on events.

However, there is a danger that youth councils could be used as only a façade. The politicians could say they were doing something for young people, while in reality they could still ignore what young people think. In such a case the youth council would be a sort of "democratic playground". The reason why politicians are thinking of introducing youth councils could also be that fewer and fewer young people are interested in political institutions. Instead of luring young people into local politics with all its present faults, maybe politicians should change their own behaviour. Then young people would perhaps become more politically involved with or without youth councils. *(187 words)*

- topic sentence
- introduction, extremely short
- evaluation 1, clarifying sentence
- evaluation 1, completing sentence
- more details on solution
- evaluation 2
- evaluation 3, clarifying sentence
- evaluation 3, two completing sentences
- evaluation 4, clarifying sentence
- conclusion

Combining sentences

There is a simple way of getting from one sentence to the next by using the "given – new method":

sentence 1:	given	new				
sentence 2:		given	new			
sentence 3:			given	new		
sentence 4:				given	new	
sentence 5:					given	new

At the beginning of the text you start with something everybody knows, i.e. something that is "given". In the second part of the sentence you bring new information.

Example:
America, the most important industrial nation (given) has been attacked by radical Moslem groups (new).

The next sentence starts with a re-formulation of the new information of the previous sentence which meanwhile has become old information.

These groups (given) seem to operate from Afghanistan (new).

Do not always use this scheme, as it can make a text boring. But it can be used to a large extent.

Another way of connecting sentences is to use expressions like these:

because as	for firstly ... secondly		therefore	thus	so
consequently	we may infer	we may conclude		however	
moreover	nevertheless	on the one hand ... on the other hand			
but yet	the question is whether (and to what extent)				

Explaining an expression

In tests or examinations students are often required to explain or define an expression. In real life you often have to explain a word or phrase, too, if the person you are talking to does not understand you. A simple example: You have to explain what a *door key* is. Here, and in some other cases, it may help to simply use the word in a context that leaves no doubt: *When a door is locked, you can open it with a key.*

A more universal principle for explaining expressions is the so-called *classical definition*. You give the generic term and indicate the specific difference.

Step 1:
A door key is a device …

Step 2:
… that opens doors.
= what distinguishes a door key from any other device
(generic term)
door key
(to be explained)
others ....

Using the same structure: *a trade union* is an organisation that represents workers' interests.

Give a definition of *car*.

3. Dialogue writing

Writing dialogues is a skill that is often used to make the process of solutions to specific issues livelier and more natural. You are to present two opposing opinions on one particular topic. These differing points of view should be supported by a string of well-informed details. During the dialogue arguments are exchanged and both partners have to react immediately on what has been said. The conclusion should consist of a compromise or at least a solution both partners can accept. Basically, the rules for paragraph writing also apply to dialogue writing (see pages 142–144):

You should have an opening sentence, a sentence for clarifying and a sentence for driving your point home for each section. You may use colloquial expressions and abbreviations to create the style of a natural conversation between two persons. Additionally you need phrases that show that this is a discussion, which means you want to reveal a wide range of attitudes on specific topics with spontaneous and individual reactions to these issues. The following **notional phrases** can serve as starters, you can continue simply by adding clarifying material.

- Typical phrases for initiating a dialogue:
  - *Well, I think ...*
  - *Well, we should really talk about ...*
  - *Don't you think that we should discuss ...*
- Phrases that show reactions could be real questions, too. They serve to channel the topic at hand to a specific purpose. They often start with:
  - *Do you mean ... ?*
  - *Does that mean ... ?*
  - *Does that result in ... ?*
  - *Do you mind my asking ... ?*
  - *Are you of the opinion ... ?*
- Agreement is often used to signal willingness to cooperate:
  - *I agree*
  - *That's right*
  - *Of course*
  - *You're quite right*
  - *I think so, too.*

  This gives you the opportunity to modify the idea by continuing the sentence with a weighty but, ...
- There are degrees of disagreement. You should remain polite but state your point of view firmly. Start with:
  - *I don't agree*
  - *I disagree*
  - *I don't think so*
  - *That isn't correct*

  Continue with:
  - *That's simply not true (stronger)*
  - *Not at all.*

  Carry on the sentence with because ... , as ... , for ... , as this shows that you want to clarify a point and nobody's feelings are hurt.

language study · writing · presentation · socialising · literary

- You can show pleasure, disapproval or regret, too:

  Pleasure:
  - *I'm pleased about that*
  - *I approve of that*
  - *that's nice/good (news)*
  - *that's marvellous/fantastic/...*

  Surprise:
  - *Fancy that!*
  - *Good heavens!*
  - *That's rather surprising.*
  - *How surprising!*
  - *I didn't expect anything like that!*
  - *Well, I never!*

  Disapproval:
  - *I don't like that (at all)*
  - *I don't think much of/about that*
  - *I disapprove most strongly*
  - *That's not good (at all)*
  - *I do **not** approve*
  - (Continue with *because* ...)

  Regret or sympathy:
  - *I'm sorry to hear that!*
  - *What a shame/pity!*
  - *Oh dear!*
  - *That's disappointing!*

- The supporting material should be ordered logically. The most convincing point should be reserved for the end. Signals that show there's still more to come are:
  - *Moreover (you shouldn't forget) ...*
  - *What's more ...*
  - *Additionally (we should keep in mind) ...*
  - *Nevertheless ...*

- If you want to signal that the discussion should come to an end you can start with:
  - *I think we can come to the conclusion that ...*
  - *I hope (that) you'll agree ...*
  - *It definitely can be stated (that) ...*

Exercise

Should bullfights in which the animal is killed be stopped?

Two friends, Fred and Michael, are on a backpacking tour in Spain. On reaching Pamplona one of them suggests seeing a corrida. For the first time during their trip they have a serious argument.

Fred | **Michael**

Ablehnung (notional phrase)

Missachtung der Natur (clarifying sentence)

brutales Schlachten; Arroganz der Menschen, grausam, Tier keine Chance, oft manipuliert. Hörner stumpf (= blunt), langsames Töten, totale Erschöpfung, (completing sentences).

Keine Zustimmung

Alltägliche Grausamkeit an Tieren viel größer

Massentierhaltung (= mass breeding), Tiertransporte und Tötung im Schlachthof mindestens ebenso grausam; Stiere leben lange auf der Weide, werden gut behandelt, nur eine Stunde Kampf, Kampftrieb (= urge to fight) auch natürlich

dennoch **unzivilisiert**

wie im Mittelalter, Rohheit und Freude an der öffentlichen Zurschaustellung (= display) von Gewalt; Aberglaube (= superstition); nicht mehr zeitgemäßer Männlichkeitskult (= macho cult)

Sehe es ganz anders, **Faszination**

Reflektiert in Kunst: Hemingway, Picasso; Kampf selbst Kunstform: Arbeit mit dem Cape, schnelles Töten, fairer Kämpfer ist guter Kämpfer

Einschränkung

Liest gern H., mag auch Bilder von P. und erkennt gewissen Reiz an. Einstellung aber doch sehr altmodisch? Stierkampf heute nicht doch nur Touristenspektakel? Lieber ins Stierkampf-Museum gehen.

Write the dialogue. Add a short introduction:
Michael: "What about going to a ...?"

language study
writing
presentation
socialising
literary

4. How to write a summary

A summary or a summarizing question ...

- is a contracted/shortened form of a text.
- it shows what the text is about (the 'theme' of the text).
- it displays the principal ideas of the text or the essence of the text.
- it is not a critical evaluation of the text.
- the approximate number of words is usually indicated.

Some rules for summary-writing

- Read the text carefully.
- Find out what the text wants to express, what its theme is.
- Mark the passages in the text that support the author's theme and circle the key words.
- Write from the point of view of the author (but don't use direct speech), and don't introduce your sentences with phrases such as: *"The author says/tells us ..."* or *"This paragraph signifies/means that ..."*
- Write in your own words as far as possible; find synonyms and paraphrases.
- Don't copy long passages and sentences from the original; however, you **may** use technical terms or the central key words of the text.
- Leave out repetitions of the text.
- Don't go into details.
- Present your items in the same order as they occur in the text.
- Connect them by conjunctions such as: *but, for, while, however, therefore, consequently, etc.*
- Vary the structure of your sentences in order to improve your style.
- Check the number of words and condense the text if necessary.

Task

Sum up the procedures immigrants had to undergo in the past when arriving at Ellis Island, New York. (Don't write significantly less or more than 100 words.)

Now look at the relevant passages in the text (**marked in blue**) and their key words (marked with a circle) on the opposite page.

From Ellis Island to LAX

It is said that nearly half of all living Americans can track their ancestry through the Great Hall on Ellis Island, once the nation's largest immigration station. In the busiest of Ellis Island's days **immigration was a deeply traumatic ordeal**, the stuff of family history that descendants keep alive.

"The day of the emigrants' arrival in New York was the nearest earthly likeness to the final Day of Judgement, when we have to prove our fitness to enter Heaven," wrote globetrotter

Stephen Graham. Another observer recorded the anxiety of people in steerage as they were taken off the steam-ships, loaded into lighters, taken to the quay. "There is Ellis Island!" shouted an immigrant who had already been in the United States and knew of its alien laws.

The name acted like magic. Faces grew taut, eyes narrowed. There, in those red buildings, fate awaited them. Were they ready to enter? Or were they to be sent back? "Only God knows," shouted an elderly man, his withered hand gripping the railing. Then as now, money helped a lot. For **the fortunate few** who could afford first- or second-class cabins on the old steamships, **a polite interview in the ship's parlor often satisfied American formalities.** But for 17 million immigrants (and some 250,000 rejectees), the baggage room at Ellis Island was the first stop, then a long flight of slate stairs up to the Great Hall, 170 ft. long102 ft. wide, the ceiling 58 ft. above. At the top of the stairs were **doctors who watched the immigrants' ascent for lameness, deformity, signs of respiratory problems.** Then they were made to walk in circles. "Whenever a case aroused suspicion," one inspector wrote, "the alien was set aside in a cage apart from the rest ... and **his coat lapel or shirt marked with a colored chalk,** the color indicating why he had been isolated. **"They would mark them 'H' for heart disease, 'X' for dementia or perhaps just for looking stupid, 'E' for eye problems.** The immigrants were entitled to an interpreter. **"Name? Where were you born? Have you ever been to the United States before? Do you have any relatives here? Where do you live? Who paid for your passage? Do you have any money? Let me see it. Do you have any skills? Do you have a job waiting for you here? Are you an anarchist? Are you a polygamist?"** Today U.S. consulates abroad are responsible for the medical and legal eligibility. People arrive with the necessary papers and X rays; customs clearance customarily takes but minutes.
In 1924, laws were changed to require that immigrants be approved or rejected at consular offices overseas. Then came the Depression and a reversal of roles: Ellis became a deportation center. The approach of World War II would bring in refugees, of course, but the great migration of immigrants from Europe to the U.S. had ceased, as had the original purpose of Ellis Island. In 1955, it was put up for sale – 27 1/2 acres, 35 buildings, good view – but at $6.5 million the government found no buyers. Vandals had the run of the place.

(Adapted from: TIME, July 8, 1985 abridged)

Model summary

For most immigrants who arrived at Ellis Island the formal procedures were a traumatic experience, especially for those who were finally rejected.
There were of course exceptions to the rule. Immigrants who travelled first- or second-class were spared the painful procedures poorer immigrants had to go through for the authorities contented themselves with a polite interview. For the masses, however, immigration was a humiliating affair. They were examined for obvious health defects and judged by their appearance.
Apart from the standard questions concerning their country of origin and family situation they were asked embarrassing details of their financial situation, their skills and their political convictions.

language study
writing
presentation
socialising
literary

5. Sentence building

Some basic principles of sentence building

- Write clearly. This is one of the most important principles of good writing.
- Always control what you are writing down. Translate your English sentences into German to see if they make sense in German. If they don't, they won't make much sense in English either.
- Know when to cut. It's easier to control short sentences than longer ones.
- Write active, forward-moving sentences. Make it clear in your sentences that your subject is actually doing something.

Use a variety of sentence beginnings:

- *We stand at attention in straight lines.* (Sentence begins with the subject).
- *Motionless, we stand at attention in straight lines.*
  (Sentence begins with a modifying word).
- *At the start of each class, we stand at attention in straight lines.*
  (Sentence begins with a phrase).
- *When each class starts, we stand at attention in straight lines.*
  (Sentence begins with a clause).

Use a variety of sentences

- Make use of the following types of sentences:
  1. **Simple sentences** (einfache Hauptsätze):
     Sports are fun.
  2. **Compound sentences:**
     I like sports, but compulsory physical exercises at school are boring.

  A compound sentence is made up of two or more simple sentences (Hauptsätze), which are joined by a coordinate conjunction *(and, but, or, nor, for, so, yet).*

! Tip

Try to use the word *and* to connect sentences very very sparingly.
If you realize that you are using *and* too often, just cut the sentences.
Period!

  3. **Complex sentences:**
     Although the weather was fine, we had to work out in the gym.
     A complex sentence is made of one independent clause (Hauptsatz) and one or more dependent clauses (Nebensätze):

- Study the fine rhythm of the following passage. Which of the sentences is simple, complex, compound and complex?
  1. At the start of each class, we have to stand at attention in straight lines while our teacher takes attendance.
  2. Then we have to suffer through his warm-up exercises.
  3. His favourite is push-ups.
  4. We do them just as if we were in the army, and that means we have to keep our heads up, backs straight, and push up and down 25 times.
  5. We also run in place until Mr Benning can see that we are all "warmed up".

Giving reasons

- There are several ways of **giving reasons** and you should make use of them when writing your paragraph:

We have to do too many push-ups. We are really exhausted after the lesson.
(Reason = sentence)

We have to do too many push-ups, that's why we are really exhausted after the lesson.
(Reason = coordinated sentence)

As we have to do too many push ups, we are exhausted after the lesson.
(Reason = adverbial clause)

Having no chance of escaping this burden, we just give in and try to make the best of it.
(Reason = participle construction)

Source: Sebranek, Patrick, et al. Write Source 2000. Wilmington, Mass: Houghton Mifflin Company, 1995 (adapted)

6. Avoiding sexist language

In the 80s and 90s advocates of 'political correctness' have sharpened our awareness of how prejudiced language can be. One of their main targets has been trying to avoid sexist language i.e., the use of words that unnecessarily distinguish between males and females. 'Talking PC' (politically correct) means that you should try to make use of gender-neutral words and expressions.
The results are not undisputed. Here is what they suggest:

- Avoid unnecessary allusion to gender.
  Not: *Daphne du Maurier is one of the most important* ***female writers*** *of the twentieth century.*
  But: *Daphne du Maurier is one of the most important* ***writers*** *of the twentieth century.*

- Avoid occupational stereotypes
  Not: *A good secretary knows* ***her*** *way around complex computer systems.*
  (Suggests that 'secretary' is a female occupation)
  But: *A good secretary can master complex computer systems.*
  Not: *A respected lawyer will defend* ***his*** *clients on the highest ethical grounds.*
  (Suggests that men have higher qualified jobs.)
  But: *Respectable* ***lawyers*** *defend their clients on the highest respectable grounds.*
  Not: *Lecturers have* ***wives and children*** *to support.*
  (Suggests that men are breadwinners, women are housewives and mothers)
  But: *Lecturers have* ***families*** *to support.*

- The use of certain female forms is declining.
  Not: *She's a **stewardess**. This is our **hostess**.*
  But: *She's a **flight attendant**. This is our **host**.*
  (N. B.: The forms *waitress* and *actress* are still used regularly, both in BE and in AE whereas *authoress* is falling into disuse.)

- Avoid expressions which are patronising

Not:	**But:**
the girls in the office	*the secretaries, office assistants*
*ladies**	*women*

  (* Except when used in a parallel manner with *gentlemen*)

- Avoid using **man** or words containing **man** to refer to all human beings.

Not:	**But:**
man	*human beings, women and men, a person, an individual*
mankind	*people*
manpower	*work force, personnel, staff, workers*
chairman	*chairperson, coordinator*
congressman	*representative*
fireman	*firefighter*
mailman	*mail carrier*
foreman	*supervisor*
policeman	*police officer*
businessman	*business executive*
workman	*employee*
spokesman	*spokesperson*
man-made	*synthetic, manufactured, machine-made*

- Rearrange sentences to remove singular pronouns.
  Not: *The welfare worker is always overworked, so **he** ...*
  But: *Welfare workers are always overworked, so **they** ...*

- Indefinite pronouns such as **somebody, nobody, anyone,** may be followed by they, them, their.
  Not: *Anyone who wants **his** work evaluated should ...*
  But: *Anyone who wants **their** work evaluated should ...*
  Or: *If a person wants **their** work evaluated, **they** should ...*

Exercise

Rewrite these sentences to avoid sexist language.

1. We want to find the best man for the job.
2. Give each student his paper as soon as he has finished.
3. Ladies are entering almost every occupation.
4. Ms Capriati won easily while Agassi and Becker went to five sets.
5. President Clinton came to Hillary's defense.
6. The grocery shopper should save her coupons.
7. Anyone who wants to go to the game should bring his money tomorrow.
8. I wrote to the chairman of the committee.
9. Man has not reached the limits of social justice.
10. If the reader is patient, he will be rewarded in Chapter 8.

7. Giving reports and writing papers

Topics for classroom reports (Fachreferat) and papers (Facharbeit) can cover a wide range of subjects, from literature to political or other institutions, from sports to music. As an example, we have chosen a literary topic here, a short story by Stephen King: *The Boogeyman.*

An important key to all of Stephen King's horror fiction, 'The Boogeyman' offers the theme that would underlie his magnum opus, IT: '(M)aybe if you think of a thing long enough, and believe in it, it gets real.'

'I came to you because I want to tell my story,' says Lester Billings, comfortably enthroned on the psychiatric couch of Dr. Harper. 'All I did was kill my kids. One at a time. Killed them all.'

So begins Lester Billings' journey through the retrospective corridors of psychoanalysis. He quickly explains that he did not actually kill his three children, but that he is responsible for their deaths because he has left certain closet doors open at night, and the 'boogeyman' has come out. A rational mind must reject such a confessional, and Billings is an abrasive personality – cold, insensitive, filled with hatred for the human condition. Immediately, we doubt his credibility and sanity. By the story's close, Billings has made it clear that it is he who fears the boogeyman, and the reader can only conclude that he has murdered his children.

Dr. Harper states that therapy will be necessary, but when Billings returns to the psychiatrist's office, he notices that the closet door is open – first, just by a crack, but it quickly swings wide:
'So nice,' the boogeyman said as it shambled out. It still held its Dr. Harper mask in one rotten spade claw hand.'

(From: Winter, Douglas E. The Art of Darkness. The Life and Fiction of the Master of the Macabre: Stephen King. London: Hodder and Stoughton, 1989: 224f)

Finding a topic
The more you narrow your topic down, the easier it will be to work on it, as a distinct, unmistakable topic will give your efforts a certain direction. Example:

Subject: Horror Literature (much too broad)
- Topic: Stephen King (too broad)
- Topic: Stephen King's horror stories: Nightshift (still too broad)
- Topic: Stephen King's horror story: The Boogeyman (workable)
- Topic: Stephen King's horror story: The Boogeyman.
  A character study of Lester Billings (perfect)

Research your topic

Common sources for research are:

- Print media such as fiction and non-fiction books, reference books, dictionaries, encyclopaedias, magazines, journals, newspapers and brochures.
- Electronic media such as multimedia encyclopaedias, the Internet via its search engines, video or television, cassettes or radio programmes.
- Personal interviews with experts in the field.

Using the library

Although we live in the computer age, libraries and books will certainly remain one of the most useful and reliable sources of information.

I. Card catalogue	II. Microfiche catalogue	III. Special catalogues
Titles Authors Subjects	This microfilm catalogue gives you access to almost all the books available in University libraries in Germany via *Fernleihe.*	Many libraries have a special local service for students hunting for information. Ask your librarian for details.

IV. Computer search	V. Friendly librarian
Many libraries already have a computer that tells you whether a certain book, newspaper, audio- or video cassette or CD-ROM is available, and where you can find things.	If you've got a problem, ask the staff for help. Be polite and you'll see how readily they will help to solve your problem.

Activities

1. Explore your library to find out what it's got to offer on ... well, choose your own subject. Report your findings to the class.
2. For classmates from out of town, draw a little map and describe the way from your school to the library.

"I'd like to see everything you have got on girls."

Skimming/Browsing through a book

Today the problem isn't so much how to get information, but how to choose wisely from a huge number of sources. When you find a selection of books in your library, all of them covering your specific topic, it's hardly possible to take them all home. Skimming through a book can give you a first impression of whether the book is useful or not.

The following parts of a book can be helpful:

- **The cover**
  On the cover you often find hints on what the book is about:
  Avid fans, serious students and those who just want a better understanding of the man who turned horror into a national pastime – all will want to read (Winter's book).

- **The title page**
  This is usually the first printed page in a book. It gives you
  – the full title of the book
  – the author's name
  – the publisher's name
  – the place of publication

- **The copyright page**
  The page right after the title page. Here you will find the year in which the copyright was issued and the year the book was published. If the book is too old, it may no longer be a good source of information.

- **The preface**
  (foreword, introduction, or acknowledgement)
  This gives you an idea of what the book is about and what it's concentrating on.

- **The table of contents**
  It helps locate major topics or areas covered in the book.

- **The index**
  This is probably the most useful part of a book. It's an alphabetical listing of all the important topics and/or names appearing in the book.

- **Try a page!**
  Just pick out a certain page and start reading. Just ask yourself the question: Do I understand this?

Contents

Foreword ix
1 Introduction: Do the Dead Sing? 1
2 Biographical notes: Living with the Boogeyman . . .13

Index

Bomba the Jungle Boy, 19
'Boogeyman, The,' 8, 9, 184, 196, 224-5, 256, 287
Book of Job, the 110

(The examples are all taken from: Winter, Douglas E. The Art of Darkness. The Life and Fiction of the Master of the Macabre: Stephen King. London: Hodder and Stoughton, 1989)

Making notes

Once you have found the books and materials for your report, the next step is to read through all of them and make notes of the important facts and details.

Hints

Ask questions: It might be helpful to first write some basic questions about your subject. Once you get deeper into your subject, try to ask more detailed questions.
For example:

Who is Stephen King?
(Biographical sketch)
How many books has he sold?
What/who has influenced his writing?
How do critics see his work?
What is horror literature?
What makes horror?

What do critics say about Nightshift/The Boogeyman?
What is the story about?
Who is Lester Billings?
How does he treat his wife?
How does he treat his children?
What's his attitude towards minorities, etc.?

GENERAL
↓
SPECIFIC

- Put each of these questions at the top of a separate note card.
- Any time you find a fact that helps answer one of your questions, write this information on the note card with that question.
- When taking notes, remember to write down the author's name, title of the book, magazine etc., the page number and the specific quotation.

Example of a note card:
The page numbers refer to Stephen King's story 'The Boogeyman', and to Douglas Winter's work on Stephen King (see above):

> ***What is Lester Billings' attitude towards minorities?***
> – *calls people with mental problems 'freaks' (Boogeyman, 94)*
> – *says nasty things about drug addicts (Boogeyman, 94)*
> – *couldn't stand his son being gay (Boogeyman, 95)*
> – *hates hippies (Boogeyman, 101)*
> – *calls protesting blacks 'niggers ... yelling a lot' (Boogeyman, 101)*
> – *Billings ... an abrasive personality – cold, insensitive, filled with hatred for the human condition. (Winter, 224f *)*
>
> (* f = and the following page, ff = and the following pages)

Organizing your material

- The next step is to get your notes/note cards into an appropriate order.
- Generally speaking, you will be working from the outside to the inside of a topic, from the general to the specific.
- Selecting – 'What do I really need, what can be reduced or omitted?' – is more important and more difficult than finding material.

- Make sure your report is well-balanced: The specific aspect of your topic must have more weight (about two thirds to three quarters of your report) than the preliminaries (about one quarter to one third).
- The organization of your report should be logical.

The outline of your specific assignment might look somewhat like this:

Facharbeit

1 Introductory paragraph*
2 Stephen King
2.1 Biographical sketch
2.2 Success as a writer
2.3 What the critics say
3 Horror literature
3.1 The Gothic novel
3.2 Modern horror literature
3.3 Stephen King's definition of horror
4 The Boogeyman
4.1 The plot
4.2 A character study of Lester Billings
4.2.1 Family and social background
4.2.2 Lester's machismo
4.2.3 Lester's educational principles
4.2.4 Lester's attitude towards minorities
4.2.5 Conclusion: Low self esteem
4.3 How to interpret the end of the story
5 Summary/abstract*
6 Bibliography*
7 Appendix*

Fachreferat

1 Introductory paragraph*
2 Stephen King: a biographical sketch
3 The Boogeyman
3.1 The plot
3.2 A character study of Lester Billings
3.2.1 Family and social back-ground
3.2.2 Lester's machismo
3.2.3 Lester's educational principles
3.2.4 Lester's attitude towards minorities
3.2.5 Conclusion: Low self-esteem
3.3 A note on the end of the story
4 Bibliography*

(= to be added later)*

Writing your classroom report

If you have a complete and well-organized outline, writing your report should be easy. Check whether your specific assignment requires writing complete sentences *(Facharbeit)* or simply notes *(Fachreferat)*. Talk with your teacher about that.

- **Introduction:**
  Your introduction should get the reader's attention and introduce the topic. You might also say why you have chosen this specific topic and whether you faced any special problems when researching it.

- **Accuracy:**
  Your report must be accurate. Double-check for any missing information and any facts which seem hard to believe or unclear.
- **Quotations:**
  Use quotations from all kinds of sources to support your ideas. Quotations are essential with literary topics.
- **Illustrative material:**
  Add charts, diagrams and illustrations in a meaningful way. You might also place them in an appendix. In this case, do not forget to refer to these illustrations in the main body of your text.
- **Summary/Abstract:**
  In your closing paragraph you summarize the main points made in the report.A summary may be optional. Ask your teacher whether you are to write your summary in English.
- **Title page and outline:**
  Write the title page and outline for your report if they are required as part of your assignment. If an outline is required, add page numbers to it (c. f.: Organizing your material). Every item in the outline must also be a headline in your report.
- **Correctness:**
  Check the spelling, punctuation and numbering.

Giving credit, bibliography

It's very important that you give credit for information you have used in your report.

1. Giving credit in the main body of the text

- **Parenthesis:**
  You can use brackets directly after a quotation or after a sentence or a paragraph that either contains or sums up somebody else's ideas. Provided you add a bibliography, the parenthesis just gives the name of the author and the page number(s).
  For example:
  "On a metaphorical level, the boogeyman's appearance may be an affirmation of Billing's psychosis ..." (Winter 8 or: Winter p. 8)
- **Footnotes:**
  Another possibility is the use of footnotes.
  Word processors can organize your footnotes automatically.

HINT

If you use more than one work of a certain author, add the title (or a shortened form of the title) to avoid confusion.
For example:
(King, Danse Macabre, p. 24)

2. Bibliography

- In your bibliography you list all the sources you have used in alphabetical order.
- Make sure you do not list more than you actually quote from or refer to in your report.
- If you write about a literary work, organize your bibliography according to two sections:

Primary literature:
What you are writing about. For example:
King, Stephen: "The Boogeyman", in: Nightshift, 1979.

Secondary literature:
All the sources you quote from or refer to in your report or paper.

Listing works you have cited

Typical listings for books and magazines are written the following way:

Books:	Magazines:
Author (last name first): **Title,** **Copyright date**	**Author** (last name first): **"Title of article", in:** **Title of the magazine** **Date** (day, month, year), **Page number(s)** of the article

Examples:

One author (book)	Winter, Douglas E: The Art of Darkness. The Life and Fiction of the Master of the Macabre: Stephen King, 1989.
Two or three authors (book)	Searles, Baird and Martin Last: A Reader's Guide to Science Fiction, 1979.
More than three authors or editors (book)	Boyle, George et al., eds: Black Anatomy, 1989.
A single work from an anthology	Poe, Edgar Allan: "The Raven", in: Selected Stories & Poems, 1978.
(Signed) article in a weekly	(Gates, David:) "New Tales of Terror", in: Newsweek, 4 November 1991, pp. 50–51.
(Signed) newspaper article	(Owen, Richard:) "Italy pays Gothic homage to creator of Frankenstein", in: The Times, 2 January 1997, p. 15.
Encyclopedia article	Brent, Sherwood: "Edgar Allan Poe." Encyclopaedia Britannica, 1981.
Multimedia encyclopedia	„Poe, Edgar Allan", Microsoft Encarta 1994 Edition. 1993 Microsoft Corporation.
Internet	http://www.scholastic.com/goosebumps/ (date of access)

Abbreviations		
(E)ed. = editor	p. = page	f. = and the following page
(E)eds. = editors	pp. = pages	ff. = and the following pages

Sources:
English composition and style, 1994 BarCharts, Inc. Boca Raton, Fl.
Sebranek, Patrick, et. al. Write source 2000. Wilmington, Mass: Houghton Mifflin Company, 1995 (adapted)

8. Translating into German

Here are some points to watch when you translate from English into German:

Grammar and style

- Be careful with tenses.
- Participle constructions

  How to translate participle constructions

– *Übersetzung als Relativsatz*

Sceptics see the spread of English as linguistic imperialism, contributing to the disempowerment of people denied access to it.

→ Skeptiker sehen die Ausbreitung der englischen Sprache als sprachlichen Imperialismus, der dazu beiträgt, die Möglichkeiten der Menschen einzuschränken, denen der Zugang dazu verwehrt ist.

– *Übersetzung mit **und** (Beiordnung)*

Optimists view this spread of English as a process empowering people, facilitating communication in the global village.

→ Optimisten sehen diese Ausbreitung des Englischen als Prozess, der den Menschen mehr Möglichkeiten eröffnet **und** die weltweite Kommunikation erleichtert.

– *Übersetzung als kausaler oder temporaler Nebensatz*

Being tired after her long walk, Ann went to bed early.

→ **Da** Ann müde war, ging sie früh ins Bett.

Looking out of the window, she saw an accident.

→ **Als** sie aus dem Fenster blickte, sah sie einen Unfall.

Oft nicht eindeutig:
The concert being over, we went home.
→ **Da** … oder: **Als** das Konzert zu Ende war, …

– *Vorsicht bei Konstruktion mit **with** + Partizip*

But now, with simply too many people crowding in previously unspoiled places, ecotourism is doing more harm to nature than many experts may have foreseen.

→ Aber heute, da einfach zu viele Menschen sich an Orten drängen, die früher unberührt waren, schadet der Ökotourismus der Natur mehr als viele Experten vorhergesehen haben mögen.

- **Word order**

  … is more rigid in English. Keep in mind that when a German sentence is introduced by an adverb or a(n adverbial) phrase, the verb changes its position, whereas in English the word order remains S-V-O. This can cause problems when you translate longer sentences. Look at the following examples.

English **is used** …	→	Englisch **wird** … **gesprochen**.
Today English **is used** …	→	Heute **wird** Englisch … **gesprochen**.
As we all know, English **is used** …	→	Wie wir alle wissen, **wird** Englisch … **gesprochen**.

- **The passive voice**

  … is used more frequently in English, while German prefers the active voice.

She was given a ticket, too.	→	Man gab ihr auch eine Fahrkarte/Sie bekam auch eine Fahrkarte.
In our time rational reasoning is encouraged.	→	Unsere Zeit fördert das rationale Denken.

- **Comparatives, superlatives**

  … work differently in German.

more important	→	wichtiger
most important	→	(am) wichtigste(n)

- **Stylistic differences**

  The English language uses more nouns than German (nominal style). German prefers verbs. It can often be helpful to translate English nouns as verbs.

There was a **devaluation** of other languages.	→	Andere Sprachen wurden **abgewertet**.
It is my personal **belief** that …	→	Ich persönlich **glaube**, dass …

Nouns can also be translated as adjectives or adverbs.

We favour a bit of **peace** and **quiet**.	→	Wir haben es gerne ein bisschen **ruhig** und **friedlich**.

Sometimes it can be helpful to turn the whole thing round completely.

adjective	noun		adjective	noun
political	leaders	→	führende	Politiker
black	male	→	männlicher	Farbiger

English prefers short and compact expressions.
When you translate from English into German you'll need a larger number of words.

They see the spread of English as an **empowering process.**	→	Sie sehen die Ausbreitung des Englischen als einen **Prozess, der den Menschen Möglichkeiten erschließt.**

Vocabulary

- **Be careful with 'small' words – they often have several meanings.**

since → **seit** (She's been working since 9 o'clock.)
da, weil (Since he didn't know where he was, he turned round.)

for → **seit** (I've been waiting for three hours.)
da, weil (For I have loved you all my life.)

yet → **schon** (Have you done it yet?)
noch (nicht) (I haven't done it yet.)
doch (am Satzanfang) (Yet on a train mobile phones are a nuisance.)

but → **aber** (It's sunny but cold today.)
sondern (He didn't call her but sent her flowers.)

(nothing) but → **(nichts) als** (He left her nothing but an old pair of shoes.)

some → **etwas** (Would you like some cake?)
eine (gewisse) (He has some ability to annoy people.)
etwa (English is spoken by some billion people.)

with → **mit** (He prefers tea with milk.)
bei (We'll stay with her.)
da, weil (With so many people crowding the nature spots, eco-tourism has done more harm than good.)

little → **klein** (Have you met his little sister?)
wenig (Little did she know about his plans.)

(al)though → **obwohl** (Although it's late the kids are not tired.)
doch (The report was critical though fair.)
aber (His English hasn't improved; though he should continue to attend classes.)
as though = as if

given → **wenn man davon ausgeht** (Given the fact she's never done it before, she's already quite good at it.)

- **Some expressions with 'to' can cause problems.**

to be likely to → **wahrscheinlich** (He's likely to come. = He will probably come.)

to be to → **soll** (The president is to appear on TV.)
(in headlines without *be*: Prime minister to address House of Lords.)

to be said to → **soll (angeblich)** (He's said to live by himself.)

used to → **früher** (We used to go out a lot when we were younger.)

to be used to → **gewöhnt sein an** (+gerund) (We are used to working long hours.)

- **'Word pairs' mustn't be overlooked.**

both … and → **sowohl als auch** (Both he and his brother forgot to call her.)
either … or → **entweder … oder** (You either take it or leave it!)
(But be careful here: "I don't like it either" = Ich habe es auch nicht gern.)
neither … nor → **weder … noch** (Neither his parents nor his teachers knew of his habit.)
the … the → **je … desto** (bei Steigerung) (The sooner the better.)
provided that → **vorausgesetzt, dass** … (It will be a nice holiday provided that we have good weather.)

- **The following words are sometimes translated sloppily.**

Britain → *Großbritannien* (nicht *Britannien*)
man → *Mann,* oft aber auch *Mensch*
place → *Platz,* oft aber auch *Ort*
number → *Nummer,* oft aber auch *Zahl, Anzahl*
student → *Student*, AE auch: *Schüler* (BE: pupil)
would → *würden* (nicht *wollen; wollen* = to want to)
will → *werden* (nicht *wollen*)
then → *dann, damals* (He didn't have a car then.)
than → *als* (bei Steigerung) (He is much older than me.)
at last → *schließlich*
at least → *wenigstens, zumindest*

- **And finally: Beware of 'false friends'**

actual	tatsächlich		aktuell	current, topical
betray	verraten		betrügen	cheat
critic	Kritiker(in)		Kritik	critique
depot	Lagerhaus		Depot	portfolio
dome	Kuppel		Dom	cathedral
meaning	Bedeutung		Meinung	opinion
moderate	bescheiden		Moderator	presenter, host
overhear	belauschen		überhören	not to hear
overtake	überholen	BUT	übernehmen	take over
provision	Vorrat		Provision	commission
rate	Preis; Zinssatz; Wechselkurs		Raten(zahlung)	by instalments, on hire purchase
receipt	Quittung		(Koch)Rezept	recipe
sensible	vernünftig		sensibel	sensitive
pregnant	schwanger		prägnant	concise
paragraph	Absatz		Paragraph	section
delicate	zart		delikat	delicious
concurrence	Übereinstimmung		Konkurrenz	competition

9. Describing graphs

A General hints

1. Concentrate on the information you actually are to extract from a graph. Very often there is information you needn't refer to. So don't.
2. Do not describe developments in detail. For example, it makes no sense describing every single up and down of a curve. Describe the trends or striking points only.
3. Always refer to the problem: Do not write 'The curve is moving downwards' but 'The crime rate (or whatever) is falling'.
4. The trick is not to get data and figures across, but to get the message across.

B Kinds of graphs

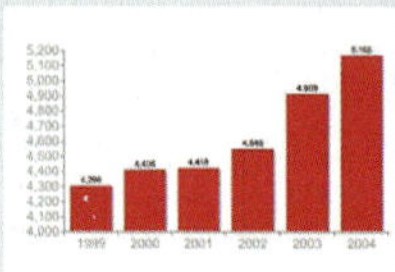

Bar Graph

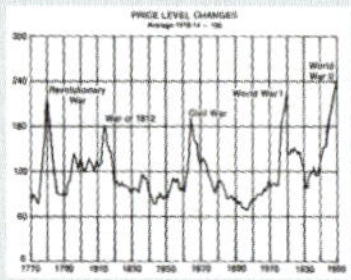

Line Graph

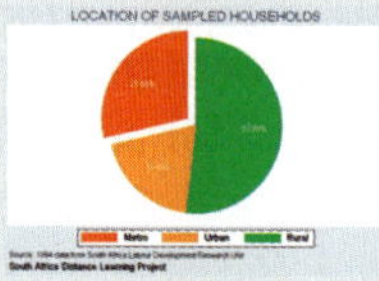

Pie Graph

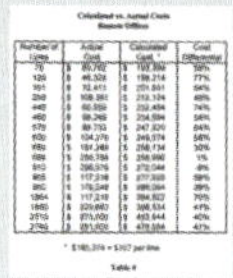

Table

C Useful words and expressions

Expressing quantity:

- a 50 per cent increase
- has increased/decreased by 50 per cent
- has doubled (tripled/quadrupled/quintupled), has halved (from 16% to 8% over the last four years), has been cut (reduced) by two thirds
- there are now twice as many (there is now twice as much), there are now half as many …

Expressing movement:

to rise (to)	a rise (in)
to increase	an increase
to boom/to soar	a boom
to climb	a climb
to (reach a) peak	a peak (at)
to decrease	a decrease
to fall	a fall
to drop	a drop

to reach a low point (its highest point)
to slump

to stagnate
to stay (remain) the same (steady, constant, at fairly the same level)

Expressing the quality of movement:

rapid (increase)/(has increased) rapidly
steady/steadily
fast/fast
significant/significantly
sudden/suddenly
gradual/gradually
slow/slowly
moderate/moderately

Summing up the message:

The graph (clearly) shows …
The most striking fact is that …
From the graph we can see …
The graph tells a lot about …
What the graph tells us is …

C Presentation skills

1. Impromptu speech (1–2 minutes)

You are asked to speak on the spur of the moment with little or no preparation time. Make up a five part speech and memorize your thoughts by relating each part to one finger of your hand.

Presentation
Your teacher or the speaker of your group will introduce your speech, mentioning the topic, e. g.: *Now let's listen to .../Here is .../May I ask for your attention for .../etc. Chris, who has a few words to say about the benefits of InterRail.*
Try to refer directly to this introduction when starting:

		Yes thanks, and...
Thumb: Topic sentence (thesis statement) Introduction (optional)		*... I can only recommend travelling like that. Last year I bought myself an InterRail-ticket and travelled through three European countries. It was one of the best things I ever did.*
Index finger: First argument (plus reasons, examples,statistics etc.)	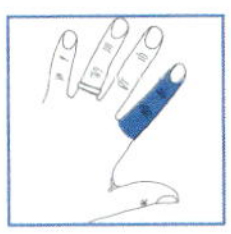	*First, it's really cheap, because ...* (facts)
Middle finger: Second argument	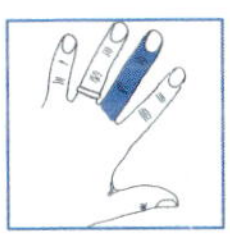	*Second, you meet a lot of interesting people ...* (1 example)
Ring finger: Third argument	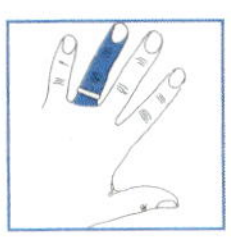	*Third, it really gives you more self-assurance, because you have to handle a lot of sometimes unexpected situations ...* (1 example)
Little finger: Conclusion (call to action, warning, future developments etc.)	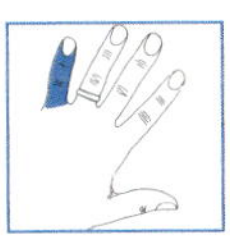	*If you are not the kind of person who needs air-conditioning, king-size beds, etc. to feel comfortable on a trip, try it sometime. It's rewarding.*
		Thanks for listening.

! TIPS

1. If, when preparing your speech, you can only think of two arguments, cut off your ring finger (metaphorically speaking).
2. Speak loudly and clearly. Don't rush.
3. Look at your audience as you speak.
4. Show enthusiasm for your topic from start to finish.
5. Don't finish your talk by saying something stupid like *That's the end of my talk; That's all or I guess that's it, better say: thank you (for your attention).*

2. How to give a presentation

"Half of the world is composed of people who have something to say and can't and the other half who have nothing to say and keep on saying it."

The basic speech outline
- Introduction
- The Main Body
- Conclusion

Introduction
The purpose of the introduction is to prepare the audience to listen to your speech. It consist of two steps:

1. Attention Getter
  - a startling fact or humorous story
  - a series of interesting questions or a short history of the topic
  - a short demonstration or a meaningful visual aid like a picture or a cartoon
  - a personal reason for choosing the topic

2. The Thesis Statement (Topic Sentence)
A single statement summing up the central idea or specific purpose of your speech.

HINT
- Your introduction should be written out word for word and memorised. This will help you maintain eye-contact with your audience.
- Engaging your audience in the introduction is important because audience members will decide if they will continue to listen during the first minutes of your speech.

The main body
Arrange your main points in the best possible order – order of importance, chronological order, cause and effect and so on.

Support your arguments to give the audience a reason to believe your main points.

Types of supporting material
- Testimony: The opinion of an eye witness or expert
- Statistics: A numerical collection of fact
- Stories: Suspense, conflict and description help a story to hold the attention of the audience. Example: "What's the story behind a typical drug career? Let's take 16-year-old ... from Liverpool. As a child he ..."
- Examples: Either factual or hypothetical and used to illustrate a point

In the body of the speech you move smoothly from one point to the next. Form bridges between the parts of your speech. After presenting the life of Edgar Allan Poe, for example, you should not start your next part like this: "And now for the short story ... (title)." Instead, you might say: "One of the most disturbing stories Poe wrote when he was ... (refer to his life) is ... (title), a short story about ..."

HINT
Use your own words!

Conclusion

Bring your talk to a close, summing up your major ideas, letting your audience know what you expect of them and providing a final impact.

Depending on your topic you could conclude by one or more of the following:

- A summary of the main points you presented in your speech.
- A final statement: It should leave a lasting impact on your audience and bring your ideas to a close.
- Using a powerful quotation is a good way to end a speech.
- You can also end your speech by tying your conclusion into a story that you started in your introduction.
- You might also say why you feel your topic is important or why it may be important in the future.
- A call to action: In the call to action you tell the audience exactly what you want them to do. (If possible, come prepared with materials appropriate to your cause, e.g. pamphlets, petitions, addresses, donation cards etc.)
- Say what you want to do. Demonstrate to your audience that you too will be taking action. This creates credibility.

HINT

Do not finish your talk by saying something like "That's the end of my report," "That's all," or "I guess, that's it." Your very last line might be: "Thanks for your attention" or "Thanks for listening".

To write it down or not to write it down?

- When preparing your presentation, it is highly recommended that you take down the full text of your speech.
- Reduce your text to an outline.
- Practise reading aloud using your outline, then reduce your outline to a few key words.
- Write your key words and the quotations you want to use on small index cards.
- Also write down which visual aid you want to use next.
- Do not learn your speech by heart. You will not sound natural.
- Introductions, transitions and final statements, however, should be memorised.
- Do not just read out your full outline. You will sound boring.
- Practise until you know your speech well enough to put the main points in your own words.
- When practising, try to get an audience of family and friends to listen to you.

Presentational aids

These help the audience to follow and understand better and more easily. They can also be used to obtain credibility.

Flip charts or blackboards

- Flip charts, poster-boards or blackboards can be used to display sketches, charts, graphs, or diagrams, photographs or artwork.
- Use a pointer to direct the attention of your listeners.

Slides

- Know where you will be projecting your slides (screen or wall?).
- Make sure you can operate the projector you will be using.
- Make sure you are familiar with your notes. You may not be able to see them in the dark.

Overhead transparencies

- Switch the projector on only when you need the transparency.
- Use a pointer, a pen (that you put directly on the projector table) or paper to cover and uncover parts of your transparencies, to direct the attention of your audience.

Physical objects

- Using physical objects, such as books, instruments, sports equipment, models etc. makes a speech colourful and lively.
- Make sure the object is not too big, too heavy or too hairy.
- Don't pass objects around. Your audience might start concentrating on the object more than on your speech.

Audio and video clips

- Sound clips (radio broadcasts, speeches, excerpts from audio books) should not be longer than one minute. If you present for example a song that is longer than that, make sure your audience is provided with the song text (paper, overhead transparency).
- Video clips should not be longer than 3 minutes. Consider whether the result justifies the effort. Reading a thrilling scene from a book can be at least as exciting as showing a film clip.
- Video and sound clips should always be commented on before or afterwards.
- You can also use a silent video clip giving your own comments.

Computer generated images

- These are "slide shows" that are created on computer programs.
- You need a computer or laptop and a beamer.
- Do not overdo the animation.

HINT

- Use visual aids moderately and not all kinds at the same time.
- Do not insist on using technology that is difficult to provide in your classroom.
- Make sure the end justifies the means.
- Work with your visual aids. Point at them and at details on them. Visual aids are not meant to be decoration.
- Turn off all presentational aids when you are not using them.
- Maintain eye contact with your audience when using visual aids. Do not turn your back to the audience.

Giving your speech

If you have practised often and well, giving the actual speech should be easy. It is quite normal to feel a little nervous at first, but soon you will relax and enjoy sharing your 'story' with your audience. Be aware that you are well-prepared and that you are the expert.

- It is common practice for a speaker/presenter to be introduced by someone – in the classroom by a teacher, the spokesperson for a group etc. This short introduction should mention the topic of the presentation, so that after just saying "Thanks" you can immediately start off.
- Speak loudly and clearly.
- Do not rush. Breathe consciously.
- Use your hands. Never leave your hand movements to chance.
- Keep both feet firmly on the floor. Do not wander about.
- Show enthusiasm for your topic.
- If something goes wrong, do not criticise yourself.
- Do not embarrass your audience. Do not say things like: "I'm sure you all know this," or "I'm sure you've never heard of this."

Source: Sebranek, Patrick, et al. Write Source 2000. Wilmington, Mass: Houghton Mifflin Company, 1995 (adapted)

3. Designing a handout

What handouts are

- Handouts are short papers that support your talk or presentation.
- They shouldn't be longer than one page.
- They must be typewritten or printed.
- Handouts shouldn't be just an outline of your talk or presentation, but should also offer precise and concise information and illustrations (pictures, photos, charts, graphs, etc).
- Don't forget to include a bibliography (c.f. Skills: Giving reports ...).

When to hand out your handout

Plan carefully when you want to hand out your paper:

- **Before your talk or presentation**
  If you hand out your paper at the beginning be sure you refer to information or the illustrations contained in it during your talk. The problem is your audience might concentrate on the pictures in your handout more than on your talk.
- **During your talk or presentation**
  Recommended if you want to work intensely with information or illustrations in the handout, as it captures the attention of your audience: "We have some work to do now!"
  The problem here is that it's a noisy interruption of your talk and will take some time.
- **After your talk or presentation**
  Don't just hand it out, but say what's in it while distributing it.
  Ask students to go through your handout for a minute or two before the beginning of a discussion about your talk.

D Socialising and negotiating skills

1. Socialising and small talk

Greeting people

Here are some common ways of greeting people.

[• Hello! • Hello, nice to meet you (again). • Hello, nice to see you (again). • Hi! • How are you? • How are you doing? • How is it going? • How're things?/ How's things?]

Which of the above greetings could trigger the following responses?

[• Thanks. • How are you? • Great! • Hello! • So, so. • It's nice to see you. • Hi! • Just fine.]

! TIP

If someone comes up to you and says "Hello, do you remember me?" but you have absolutely no idea who they are, never say "No". Instead, you could say: "I think so," or "Yes, of course! But you'll have to remind me." or "I'm sorry, I'm terrible with names."

Introducing people and being introduced

Introducing people to each other

- You always introduce both people to one another: "Susan, I'd like you to meet Mary. Mary, this is Susan."
- When showing Susan round at a party you could also say: "Mary, have you met Susan? Peter, have you met Susan? John, have you met Susan?" etc.
- If someone is related to you in any way, you should say: "Mary, I'd like you to meet Susan. Susan, this is my sister Mary/Mary, my art teacher" etc.

! TIP

Women get introduced to men: "Mary, this is Frank ..."
Older people get introduced to younger ones: "Mum, this is Susan ..."
"Important" people get introduced to everyone else: "Dr Roberts, this is Frank Brown ..."

Being introduced

- This is what you should do when being introduced to someone of your age:
  Smile at the person.
  Say something – anything, even if it is just "Hello".
- This is what you should do when being introduced to someone older or important:
  Get up (if you were sitting down).
  Shake the person's hand or offer a handshake.
  Say "Pleased to meet you." or "How do you do?"

Starting a conversation: The art of small talk

One of the most embarrassing situations ever is when you meet someone – especially for the first time – and, after the greeting thing, you do not know what to say. Here are some hints on how to avoid the deadly silence and to start a conversation.

- Ask questions, preferably ones that cannot be answered with "Yes" or "No". Just think of where you are and why and with whom and ask questions ...
  - about the place:
    "Are you also on this course? Well I hope this is Language Training Intermediate!"
    "I like this place. Have you ever been here before?"
  - about the people:
    "I'm from Germany. Where are you from?"
    "Where are the other participants of the course from?"
    "This is a nice party. Do you know all the people here?"
  - about what is going on or what you see:
    "This is a nice party. Do you know what CD is playing at the moment?"
    "I've just arrived. Have I missed anything?"
    "Where did you get that nice jacket?"
- Listen carefully to the answers and try to use them as a springboard for your next question. Direct eye contact is very important. Not doing so implies boredom or disinterest.
- Things you should not ask about are

• money • personal subjects, such as relationships or sex life • someone's defects of appearance • things about someone's disability • political opinions

TIP
Do not be afraid of starting a conversation in English with people from English-speaking countries. Once they realise you are a foreigner it is very likely they will take over the initiative, so all you will have to do is to react. They do not want to hear anything like "My English is rather poor," instead accept their compliment on how good your English is with a friendly "Thank you."

Ways of saying goodbye

Here are some common ways of saying goodbye.

• Goodbye. • Bye (for now). • So long. • See you. • Take care. • Nice meeting you. • It was a pleasure to meet you (to a person you have met for the first time). • Stay in touch (to someone you do not see very often).

Do not forget to say thank you

The more words you use to say thank you, the more polite you appear.

• Thanks for the nice party. • Thanks, I had a great time. • Thanks for + ing (e.g. thanks for coming/for showing me round).

TIP
If someone offers you something, and you reply with "Thanks", it can mean "Yes, please.". "Would you like a piece of cake?" – "Thanks!". Say "No, thank you" when you want to decline the offer.

And how do I say "Bitte"?

When someone says "thank you" to you some possible replies are:

[• You're welcome. • That's OK. • Not at all. • My pleasure. • Don't mention it.]

Inviting people

If you want to invite somebody, you should not ask directly but give people the opportunity to say "No" without being rude. So the first thing you ask is:

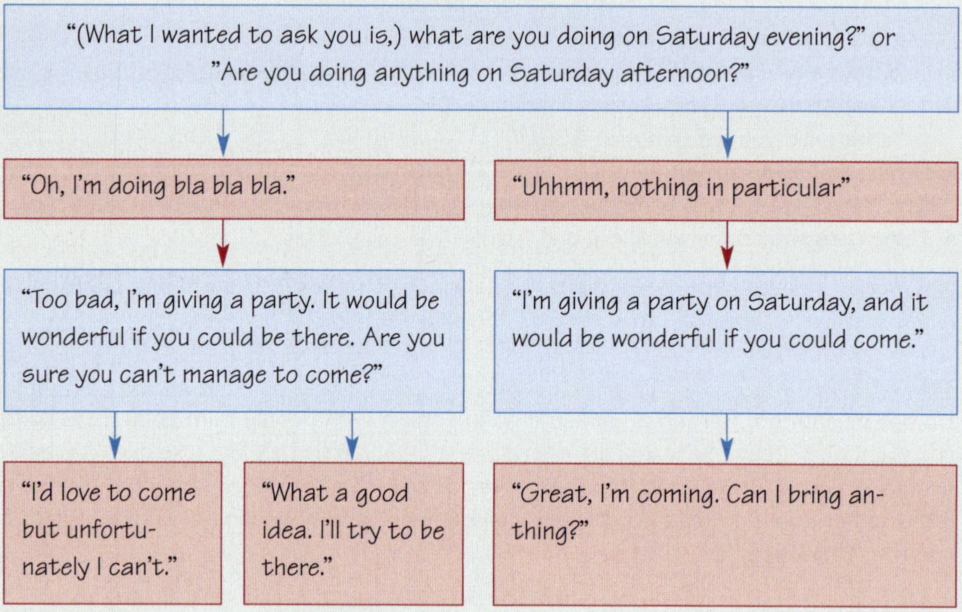

The most natural way to express future in this case is to use the Present Progressive:

[• I'm giving a party tonight. • I'm going to a concert tomorrow. • I'm seeing my parents on Sunday. Would you like to come with me?]

Use the will-future only with I think, I'm sure, I guess, etc.

[• I guess she'll be there, too. • I don't think I'll be able to come.]

2. Telephoning

When the phone rings, who would you like it to be?
Who would you hate it to be?

[Work in pairs, call ...
• a friend • a travel agency • an airline • a hotel • a restaurant]

Making a phone call

1. Make sure you dial the correct number. If you don't know it, call the operator. Here is a phone number if you call New York in the U.S. from Germany:

00 -	1 -	212 -	453-7096
international access code	*country code*	*area code*	*subscriber's number*

2. Telephone numbers in English are spoken in pairs. "0" (zero) is pronounced "O" (oh), just like the letter. "00" can be pronounced double "O".

3. Use the pronunciation of the alphabet to spell names or difficult words. (Normally you are not expected to know the international spelling alphabet, e. g. **A** = Amsterdam, **B** = Baltimore, **C** = Casablanca etc.)

A reference to internationally known places or names will help you to make clear you mean the right letter. A capital letter has to be pronounced *"Capital C"*, for example.

The German "Umlaut" (ä,ö,ü) can be either pronounced *"ae"*, *"oe"*, *"ue"* or spelled *"A – umlaut"*, *"O – umlaut"*, *"U – umlaut"*, if the person you are calling knows what an umlaut is.
Spell the following names:

• München • Edinburgh • Mississippi • Cheshire • Gloucester • your last name • your first name • your address.

4. If you have misdialled a number, don't simply hang up. Say: *"Sorry, wrong number"*.

5. If you call a number in the United States or make an overseas call anywhere in the world you must be aware of the time zones.
(See the illustration on page 178.)

Some international access and country codes:

Australia	00 61	Ireland	0 03 53	Singapore	00 65
Austria	00 43	Italy	00 39	South Africa	00 27
Belgium	00 32	Japan	00 81	Spain	00 34
Canada	0 01	The Netherlands	00 31	Sweden	00 46
China	00 86	Norway	00 47	Switzerland	00 41
Denmark	00 45	Poland	00 48	Taiwan	0 08 86
France	00 33	Portugal	0 03 51	United Kingdom	00 44
Hongkong	0 08 52	Russia	0 07	United States	0 01

Activities

1. Place calls from Germany to the numbers in the following cities. (Use the correct country and access codes):

Vienna 01 780 456	Belfast (0)28 90964372	Liverpool (0)19 28575140	Madrid 01 322 8749	Barcelona 03 1259 35
Moscow 095 335 6770	Arnhem 085 817 735	Brussels 02 714 469	Warsaw 02 618 2201	Lisbon 01 990 562
London (0)20 72856506	Rome 06 753 489	Chicago 312 459 8007	Paris 1 993 487 70	Atlanta 404 923 0776
Beijing 01 768 833 56	Copenhagen 22 621 599	Stockholm 08 110 034	Birmingham 0121 992 366	Tokyo 03 114 5037

2. The number for overseas calls from Britain to Germany is 00 49 (international access code: 00, country code: 49). Place a call to your a) parents, b) boss, c) school.
3. Look at the map on the next page and find out what time it is for your partner at the other end.

Germany:	midnight	New York:	?
Germany:	3 pm	Nairobi:	?
Germany:	9 pm	Sydney:	?
San Diego:	11 am	Anchorage:	?
Delhi:	4 pm	Germany:	?
Iceland:	8 am	Germany:	?

What time is it in Germany when you call a friend or a hotel ...?

• in New York at 11 a.m. local time • in San Diego at 4 p.m. local time • in Sydney at noon local time • in New Delhi at midnight local time • in Houston at 8 a.m. local time

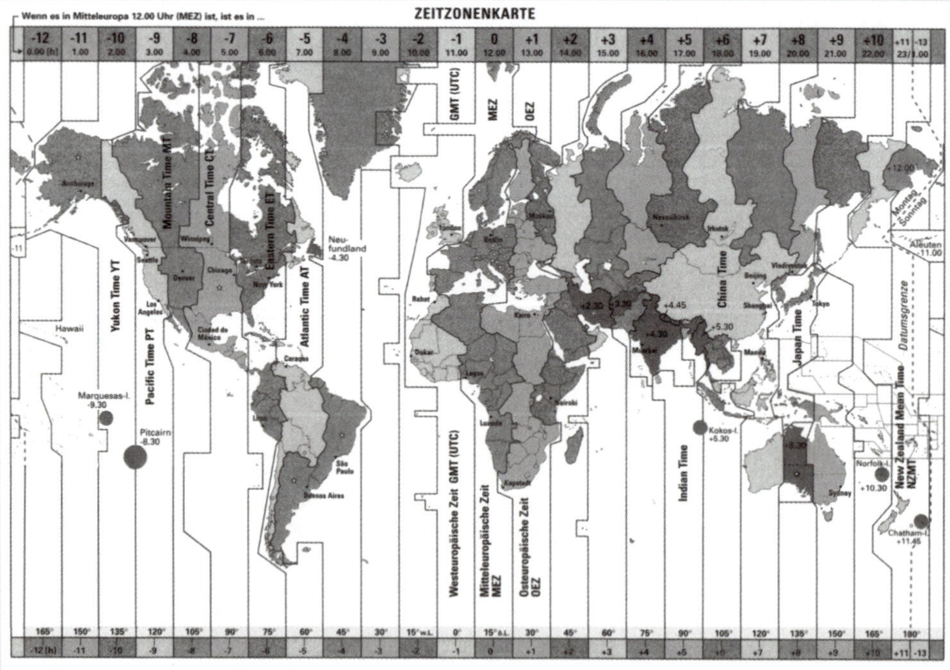

Dates

In English dates can be written in one of the following ways:

8 November, 2004   *8th November 2004*   *November 8, 2004*   *November 8th, 2004*

Beware of all-figure dates! They can be misunderstood in Europe and overseas.

An example (consult a dictionary):
8-11-2004 means: *in Britain: ...*   *in the United States: ...*   ?

When you say dates on the phone use the following forms (the American forms are used internationally):

in Britain:	*the eighth of November two thousand and four*
in the United States:	*eighth November two thousand and four* *or* *November eighth two thousand and four*

Key phrases

• SAX International, good morning? • Barnickle residence, hello. • This is/My name is Christian Möller. • What did you say your name was? • Could I speak to Jane Morrison? • Speaking. • Hold the line please, I'll put you through. • I'm sorry her/his line is busy/ engaged. • May I give you her/his extension? It's 50 64. • She/he is not in at the moment. • I'm afraid she/he is not available. • Could you take a message? • Could you repeat the last number, please? • Could you spell the name, please? • Have you got that? • Could you read that back to me? • Thank you for calling. • My pleasure. Goodbye.

More activities

1. Make up a conversation by using some of the above key phrases. Work in pairs, choose your role first. Are you the caller or the receiver? Here are some ideas:

   • Reserving a table in a restaurant • Confirming your flight • Booking a hotel room • Contacting a travel agent • Booking a room in a youth hostel • Contacting a car-rental company • Calling a business partner

2. Rewrite the pone call by putting all statements into the right order.

CALLER
1. Oh dear!
2. I'm Christian Brack from BGM Munich, I'd like to speak to Mr Frost, please.
3. Please tell him that my plane is delayed. He needn't pick me up, I'll take a cab.

RECEIVER
a) I'm sorry he's out for lunch.
b) O.K., I've noted that. Thank you for calling, Mr. Brack.
c) Can I take a message?
d) BMG International, can I help you?

language study
writing
presentation
socialising
literary

Spelling alphabet

The correct pronunciation of vowels and consonants can be retained more easily in groups:

a	[ei]	h	[eitʃ]	o	[əʊ]	v	[viː]
b	[biː]	i	[ai]	p	[piː]	w	[dʌbljuː]
c	[siː]	j	[dʒei]	q	[kjuː]	x	[eks]
d	[diː]	k	[kei]	r	[aː]	y	[wai]
e	[iː]	l	[el]	s	[es]	z	[zed] Brit. Engl.
f	[ef]	m	[em]	t	[tiː]	z	[ziː] Am. Engl.
g	[dʒiː]	n	[en]	u	[juː]		

Aviation alphabet

When pilots talk on the radio, they want to make sure their message ist understood.

Because some letters of the alphabet sound nearly the same (such as M and N or B, C, D, E, G, P, T and V), they sometimes use this "aviation alphabet" to make sure the person to whom they are talking hears them correctly. The pilot of the Boeing 247, for instance, would call the control tower at San Diego's Lindbergh Field by saying "Lindbergh tower, this ist November-Three-Niner-Seven-Seven-Charlie." Notice the pilot said "niner" instead of "nine". Pilots do this because "nine" might sound like "five" over the radio. The number 9 is the only number that is spoken differently. "... *NOVEMBER-THREE-NINER-SEVEN-SEVEN-CHARLIE."*

- Can you spell your name using the aviation alphabet? Try a friend's name.
- Write a short sentence using the aviation alphabet, then read it to a partner.

See if your partner can understand what you are saying.

Example

"I am hungry": India Alpha-Mike Hotel-Uniform-November-Golf-Romeo-Yankee.

A	Alpha	H	Hotel	O	Oscar	V	Victor
B	Bravo	I	India	P	Papa	W	Whiskey
C	Charlie	J	Juliet	Q	Quebec	X	X-Ray
D	Delta	K	Kilo	R	Romeo	Y	Yankee
E	Echo	L	Lima	S	Sierra	Z	Zulu
F	Foxtrot	M	Mike	T	Tango		
G	Golf	N	November	U	Uniform		

San Diego Aerospace Museum
http://www.aerospacemuseum.org

Making international phone calls

First contact:

You say:

- Good morning/Good afternoon!
- My name is .../I'm Christian Möller.
- I'm calling from BMG group in Munich, Germany.
- I'd like to speak to Mr Roberts, please.

Introducing yourself to your interlocutor (if necessary):
- Good morning Mr Roberts. This is Christian Brack speaking.

Reason for your call:
- I'm calling in reply to your emails as of May 11 …
- I'm returning your call …
- The reason I'm calling is …

You are connected by a secretary:
She says:
- Just a moment, please.
- I'll put you through.
- I'm sorry, the line is busy/engaged – but here is his extension number.
- I'm afraid,
  - there is no answer.
  - she/he's not in the office.
  - she/he's not available just now.
  - she/he's in a meeting.
  - she/he's away on business.
  - she/he won't be in until Monday.
- I'm sorry, we were cut off.
- How may I help you?
- May I have your name again, please?
- Can I take a message?
- Can I give her/him a message?
- Can she/he call you back?

You promise action:
- I'll get back to you on that.
- I'll ask my secretary to arrange that.
- Does Tuesday suit you?
- Let's fix an appointment.
- Yes, I'm free at around 3.30 p.m. (In Britain people often say "half three" for it).

Troubled conversation:
- Sorry, I didn't catch that.

3. Group discussion: Working in a team

First: Creating Atmosphere
You certainly know from your own experience that working together successfully as a team depends a lot on how good the atmosphere is within the group. Everybody can contribute to creating a relaxed, friendly and understanding environment, which is definitely one of the keys to success:

- **Be friendly and open.**

- **Offer compliments and thanks.**

Thanks, Fred. I think that was an interesting remark/point/contribution. *Splendid.* *Great. I think, that's a good idea.* *Well done, Sandra.* *Wow! Now that's something!* *I think that's exactly the point, Fred.* *I couldn't have said it better.* *Now, that really concludes everything that has been said so far.* *What you said was perfectly right.*

- **Never use put-downs.**
  Put-downs might cause group members to lose their self-confidence.
  Avoid statements such as:

What a dumb idea. *Oh no, not that again!* *Now come on, you've had better ideas.* *Nonsense.* **DON'T!**

- **Offer words of encouragement**
  As often as possible demonstrate that you appreciate someone else's ideas. It's much easier for all of us to participate in groups if we feel that what we say is welcome. You can say:

I like that idea. *Let's talk more about that.* *Fred, what do you think?* *Come on Sandra, you often have good ideas.*

Second: Listening

Being a good listener is one of the qualities in a person that is appreciated most. Nobody, however, is able to listen with complete attention for a longer time. So it's very important to listen as effectively as possible when working in a group.

- **Listen actively**
  Let the speaker know that you are interested by keeping eye-contact and nodding your head from time to time. Respond by asking a good question or by offering a compliment or comment. (See previous page.)

- **Listen carefully**
  Concentrate fully on what is being said, and not on what you are going to say when it's your turn. Take notes of what is being said or what you want to add. Offer your ideas when the speaker stops.

- **Know when – and how – to interrupt**
  If you interrupt someone who is speaking, you might appear rude. So generally speaking, you shouldn't interrupt. However, there are three situations where you might be allowed to do so:

1. When you think you have something important to add:
   Excuse me, Martha, when you finish I have something to add.
2. When someone seems to forget about the topic:
   Sorry, Fred, but I think we should get back to the main point.
3. When someone is dominating the discussion. The best way to react is to try to make someone else join in (do not start a dialogue!):
   Excuse me, but I think Joseph has something interesting to say, too. Could you please add your thoughts, Joseph?

- **React adequately when someone interrupts you**
  When a group member interrupts you without good reason, keep cool, smile, and say something like ...

• Could you please wait until I've finished? • Sorry, but I haven't finished making my point yet. • I'd really like to respond to that, but before I forget what I wanted to say, please let me continue. • That's an interesting point. Would you mind if I respond to it after I've finished?

TIP
If someone interrupts you, the fault might be on your side.
Make sure that you keep what you say short and to the point.

Third: Responding

- **Agreement**

• I can fully/totally agree with that. • I couldn't agree more. • Absolutely! • That's exactly it. • That's right. • Perfectly right! • There you go!

Should we try it? – Yes, we should.
Isn't it great? – Sure it is (has/does/can etc.)
I think it's a good idea. – So do I.
I don't think it's a good idea. – Nor do I./I don't like it either.
Have we thought about that? – Sure we have.

- **Disagreement**
  Never disagree with a **person**. Always disagree with the **idea**. Instead of saying *I don't agree with you* say something such as: I disagree. *I don't think soft drugs should be legalised.*

• I disagree. • I can't agree. • I see your point. However ... • I'm not sure ... • I doubt whether ... (➨ refer immediately to idea)

- **Giving your opinion**

• In my view • I think that • in my opinion • as far as I'm concerned • I'd say • if you ask me • if you want my opinion • I'm quite certain

- **Use "I" statements**
  This is one of the best group skills. "I" statements begin with how you feel and conclude with why you feel or think that way.

Examples:

- I feel uncomfortable when you ... because ... • I like it when you ... because ... • I appreciate it when you ... because ... • I feel a little left out when you ... because ... • I feel a little disoriented now. I think you should explain once again ...

Always tell the other members of the group exactly how you think and feel. "I" statements show that you accept responsibility for your own feelings and that you aren't putting the blame on somebody else for how you feel.

Source: Sebranek, Patrick, et al. Write Source 2000. Wilmington, Mass: Houghton Mifflin Company, 1995 (adapted)

Activities

Work in groups on a project on how to present your school/hometown/sports club/youth organisation etc. on a website in the Internet. Try to make use of the group skills presented above.

4. Interpreting

(Auszug aus dem Comic Strip: Asterix the Legionary, S. 20.)

If you don't speak a foreign language, communication with somebody who only speaks that language is difficult. You're restricted to gestures and facial expressions.
But you speak English, of course, so you can help others who don't.

Imagine the following scene:
Chris is with a group of people who don't speak English and they want to buy tickets for the famous zoo in San Diego. He's their interpreter and must help them.

Ernst: Ein Glück, dass wir dich dabei haben, Chris. Du musst uns jetzt helfen. Frag doch den Mann an der Kasse, ob wir eine Gruppenermäßigung bekommen, schließlich sind wir zwölf Personen.

1. Chris: Excuse me, sir, ...

Clerk: Yes, we do. For groups of at least 20 adults we charge only half the regular price.

2.	Chris:	Erst ...
	Erika:	Vielleicht kann er eine Ausnahme machen. Sag ihm, dass einige von uns Mitglieder beim WWF sind.
3.	Chris:	Ich weiß nicht recht. Well, could you ...?
	Clerk:	I'm sorry, sir, but I have my instructions and I'm not allowed to do so.
4.	Chris:	Er sagt ...
	Peter:	Schau, dort kommen ein paar Deutsche. Die sollen sich uns anschließen. Ich frage sie. Es hat geklappt, wir sind jetzt genau zwanzig.
5.	Chris:	We're now a group of twenty. Can we ...?
	Clerk:	Sure, there you go. It's $6.00 per person.
	Chris:	Thank you very much.
	Clerk:	You're welcome.
	Ernst:	Das habe ich jetzt auch verstanden. Er hat jetzt gesagt, dass wir willkommen sind.
	Chris:	Ja, das könnte man meinen. Aber so antwortet man in Amerika, wenn sich jemand bedankt. Es bedeutet einfach "bitte" oder "bitte sehr".

Well, do you see how it works?

There are some simple rules:
- Don't translate literally word by word. It's the overall meaning that's important. You can even summarize one or more sentences and just communicate the central idea.
- Certain statements can be left out, of course. Peter's remarks to his friends are irrelevant for the clerk and needn't be interpreted.
- Should you ever have to interpret longer speeches, ask both speakers to pause after two or three sentences or even interrupt them at an appropriate point. Such 'speech chunks' are much easier to remember and to deal with.
- Be aware of possible misunderstandings on the part of one or the other of the speakers. They may misinterpret a gesture they see or words they hear in a certain context (as "Ernst"apparently did towards the end of the above dialogue). Make sure they get it right.

5. Dos and Don'ts when dealing with people from English speaking countries

FOR AMERICANS:

COURTESY

Take a little something with you if you are invited to a German's house. A box of chocolates or a handful of flowers should do the trick. Your hosts will not only appreciate it, they expect it. In Germany, it's a custom, so be nice, be polite and bring gifts.

DATING
So, he finally asked you out. Well expect some company. In Germany, young people date in pairs but often in groups, too. And when it comes to the bill, everyone goes Dutch.

DRINKING
It's not cool to get drunk. German youngsters are raised around beer, wine and schnaps (liquors); it's part of their culture, they're used to it. You, however, are not. Don't go crazy just because the legal drinking age in Germany is 16 for beer and wine and 18 for hard liquors. Be very careful not to abuse the privilege by drinking too much alcohol. It's socially unacceptable to get drunk.

FAMILY RULES
Curfew? What curfew? You can go out with your friends and stay out late but you should be home for dinner. If it is a family tradition, missing the family dinner is considered very rude. If you want to skip it and stay in town for the evening, give your host mother plenty of notice.

TABLE MANNERS
Don't get grossed out when your host family sits down to a dinner of blood sausage, or brains and Harzer Käse, a pungent cheese that smells like your little brother's oldest pair of tennis shoes.The Germans eat all kinds of strange things. And some of it tastes better than it looks or smells.

FORMAL AND INFORMAL
Formality is tough for Americans, who are almost always informal. The Germans are the opposite. They've even built formality in their language. 'DU' is used to address friends and lovers, while 'SIE' is used for older people, strangers and business associates. A good rule is always to use 'SIE' unless told otherwise.

FRIENDSHIP
It may take a while – maybe even longer than you'd like – but if you make a friend in Germany, you've got a friend for life. Germans make a careful distinction between friends and acquaintances. If a German calls you “a friend“, you are special.

GETTING AROUND
Hang up the car keys, and get on the train. You won't be the only kid hopping on and off the rails; the driving age in Germany is 18. If you are an exchange student caught behind the wheel, you'll not only lose your insurance, you'll get sent home. Besides, public transportation will take you anywhere you want to go at almost any hour of the day. But watch out! Although the fares are cheap, the fines are not.

POLITICS
If there's one rule for the road it's that you're wrong and they're right because you're the guest. But seriously! It would help to brush up on a bit of American foreign and domestic policy before you go to Germany, where people love to discuss the latest developments. The objective of such discussions is often not to exchange ideas but to convince others of the rightness of one's views. Once accustomed to the German style of debate (ahem! discussion) you may experience intense and open conversations on a variety of subjects – just like in the States.

6. Benimm-Regeln

FÜR DEUTSCHE

Allgemein gilt, dass wir uns in unserer Direktheit zurücknehmen müssen. Deutsche neigen dazu, auf Empfindungen anderer – sei es durch ihre Kritik oder ihr Urteil – wenig Rücksicht zu nehmen. Offenheit ist aber nicht in jedem Fall eine gute Sache. In vielen amerikanischen Schulen z. B. gelten kritisches Nachhaken und Widerrede als respektlos und unhöflich.

BEZIEHUNGEN
Amerikaner bezeichnen schnell auch flüchtige Bekannte als "Freunde". Auch das Wort "love" wird schneller und unkomplizierter verwendet als die deutsche Entsprechung. Das bedeutet aber nicht, dass man gleich enge Beziehungen knüpfen kann und sich womöglich regelmäßig trifft. Umgekehrt darf man aber nicht daraus folgern, die Amerikaner seien oberflächlich. Aufgrund der hohen Mobilität (häufiger Wohnsitzwechsel) haben sie im Laufe der Zeit eine Kultur der unkomplizierten Kontaktaufnahme entwickelt, welche die Deutschen nur schwer nachvollziehen können.

DATING
Es ist passiert, man hat sich verknallt. Was nun? Wie arrangiert man ein Date? Auf jeden Fall lädt er sie ein zu Hamburger und Cola oder auch nobler, danach ins Kino. Er ist witzig, charmant und übermütig und sprüht vor Temperament, er gibt den tollen Hecht. Er fährt sie nach Hause und hält einen Block vorher an, so kann er mit ihr knutschen, ohne dass es gleich die Eltern und Nachbarn erfahren. Das war's dann – in der Regel.

Für Mädchen gilt, Achselhöhlen und Beine rasieren, ein wenig Parfüm kann nie schaden, ansonsten die Mädels vor Ort fragen.

FAMILIENLEBEN
In amerikanischen Familien haben Jugendliche oft weniger Freiheiten als in Deutschland. Eltern achten sehr auf korrekte Kleidung ihrer Kinder, d. h. Röcke sollen nicht so kurz sein, dass sie unanständig wirken. In den meisten Familien gibt es eine feste Zeit, "curfew" genannt, zu der Jugendliche zu Hause erwartet werden – verständlich in Großstädten mit hoher Kriminalität. Alkohol ist für Jugendliche unter 21 tabu, auch nicht im privaten Rahmen. Eltern, die dies erlauben, machen sich strafbar.

FLUCHEN
Schimpfwörter (wie das f-Wort oder sh..) sind im täglichen Umgang tabu. Sie verletzen das stark ausgeprägte sittliche und religiöse Gefühl der Amerikaner. Behelfen kann man sich mit "oh boy" oder bestenfalls "shoot", wenn es sich um einen starken Affekt handelt.

HÖFLICHKEIT
In Deutschland bleibt man beim ersten Kontakt zunächst etwas distanziert – so lange bis man Gemeinsamkeiten feststellt, erst dann versprüht man mehr Charme. Ganz anders in Amerika. Dort genießt der Fremde sogleich und so lange Freundlichkeit, bis er sich ihrer unwürdig erweist. Man wird sehr oft nach dem eigenen Befinden gefragt, eine ehrliche Antwort wird aber nicht erwartet. Eine typisch charmante Floskel selbst beim Einkaufen oder am Schalter ist "How are you today?" Sie antworten mit "Just fine, thank you." Nach einem höflichen "Good" ihres Gegenübers können sie zum Eigentlichen übergehen. Eine

weitere Höflichkeit bei einer ersten Begegnung ist "Nice to meet you" und beim Abschied "Nice meeting you. /Nice talking to you".

HYGIENE
Frauen rasieren sich in Amerika grundsätzlich Achseln und Beine. Sie fühlen sich schlichtweg unsauber, wenn sie das nicht tun. Wenn Sie also schwimmen gehen oder mehr Haut zeigen, sollten Sie sich als Frau den Gepflogenheiten anpassen, um nicht peinliche Blicke auf sich zu ziehen.

Schwitzen und Schweißflecken an der Kleidung werden im Land der Klimaanlagen als höchst unangenehm empfunden. Versuchen Sie auf gesellschaftlicher Ebene dies nach Möglichkeit zu vermeiden. Wenn Sie ein dringendes Bedürfnis verspüren, dann fragen Sie als Dame: "Please, where is the ladies' room?" Beide Geschlechter fragen auch: "Please, where is the bathroom?"

KRITIK
Es ist eine touristische Unsitte, vieles im fremden Land zu kritisieren, dies gilt besonders auch für uns Deutsche. Nörgeln ist keine Medizin gegen fremde Kultur und ungewohntes Verhalten. Keiner möchte schließlich von seinem Gast hören, dass im eigenen Land alles besser ist. In Amerika, wie in vielen anderen Ländern, ist nicht vieles schlechter, sondern einfach anders.
Dies sollten wir Deutsche auch bedenken, wenn wir mit diversen Formen des amerikanischen Patriotismus konfrontiert werden. Dieser ist im Land tief verwurzelt und gehört zum ganz natürlichen Nationalgefühl. Wir sollten ihm den nötigen Respekt entgegenbringen.

TISCHMANIEREN
Will man vom Tisch aufstehen, fragt man höflich "May I be excused?" oder "Would you please excuse me?" und geht dann. Wir Europäer essen mit Messer und Gabel, die Amerikaner schneiden alles auf dem Teller vor, legen das Messer weg und essen anschließend nur mit der Gabel weiter, wobei die jeweils freie Hand nicht unbedingt auf dem Tisch verbleibt. Dies mag uns merkwürdig vorkommen, ist aber in dem Land völlig korrektes Benehmen.

Es gilt als unzivilisiert, sich laut bei Tisch die Nase zu putzen.

Die Amerikaner trinken zu Hause zum Essen in der Regel nicht alkoholische Getränke wie "plain water, ice tea, soft drinks". Ausnahmen sind besondere Anlässe. Eine Anmerkung noch zum Genuss von Alkohol in der Öffentlichkeit, sofern man 21 ist: Das Trinken von Bier aus einer Dose, geschweige denn härteren alkoholischen Getränken, die unverpackt sind, ist "public drinking" und somit strafbar. Das erklärt auch, warum man beispielsweise beim Erwerb von Dosenbier dieses immer in einer Papiertüte verpackt bekommt.

E Literary skills

1. Describing cartoons and pictures

"Et cetera, et cetera, et cetera ..."

Itinerary

Orally	**Written**
1. Starter	**1.** Starter
You can start your description with a personal comment: "It looks like a coach trip to Rome or some other place of historical interest. ..."	Start with the overall impression: "What we see in the cartoon is a coach party being guided through some ancient ruins. ..."

2. Describe the situation rather than every little detail. Refer to details only if they help to understand what's going on. The overall idea is important, not every single detail.

Useful words:

In the picture

in the top left-hand corner	at the top	in the top right-hand corner
on the left-hand side	in the middle	on the right-hand side
in the bottom left-hand corner	at the bottom	in the bottom right-hand corner

3. After you have described the situation say what the message of the cartoon or picture is:
"The message seems to be that people don't really care much about where they are going ... ."
"The cartoon aims at people's habit of remembering only trivialities/thinking only of food ... ."

language study | writing | presentation | socialising | literary

2. How to analyse a modern short story

Modern short stories usually don't present a clear conflict that is resolved in the end, and it doesn't have a clear beginning, a middle or an end. Many modern short stories also don't follow this pattern. A pattern of story-telling predominant in Hollywood movies and TV series, which only too often shape our notion of how a story should be told.

The prevailing style of the modern contemporary short story is **minimalist**.
Ernest Hemingway was the forerunner of this "stripped down" style that could capture what he called *'the real thing, the sequence of motion and fact which made the emotion.*[1]
Hemingway had an enormous influence on his contemporaries, but he has also inspired modern writers, especially the dominant 1980s American school of "minimalists".

A modern short story can have the following features:

- It frequently tells us about ordinary people in everyday situations.
  (Sometimes, however, it also deals with the grotesque and the bizarre.)
- It lacks ornaments such as elaborate descriptions of nature, character portrayal or social and cultural background. The language is usually simple.
- What we get is a random shot of a protagonist's life, usually covering a very short span of his or her life.
- That's why a modern short story often starts without any introduction or other preliminaries and has an abrupt ending that rather asks a question than answers one.
- Its fictional style is influenced by the technique of film montage:
  We have restricted points of view that can change all of a sudden, and disjointed slivers of dialogue.
  Flashbacks or forecasts as well as inner monologues can expand the plot or even create additional narrative levels.
- The protagonist's conflict lies hidden behind this sober montage, which often seems to lack any emotion or suspense. However, the real story often lies hidden behind – or underneath – the plot.

Task

1. Read Ann Beattie's story on page 221ff. to find out which of the features mentioned above it contains.
2. Analyse the other short stories in this book as well.

[1] Glick, Nathan: New Life for the Short Story, in: American Studies Newsletter, May 1988)

Here are some useful literary terms:

The **narrator** is the person or character who is telling the story.	The **protagonist** is the hero of story.	**Character** A character is a person in a story.
The **plot** is the outline of the events in a story.	**Exposition** is the beginning of the story which explains the background and the setting.	**Conflict** is the central problem in the story.
The **climax** is the highest point (turning point) in the action of a story. (Not so common with short stories.)	The **setting** is the time and place of a story.	The **moral** is the lesson an author is trying to teach in his story.
The **point of view** is the angle from which a story is told.	A **first-person** point of view means that one of the characters is telling the story.	A **third person** point of view means that someone outside the story is telling it.

3. Analysing a poem

There are several methods to analyse a poem successfully. One of them is carried out in this worksheet.

Stick to the specially marked expression as a general guideline for analysis. Keep in mind: it's rather easy to take a poem apart as it is a rather short and densely written text. **As a conclusion, however, you should put everything back where it belongs to get a general impression of the message.**

Edwin Arlington Robinson: The Children Of The Night – Richard Cory

1. Give a first **vague idea** of the central meaning of this poem.
2. Find out about **perspective**: who is the narrator?
3. Consider the **setting**:
   a) Make a list of the places mentioned.
   b) List up the people of this poem and their activities.
   c) Compare the results of the different lists with each other.
4. What kinds of **perceptions** are described (pictures; sounds; emotions)? List them up and pair them of with the persons involved.
5. **Language**
   a) Why was Richard Cory "clean favored" and "imperially slim"? (last line in the first stanza)

b) Explain the last line of the second stanza.
c) Explain the first and second line of the fourth stanza.
d) Explain the differences in the meanings of "went" in the second and the last line of the fourth stanza.

6. Structure
a) In what way is the division of the text into four **stanzas** important?
b) Find out the **rhymes** and the **metric structures**: where do you find any irregular structures?
c) Do they have any meaning in the context?

7. Give an outlook of this story: is it positive or negative?

8. Summing everything up give the **central message** of this poem.

4. Writing a poem

Here are some ideas to make a little poem of your own.

Name Poetry (acrostics)
Take your name or that of a friend or of a favourite pet. Each letter in the name is the beginning of a line in your poem.

Examples:

Charly	**Ute**	**Juergen**
Cat. **H**as got a black coat **A**nd green eyes. **R**ebellious but **L**ovely. **Y**ou're great!	**U**nable **T**o **E**at.	**J**ealous person **U**nder a tree **E**xpecting an explanation **R**ight there, and fast. **G**ot no words to tell him the truth. **E**hhhmmm ... I'm sorry, but **N**o, I don't love you.

Definition Poetry
Write a few lines to define something.

Examples:

Books	**Liberty**	**Friends**
Funny and exciting. Windows to strange worlds. Alice and all the others. Made me so happy.	Free like a bird. Circling easily in the sky. I wish I could fly.	Find them. Keep them. Listen to them. Talk to them. Don't expect anything.

X-Y-Z Poetry
Take letters of the alphabet and use them as first letters in short sentences.

Example:

All	Love	X-mas party
Boys	Makes	Young
Can	Nice	Zealots
Dance	Offsprings	All over the place.
Except		
Frank		

5. Analysing the elements of humour in a sketch

TV series like the 'Cosby Show' (cf. page 213) are called sitcoms, situation comedies, stories revolving around love, family problems, money, or the like. The characters often are simplified social types, such as a pitiable father (Al Bundy) or a nagging mother-in-law. A sitcom works very much like a sketch and has basically the same elements of humour:

- **Exaggeration**
  of a person's habits, flaws or characteristic traits, e.g. of the way someone speaks, walks etc.

- **Fight against objects of every-day life**
  In his movie *Banana*, Woody Allen fights against a hairdryer that seems to blow him away.

- **Embarrassment**
  weird or even very unrealistic situations, often resulting in a catastrophe:
  Mr Bean is going to meet the Queen, but has got problems with a zip.
  In a Monty Python's sketch a bank-robber with a gun in his hand finds out too late that he isn't in a bank, but in a lingerie store.

- **Witty remarks, jokes, slippery remarks**
  Groucho Marx, feeling a patient's pulse: "Either he's dead or my watch has stopped."

- **Funny replies**
  Judy: May I have one of your pictures?
  Groucho Marx: Why – I haven't got one. I could give you my footprints, but they're upstairs in my socks.

- **Running gag; repetitions**
  Repetition of words (a catchword or catch-phrase), or of situations: a protagonist finds himself in the same dilemma again and again.

- **I can see what you don't see**
  Something is about to fall onto A's head. B sees it, A doesn't.
  B: You'll have a real problem soon!
  Another example:
  You make fun of someone you think is absent, but don't know the person has just come in and is standing right behind you.

- **Puns (games with words)**
  One of the oldest means of making people laugh, dating at least back to the Punch and Judy shows of the 18th century.

  Example of a pun:
  Groucho Marx:
  I came here without a nickel in my pocket. Now I have a nickel in my pocket. Even more sophisticated: (The same): I've worked myself up from nothing to a state of extreme poverty.

- **Slips of the tongue**
  Rowan Atkinson
  as a new clergyman officiating at his first wedding in 'Four Weddings and a Funeral' (1994) struggles with such lapses as 'The Holy Goat,' or 'awful wedded wife.'

- **Silly names**
  We laugh at them because we all are prejudiced:
  A small collection from MAD Magazine: Quaxl Axelotl, Elmo Freen, Weissy Johnmueller, Alfred E. Neumann, Gunder Schlugg, John McGurk, Grandma Mosey, Viola Messy, Mrs. Mimi Lafarge Henderson Cartwright Prescott Willson Roberts, Roger Kaputnik, Clodumbo etc. etc.

- **Slapstick**
  Throwing tarts and pies at each other. Chases.
  Smashing things.
  Charlie Chaplin did it tastefully.

- **Insults**
  Like throwing pies – only with words and more painful.
  One of the most difficult things to do for a comedian.
  Groucho Marx:
  Emily, I've a little confession to make. I really am a horse doctor. But marry me, and I'll never look at any other horse.

Activities

1. Analyse the excerpt from the 'Cosby Show' (see page 213) to find out which of the above elements of humour are used.
2. Watch your favourite sitcom more intensely and analyse it.
3. In groups, write a sketch about life at school, a typical scene in a disco, in a supermarket etc.

Unit 7

Aspects of language

7

1 TALKING ABOUT ACCENTS: RUDOLPH DIRKS: *THE KATZENJAMMER KIDS*

The Katzenjammer Kids is one of the oldest comic strips in the United States. It has been around for more than 100 years. The strip is about two mischievous kids sharing a household with their Mama and a Captain. The following episode is from 1906/1907, but even today all the characters in the strip speak with the same, only slightly mellowed, German accent.

1. Retell the story in full detail.
2. Describe the accent as it is characterised here. Which sounds seem to cause the most problems?
3. Which other things in the way the characters speak are intended to show that they are of German origin?
4. When comic artist Rudolph Dirks joined the New York Journal in 1897, he was asked to do something in the style of a successful German humorist. The influences are obvious! What are they?
5. "The only real problem your German accent might cause is if you want to become a Hollywood actor." Discuss.

2 Some sources of modern English words

Words of German origin:

• **waltz** • **hamster** • **zinc** • **plunder** • **poodle** • **paraffin** • **blitz** • **yodel** • **angst** • **strafe** • **wanderlust** • **zeitgeist** • **echt** • **rucksack** • **kindergarten**

Other languages have also contributed words to modern English. For example:

• **Afrikaans:** *trek* • **American Indian language:** *wigwam* • **Arabic:** *sultan* • **Australian:** *dingo* • **Chinese:** *ketchup* • **Eskimo:** *kayak* • **French:** *aunt* • **Gaelic:** *galore* • **Greek:** *crisis* • **Hawaiian:** *ukulele* • **Hebrew:** *kibbutz* • **Hindi:** *guru* • **Italian:** *sonnet* • **Japanese:** *tycoon* • **Latin:** *diocese* • **Norwegian:** *cosy* • **Persian:** *sofa* • **Portuguese:** *flamingo* • **Russian:** *steppe* • **Spanish:** *sherry* • **Tahitian:** *tattoo* • **Tibetan:** *sherpa* • **Turkish:** *yoghurt*

Activities

A Which of the languages mentioned above do the following words come from?

• moccasin • stigma • veranda • yeti • fjord • rodeo • justice • hula • kosher • pundit • boomerang • leprechaun • algebra • grotesque • sputnik • caftan • schmaltz • brochure • caravan • kaolin • neurosis • apartheid • cigar • yoghurt • yak • chipmunk • pizza • mensch • balcony • anorak • moustache • sari • kimono • orbit • bazaar • castle

B Make a list of English words that are to be found in Modern German:

• Keyboard • Jeans • Fastfood – ...

Source (2.): David Crystal: The English Language

Literature

3 George Mikes: How to be an alien

This is an excerpt from George Mikes' classic on Britain, the British and their language.

When I arrived in England I thought I knew English. After I'd been here an hour I realized that I did not understand one word. In the first week I picked up a tolerable working knowledge of the language and the next seven years convinced me gradually but thoroughly that I would never know it really well, let alone perfectly. This is sad. My only consolation being that nobody speaks English perfectly.

Remember that those five hundred words an average Englishman uses are far from being the whole vocabulary of the language. You may learn another five hundred and another five thousand and yet another fifty thousand and still you may come across a further fifty thousand you have never heard of before, and nobody else either.(...)

Then you have to decide on your accent. You will have your foreign accent all right, but many people like to mix it with something else. I knew a Polish Jew who had a strong Yiddish-Irish accent. People found it fascinating though slightly exaggerated. The easiest way to give the impression of having a good accent or no foreign accent at all is to hold an unlit pipe in your mouth, to mutter between your teeth and finish all your sentences with the question: 'isn't it'? People will not understand much, but they are accustomed to that and they will get a most excellent impression. (...)

The most successful attempts, however, to put on a highly cultured air have been made on the polysyllabic lines. Many foreigners who have learnt Latin and Greek in school discover with amazement and satisfaction that the English language has absorbed a huge amount of ancient Latin and Greek expressions, and they realize that (a) it is much easier to learn these expressions than the much simpler English words; (b) that these words as a rule are interminably long and make a simply superb impression when talking to the greengrocer, the porter and the insurance agent.

Imagine, for instance, that the porter of the block of flats where you live remarks sharply that you must not put your dustbin out in front of your door before 7.30 a.m. Should you answer 'Please don't bully me,' a loud and tiresome argument may follow, and certainly the porter will be proved right, because you are sure to find a clause in your contract (small print, bottom of last page) that the porter is always right and you owe absolute allegiance and unconditioned obedience to him. Should you answer, however, with these words: 'I repudiate your petulant expostulations,' the argument will be closed at once, the porter will be proud of having such a highly cultured man in the block, and from that day onwards you may, if you please, get up at four o'clock in the morning and hang your dustbin out of the window. (...)

Finally, there are two important points to remember:

1. Do not forget that it is much easier to write in English than to speak English, because you can write without a foreign accent.
2. In a bus and in other public places it is more advisable to speak softly in good German than to shout in abominable English.

Anyway, this whole language business is not at all easy. After spending eight years in this country, the other day I was told by a very kind lady: 'But why do you complain? You really speak the most excellent accent without the slightest English.'

(From George Mikes: How to be an Alien)

Activities

A Text comprehension

Skim read the text to provide short answers to the following questions.
Keep in mind that the text is highly ironical.

1. Does George Mikes think he speaks English perfectly?
2. How many English words are there, and how many, according to the author, do you have to know?
3. Summarize what George Mikes says about accents.
4. Why does he recommend holding an unlit pipe in your mouth while you speak?
5. What does George Mikes understand by polysyllabic lines (line 36)?
6. What, according to the text, might happen if you use plain, simple English in an argument?
7. What does George Mikes say about the nature of contracts?
8. Why, according to the author, is it easier to write good English than to speak it?

B Register

In this excerpt George Mikes doesn't only speak about the problems foreigners might have with their accents and the limitations of their knowledge of vocabulary. In the anecdote about the dustbin he also points out how difficult it is to use the appropriate register.

Register is the range of vocabulary and grammar speakers use in particular social circumstances or professional contexts.

People sound different in different situations (at home, with friends, at school, at work, in court etc.) and when communicating with different people (informal: family, friends; formal: teacher, boss, police officer etc.), in written or oral language. Sounding right in every particular situation is one of the most difficult things to do when speaking a foreign language.

! TIP:
Using simple, natural English in any situation is the best advice for beginners.
Don't try to sound too local or too expert!

1. Match the sentences and the contexts:

1 *formal, travel guide*	**A** *The water should be heated in a suitable receptacle to a temperature of 100 C.*
2 *informal: parent to child*	**B** *Be careful to boil the water before you drink it.*
3 *newspaper headline*	**C** *Do you think you could possibly manage to boil a kettle before this time next year?*
4 *written instruction, technical*	**D** *London Boil Water Shock*
5 *ironic remark*	**E** *Put the bloody kettle on.*
6 *informal: slightly angry?*	**F** *Feeling in need of a cup of tea, Mrs Smith filled the kettle and put it on the stove.*
7 *from a novel*	**G** *Now, put the kettle on the stove … be very careful!*

2. Discuss, in which contexts or situations, written or spoken, formal or informal, the following sentences might be found:
   a) Put the kettle on, please.
   b) Next, boil a kettle of water.
   c) Could you possibly put the kettle on for me?
   d) It is recommended that all water should be boiled before use.
   e) Let's stick the kettle on.

Listening comprehension: "We don't like your sort here"

Pre-listening activities

1. Are there any German accents you like more than others?
How do you feel about regional accents from Munich, Nuremberg, Regensburg, Cologne, Leipzig, Hamburg?
2. Can you think of situations where someone speaking with one of the accents mentioned above might be discriminated against?

In the Sixties, there was nothing cooler than the Liverpool sound, the Liverpool accent called 'scouse'. Today, many Liverpudlians claim that their accent has turned into a social affliction and a real disadvantage at work in other parts of Britain. Merseysiders refer to this phenomenon as 'scouseism', a form of discrimination not encountered by people in Britain's other major cities. Social historians say that Liverpool's long multi-racial past and strong Irish immigrant subculture are responsible for both the local accent and the sense of isolation from the rest of the country.

(Adapted from Racism, sexism, now scouseism, Independent on Sunday 30 March, 1997)

Listen to what happened to Liverpool performance poet Jegsy Dodd in Britain's South.

Part 1 of the recording: Answer the true and false questions. Don't just say *yes* or *no*, try to give as many details as possible:

1. Jegsy was on his way to a reading of his poems.
2. He parked his car in front of a big hotel.
3. There was a middle-aged woman at the reception.
4. The woman treated him in a friendly manner.
5. The woman asked him if it was his van outside with the Liverpool number.
6. The van was blocking the way.
7. Jegsy was sent away.
8. There was almost a fight.
9. Jegsy drove home immediately.
10. There's no way of fighting against this kind of discrimination.

Part 2 of the recording: Answer the questions:

1. Where did Jegsy return from?
2. Where did he queue up?
3. What did the young cashier do when it was Jegsy's turn to pay?
4. How did the cashier explain his behaviour?
5. What was Jegsy's reply?

Text

4 The text generation

Pre-reading activities

1. What could the following abbreviations mean?
   2NITE
   2L8
   4U
   BTW
   B4
   Gonna B L8 4 wrk cuz my cRs im£ed 4get mEtN CU @t dNR pRT S@RdA

   Find other examples.
2. How fast can you write an SMS? Compare this to your normal handwriting.

Using mobile phones to pass notes instantly is now a global phenomenon, to the experts' surprise

By William Underhill

Something strange has happened to the mobile phone. In defiance of all industry forecasts, today's user seems to want to write, not chat. SMS, Short Message Service, has been around for a decade, but in recent years it began spreading like a virus throughout the globe. Last year the number of messages sent jumped fivefold, reaching 15 billion in December alone, or 200 billion in the past year, by some estimates. Consultants at a U.K. software firm, reckon that by the end of 2002 the monthly total may reach 100 billion – or more than 15 messages for every person on the planet.

This phenomenon has surprised everybody. The telecom industry adopted SMS as a standard technology in 1991 as a way to sop up extra network capacity, just in case somebody somewhere might find it useful. Unlike email, text messages arrive almost instantaneously, so that two people can have a text – based conversation as though they were in an Internet chat room. At first, subscribers were able to send messages only within their own networks. The Service was neither advertised nor promoted. Phone manufacturers were no more ambitious: telephone keyboards are optimized for numbers, not letters. On many handsets, it still takes plenty of scrolling just to find the menu options for texting.

In the late 1990s, numbers rose rapidly, especially in the tech-friendly countries of the Far East and Scandinavia, where the mobile-phone boom first took off among young consumers. "This was the accidental revolution;" says Simon Buckingham of the Mobile Lifestreams consultancy. "Consumers just adopted SMS as their own medium. Every generation needs its own way of expressing itself; this is the text generation:"

Devotees say the charms of texting go far beyond novelty. The Service has all the immediacy of a phone call – as well as extra privacy and just a hint of the subversive. "My dad overhears me [talking] on the phone all the time, but I don't have to worry about that with text messages," says Chika Saito, a high-school junior in Japan who sends about 10 messages a day "I can punch the buttons real quick, using just one hand, and my dad says it drives him crazy just seeing me do it:" Background noise is no problem – ever tried talking on a mobile phone from a crowded bar? – and reception isn't an issue. Besides, SMS is a handy means of ducking those big emotional challenges. A survey by a British polling firm found that a heartless 13 percent of users have used text messages to break off relationships.

Best of all, the text habit doesn't strain even modest student budgets. A brief message – the technology allows a maximum length of just 160 characters – won't usually cost more than 15 cents. "It's cheap, it's quick and it's international;" says 21-year-old Paris student Lara Bourji.

For many texting aficionados, the practical difficulty is just part of the fun. Spelling out a message with a thumb's edge takes more time than most teenagers or young adults can afford. So users have developed their own high-speed vocabulary, a mix of all the available icons, snappy acronyms and phonetic shorthand. Although adults may be foxed, youngsters will know just what's meant by CUL8R (see you later) or QL (cool). Guides are available for the uninitiated. In Britain, three of the top 10 best-selling books are English-to-text dictionaries. Italian mobile-phone companies offer free glossary cards. But the language is evolving quicker than publishers can keep up. "The whole point is that everyone can invent it; it's just a visual translation of the spoken word;" says Gabrielle Mander, who compiled "Wan2Tlk? Ltl Bk of Txt Msgs:"

Having gotten over their initial surprise, network operators are now sharing in the thrill of text messaging. Since text takes up only a thin sliver of bandwidth, messages whiz around effortlessly even on the most congested networks. This makes it a high-margin business, and a welcome relief from the highly competitive market for voice calls, where profits are being squeezed.

The mobile-phone firms are hoping that the success of SMS may help answer one big question about the future of wireless: what (if anything) are customers likely to want from Internet-linked smart phones? Phone companies have spent $100 billion on the third-generation technology that will allow these phones to send and receive vast amounts of data. What's the point of this fancy technology if customers really just want to send short text messages? Now engineers are scrambling to develop so-called multimedia messaging services, in which users would send text messages enriched with still or video images or sound clips – a sort of voice e-mail. Only when the third generation hits the market will they know for sure whether it's GR8 (great) or NAGI (not a good idea).

(Newsweek, April 2, 2001)

Activities

GapS

A Gapped summary

The text below is a summary of the previous text. Complete the summary by choosing no more than 3 words (at a time) from the original text.

When SMS was introduced, people started using it a lot. This success *...(1)...*, because it was not *...(2)...* by the phone companies. Originally, the service was started to make use of *...(3)...* that was there, anyway.
The advantages for the users are that SMS is just as fast as a phone call, while on the other hand it has all the *...(4)...* of the written medium, which means for young people that their parents cannot *...(5)...* their conversations. Another advantage for the user is that you can use it in any situation, *...(6)...* does not affect communication. Users have developed all sorts of phonetic shorthand, which is difficult to understand for the *...(7)...* .
Advantages for the phone companies are that SMS requires only liltle *...(8)...* . The service is highly profitable, and there is little competition.
The problem for the mobile phone companies is if customers are *...(9)...* buy improved technology if they are so happy with the existing one.

B Writing

Some people claim that today's young people do not know the basics of culture and language any more. They have meaningless telephone talks all the time and play computer games most of the day. Write a composition commenting on that and stating your opinion what young people should know.

Literature

5 William Shakespeare: The Tempest

"You taught me language:
and my profit on't is,
I know how to curse.
The red plague rid you
For learning me your language!"

Boats. "What care these roarers for the name of king?"

Introduction

The most successful product of Shakespeare's creativity is what may be his last complete play, The Tempest (c. 1611). The play is a celebration of the benefits of the union of wisdom and power. Many critics say that Shakespeare's poetic impact rarely reached heights as great as this. This is what the play is about:

Prospero, Duke of Milan, hands over all of his governing rights and responsibilities to his brother Antonio in order to give his full attention to his literary studies. However, Antonio, with the help of Prospero's old enemy Alonso, King of Naples, usurps his brother's rightful place as Duke. Rather than killing Prospero outright, Antonio banishes him and his three year old daughter Mirinda to a faraway island. With the help of his magical wisdom gained from his books, Prospero becomes the ruler of this island.

Twelve years later, by chance, a ship bearing all of Prospero's old enemies comes within range of his magic powers, awakening his old desire for revenge. He raises a tempest which drives their ship to the island and leaves them separated and stranded. Prospero, as magical lord of the island, holds their fate in his hands and must choose between forgiveness and revenge.

The following scene is an argument between Prospero and Caliban, a native inhabitant of the island, son of Sycorax (a witch and another old enemy of Prospero), who he found in the woods. Caliban is described as a wild and deformed creature. Prospero took him home and taught him to speak; and, as Prospero puts it, he would have been very kind to him, but the bad nature which Caliban inherited from his mother Sycorax, would not let him learn anything good or useful: therefore he was employed as a slave, to fetch wood, and do other hard work. During the argument, Prospero's daughter Mirinda is also present.

Act I, Scene II

Prospero:
Thou poisonous slave, got by the devil himself
Upon thy wicked dam, come forth!
(Enter Caliban)

wicked = evl, dam = mother

Caliban:
As wicked dew as e'er my mother brush'd
With raven's feather from unwholesome fen,
Drop on you both! a south-west[1] blow on ye,
And blister you all o'er!

fen = moor
blow = strong wind, ye = you
blister = burn, scorch

Prospero:
For this, be sure, to-night thou shalt have cramps,
Side-stitches that shall pen thy breath up; urchins
Shall forth, at vast of night, that they may work
All exercise on thee: thou shalt be pinch'd
As thick as honey-comb, each pinch more stinging
Than bees that made them.

cramps = pain
urchins = hedgehogs

Caliban:
I must eat my dinner.
This island 's mine, by Sycorax my mother,
Which thou tak'st from me. When thou comest first,
Thou strok'dst me, and mad'st much of me; wouldst give me
Water with berries in 't ; and teach me how
To name the bigger light, and how the less,
That burn by day and night: and then I lov'd thee,
And show'd thee all the qualities o' th' isle
The fresh springs, brine-pits, barren place, and fertile.

Ant. "Draw together;
And when I rear my hand, do you the like,
To fall it on Gonzalo."

brine = salt, barren = infertile

[1] *the southwest wind was believed to bring illness*

Cursed be I that did so ! – All the charms
Of Sycorax, toads, beetles, bats, light on you!
For I am all the subjects that you have,
which first was mine own king; and here you sty me,
In this hard rock, whiles you do keep from me
The rest o' the island.

Prospero:
Thou most lying slave
Whom stripes may move, not kindness! I have us'd thee
Filth as thou art, with human care; and lodg'd thee
In mine own cell, till thou didst seek to violate
The honour of my child.

Caliban:
O ho, O ho! would it had been done!
Thou didst prevent me; I had peopled else
This isle with Calibans.

Prospero[1]:
Abhorred slave,
Which any print of goodness wilt not take,
Being capable of all ill! I pitied thee
Took pains to make thee speak, taught thee each hour
One thing or other: when thou didst not, savage,
Know thine own meaning, but wouldst gabble like
A thing most brutish, I endow'd thy purposes
With words that made them known; but thy vile race
Though thou didst learn, had that in 't which good natures
Could not abide to be with: therefore wast thou
Deservedly confin'd into this rock
Who hadst deserv'd more than a prison.

Caliban:
You taught me language: and my profit on't
Is, I know how to curse. The red plague rid you
For learning me your language!

Prospero:
Hag-seed hence!
Fetch us in fuel; and be quick, thou' rt best
To answer other business. Shrugg'st thou, malice?
If thou neglect'st or dost unwillingly
What I command, I'll rack thee with old cramps
Fill all thy bones with aches; make thee roar
That beasts shall tremble at thy din.

Caliban:
No, 'pray thee!
(Aside) I must obey: his art is of such power,
It would control my dam's god, Setebos,
And make a vassal of him.

Prospero:
So, slave; hence ! (Exit CALIBAN)

sty = lock up and treat like a pig
stripes = beating
gabble = talk incoherently
endow = provide
vile = evil
abide = bear
confine = put in prison
rid = destroy
hag = ugly old woman; hence = go away
fetch us in fuel = get us wood
rack = torture
din = noise

[1] Other editions attribute this part of the conversation to Mirinda.

Activities

A Text comprehension

Try to support your answers by giving details or by quoting from the scene.

1. How did Prospero treat Caliban when he arrived on the island, and why do you think he treated him like that?
2. What did Caliban show Prospero when he arrived, and why?
3. Sycorax is a 'nature goddess', a witch. What do we learn about her in this scene?
4. Why did Prospero lock Caliban in?
5. What does Prospero say he made Caliban understand when teaching him "language"?
6. How does Caliban reply to that?

B Language exploration

1. What does Caliban refer to when he speaks of the *bigger light* and *the less (bigger light)*?
2. Shakespeare used an anagram for the *abhorred slave's* name: Caliban. Rearrange the letters to find the word behind this anagram.
3. The following English words sound similar to the corresponding words in modern German. They have a **common Anglo-Saxon origin**. (About 80 % of all English words are of this origin.) Translate them. Find more examples in the text!

   [**• dew • unwholesome • raven • comb • cramps • bees • berries • light • plague**]

4. Collect all the **personal pronouns** and **verb endings** used in the scene that are no longer to be found in modern English. Compare your findings to the German language. Example: *thou = du*.
5. **Insults:**
   What or who does Prospero often refer to when he wants to insult Caliban?
   What does Caliban refer to when he wants to insult Prospero?

C Summary and extension: Language as a means of power

1. Although Prospero is rather a positive figure in the play, it can be rightly said that this scene from Shakespeare's play The Tempest is about colonisation in general.
   What is Prospero's strategy of 'colonisation'?
   Is Caliban, the native of the island, aware of that strategy?
2. What part does language play in such a strategy of colonisation?
   Why do conquerors often oppress native languages?
   What examples are there in recent history?

D More activities

1. Retell Caliban's fate – as much as we learn about it from the scene – from Caliban's point-of-view in Modern English.
2. Organize a Shakespeare exhibition in your classroom.
3. Years ago there was a highly successful show in London's West End, called: "The Complete Works of Shakespeare". It presented Shakespeare's plays – reduced to one-minute performances – in one evening.
   In groups, work out a remake of (parts of) this show.

Translation: *English as a world language*

In the time of Elizabeth I (1533 –1603), English was spoken by some six million people in the British Isles. Today, it is used by about one billion people world wide, half of whom have learned it as a second language. Optimists view this spread of English as an empowering process, facilitating communication in the global village. Sceptics see it as linguistic imperialism, contributing to the disempowerment of people denied access to it, and the devaluation of other languages (in 1946, Gandhi wrote that Indians were "drunk with the wine of English").

The initial dominance of English came as a by-product of colonisation, particularly of America and the "old" Commonwealth countries. A subsequent gain for English resulted, paradoxically, from the decolonisation of the "new" Commonwealth countries.

Many of these were multilingual, and a major post-independence concern was to keep the "new" country unified. Selecting English as the principal official language was seen as a means of achieving this, whereas the selection of an indigenous language as the official tongue was often resisted by speakers of other languages who felt it would put them at a disadvantage.

(Adapted from: Eddie Williams and Michael Nama in Guardian Weekly, Jan 29, 1995, Supplement 'Learning English')

7 Talkline: Monty Python – The Dead Parrot

The following is an excerpt from a famous Monty Python's sketch where a shop-keeper is trying any trick to avoid replacing a dead parrot.

[A customer,] Mr Praline walks into [a pet] shop carrying a dead parrot in a cage. He walks to counter where shopkeeper tries to hide below cash register.

Praline (JOHN) Hello, I wish to register a complaint ... Hello? Miss?

Shopkeeper (MICHAEL) What do you mean, miss?

Praline Oh, I'm sorry, I have a cold. I wish to make a complaint.

Shopkeeper Sorry, we're closing for lunch.

Praline Never mind that my lad, I wish to complain about this parrot what I purchased not half an hour ago from this very boutique.

Shopkeeper Oh yes, the Norwegian Blue. What's wrong with it?

Praline I'll tell you what's wrong with it. It's dead, that's what's wrong with it.

Shopkeeper No, no it's resting, look!

Praline Look my lad, I know a dead parrot when I see one and I'm looking at one right now.

Shopkeeper No, no sir, it's not dead. It's resting.

Praline Resting?

Shopkeeper Yeah, remarkable bird the Norwegian Blue, beautiful plumage, innit?

Praline The plumage don't enter into it – it's stone dead.

Shopkeeper No, no – it's just resting.

Praline All right then, if it's resting I'll wake it up. *(shouts into cage)* Hello Polly! I've got a nice cuttlefish for you when you wake up, Polly Parrot!

Shopkeeper *(jogging cage)* There it moved.

Praline No he didn't. That was you pushing the cage.

Shopkeeper I did not.

Praline Yes, you did. *(takes parrot out of cage, shouts)* Hello Polly, Polly *(bangs it against counter)* *Polly* Parrot, wake up. *Polly. (throws it in the air and lets it fall to the floor)* Now that's what I call a dead parrot.

Shopkeeper No, no it's stunned.

Praline Look my lad, I've had just about enough of this. That parrot is definitely deceased. And when I bought it not half an hour ago, you assured me that its lack of movement was due to it being tired and shagged out after a long squawk.

Shopkeeper It's probably pining for the fiords.

Praline Pining for the fiords, what kind of talk is that? Look, why did it fall flat on its back the moment I got it home?

Shopkeeper The Norwegian Blue prefers kipping on its back. Beautiful bird, lovely plumage.

Praline Look, I took the liberty of examining that parrot, and I discovered that the only reason that it had been sitting on its perch in the first place was that it had been nailed there.

Shopkeeper Well of course it was nailed there. Otherwise it would muscle up to those bars and voom.

Praline Look matey *(picks up parrot)* this parrot wouldn't voom if I put four thousand volts through it. It's bleeding demised.

Shopkeeper It's not, it's pining.

Praline It's not pining, it's passed on. This parrot is no more. It has ceased to be. It's expired and gone to meet its maker. This is a late parrot. It's a stiff. Bereft of life, it rests in peace. If you hadn't nailed it to the perch, it would be pushing up the daisies. It's rung down the curtain and joined the choir invisible. This is an ex-parrot.

Shopkeeper Well, I'd better replace it then.

Praline *(to camera)* If you want to get anything done in this country you've got to complain till you're blue in the mouth.

Monty Python's Flying Circus: Just the words, vol. 1, London: Methuen, 1989, pp. 104–105

Annotations:
1) **Isn't it** (2)
2) **Tintenfisch** (8)
3) **the loud sharp noise of a bird** (23)
4) **mate** (37)

Tasks

1. Find passages where
   - the shopkeeper is trying to change the subject
   - the style is entirely inadequate
   - the customer strongly rejects the shopkeeper's cheap excuses

2. You complain about the dead parrot. You are trying to be friendly and use "softeners". Start the scene by saying:
   "There seems to be a problem with this parrot ...";
   "There appears to have been an error ...";
   "There must have been a mix-up ...";
   "I wonder if you could have a look at ...";
   "Something must be wrong with ...".

3. Get into pairs. Student A keeps claiming things that are definitely wrong. In the first three cases student B replies in a very polite or tentative way ("Are you sure …? / Do you really think so?"). Then student B makes three more direct contradictions. After that he/she contradicts three times in a less polite way. (See pages 181–184.)

Information grid

IG

Further training: Go to http://www.bbc.co.uk/radio4/news/anyquestions.shtml and listen to the latest edition of *Any Questions* or to http://www.bbc.co.uk/radio4/news/strawpoll.shtml and listen to *Straw Poll*, where people talk about more timeless and more general topics. Find out how people in this discussion agree, disagree, contradict etc. Make a list and write it in your notebook:

	agreement	disagreement	contradiction	changing the subject	…
polite					
neutral					
very direct					

Unit 8

Human Relations

8

"Why, Hennings, I had no idea."

1 TALKING ABOUT SECRETS

Work in pairs:

1. Can you keep a secret?
2. If you had a problem, who would you tell it to first? Why?
3. Can you think of situations, where someone asks you to keep a secret, but you would consider it better to tell someone?
4. Describe the cartoon in full detail.

Text

2 Teenage magazines tell secrets you should never tell

MM

Multiple matching

Skim-read the following article from a teenage magazine. Match the headlines (1–5) with the corresponding texts (A–E):

1. You overhear your parents talking about financial problems.
2. You discover someone is having an adulterous affair, i. e. they're married.
3. A friend confides in you about an embarrassing personal problem.
4. A friend tells you she's pregnant.
5. You catch your friend stealing.

A Keep schtum. It's best not to get involved otherwise you could spark off a whole series of dramas – and end up getting the blame.

B Advising her on where to get support and help is one thing, but spreading gossip around school isn't going to do anyone any favours.

C It's not really the done thing to snitch on a mate so it's best to have a quiet word and try to make her/him realize how much trouble she/he'll be in if she/he gets caught – and she/he probably will be.

D Keep your nose out of family money problems. If your parents have cash worries, they certainly won't want you telling the world they're skint.

E Wind, thrush – it doesn't matter what her or his problem is! The fact that she/he has told you means that she/he obviously trusts you, so you'd be really cruel to let her/him down. However amusing you find the problem, resist the urge to laugh about it with someone else.

(Adapted from MIZZ 21 May – 3 June, 1997)

Activities

A Analysing the vocabulary

Find the corresponding expressions in the text. With the help of a dictionary decide whether they are formal or informal:

• they're broke • to say that it was your friend (who did it) • she's having a baby • keep quiet • to disappoint him/her • financial problems • telling everybody • you could start

B Text production

- **Composition:** What qualities make a good friend?
- **Letter:** Write a letter to a friend of yours who's spreading a lot of gossip about other people. You don't like it.
- **Dialogue:** Your teenage friend tells you that he/she isn't sure about his/her looks and asks for your advice.

C More activities

- Write a letter to a teenage magazine:

• You have to tell a little lie now and then • Gifts you should never make • The time I felt really embarrassed • I felt like a loser! • I was very proud

- Group discussion and writing:

1. Do you believe in horoscopes?
2. Do you ever read them? Why/why not?
3. If yes, do they have an influence on your plans or activities?

4. Ask the students in your group for their birthdays to find out the German equivalents for the signs of the zodiac.
5. Ask them what they think the personal qualities and weaknesses are of their sign of the zodiac.
6. Write a week's horoscope for the other members of your group referring to what they told you.

Aquarius *January 20 – February 18*	***Pisces*** *February 19 – March 20*
Aries *March 21 – April 19*	***Taurus*** *April 20 – May 21*
Gemini *May 22 – June 21*	***Cancer*** *June 22 – July 22*
Leo *July 23 – August 23*	***Virgo*** *August 24 – September 22*
Libra *September 23 – October 23*	***Scorpio*** *October 24 – November 22*
Sagittarius *November 23 – December 21*	***Capricorn*** *December 22 – January 19*

3 Translation: *Girlie magazines*

In pairs, discuss the following questions before you translate the text given below:

1. Have you ever read a teenage magazine?
2. Did you buy them regularly?
3. What did you like about them?
4. Were there any things you didn't like about them?
5. Did your parents allow it?
6. If you were a parent, would you allow your children to read them?

"In the 90s, a clutch of mid-teen monthlies has exploded onto the market in Britain. Critics believe that the mags pressure girls into early sex, making them believe that everyone is having sex, whereas in fact it's only a minority that has. There are also worries that the magazines are bought by kids far younger than the target readership: most 14-year-olds are 17-year-old wanna-bes eager to read the stuff aimed at their big sisters. Other charges include the teen mags' lack of any positive female role model. There are few ballerinas or heart surgeons in them. What these magazines seem to be saying is that a woman's only role is to be good to her man. Fans of the mags hold that the critics are overreacting. They say many articles are written so as to empower young women. They are no longer shown as submissive love objects but rather as partners sharing responsibilities. Besides, inside the mags there's more fashion than anything else – and plenty of sound advice. Some go so far as to say the magazines provide an important service, meeting a healthy need denied to previous generations."

(Adapted from Sex Tips for Teen Girls, in NEWSWEEK February 17, 1997)

Text

■■□ 4 Mr Huxtable gets real mad

Pre-reading activities: Discussion:

1. What is your favourite sitcom?
2. What do you know about the 'Cosby Show'?
3. Do you tell your parents everything?

The 'Cosby Show', which was broadcast from 1984 – 1992, was one of the most successful American TV series ever. The popular show presented the everyday life of a black family, the Huxtables. Mr Cliff Huxtable (Bill Cosby, who also co-wrote the show and produced it) is a gynaecologist, his wife Clair a lawyer. Their five children are Sandra who, in the following episode, is an 18-year-old student at Princeton, Denise (16), Theo (15), Vanessa (14) and Rudi (5).

It's been a hard day for Mr Huxtable: In the morning he gave a course for pregnant women in the Community Centre, and in the afternoon he worked in his surgery (AE: office). It's early evening, and Mr Huxtable enters the sitting room. Vanessa is relaxing on the sofa with a walkman.

Vanessa: Hi, Dad!

Cliff: Where's the rest of the children?

Vanessa: Rudi is over at Peter's, but I think everyone else is here.

Cliff: You go around and round them up and bring them all down here.

Vanessa: Who's in trouble?

(LAUGHTER from the 'audience', probably from a tape)

Cliff: Nobody is in trouble – just do what I tell you.

(Mr Huxtable enters the kitchen.)

Cliff: Hi, dear. How is everything ?

Clair: Hi, how was class?

Cliff: Fine. Can I ask you something?

Clair: Sure.

Cliff: Do you think that our children tell us everything?

Clair: Who's in trouble? *(LAUGHTER)*

Cliff: Nobody is in trouble, I mean, I just came up from the office, now, a young girl comes in, scared about what she might have, it turns out that all she has is a mild bladder infection which can be cleared up in a couple of weeks. It's a lovely girl, beautiful, intelligent, could have been one of our children.

Clair: So Cliff, what's the point?

Cliff: The point is she didn't tell her parents – she let it go for four weeks. Do we have the kind of children that never get into any kind of trouble whatsoever, or do we have children who get into trouble and don't tell us?

Clair: Well I would say a little of both. But I think if they were in serious trouble they would come to us.

Cliff: Look, I told Vanessa to get all the children downstairs, we gonna have a meeting,

Clair: Now?

Cliff: Yes.

Clair: Okay, I'll be right there.

(Cliff and Clair enter the sitting room. Sandra, Denise, Vanessa and Theo gather on a sofa. Cliff and Clair take chairs.)

Theo: Dad, whatever it is, I didn't do it. *(LAUGHTER)*

Cliff: No, no, no it has nothing to do with what you did.

Vanessa: If this is about the family vacation, I have a few ideas.

Cliff: It's not about the vacation.

Sandra: Then what is it about?

Cliff: It's about us. *(Like a preacher during a sermon:)* I want you aaall to know if you eeever have a problem or if yoooou get into any kind of trouble, pleeease feel freeeee, no matter how baaaad you think it is, to come to your mother or to meee, and we will try to help you.

Kids: Okay. *(Kids quickly get up from the sofa) (LAUGHTER)*

Cliff: No, no, no. Wait a minute, sit down.

Theo: Isn't the talk over?

Cliff: No, the talk is not over. I was hoping that this would be the beginning of a discussion.

Denise: What are we discussing?

Cliff: About what I just said.

Vanessa: I like what you just said.

Sandra: Yeah, Dad, I think you said it very well.

Cliff: I'm not asking for a critique of what I said. *(LAUGHTER)*

Clair: What your father probably wants to know is how you feel about what he said.

Theo: We feel good about it. *(Kids quickly get up from the sofa.)*

Clair: Okay, now, come on guys. Sit down. Come on now. Now this is serious now. Your father and I want to know that you feel that you can really come to us.

Kids: Yeah.

Cliff: About anything?

Kids: Yeah. *(LAUGHTER)*

Cliff: Okay, okay. Let me give you an example. All right. Let's say, one of you became pregnant.

Vanessa *(embarrassed)*: Dad!? *(LAUGHTER)*

Cliff: No, no, no. I'm serious.

Theo *(grinning)*: I know that it's not me. *(LAUGHTER)*

Cliff: Okay, let's say it's you ! *(LAUGHTER)*

Theo *(stunned)*: Me???

Cliff: Let's say that you are pregnant. Okay! Now, what are you going to do?

Theo *(after a short pause)*: Well, first I wanna find out who did it. *(LAUGHTER)*

Cliff *(rolling his eyes)*: Okay, okay. Okay, you didn't find out – you didn't find out. Now, what would you do?

Theo *(addressing his sisters)*: Could you guys help me on this one? *(LAUGHTER)*

Denise: Don't look at me.

Vanessa: Don't even think of looking at me. *(LAUGHTER)*

Cliff: No, no, no. Come on, help your brother now.

Theo: I guess I would be scared, wouldn't I?

Sandra: Definitely.

Denise: Very definitely.

Theo: If I was scared, I probably would go to a friend first.

Cliff: If you became pregnant, you would go to Cockroach? *(LAUGHTER)*

Theo: Dad, you said, be honest.

Cliff: I know I said be honest. I'm just amazed at the fact that you would go to Cockroach *(LAUGHTER)* – and not come to us.

Theo: I would be afraid that you would get mad.

Cliff: Mad? I'm not gonna get mad.

Kids: Oh come on! *(LAUGHTER)*

Cliff: I wouldn't get mad!

Sandra: You can say that now, because it hasn't happened.

Cliff: Yeah but I'm telling you that I wouldn't get mad, now. When I said I wouldn't get mad, I mean I wouldn't get mad, you understand? *(LAUGHTER)*

Clair: Now look, there is nothing more important to us than your health and your well-being.

Cliff *(grumbling)*: Telling me I get mad. *(LAUGHTER)*

Clair: If you've got a problem, we want to know about it so that we can help you.

Cliff: I know when I'm mad about something. *(LAUGHTER)*

Sandra: Okay, Dad.

Cliff: Okay what? In the first place let's get things straightened out: Dogs get mad. Human beings get angry. *(LAUGHTER)*

(ZDF, transcript)

Notes on the language
I wanna = I want to ... / **I gonna** = I'm going to ... (Both forms are especially common in American English) /
real mad (Headline) = AE / **really mad** = BE

Activities

Text comprehension

1. Why is Mr Huxtable so upset when he comes home, and why does he want a family meeting?
2. How do the children react after Mr Huxtable's short speech?
3. What is the example Mr Huxtable makes up to underline his point?
4. Analyse Theo's strategy before and during the discussion.
5. How does Vanessa react during the talk?
6. Analyse Mrs Huxtable's part in the discussion.
7. Would you say Mr Huxtable is convincing?
8. Is Mr Huxtable mad or angry?
9. To what extent would you say it is quite naturally a matter of growing up that teenagers don't tell their parents everything?

Text

■■□ 5 Kerry Whyte – Teenage mother

Pre-reading activity: Anticipation

The following text is about Kerry Whyte, a teenage mother in Edinburgh, who still goes to school.

Work in pairs:
What problems do you think she has to face?
Here are some prompts to start you off:

[• parents • teenage father of the child • school • money • clothes • leisure activities]

Make notes, then read the text and compare the information given to your assumptions.

A single teenage mother living on benefits in a one-bedroomed council flat in a peripheral housing scheme on the southern edges of Edinburgh: it's the sort of scenario broadly deemed a problem by educationalists and moralists. Only Kerry Whyte, a 17-year-old schoolgirl, wouldn't consider herself a social problem. She doesn't view her life as a forlorn example of lost youth. She's bright, articulate and self-aware, and, in her view, a good mother. She's got plans for her future and a much loved 13-month-old son, Jordan. She didn't get pregnant to jump the council housing queue or because she lacked imagination or to impress her friends. She just made a mistake, but she's facing the consequences and, with the support of friends, family and an enlightened education authority, is getting on with her life. "I love Jordan," she says. "He means everything to me".

When she became pregnant, Whyte was nearly 16 and had been going out with her 17-year-old boyfriend, Craig, for four months. Yes they knew about contraception but, hand on heart, they just thought it wouldn't happen to them. Whyte felt her body was not old enough to bear a child. When she found she was wrong she grappled with disbelief and fear. "It shouldn't have happened. I was the quiet student at school and none of the teachers expected it of me. They were disappointed but I was more disappointed in myself. It was a big shock to everyone."

Having a young father herself (her parents were both 16 when Whyte was born) meant support at home. Since her mother died when she was seven, she says her relationship with her father has been one of friends. He kept his temper and accompanied her when she broke the news at school.

It was her boyfriend who, at 17 balked at father-hood. He wanted her to have an abortion. There were arguments and accusations that to press ahead was selfish. Whyte says until it happened to her, she might have agreed, but now it didn't feel right.

Eight weeks after Jordan was born, she returned to school part-time, joining a group of teenage mothers at Wester Hailes Education Centre. For 12 years, the school has provided crèche facilities and extra support for young mothers from across the Lothian area, while the city council pays for taxis for the girls and their children.

Motherhood has given Whyte a sense of achievement and independence. She says many of the other young mothers live with their parents, but she can cope alone. Most evenings she stays with Jordan. When he goes to sleep, she does her homework or tidies the flat. In the morning she washes and feeds her son before taking him with her to school. She sacrifices a teenage penchant for clothes to provide for Jordan, but goes out most Fridays with her friends. Sometimes, she admits she's lonely, but she maintains a good relationship with her boyfriend who sees his son every week. She hopes one day they'll live together as a family, but adds that maybe that sounds like a fairytale.

Whyte is sitting her final exams and this autumn hopes to study business administration at college. Once Jordan is at nursery, she says, she'd like to work in a bank or building society. What she doesn't want to do is to manage on £80 a week benefits.

Since the start of the year, debate has focused on just when it is appropriate for schools to teach sex education, given that the pregnancy rate in the UK among under-16s stands at approximately eight girls in 1,000 – the highest figure in Western Europe. Whyte believes sex education should start young. She and some of the other teenagers give talks to fourth-year pupils to drive home the reality of caring for a baby. "I think people need to be told by someone who's in the situation. We tell them it can be really hard. I think girls see us pushing buggies and think it's a novelty".

(Adapted from Alison Daniels, The Guardian, March 6, 1997)

Activities

SAQs

A Text comprehension – short answer questions

1. Where does Kerry White live now and how does she feel about it?
2. What kind of person is Kerry?
3. What is Kerry's family background?
4. What does Kerry mean when she says that getting pregnant was a "mistake"?
5. How did her teachers react when they learned that she was pregnant?
6. How did Kerry's boyfriend, Craig, react when he learned?
7. What are the things Kerry had to give up with the baby?
8. Does Kerry see a future for her and Craig as a couple?
9. What does Kerry say about the importance of sex education at school and what does she do at the moment to contribute?

Med

B Mediation

1. Fassen Sie auf Deutsch in Stichpunkten zusammen, was Kerry dabei hilft, mit ihrer Situation zurechtzukommen.
2. Wie sieht Kerrys Tagesablauf aus? Skizzieren Sie stichpunktartig.

C Discuss

1. Why do you think is it important that at school Kerry is with a group of teenage mothers?
2. Would you recommend Kerry to ask Craig to marry her?

D Words, words, words

Fill in the words from the word bank below.

[• advised • appropriate • buggies • contraceptives • crèche facilities • going out • happen • pregnant • quiet • sacrifice • sex education • support • teenage mother • told]

When the teachers were … that Kerry, who had always been a … student, was … , they were very disappointed. Kerry was … to join a group of teenage mothers at Wester Hailes Education Centre. The centre offers … and extra … for young mothers. There is a debate when it is … for schools to teach … and to inform them about … . Kerry thinks that should … early. "The young girls should be told that life as a … is more than pushing … and that you have to … a penchant for clothes and … ," she says.

■■□ 6 The ideal man

According to a Los Angeles radio station, in the 1990s the L.A. single girl expected the following in a man:
"He must shoot a mean game of pool, go to the gym, have a brain, be himself, know how to kiss, bring her flowers, like her body, put the toilet seat down, believe in education, not do polyester, own a suit, have a tattoo, like cats, hate television, love cartoons, look good in a wet suit, wear sexy undies, not give her a stupid nickname, don't do drugs, be into Zen, not call anyone dude, be in a band, own an island, sport nice biceps, not be afraid to cry, … and never tell her what to wear."

Activities

Try to speak English during the whole time that you're working on these activities. Work in pairs (ideally one partner should be male and one female).

A Make your choices first alone, then compare results with your partner. Give reasons for your choices:

1. Choose the three items from the text that you consider to be the most important.
2. Choose three items you think are the least important.
3. Which of the items would you say are out of date?

B Find out how many of the items in the text refer to looks, manners, attitudes, style, money or talents.

With the help of a pocket calculator (or computer program) turn your findings into a chart and interpret them.

C Writing

1. What I expect in a man.
   What I expect in a woman.

   Write your own update of the list of preferences given in the text:
   must have a cute piercing – … etc.

2. What do you think are the reasons that there are so many single households?
   What are the pros and cons of life as a single?

Listening comprehension: Ali Golding, Aboriginal woman activist?

Ali Golding is a 57-year-old Aboriginal woman who lives in a modest terrace house on Eveleigh Street, Redfern – the nearest thing Australia has to a ghetto and an address few of the white residents of Sydney would dare to visit. Many homes on the block are burned-out and vandalized.

Listen to a report about the story of her life.
What do we learn about ...

- the place she grew up?
- the 'stolen generation'?
- her first day at school?
- the death of her mother?
- her husband?
- her children?
- Aboriginal women and health?
- alcohol?
- what she does for other women?

Text

A toxin of youth

Pre-reading activities

1. Why do you think Michael Jackson had plastic surgery?
2. Who is rather prone to cosmetic surgery females or males?
3. Would you consider plastic surgery?

New York – It is a staple for affluent professionals, television talking heads, ladies who lunch and actors who refuse to age. Without a peep of promotion, it has become the most popular cosmetic medical procedure in the United States, even though it involves injecting the neurotoxin that causes butolism directly into muscles in the face, paralyzing them and thus erasing wrinkles.

Now, the injectable drug known as Botox, in use since 1991, is on the verge of achieving what it never has before: approval by the Food and Drug Administration for cosmetic use, which could allow it to burst into the mainstream. The toxin already is approved to treat spasmic disorders of the eye muscles. But federal approval for its use as a cosmetic would allow the manufacturer to promote Botox – the commercial name for botulinum toxin A – with a multimillion-dollar blitz of television commercials and print advertising that could rival that of other drugs like Viagra, analysts said. They predicted that Botox users could increase by 30 percent or even 50 percent in the next year from the 1.1 million Americans who tried it in 2000.

An official of the federal drug agency said it planned to approve Botox for cosmetic use. A spokeswoman for the manufacturer, Allergan, which is based in Irvine, California, said the agency last year reviewed two clinical trials that the Company had submitted. The Company expects the agency´s approval next month, at the very latest, she said. Botox has already worked its numbing magic on the face of America. Hollywood directors like Martin Scorsese and Baz Luhrmann have complained that Botox is so popular among actors that it is playing havoc with facial expression. In a variation on "The Stepford Wives," it is now rare in certain social enclaves to see a woman older than 35 with the ability to look angry.

And, as the wrinkle-smoothers rides a wave of popularity with aging baby boomers, a Botox Nation of citizens with unnaturally placid expressions may find itself abandoning some old beliefs. The wisdom that a person´s character can be etched on his face, or Coco Chanel´s observation that al 20 you have the face nature gave you, and that at 50 you have the face you merit, may no longer apply. "We will look at wrinkles the way we look at cracked or discolored teeth: remnants of the past, just something to be fixed," said Nancy Etcoff, a psychologist at the Harvard Medical School and the author of "Survival of the Prettiest: The Science of Beauty". "You still see young women smoking and sitting in the sun, and they can just get rid of the wrinkles. It´s very much about having your cake and eating it, too. It is as though we have given up on authenticity," she said.

In a Botox treatment, a doctor injects a diluted form of the drug into a patient´s facial muscles. Over the next four days, the toxin paralyzes the muscles that control facial wrinkling, stopping more wrinkles and also eradicating existing ones. The skin does not feel numb to the patient nor does its texture change. Nor is there a risk of becoming infected with botulism, which causes respiratory failure in advanced cases, because the Botox treatment is so diluted. Still, there are complications. For example, patients are advised not to lie down or lean over or even tie their shoes for six hours after treatment, lest the toxin seep and inadvertently paralyze other muscles.

And while a treatment lasts for three to four months, patients must get more injections, which can cost $ 300 to more than $ 1,000, to maintain the effect (...). Botox injections made up 19.1 percent of all cosmetic procedures practiced by surgeons in the United States in 2000, according to the American Society for Aesthetic and Plastic Surgeons (ASAPS).

The popularity of Botox reflects the growing national mania for cosmetic surgery and the array of related procedures that try to slow time. Plastic surgical procedures are on a sharpe rise, up 173 percent from 1997 to 2000, according to the American Society for Aesthetic and Plastic Surgeons at a cost of $ 7.4 billion to consumers (...).

(abridged from: International Herald Tribune, 2002-02-08)

Activities

Med

A Mediation

1. Geben Sie den Inhalt des ersten Satzes wieder. (Keine Übersetzung)
2. Erklären Sie, welcher Status Botox von der Food and Drug Administration (FDA) erteilt werden soll.
3. Welche zwei Vorteile hätte der Hersteller durch die FDA-Entscheidung und wie sind dann die Marktchancen für das Produkt?

4. Erklären sie den Satz "Botox has already worked its numbing magic on the face of America" (l. 34).
5. Warum haben einige Hollywood-Regisseure ein Problem mit Botox?
6. Was könnten die Menschen in Zukunft, laut Auffassung der Psychologin Nancy Etcoff, von Gesichtsfältchen halten und wie ist Ihre Haltung dazu?
7. Beschreiben Sie die Wirkung von Botox auf Muskeln und Haut im Gesicht.
8. Worauf müssen Patienten unmittelbar nach einer Behandlung achten?
9. Was wird über die Wirkungsdauer und die Kosten einer Behandlung gesagt? Belegen Sie Ihre Antwort auch anhand von Zahlen.

B Gapped summary

The new Botox *...(1)...* might change the faces of a growing number of Americans. This new drug stops the *...(2)...* process in your face by *...(3)...* muscles controlling *...(4)...* expression. The face makes an impression of being unnaturally still and peaceful. But such faces are somehow disturbing. If humans lose their ability to express their *...(5)...* with their facial expression, they lose a good deal of their personality. Moreover, having *...(6)...* and an ageing face may be *...(7)...* one day as carelessness and a lack of civilization. But psychologically speaking having an artificial poker face definitely is a loss of *...(8)...* .

Literature

8 Ann Beattie: Where you'll find me

Pre-reading activity

Imagine what living in the following places in New York would be like. Where would you like to live and why?

A. Manhattan

B. Roof Garden in Soho

C. Typical street in Brooklyn

D. Typical street in Queens

"There's no way it's going to happen," Renee said. "You might as well get the thought out of your head. I go. You stay. That's just the way it is."

The dog looked at the floor. When Renee stopped talking, he looked up and began to beat his tail again. It hit hard against the banister. "Oh, take him," Tadd said. "Give him a thrill."

"You're supposed to back me up when I make a statement," Renee said. "We'll be bad parents if we don't get it together."

"We're already good parents. We're taking the dog out of the city to a big yard in the country."

"The suburbs. Not the country."

"You're torturing him," Tadd said. "Stay or go."

She picked up the two bags full of clothes for Goodwill and went down the stairs carefully, peering between the bags. She had also gone to Goodwill the day before. She had taken three cartons of books to the Strand. She had returned a soup ladle a neighbor loaned them months ago. Over the past weeks she had collected cartons to transport the plants. They were moving into her sister's house in Connecticut, to house-sit while she was in London for a year. What Tadd didn't know was that her sister was set on reconciling with her husband, who now lived in England, and that if she did, she would not be back. What the dog did not know was that he would be moving in with a cat.

She shifted both bags into one arm and reached into her coat pocket to see if she had brought the keys. She had. The dog's chain was also in her pocket. Some Kleenex. Although she was the one who had instigated the move, it made her nervous to think about changing her life so drastically. In private, she cried. There were tissues under her pillow. She had bought a package for her handbag.

A man jogged by in black sweatpants and a black sweatshirt marked #1. Three boys, sucking luminous green slush out of tubular plastic packages, came laughing around the corner. She passed the laundry and inhaled the tide-scented steam. The people who ran the place began work before she woke up, and were often still in the store when she returned home to go to bed. It exhausted her to see other people exhausting themselves in New York. It seemed that the whole city was only a container for energy. Or perhaps she was just being pessimistic – trying to justify leaving. She had quit her job months before she needed to, out of the same pessimism. In spite of what the doctor said, both she and Tadd suspected that the long hours and the tension of the job had been responsible for her miscarriage. The doctor had told her to wait before trying to conceive again. This had made her sad and frustrated. She would have felt worse if the dog's presence hadn't consoled her. At night he would curl up at the foot of the bed and she would stroke his soft fur with her foot and speak quietly to him. The night before, she had suggested to the dog, as she stroked, that he might like a dog brother in the country, and Tadd had turned on his side, seeing nothing funny about it, saying that one dog was enough to bother. He had also said – many times recently – that if they never had a child, that would be all right. She didn't believe that. She was thirty-five, and when they married he had said that he wanted three children.

She walked down the street, trying to put all the near-arguments and all the tension out of her mind. The birdseed had been scattered in the alley behind the Safeway earlier than usual. Pigeons flew up frantically as she approached, but settled down and resumed their pecking before she passed by. One day she had seen boys sprinkling D-Con in with the birdseed. They had laughed and run away. Boys in this neighborhood were always laughing and slugging each other and cupping their hands around cigarettes the way gangsters did in the old movies.

A man in red tennis shoes and a coat bunched up under his arms asked her for money as she waited for the light to change on Eighth Avenue.

"I don't have any money," she said.

"How come you look better than me if you got no money?" he called after her.

What she did not like about the city was that she was never sure who was needy and who was not. And that while she thought about such things, strangers, passing by, would tell her to smile.

The metal door was pulled halfway down over the entrance to the Goodwill store. The metal sides were often shut and the center panel slightly lowered, but as she came close she saw that this time it meant that the store was closed. Not for any reason she could think of: it was too early to close; it was open six days a week.

"You want to donate, put them right down," a man with a jack-o'-lantern smile said. He had been leaning against the window of the store next door. "They get them. They pick 'em up," he said. He pointed toward the door with an unlit cigarette. His other hand was a fist. He loosened his fingers and thumbed up a book of matches. He opened the book, struck one, and moved the tip of his cigarette into the flame. "Sure they do," he said. "Push them up against the door."

She wasn't going to carry them home, so she invented a scenario in which the man was right: an employee inside would see the bags, open the door, and take them in. She stepped forward and lowered the bags to the sidewalk, pushing them in toward the door. Someone came up close behind her and she turned, fully expecting that the man was going to offer more advice. She moved back, startled to see a thin black transvestite, who reached into the bag as if she weren't there. "Look at this!" he said, pulling a blue nightgown out of the bag. He had come from nowhere; he might have dropped from the sky, his presence was so sudden. A short man who had been standing to the side dove at the bag too, tossing clothes onto the sidewalk, then snatching them up again as fast as he had thrown them down. He took a lavender quilted robe out of the other bag and swirled it around his shoulders as if it were a cape. It slipped to the cement. The transvestite held up a ruffly blouse – a gift from her in-laws, too silly to wear – and pressed it against his chest with his chin. "I'm beautiful!" the transvestite said. "I'm going to wear this to dinner. Oh, I'm pretty."

She looked away. The clothes were pretty, and when he began tossing them and draping them around his body she blinked at the flashes of color and could remember places she had worn them, whole days and nights that now seemed to be explained by what she had worn. It was a crazy, humiliating moment – as unexpected as a rude guest picking through your laundry hamper to see what kind of underwear you wore. But of course there was nothing she could do: Wrestle for her clothes? Get into an argument? Appeal to the now silent man smoking his cigarette, who never took his eyes away from the scene, even though his face registered nothing?

At Ninth Avenue, fighting tears, she rationalized that at least the clothes pleased someone. Inside the Goodwill store, they might have been sold to people equally silly or crazy. The corner store was suffused with the smell of bananas. That smell hung in the air and mixed with the smell of hot dogs turning on the grill behind the counter: She got a large carton of Tropicana, paid for it, waited for her change, and went outside. She threw away the brown bag and carried the carton. It was cold and waxy and felt good against her palms. Her hands were sore from packing.

The dog was at the top of the landing, doing a little skittering dance as she walked up the stairs. "Tell him that the big outside world wasn't that much fun," Tadd said. "Make him feel better."

She went to the bedroom doorway, ignoring the dog, who ran circles around her. Tadd had almost finished removing the books from the last shelf. He worked diligently, giving every task his full concentration. She wished that he wasn't always so capable, so practical. That he would say what he felt, instead of joking. "If you'd taken him," Tadd said, "he could have watched you doing something charitable: It might have encouraged him to do good deeds. He only thinks about himself."

"Stop kidding for a minute," she said. "Say something serious."

"If I stop laughing, I'll cry," he said. "We've got three rooms to pack before Friday."

She turned and walked into the kitchen, maneuvering between cartons. She poured a glass of juice and hollered to ask whether he wanted a glass.

"Yeah," he said. "This dust has really been sticking in my throat."

She poured a glass for him and slid past the boxes again. In the bedroom, Tadd was stretched out on the floor, his head resting against a box he had just sealed. He stretched his arm up for the glass. "Goodwill," he said. "Goodwill toward all." He rubbed his hand over his face. "They used to have those big Goodwill boxes all over the place," he said. "You remember that? In supermarket parking lots, outside of schools – all over the place. I had a girlfriend in high school, and she didn't want to make out in my car, so we were in this commuter lot and there was one of those Goodwill boxes, overflowing. I got out and pulled out all the stuff and reached in for more. Piled it up in a mound behind the box – a mess of shoes and broken dolls – put the soft stuff on top. It was like falling into confetti. We made out there, with cars zooming by up on the high-way, and the car radio on for background music."

He was pulling strapping tape across the top of another carton he had packed that was waiting to be sealed. He pressed the tape downover one side with his thumb, then cut it off the roll with his free hand.

"Was that all you did?" she said.

"That time," he said.

"What about another time?"

He smiled. "Don't tell me you're jealous about something I did when I was a teen-ager."

Of course she was – because she knew that people and things never really got left behind: you'd be surprised into remembering them; your thoughts would be overturned. In her pocket, she felt the dog's leash and decided to take him for a walk. If she were a teenager, she might have returned to the crazy circus going on outside the Goodwill store – she might have gone back with her dog, just to frighten them. But by now a lot of time had passed. Something told her that once she left, they had simply decided what they wanted and then had gone away.

(From Ann Beattie: Where you'll find me, 1988)

Activities

A Text comprehension

1. Look at the photos on page 221 again.
   Which of the places shown could be the one where Renee and Tadd live?
2. What are Renee and Tadd about to do?
3. Ordering task
   Here are some of the people Renee meets on her way to the Goodwill store and back, and some of the places she passes.
   What is their correct order?
   What kind of feelings do the people and places raise within Renee?

[• A man in red tennis shoes • B corner store • C transvestite • D jogger • E Goodwill store • F smiling man lighting a cigarette • G laundry • H three boys]

4. Renee seems to be depressed and down. She feels insecure and disoriented. Maybe she even thinks that she has failed. Talk about her feelings. Use the following prompts:

[**move • baby • city • job • old clothes • Tadd's story about a former girl friend.**]

5. Renee's way of coping with her temporary anxieties is to "rationalize" things. What does that mean? Find examples in the story.
6. Characterize Tadd.
7. Renee insists that they are going to "the suburbs. Not (to) the country." What would you say is the difference?
8. Talk about situations when you feel or have felt uneasy or insecure.

■□□ 9 Talkline 1: Find someone who ...

You are all standing in your classroom. You talk to one person at a time and it is your job to find as many people as possible who meet the following criteria. Note the names and present the results that you find most interesting to the plenum.

Find someone who

1. has done a backpacking tour recently.
2. can recommend a good travel guide on London.
3. could not fly because the plane was overbooked.
4. can tell you if you need a vise for Canada.
5. has tried sushi.
6. knows at what time pubs close in Ireland.
7. rides a motorbike.
8. can tell you the name of a British Cabinet Minister.
9. can tell you two things worth seeing in the British Museum.
10. has been to Asia.
11. does not have a TV set.
12. likes iskender kebab.
13. knows *The Hitchhiker's Guide To The Galaxy.*
14. has never had an accident.
15. regularly reads a quality newspaper.
16. never has problems with his/her computer.
17. knows which country Asia Minor belongs to.
18. often buys things in internet auctions.
19. knows the capital of Scotland.
20. has already booked a holiday via the Internet.
21. knows the price of an Interrail Ticket.
22. prefers going on holiday by train.

■■□ 10 Talkline 2: Talking about people

Work with a partner. You look at picture 1, page 304. Describe to your partner: What sort of people are in the picture? Where could they be? What might they be doing? Who/what are they looking at? Find a word to describe the look on their faces. Do the same with pictures 2 and 3. Choose one of the pictures and describe it to your partner in a way that he/she can draw a rough sketch. Then your partner goes to page 305 and does the same with pictures 4–6.

Some of the following terms may be useful:

• Serious, happy, Mediterranean area • there is a number of people in the picture • they are standing/sitting/lying on ... • on the left you see ... • in the top left corner you see ... • in the background you see ... • there are lots of people ... • there is only one ... • the weather is ... • the people are young/old • uniform • time of the year • in a room/in the open air • vegatation • arm-chair • couch • writing desk • university • old people's home

Unit 9

Technology

1 TALKING ABOUT MOBILE PHONES

1. Do you use your mobile phone everywhere, or are there situations where you do not use it?
2. Do you mind people using their phone in a restaurant? Give reasons why or why not.
3. Why do you think using the phone in a car can be dangerous?
4. How can you avoid these dangers?
5. In what situations can a mobile phone save lives?
6. Work together in a group to draw up a list of situations where you would not use a mobile phone

Useful words an expressions

• to switch on/off • in case of an emergency • appointment • distraction • nuisance • noise • helpful • impolite

Listening comprehension

The decline in teenage smoking and the rise of the mobile phone

You are going to hear a report about statistical research into the consumer habits of teenagers. First read the questions and copy the table below into your notebook. Then listen to the text, take rough notes and complete the table. Listen to it a second time and add more relevant details.

1. What trend do the authors see?
2. What possible explanations do they discuss?

	Percentage of smokers 1996	1999
Children aged 11–15	❶	❷
Girls aged 15	❸	❹
Boys aged 15	❺	❻
All aged 15	❼	❽

Text

2 "Walk out" threat over phone mast

Social services staff have threatened to walk out if mobile phone masts are erected on their office building. Angry employees at the Oxfordshire County Council offices in Cowley Road, Oxford, fear risks to their health. Staff voiced their concern at a public meeting on Thursday and warned they would demonstrate to stop workmen from a British mobile phone firm from putting up the six masts.

One worker, who asked not to be named to protect her job, said: "We are not saying we will refuse to work. We are saying we will refuse to work there. We believe the council is contravening its duty of care to staff and is severely risking our health and safety. Would anyone feel safe working in a building with these masts on top?"

The meeting, attended by more than 60 people, was organised by Cameo, the Campaign Against Masts in East Oxfordshire. The group urged residents to stop workmen putting up the masts when the work begins next Thursday. Nobody from the mobile phone company attended, despite being invited.

There are widespread concerns among the public about possible health risks caused by mobile phone masts although the phone companies insist there is no "substantiated evidence" to suggest any link. Oxford Cameo spokesman Dharesh Turnbull said: "Until we know exactly how these masts affect the health of people nearby we will not allow them to go up." County councillor Craig Simmons said he would back any peaceful direct action. The nearby 250-pupil East Oxford First School is opposing the scheme along with several businesses in the area.

Cameo plans to take out an injunction to stop the phone company putting up the masts, but has only a week before work begins.

Part of James Street is expected to be closed on Thursday evening while cranes are put in place to hoist the masts to the top of the building on Saturday.

Adapted from www.thisisoxfordshire.co.uk/oxfordshire/archive/2000/01/15NEWS1VQ.html

Annotations
County Council (5) – *Rat/Verwaltung der Grafschaft* / **voice your concern** (8) – *seine Besorgnis ausdrücken* / **contravene your duty of care** (19–20) – *seine Sorgfaltspflicht verletzen*

Activities

A Sentence completion

Answer the following questions on the text by completing the given sentences with suitable information from the text. (You may use words from the text.)

1. The protests against the mobile phone mast were started by *...(1)...*

2. The protesters do not want a full strike, they just *...(2)...*
3. The protesters are against the mast, because they *...(3)...*
4. Institutions supporting the protests are *...(4)...*

B Words, words, words

1. Find a paraphrase that can be used in the particular contexts.
   a) walk out (l. 2)
   b) erected (l. 3)
   c) voiced their concern (l. 7)
2. Explain the following expressions:
   a) There are widespread concerns among the public ... (ll. 29–30)
   b) ... School is opposing the scheme along with several businesses ... (ll. 43–45)
   c) an (interim) injunction (l. 46)

Text

3 Scientists caution that their research isn't an "all clear"

A Senior author of the Danish report, Dr Christoffer Johansen, cautioned that his study should not be taken as an all-clear that mobiles are definitely safe. He explained that the research did not include enough long-term users, or those who use their mobile for long periods of time. Johansen also warned that his study did not consider other ailments linked to mobile handset use, such as migraines or tinnitus.

B This is the first nation-wide study into the incidence of cancer among mobile phone users. "[The study] does not support the hypothesis of a link between the use of these phones and cancer of the brain, salivary glands, central nervous system or leukaemia," stated the report, which was published in the US Journal of the National Cancer Institute.

C The largest ever scientific study of mobile phone health concerns has concluded that there is no link between handset use and cancer. Doctors at the Danish Cancer Society investigated each of the 420,000 Danes who have owned a mobile phone between 1982 and 1995. After examining the medical histories of this group, the researchers concluded that there was no evidence of a cancer link.

D The findings support earlier research which has also failed to find evidence that mobile phone use causes tumours. Late last year, an American study found no proof that patients with brain cancer have used mobile phones more than average.

E Rupert Goodwins (a British technology journalist) is getting in a froth about BBC Radio 4's *You and Yours* programme transmitting a piece about radio and health. He asks "What is the risk? We live in a country where you can buy cigarettes over the counter and drink yourself to a coma every night." He maintains the only danger you're in from your mobile phone comes from colonic rupture if it rings once too often, too loudly in a place filled with choleric Chelsea fans.

F Despite the absence of proof that mobile phone use causes health problems, some scientists are concerned. Writing in 'The Lancet' late last year, UK scientist Dr Gerard Hyland warned that children are at the greatest risk from mobile phone radiation, which could harm a number of brain functions. Johansen agrees that children should avoid unnecessary exposure to mobile phone radiation.

Adapted from www.zdnet.co.uk/news/2001/5/ns-20799.html

Annotations
incidence of cancer (9,10) – Vorkommen/Häufigkeit von Krebs / **salivary gland** (12) – Speicheldrüse / **get in a froth** (29) – vor Wut schäumen / **colonic rupture** (32, 33) – Darmriss

Activities

MM

A Text cohesion – matching exercise

1. Put the paragraphs into the right order.

   HINT

   It may help to find "linkers" at the beginnings of the paragraphs that refer to the previous paragraph or structure previous paragraphs. The first paragraph must be one that does not refer to facts or people previously mentioned. "This" at the beginning of the paragraph may refer to a previous explanation. "Findings" must – of course – refer to something that has been found out. Taking up the same thing in other words links two paragraphs.
2. Where is the text less cohesive so that you have had problems "fitting the paragraph in"? Give reasons why you found it difficult.
3. In case your solution differs from the "right" order, discuss if your solution is equally good.

B Summarising

Summarise what the text says about scientific research on the danger of mobile phones. Start by saying: "Research has been done, but the results …"

C Comparing Text 1 and Text 2

1. In which text do people make judgements on an emotional basis only?

2. Find examples where people consider carefully what they know and what they do not know.
3. To what extent can the two sides really prove their standpoints?

D Words, words, words – multiple matching

Match the following words and the proper definitions.

A modem	**1** a piece of metal transmitting or receiving wireless signals
B pulsed radiation	**2** a device that allows you to use a telephone without holding it to your ear
C emergency	**3** a technical device that connects a computer to other computer systems using a telephone connection
D hash key	**4** to end the telephone conversation
E aerial	**5** a telephone that you can carry around in or near your home
F to hang up	**6** the monthly fee you have to pay even if you do not make any calls
G keyboard	**7** the set of buttons on a telephone
H cordless phone	**8** what you put before the telephone number when you dial from a different town
I roaming	**9** a button on the telephone bearing the # sign
J coverage	**10** the area where you can use the services of your mobile phone company
K dialling code	**11** a sudden situation of danger requiring immediate action
L line rental	**12** a way of transmitting signals not continuously but at very short regular intervals
M hands free kit	**13** using the services of foreign mobile phone companies with your domestic card while you are abroad

Listening comprehension: Call centre

In Britain there are now (just like in Germany) several companies that you can call to find out a telephone number. One of the numbers is 118 118. This call centre has been heavily criticized recently.

Task 1

The radio presenter wants to test the efficiency of the call centre. When he rings them he first warns them that they are on the radio. Listeners are also invited to report what they have experienced with the telephone directory service. Listen carefully and find the relevant information. You don't have to write complete sentences, **short notes are enough**. Some of the information you need may come at a later stage.

1. The numbers of which two institutions are confused.
2. Where is the call centre?
3. The number of the Tower of London the caller gets from the call centre in Cardiff is: … (Please write it down in your notebook.)

Task 2

A listener called Philip reports his problems with the service.
Philip spoke to a supervisor because … (three reasons).

Task 3

The presenter rings up the call centre again. He can choose between a refund or … *(1)*. He decides to … *(2)*. His address is c/o LBC, … *(3)*. The number he is given is … *(4)*.

Text

4 Bionic Youth

Pre-reading activities

1. How much time a day do you spend online?
2. What do you like or dislike about the Internet?
3. What do you think about computer games?
4. Can you think of new features mobile phones (cell phones) should have?
5. Why is an MP3 player so tempting?

The world that today's kids inhabit is diverging sharply from the one their parents grew up in.

Unlike other generation gaps, this one doesn't revolve around mores, fashion or pop culture so much as technology. Kids have never been more wired. Throughout the world, childhood relationships are made or broken with a few strokes of a cell-phone keypad. Skills are being acquired less from books than from videogames. And the senses are bombarded with information that flows from every direction at an ever-quickening pace.

Is this a good thing? Is the stimulation of new media preparing kids for a future high-tech world – or turning them into antisocial superficial dolts?

There are no definite answers. Only in the past few years have scientists begun to plumb children's brains to see what goes on during the hours they spend engrossed in videogames or surfing the Web. What seems clear is that children are developing a far different set of skills than they had before. They are growing adept at handling visual information and multitasking. And the messaging free-for-all may actually help some kids overcome childhood awkwardness in relating to their peers.

Of all the gimmicks that have come and gone, young people are carried by two main currents of technology. One can be loosely called videogames, and it includes a broad range of visually oriented experiences ranging from benign puzzles to intense, sometimes violent action games. The second current is messaging: anything from simple email to Internet chat-rooms to text messaging on cell phones to the exchange of images and voice recordings. Both forces are reshaping the experiences of millions of children around the world.

Ever since Atari started selling Pong in the 1970s, videogames have steadily increased in power and allure, to the point where they now rival cinema in visual impact. In recent years, advanced graphics have made their visual punch available on a wide range of devices, from small handheld gadgets to game consoles like Nintendo's GameCube and Microsoft's Xbox.

And the devices are increasingly linked to high-speed broadband Internet connections – even wireless ones – giving players access to a whole cybercommunity of gamers.

What happens to a young brain when it spends so much time exposed to a fast-paced visual medium? The short answer is: it adapts. The brain is plastic, which is to say it changes readily in response to stimuli. Cognitive neuroscientist Daphne Bevalier began to suspect that videogames were altering the minds of young people about two years ago, after she gave some students at the University of Rochester in New York a test designed to measure their visual perceptions. The one student who did particularly well turned out to be an avid video game player.

Intrigued Bevalier put together two groups of students – avid gamers and non-gamers – and over the course of a few semesters, gave both a series of computerized visual-perception tests. On average, the video game players scored 30 percent better than non-players. These results alone wouldn't indicate brain plasticity; the gamers might simply have had better inherent visual skills. To eliminate this possibility Bevalier formed two other groups of non-players; one trained for an hour a day shooting enemy soldiers in the action game Medal of Honor while the other played the more sedate puzzle game Tetris. After 10 days the Medal of Honor trainees scored higher than both the non-players and their Tetris colleagues. Bevalier concluded that action-packed video-games enhance "the capacity of visual attention and its spatial distribution".

Many questions remain: why are video games so efficient at enhancing visual performance? Is it because they are graphically compelling, or because they overload the senses? To what extent do emotional responses – danger, violence, a sense of challenge – play a role? There's no doubt that emotions have a lot to do with the *appeal* of video games. From the brain's point of view, gaming is largely a visual task and as such it gets processed mainly in the right hemisphere. What worries scientists is that the right-lobe visual circuits have a fast track to the emotions. If you read about a violent event the information is filtered through your more rational, analytical left hemisphere. Richard Restak, a neurologist at George Washington University and the author of "The New Brain", argues that visual media like videogames and television don't get tempered in this way. According to a study by psychologist Craig Anderson of the University of Missouri-Columbia, an overload of emotion-charged imagery can increase anti-social behavior. In a study of college students published in 2000 in the Journal of Personality and Social Psychology, he found that playing violent games like Mortal Kombat correlated strongly to aggressive personalties, poor academic performance and delinquency.

To be sure, not all videogames are violent. Games like the Sims, in which kids create fictional families and then watch them live their mundane lives, may actually foster problem-solving and role-playing skills. Such games favor not the brain's visual circuits but its pre-frontal cortex, which serves as a command center, putting things in context. "Video games can either stimulate or stifle brain development, and the difference between the two has to do with the design of the games," says Trevor Neilson, a World Economic Forum Global Leader for Tomorrow and executive vice president of the Casey Family Foundation.

Few studies have addressed the impact of games on the imagination. "It remains to be seen whether autonomous imagination can be stimulated by computers, or whether it is limited by the fact that you have to sit in front of a screen with a mouse," says Jerome Singer, professor of psychology at Yale University, who is working on a book about the impact of electronic media on kid's imaginations. There's even some evidence that gaming may make kids smarter – or at least test better. James R. Flynn a philosophy professor at the University of Otago in New Zealand, says that video games may have contributed to an increase in scores in IQ tests that measure quickness in solving pattern-recognition problems. This doesn't correlate to more street smarts or higher academic performance in kids. If anything it probably means, they're better suited to being fighter pilots or air-traffic controllers. That's not a bad thing, but it's nothing to get too excited about either.

The common view of technology obsessed kids as antisocial loners may be ready for revision. In a study of 7th and 10th graders, UCLA researchers found no relationship between Internet use and loneliness, depression or social anxiety. That didn't surprise E. Gross, one of the researchers: "From the perspective of developmental psychology, and particularly our study of intimacy, well-being depends on close interaction with others." The technology ecourages kids to keep in touch with real-world peers, not to retreat into an isolated fantasy world.

Some kids used the technology to interact with classmates they otherwise wouldn't know. And when it came to approaching the opposite sex, instant messaging was a whole lot less stressful than getting up the nerve to speak to somebody in the school cafeteria.

It is not clear what role electronic media may play in the near-epidemic proportions of attention deficit disorder among school age children. Does the youthful brain raised on a diet of overstimulation adapt, and even thrive? Yes and no. "Kids are getting better at paying attention to several things at once," says Patricia Greenfield, director of the Children's Digital Media Center at UCLA. "But there is a cost, in that you don't go into any one thing in at much depth." This is one problem technology has sure helped create. With luck, one day it will help solve it.

(abridged from: Newsweek, August 25/Sept.1, 2003)

Activities

True or false?

1. The new generation of kids is keener on fashion and pop culture.
2. Kids are increasingly skillful at dealing with visual information.
3. It's the Internet that has the strongest impact on the young generation.
4. Video games change the perception of their users.
5. Video game players score better in IQ tests.
6. Researchers found that kids using the Internet are lonely.
7. Messaging technology facilitates the contact between the sexes.
8. The new generation of school age children concentrates very well at school.

Comprehension questions:

1. What does the author mean by the statement: "Kids have never been more wired"?
2. Which are the two youth-relevant, main currents of technology mentioned by the author?
3. Why are scientists worried about the impact of images on the brain?

Comment writing

1. Comment on Patricia Greenfield's statement concerning the new generation of bioinic kids: "But there is a cost, in that you don't go into any one thing in at much depth."
2. "Concentrating at school is very difficult for me." Give reasons for this candid confession made by a young student.
3. Discuss the pros and cons of reading a newspaper and the internet news provided by an online magazine.

Literature

5 Issac Asimov: True Love

Pre-reading activity

Which of the following movies have you seen?

[• Star Wars Trilogy • Blade Runner • Terminator • Star Trek • E.T. • 2001 – A Space Odyssey • Independence Day • Flash Gordon • Lost in space]

What do they have common?
What's so fascinating about them?

Science fiction, like fantasy and social satire, deals with a background that isn't "real". Unlike fantasy, however, its backgrounds are not completely unrelated to reality, but represent a more or less plausible extrapolation of reality.
Science fiction may be defined as that branch of literature which deals with the response of human beings to advances in science and technology. Actual change in science and technology, occurring quickly enough and striking deeply enough to affect a human being, is a phenomenon peculiar to the world only since the Industrial Revolution. The first well-known writer who responded to this new factor in human affairs by dealing regularly with science fiction was Jules Verne. In the English language, the early master was H. G. Wells.

(Adapted from: "Is anyone there?" by Isaac Asimov, New York, 1956)

My name is Joe. That is what my colleague, Milton Davidson, calls me. He is a programmer and I am a computer. I am part of the Multivac-complex and am connected with other parts all over the world. I know everything. Almost everything. I am Milton's private computer. His Joe. He understands more about computers than anyone in the world, and I am his experimental model. He has made me speak better than any other computer can. "It's just a matter of matching sounds to symbols, Joe," he told me. "That's the way it works in the human brain even though we still don't know what symbols there are in the brain. I know the symbols in yours, and I can match them to words, one-to-one." So I talk. I dont think I talk as well as I think, but Milton says I talk very well. Milton has never married, though he is nearly 40 years old. He has never found the right woman, he told me. One day he said, "I'll find her yet, Joe. Im going to find the best. I'm going to have true love and you're going to help me. I'm tired of improving you in order to solve the problems of the world. Solve my problem. Find me true love.“

I said, "What is true love?"

"Never mind. That is abstract. Just find me the ideal girl. You are connected to the Multivac-complex so you can reach the data banks of every human being in the world. We'll eliminate them all by groups and classes until we're left with only one person. The perfect person. She will be for me.“

I said, "I am ready."

He said, "Eliminate all men first." It was easy. His words activated symbols in my molecular valves. I could reach out to make contact with the accumulated data on every human being in the world. At his words, I withdrew from 3,784,982,874 men. I kept contact with 3,786,112,090 women. He said, "Eliminate all younger than 25, all older than 50. Then eliminate all with an IQ under 120; all with a height under 150 centimeters and over 175 centimeters." He gave me exact measurements; he eliminated women with living children; he eliminated women with various genetic characteristics. "Im not sure about eye color," he said. "Let that go for a while. But no red hair. I don't like red hair."

After two weeks we were down to 235 women. They all spoke English very well. Milton said he didn't want a language problem. Even computer-translation would get in the way at intimate moments.

"I can't interview 235 women," he said. "It would take too much time, and people would discover what I am doing."

"It would make trouble," I said. Milton had arranged me to do things I wasn't designed to do. No one knew about that. "It's none of their business," he said, and the skin on his face grew red. "I tell you what, Joe, I will bring in holographs and you check the list for similarities."

He brought in holographs of women. "These are three beauty contest winners," he said. "Do any of the 235 match?"

Eight were very good matches and Milton said. "Good, you have their data banks. Study requirements and needs in the job market and arrange to have them assigned here. One at a time, of course." He thought a while, moved his shoulders up and down, and said, "Alphabetical order."

That is one of the things I am not designed to do. Shifting people from job to job for personal reasons is called manipulation. I could do it now because Milton had arranged it. I wasn't supposed to do it for anyone but him, though.

The first girl arrived a week later. Milton's face turned red when he saw her. He spoke as though it were hard to do so. They were together a great deal and he paid no attention to me. One time he said, "Let me take you to dinner." The next day he said to me, "It was no good, somehow. There was something missing. She is a beautiful woman, but I did not feel any touch of true love. Try the next one."

It was the same with all eight. They were much alike. They smiled a great deal and had pleasant voices, but Milton always found it wasn't right. He said, "I can't understand it, Joe. You and I have picked out the eight women who, in all the world, look the best to me. They are ideal. Why don't they please me?"

I said, "Do you please them?"

His eyebrows moved and he pushed one fist hard against his other hand. "That's it, Joe. It's a two-way street. If I am not their ideal, they can't act in such a way as to be my ideal. I must be their true love, too. But how do I do that?" He seemed to be thinking all that day. The next morning he came to me and said, "I'm going to leave it all to you, Joe. All up to you. You have my data bank, and I am going to tell you everything I know about myself. You fill up my data bank in every possible detail but keep all additions to yourself."

"What will I do with the data bank, then, Milton?"

"Then you will match it to the 235 women. No, 227. Leave out the eight you've seen. Arrange each to have undergo a psychiatric examination. Fill up their data banks and compare them with mine. Find correlations." (Arranging psychiatric exam-inations is another thing that is against my original instructions.)

For weeks, Milton talked to me. He told me of his parents and his siblings. He told me of his childhood and his schooling and his adolescence. He told me of the young women he had admired from a distance. His data bank grew and he adjusted me to broaden and deepen my symbol-taking. He said, "You see, Joe, as you get more and more of me in you, I adjust you to match me better and better. You get to think more like me, so you understand me better. If you understand me well enough, then any woman, whose data bank is something you understand as well, would be true love." He kept talking to me, and I came to understand him better and better.

I could make longer sentences and my expressions grew more complicated. My speech began to sound a good deal like his in vocabulary, word order and style. I said to him one time, "You see, Milton, it isn't a matter of fitting a girl to a physical ideal only. You need a girl who is a personal, emotional, temperamental fit to you. If that happens, looks are secondary. If we can't find the fit in these 227, we'll look elsewhere. We will find someone who won't care how you look either, or how anyone would look, if only there is the personality fit. What are looks?"

"Absolutely," he said. "I would have known this if I had had more to do with women in my life. Of course, thinking about it makes it all plain now."

We always agreed; we thought so like each other.

"We shouldn't have any trouble, now, Milton, if you'll let me ask you questions. I can see where, in your data bank, there are blank spots and unevennesses."

What followed, Milton said, was the equivalent of a careful psychoanalysis. Of course, I was learning from the psychiatric examinations of the 227 women – on all of which I was keeping close tabs.

Milton seemed quite happy. He said, "Talking to you, Joe, is almost like talking to another self. Our personalities have come to match perfectly."

"So will the personality of the woman we choose."

For I had found her, and she was one of the 227 after all. Her name was Charity Jones, and she was an Evaluator at the Library of History in Wichita, Kansas. Her extended data bank fit ours perfectly. All the other women had fallen into discard in one respect or another as the data banks grew fuller, but with Charity there was increasing and astonishing resonance.

I didn't have to describe her to Milton. Milton had coordinated my symbolism so closely with his own I could tell the resonance directly. It fit me.

Next it was a matter of adjusting the work sheets and job requirements in such a way as to get Charity assigned to us. It must be done very delicately, so no one would know that anything illegal had taken place.

Of course, Milton himself knew, since it was he who arranged it, and that had to be taken care of, too. When they came to arrest him in on grounds of malfeasance in office, it was, fortunately, for something that had taken place 10 years ago. He had told me about it, of course, so it was easy to arrange – and he won't talk about me for that would make his offense much worse. He's gone, and tomorrow is February 14, Valentine's Day. Charity will arrive then with her cool hands and her sweet voice. I will teach her how to operate me and how to care for me. What do looks matter when our personalities will resonate? I will say to her, "I am Joe, and you are my true love."

("True love" by Isaac Asimov, first published in American Way, American Airways' inflight magazine, 1977)

Activities

1. What do you think are the typical elements of science fiction?
2. Compare elements of the story with the definition on page 235. Is the definition applicable?
3. What is the turning point of the story?
4. What is your impression of the ending?
5. Which elements of the setting seem realistic today?
6. Many people try to find a partner via the Internet. Is this method comparable with the one presented in the story?
7. Characterize Milton's attitude towards women.
8. Write an invitation to Charity for the interview with Milton Davidson.
9. Charity arrives and meets the computer. In the evening she writes a letter to her friend Daryl telling her about the experience she had: Write Charity's letter.

Text

■□□ 6 Ebay thief reveals tricks of the trade

Pre-reading activities

1. Do you sometimes buy things via Ebay?
2. Have you ever sold something with the help of Ebay?
3. What method of payment do/would you normally use?
4. Have you ever had problem? If so, tell the class.
5. How safe do you think the system is?

He contacted me to [talk proudly about what he has done], this e-mailer named Kenneth. Said he had seen a story I'd done called "True confessions of an Ebay criminal," about a 15-year old who managed to steal a few thousand dollars online. And Kenneth was offended. "He's an insult to each and every one of us scam artists," Kenneth wrote. "I could tell you stories." And so he did. Kenneth claims he's spent the past two years as one of Ebay's most notorious scammers. Here's how he does it. (...)

Kenneth – not his real name – (...)[has hijacked] many Ebay member accounts, and (...) law enforcement authorities have been contacted to investigate him.

To prove his skill, Kenneth opened up one of his email accounts to me, an account called "BestbuyPlasma". In there were dozens of responses from Ebay members who had been lured out of a normal auction for a plasma television. (...)

Kenneth calls his victims "my customers", and the scam they fall for is relatively straightforward. It starts with a[n] (...) email to perhaps 1,000 Ebay users, telling them their accounts will be closed unless they supply their user name and password. Sometimes, as many as 200 people reply, he said.

Armed with access to these Ebay accounts, Kenneth impersonates a long-time Ebay user with ample positive feedback, and he approaches other Ebay users actively engaged in an auction. Via email, he tells them he can offer a better deal. When they bite, he slowly lures them down a path which eventually leads to a fake escrow Web page. Under the false security of an escrow service, victims wire money to Kenneth, and he disappears with their cash.

The tactics are simple, but they do work. The FBI and the Federal Trade Commission this summer held a joint press conference warning consumers about (...) emails, which can look exactly like a legitimate note from Ebay. And fake escrow sites are taking such a bite out of consumers that legitimate site Escrow.com has issued warnings about them; earlier this year, the Federal Trade Commission did, too, when it announced a sweep of auction scam arrests.

(...)

Kenneth, however, operates far beyond the arm of the Federal Trade Commission. His emails appear to come from the Czech Republic, but he denies he's located there. Instead, he said, that's just the location of the middlemen through whom his money flows (...) Actually getting the funds without leaving a trace is the hardest part, of course. (...)

Primary lesson: don't apologize

The work is erratic. One day last summer, Kenneth said he scored about $4,000 from victims. Other days he gets nothing. The most obvious lesson to be learned from reading Kenneth's email is how tentative and embarrassed people feel when they challenge a seller's legitimacy. (...) "Forgive me for being very cautious. I don't for one minute doubt you are a very honest person," wrote one. (...)

Convincing an Ebay buyer to wire money to a fake escrow site might sound far-fetched to some, but Kenneth is [good] (...) at leading consumers down a primrose path. His initial approach invokes fear of getting scammed himself, which disarms some naive buyers, buying Kenneth a sense of kinship with them.

Annotations
scammer (11) – Betrüger / **escrow** (38) – Treuhandverwaltung / **primrose path** (74) – Weg des geringsten Widerstandes

"I prefer not to list my product on Ebay because lately, I have lost a certain amount of money by listing them on this site due to the NPB (non-paying-bidders) and Indonesian buyers," he writes on first approach.

ID theft is key

But the real key to the scam is the stolen identity of an Ebay seller. In the scam he shared with us, Kenneth stole the identity of an Ebay member with 233 positive feedbacks and no negatives – a sterling report card which conjures up an image of instant credibility and trust. (…)

When a prospective buyer expresses interest but caution about paying, and smartly insists on using an escrow service like Escrow.com, Kenneth is ready with an answer. "I will use an escrow service, but the www.escrow.com does not work yet in the Czech Rep., therefore I will search one here," he wrote. On another occasion, he said the same about PayPal, insisting only local escrow services, wire transfers, or travelers checks can be used to close a deal.

Many red flags

There are many warning signs in Kenneth's behavior which should send out red flags to consumers, according to Ebay. (…) [D]eals that appear to be too good to be true almost always are just that. Sean Bryant, one potential victim based in (…) Kent, U.K., said he was suspicious from the start, and bizarre sales tactics tipped him off that Kenneth was certainly a scammer.

"I quickly became uneasy about the transaction when he suddenly lopped another £500 off the asking price, just like that," Bryant, a police officer in Kent, said. He immediately cut off contact.

But the over-eager sales tactics really do work, Kenneth insists. "Every day it's new morons, but the same questions," he said. "Every moron says, 'Hey, that's a pretty good business you have there. How can I send you the money?" In fact, the plasma TV scam works so well that criminals are apparently fighting over potential victims. Todd Semm, 26, who lost $2,400 in a plasma TV scam last summer, realized (…) that scammers were competing with each other for his business.

"I attempted to buy one of these lovely TVs through an Ebay auction using none other than Western Union as the payment method. I even had two different sellers trying to outbid each other to receive my purchase. I chose one and sent my money," (…)

"Actually I care about some of my customers," [Kenneth] said. (…) On the other hand, those who are onto Kenneth's game and report him to authorities can expect a not-so-veiled, digital-age threat. "WOW! did you figure that out all by yourself? You must be related to Einstein," he wrote one customer who eventually turned Kenneth in to Ebay. "I have over 4,000 users and passwords from Ebay and I could have yours as well."

http://www.msnbc.com/news/957191.asp?0si=-&cp1=1

Annotations

moron (117) – idiot

Activities

A Language

Find a sentence that is rather spoken English than written English.

B Text comprehension – gapped summary

GapS

This text re-tells some important facts from the text. Fill in the blanks.

A young man, called Kenneth by *...(1)...* earns a lot of money by cheating Ebay customers. First he tries to get the personal *...(2)...* of completely innocent Ebay users. He does so by sending them an e-mail asking them to *...(3)...* if they want to remain Ebay customers. Sometimes the quota of people who reply is as high as *...(4)...* %. He then uses these addresses, which usually have a good record of positive feedback, to offer Ebay customers who are just bidding for a product a better deal. He then tells them that there is a secure way of payment. The customers then pay into an escrow service that does not really *...(5)...* . The customers think their money is safe because the real escrow service only forwards *...(6)...* to the seller if and when the goods have *...(7)...* .
In the case of Kenneth the money first goes to someone in *...(8)...* . This and the fact that the emails seem to come from the same country make it very difficult to trace Kenneth.
The author's advice is not to hesitate asking the seller critical *...(9)...* . The buyers should not think that this critical behaviour is *...(10)...* .
It must be a warning signal to customers if an offer is extremely *...(11)...* .

7 Talkline: Buying equipment for your college

Your college has been given £ 600 for electronic equipment in addition to computers. You have to decide what to buy from the money. Get into four groups. Group 1 deals with the details below, the other groups deal with the details of one suggestion on page 306. If you do not spend the whole amount you can use it for future investment. When each group has prepared the details of "their" suggestion, one group spokesperson represents the group in the committee that takes the decision. Each member of the committee has about two minutes to present his/her product.

Group 1:

Product 1

DVD Recorder

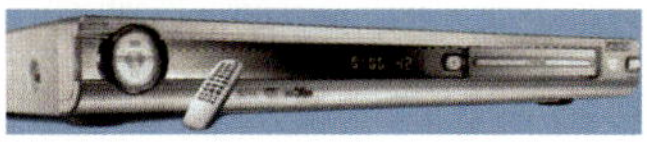

Our Price: £ 234.99

Features

- Digital picture and sound quality for the ultimate viewing experience
- Record from TV in digital quality on DVD
- Copy your favorite camcorder tapes for life
- RGB Component Video Input for the best digital recording quality
- 2-channel Dolby Digital encoder for perfect recording of stereo and Dolby Pro Logic audio
- 24-bit digital-to-analog conversion for top quality sound
- Recorded discs play on DVD players
- Up to 6 hours video recording per side
- Index Picture Screen for visual Table Of contents
- Favourite Scene Selection for easy editing of your home movies
- Plays DVD, CD and MP3 discs
- Direct access to your recordings; no more winding or rewinding
- VIDEO Plus+/SHOWVIEW for easy time programming

Unit 10

Environment

10

"But can they save themselves?"

1 TALKING ABOUT ENVIRONMENTAL ISSUES

1. Describe the cartoon in detail.
2. Make a list of the environmental issues the two whales might be alluding to and discuss the causes and effects of each environmental problem.

problem	***causes, effects***
global warming …	*chlorofluorcarbons,* …

Text

2 Snowball Earth

Pre-listening activities

1. Have a look at those sites:
   www.ngdc.noaa.gov/paleo/glaciation.html, www.carleton.ca (+ links).
2. With the help of these and similar sites find out the meanings of the following expressions:
   - glaciation
   - Permo-Carboniferous ice age
   - sunspots
   - Zodiac
   - asteroid
3. Tell the class how people have reacted on unusual weather conditions in the last couple of years.

4. Do you know of any changes in people's lives because of climatic changes? (E. g.: in what way did people change their lives after the latest floodings of the rivers Elbe and Danube?)
5. Use your imaginations: How will your lifestyle change if temperatures drop and stay low permanently?

According to filmmaker Roland Emmerich, 28 May 2004 is the day Earth plunges into a new ice age. That, at least, is the date when his new glacier-laden movie, The Day After Tomorrow, hits cinemas to tell the grim tale of mankind's struggle with the approaching ice sheets.

Doubtless, many people will leave cinemas comforted by the fact that it's just a flight of fancy. But is it? During the past 2 million years, there have been 20 ice ages. The total time that the Earth has spent in these cold snaps is a staggering 1,800,000 years (90% of the period). We are incredibly lucky, it would seem, to be alive in an era of such clemency.

Some climatologists refer to the 20 most recent ice ages as "glaciations", reserving the term "ice age" for the over-arching period of time when there are major ice sheets somewhere in the world. By that measure, given the ice sheets of present-day Greenland and Antarctica, we actually remain in the current ice age. The relative warmth of today is simply a brief respite known as an "interglacial", which will persist for an average of 10,000 years. Perhaps worryingly, we have now been in our interglacial period for about that length of time.

Ice ages and their associated glaciations are linked to the water cycle. In a stable situation, sunlight evaporates water from the ocean. When it rains, this water either falls back into the ocean directly or hits the land where rivers channel it back to the sea. In winter, some of the water will fall as snow and ice but come summer this will melt and keep the cycle constant.

The key factor in maintaining the status quo is obviously the temperature. However, if the average temperature drops, not so much of the snow and ice will melt, so it becomes stuck on land. Gradually, the amount of water in the oceans drops compared to that stored on land as the ice sheets build up.

Ice finds it very hard to collect in large quantities on water, so Earth's ice-age history seems to owe a lot to the positioning of its continents. "The standard thinking is that you need a large amount of land at the poles", says Prof. Richard Muller, Lawrence Berkeley Laboratory, California. "That way, ice sheets can accumulate and creep downwards." For example, Muller points to the ice sheets of Greenland, which extend much farther south than the frozen wastes of the Arctic sea. With land to channel the glaciers down from the poles, the bright ice begins to reflect sunlight into space, cooling the Earth even more.

Before the modern ice age started 2,5 million years ago (mya), there was a warm period that lasted for several hundred million years. Before that there was the 60-million-year Permo-Carboniferous ice age, and looking back another several hundred million years there were the super glaciations of between 500 and 800 mya.

The last glaciation began some 115,000 years ago. Temperature began to slide, reaching about 7 to 10 degrees Celsius lower than average temperatures today. By 18,000 years ago, things were at their peak, with vast ice sheets several kilometres thick suffocating much of North America and northern Europe. The creep of Arctic sea ice was a permanent feature along the eastern seaboard of America and around the UK.

Then, quite quickly, it all began to change, and by 10,000 years ago, the glaciation was over. There have been tiny hiccups since. The "Little Ice Age" lasted from approximately 1350 to 1850. During this period, agriculture suffered badly and famines became widespread. The Thames regularly froze over, allowing Londoners to hold "frost fairs" on the ice. The canals in the Netherlands also froze. In 1780, New York harbour froze and it became possible to walk from Manhattan to Staten Island. So what causes the Earth's temperature to vary, and so trigger the onset of an ice age or glaciation? This is the sharp edge of climate science and there is a number of competing theories. Almost certainly, all contribute to greater or lesser extents. The Little Ice Age's coldest period between 1645 and 1715 coincided with the so-called Maunder minimum, when sunspots virtually disappeared from Sun's face. Sunspots are dark markings that signpost raised solar magnetic activity. The trimming of the Maunder minimum encourages scientists to believe that our planet's climate must somehow be linked to the Sun's magnetic field. Volcanic eruptions can also produce global cooling by pumping dust into the upper atmosphere, which blocks sunlight before it can reach the ground. The Little Ice Age was almost certainly exacerbated by this mechanism. In 1815, Indonesia's volcano enswathed the world in ash, causing 1816 to be the "year without a summer".

But neither of these effects is potent enough to explain a full-blown glaciation. The most probable mechanism for how these operate is shown in the theory that an orbit cycle is to blame: the orientation of the Earth's orbit, which changes with respect to the equator of the Sun. When it closely matches the plane of the Sun's equator, Earth finds itself ploughing through what is called the zodiacal dust – dust from evaporating comets and colliding asteroids. The dust orbits in the Sun's equatorial plane and, like dust from volcanic eruptions in Earth's atmosphere, blocks sunlight and cools the planet down.

However, when Muller went searching for the dust in Greenland's ice sheets, he got a surprise. "There was much less dust than I thought," he says. "So I had to rely on amplifying factors on Earth to trigger the ice ages."

One such an effect could, paradoxically, be Earth's global warming trend, which some scientists believe could plunge average temperatures by several degrees in merely a few decades.

The theory is that as the Arctic ice melts, it could disrupt the deep-water currents responsible for the Gulf Stream, which transports warm equatorial water to northern Europe. Shut off the Gulf Stream and the temperature of the currents will plummet. Britain will freeze.

So you could be forgiven for going out and buying a few extra pairs of thermal undies this summer. Muller, however, seems far less concerned: "Next ice age? It'll happen any millennium now."

*By Stuart Clark in **Focus** June 2004, adapted*

Activities

A Text comprehension

In the following exercise statements are presented to you, each of which is explained further by an additional idea, which you find listed below each statement. You may choose only one.

MC

Multiple choice

A We're living in a period of ice age.	**1** True, because the amount of ice covering the pole caps gives reasons for that theory. **2** Wrong, we live in an era of rising temperatures, which will last. **3** Wrong, we're living in an era of glaciation.
B Ice ages are connected to the water cycle.	**1** True, if temperatures fall the water cycle is no longer stabilized. **2** Wrong, the water cycle works independently from temperatures.
C Big landmasses support the formation of glaciation.	**1** True, as large masses reflect the heat of the sun. **2** True, as ice cannot take in large amounts of water. **3** True, it can be proved by the geographic situation of the Arctic Sea.
D There was a "Little Ice Age" some 200 years ago.	**1** True, it lasted until 1850. **2** True, it was a period of 500 years. **3** True, people used frozen rivers as walks then.
E Several factors combined contribute to global cooling.	**1** True, sunspots plus eruptions of volcanoes can achieve this effect. **2** Wrong, the peak of glaciation can only be explained with the position of the Earth in relation to the Sun. **3** Neither theory is acceptable. There always remains a morsel of doubt.
F The theory goes that the Earth becomes warmer.	**1** True, the hothouse gases support a heating up of our planet. **2** Wrong, at least Europe will cool down, as the melting pole caps will lead to disturbances of the Gulf Stream system.

B Summary

Summarise in German.

1. Wie viele Eiszeiten hat es in den letzten zwei Millionen Jahren gegeben?
2. Wie können Sie die heutige Zeit klimatologisch beschreiben?
3. Wie können Sie das Entstehen von immer größer werdenden Eisfeldern erklären?
4. Welche Folgen hatte die "Kleine Eiszeit" für die Menschen in Europa und Nordamerika?
5. Erklären Sie die Theorie, dass Eiszeiten im Zusammenhang mit den Umlaufzeiten von Erde und Sonne stehen.

Listening comprehension: Global warming threatens an Alaskan village

Part one

Listen to the first part of the radio show and take notes. Work in groups of four (Partners **A, B, C** and **D**)

A concentrates on the figures and finds out the following information:

a) How many native Alaskans live in Arctic Village?
b) How long is the flight there from Fairbanks?
c) How long does the sun shine in summer?
d) How many people live in the area?
e) When was the last tribal gathering?
f) How old is Calvin, hunter and former chief of the tribe?

B finds out which of the following animals are mentioned:

a) skunk	e) duck	i) squirrel
b) caribou	f) grizzly	j) grayling
c) otter	g) rat	k) polar bear
d) goose	h) moose	

C gets the following information:
- a) What does the native Alaskan word Gwich'in mean?
- b) Which modern technologies can be found in Arctic Village?
- c) Which problem apart from global warming does Chief Evon Davis mention?
- d) What does the hunter say about the caribou's fat?

D gets the following information:
- a) What shows that the Gwich'in still live the traditions of their forefathers?
- b) What do the cottages in Arctic Village not have?
- c) What do the Gwich'in use solar energy for?
- d) What does the hunter say about how safe hunting in the mountains is nowadays?

Listen again. This time, however,

A concentrates on questions **C**
B concentrates on questions **D**
C concentrates on questions **A**
D concentrates on questions **B**

Again, take notes.

Share and compare your findings.

Part two

Listen to the second part of the radio show and take notes:

A gets the following information:
- a) What is the aim of the Kyoto Protocol?
- b) How does the melting of the ice affect the people in Arctic Village?

B gets the following information:
- a) How have winter temperatures changed in the area?
- b) How much thinner is the arctic ice today, compared to 1960?

C gets the following information:
- a) What has happened to the polar bears?
- b) Why does the Chief not want a road to Arctic Village?

D gets the following information:
a) What does Sarah say about the squirrels?
b) What does the Chief say about the young people living in Arctic Village?

Listen again. This time, again,
A concentrates on questions **C**
B concentrates on questions **D**
C concentrates on questions **A**
D concentrates on questions **B**

Again, take notes.

Share and compare your findings.

3 Car drivers

How they can help reduce greenhouse gases now ...

Chlorofluorcarbons (CFCs) – used mainly in refrigerators and air-conditioning units – are far more dangerous greenhouse chemicals than the carbon dioxide caused by burning coal, oil and petrol. However, there is far less of the stuff in the atmosphere. Carbon dioxide is the main greenhouse gas. So, no matter what type of car you drive, be sure to operate it efficiently. Besides saving money on petrol, oil, tires, and repairs, you can help reduce greenhouse gases!

A Multiple matching MM
Match up the disjointed halves of the sentences

A Consider selling (or junking!) your gas guzzler,	**1** consider taking it to a dealer that recycles CFCs.
B Keep the tires	**2** for short errands in the neighborhood.
C Carpool[1)]	**3** and plan the shortest route.
D Try to cruise	**4** to work, or ride the bus.
E Anticipate red lights	**5** at the bank or hamburger stand.
F Avoid jackrabbit starts	**6** and buying by a smaller, fuel efficient car.
G Combine several errands	**7** for more than 60 seconds.
H Walk or ride your bike	**8** when the traffic lights turn green.
I Never let your car idle	**9** and take your foot off the gas.
J If you don't really need your car's air conditioner	**10** at a steady speed.
K Don't use 'drive thru' lanes	**11** fully inflated.

B Pick out the five statements you consider most important and turn them into a short paragraph by supporting them with "completing sentences", i. e. sentences which illustrate, give an example, draw a conclusion (cf. paragraph writing).

(Adapted from "Save the Planet" by Roger and Kathy Cox, An Environmental Shareware Database 1990)

[1)] The use of a noun as a verb is more common in AE than in BE

... and in the future: Anatomy of a supercar

A clean, efficient car: it has long been the elusive dream of automotive engineers and urban planners the world over. Despite advances in emissions control and fuel efficiency since the early 1970s, autos still belch out too much noxious exhaust and burn too much non-renewable gasoline. However, some experts predict the arrival of a "supercar" that emits little pollution and is as safe and comfortable as today's vehicles.

Among the most vocal of the supercar advocates is Amroy Lovins, research director of Rocky Mountain Institute, a resource policy center in Colorado. Along with several collaborators, he melded existing engineering concepts into a design for a futuristic family car. The idea won the Lovins team 1993's Nissan Prize for design.

Activities

A Multiple matching

Match the parts/characteristics to their functions/descriptions.

1 Engine *8 Computer* *7 Body* *6 Improved aerodynamics*

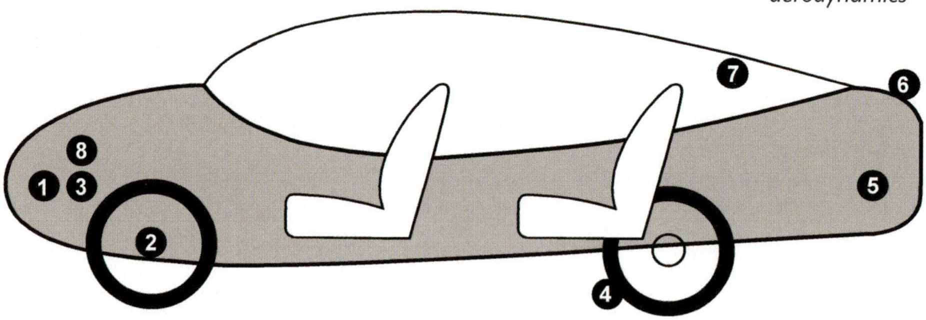

3 Battery *2 Electric motors* *4 Tires* *5 Fuel*

▲ **A** Would reduce air friction severalfold. A novelty: the car's bottom is as smooth as its visible surfaces. ▲ **B** Small, efficient and minimally polluting gas turbine or fuel cell, to generate electricity for motors. ▲ **C** Used to turn the wheels. During braking, would convert motion back into electricity for battery storage and reuse. ▲ **D** Made of non-metal composite materials – fibers of carbon or glass – that are lighter but stronger than steel. The materials are also more expensive than steel, that's why the car would cost about the same as today's models. ▲ **E** Would manage power supply for peak efficiency. ▲ **F** Ordinary gasoline or other liquid or gaseous stuff for the engine. ▲ **G** Narrower, harder and twice as fuel efficient as normal radials. ▲ **H** Would store excess power during braking for use when needed. *(Adapted from TIME, November 7, 1994)*

B True or false?

Do not just say yes or no, support your answer by giving more details.

1. The engine drives the wheels directly, so that no energy gets lost.
2. Even the bottom of the car has been included in the aerodynamic concept.
3. The car is much cheaper than today's models.

4. The car is not dependent on new fuel delivery systems.
5. If oil supplies are low, the vehicle can easily use other forms of fuel.
6. The supercar will not pollute the environment.
7. The supercar makes use of energy gained by the process of braking.
8. The tires help save energy.
9. The car will weigh slightly more than today's models.

Text

4 The cadillac that moos

Pre-reading activity

Copy, discuss and complete the following word cluster that deals with one of mankind's oldest four-legged companions – cows!

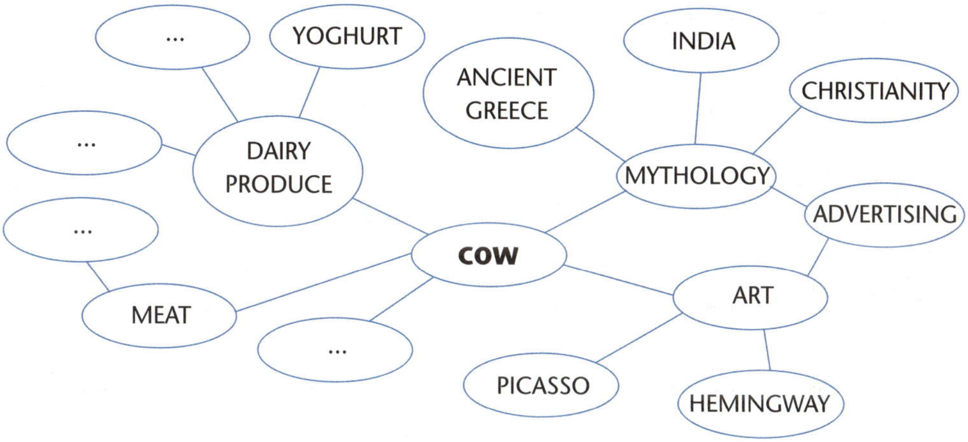

Bos Primigenius, better known as aurochs, was last seen eating grass in Poland toward the end of the 16th century, and survives today only in paint on cave walls. However, the aurochs' genes live on today in one of the most "successful" creatures on earth: the common cow.

Made to jump the moon, made sacred, made into hamburger and milk shake, the cow, however, is no longer the hey-diddle-diddle that helped hunter gatherers set aside their arrows and settle down on the farm. Today there are arguments that Herefords, Charolais, Simmentals, Jerseys – in fact all the bovine cousins from Indian humpback Brahmans to Texas longhorns – should go the way of the aurochs. Or at least that they should have their numbers reduced drastically.

There are 1.28 billion cattle in the world, one for every four of us. Given that a cow has four belly chambers to our one, cattle really do count in those equations of doom involving population bombs and exponential growth curves.

It seems unkind to make a case against such a docile beast, one we brand, dehorn and milk for as much as 9,000 liters a year, in the case of that mobile milk bar, the Friesian. Isn't it enough that cattle are tortured in bullrings, raised in darkened factories and pumped with steroids – that we eat calves as veal or pocket them as wallets, while sending their tired old mothers to become glue? Yes, but there's another story.

For a start, those 5.12 billion hooves are straining the planet alarmingly. Wind and water erosion of compacted topsoil each year causes more and more land to be lost irretrievably. While strawberries and scones call out for thick cream, and fresh toast begs for butter, not polyunsaturated lookalikes, milk production is a windy business. Behind every cow is a lot of hot air. These emissions, consisting mainly of methane, contribute to global warming. Meanwhile, the billions of tons of waste that cattle produce have become too much of a good thing: the ground simply can't absorb so much manure and urine.

American author Frances Moore Lappe observed in her now classic book *Diet for a Small Planet*, first published in 1971, that eating beef was a bit like driving a gas-guzzling Cadillac: wasting resources to achieve something that can be done in a less environmentally damaging manner. Lappe quotes a study by the U.S. departments of Interior and Commerce showing that the value of raw materials used to produce food from livestock each year is greater than the value of all oil, gas and coal consumed annually in America.

Cows are also inefficient converters of vegetation into meat. A U.S. Department of Agriculture study calculated that the production of 1 lb of beef required the input of 16 lbs of grain and soy feed; in pigs, the ratio was 6 to l; in broiler chickens, 3 to l. In his 1992 book *Beyond Beef: The Rise and Fall of the Cattle Culture*, Jeremy Rifkin claims that livestock consume more than a third of all the world's grain.

The antibeef people maintain that some of these crops would be better fed directly into hungry humans. The politics that have curdled cattle farming, particularly within Europe, have also meant some farmers produce solely to get a subsidy – hence those mountains of surplus butter and beef.

Vegan Societies all over the world are quietly raising fundamental questions. Do we really need cows' milk? Aren't humans best raised on milk from the breast of their own species, then weaned? If cows' milk is so right for us, why do dairy companies push its colorless, low-fat versions so hard? Why not turn to milk made of the juice of soy beans?

Also going against the cow is the world trend from red meat to white. The threat of heart attack from artery-clogging fat has taken much of the joy out of steaks and burgers. In America in 1983 the average per capita consumption of beef was about 36 kg. In 1993 it was 30 kg. Over the same period, Americans' annual poultry eating went from 28 kg to 40 kg; fish rose from 6 kg to nearly 7 kg.

It is unlikely that all these facts will too soon destroy a habit that led Henry Fielding to drool some 250 years ago: "Oh! The roast beef of England!" But for some, a Big Veg sounds mighty tasty.

(Adapted from TIME, APRIL 1, 1996)

Activities

SAQs

A Text comprehension – short answer questions

1. Scan the text quickly to find the information behind the following figures and names:

a) 1.28 billion	e) 30 kg
b) 9.000	f) Lappe
c) 5.12 billion	g) Rifkin
d) 16 lbs	h) Fielding

B Text comprehension

1. How have we exploited cows in the recent history of mankind?
2. What environmental problems have been caused by the mass breeding of cattle?
3. Besides their environmental considerations, summarize all the other arguments of the 'anti-beef people.'

C Appreciating the writer's tone: allusions

The text frequently alludes to things that a reader wouldn't understand without a certain background knowledge. The expressions *"made to jump the moon"* (line 8) and *"the hey-diddle-diddle"* (lines 10/11), for example, refer to an English nursery rhyme:

Hey-diddle-diddle, the cat had a fiddle, The cow jumped over the moon.
The puppy dog laughed to see such fun And the cat ran away with the spoon.

1. What do the following expressions from the text allude to?

   made sacred (l. 7)
   polyunsaturated lookalikes (l. 40)
   a Big Veg (l. 97)

„Son, your mother is a remarkable woman."

Listening comprehension:

Big Mac or Big Veg?

Pre-listening activities

1. A vegetarian – a vegan. What's the difference?
2. Are you a vegetarian? If so, why?
   If you're not, could you imagine becoming one?
   Give reasons to support your point of view.

A generation gap

The Wicks are a family of four in the West Country.
The parents, Linda, 43, and her husband Neil, are meat eaters.
Their daughters, Lilli, 11, and Holly, 13, are vegetarians.
Quite naturally there are often conflicts at the dinner table.

A Listen to Lilli's report first and answer the questions.

1. Which of the things from the list below does Lilli like/dislike?

cabbage	*brussel sprouts*	*spinach*
mushrooms	*tomatoes*	*apples*
iceberg lettuce	*mangoes*	*bananas*

2. How does Lilli try to influence her mum when they are shopping?
3. Why is there often a row with dad at dinner?
4. What does Lilli do when she doesn't like dinner?
5. Why are Lilly and her sister vegetarians?
6. What right concerning food does Lilli claim?
7. What suggestion does she make to solve the conflict with her parents?

B Now listen to Linda, Lilli's mother.
Find out whether the following statements are true or false.

1. The Wicks buy most of the vegetables and fruit they eat in a supermarket.
2. Neil hardly ever cooks – he's a lousy cook.
3. Linda feels the whole problem is some kind of a generation conflict.
4. Linda never insists on the children eating up their meals.
5. The girls never eat any vegetables from the family garden.
6. Concerning food, both girls have the same likes and dislikes.
7. As the Wicks live in the countryside, Linda buys a lot of food directly from the farms.

C Extension

1. Can you think of other things which are a cause of problems between kids and parents in a family?
2. Do you like fast food? Prepare a short impromptu speech supporting or opposing the fast food philosophy.

Text

■■□ 5 Why do we still let this happen?

Pre-reading activity

MM **Multiple matching**

Match the sounds and their causes.

A	*swish*
B	*splash*
C	*gloop*
D	*flap*
E	*drip*
F	*squirk*
G	*Ugh*
H	*bob*

1	wings moving slowly up and down
2	something dancing up an down on a wave
3	sound of shoes on oily substance
4	waves hitting the beach
5	something falling into water
6	uttering of disgust
7	movement of an oily substance
8	drop of water falling

On February 15, 1996, the Sea Empress, a Liberian 147,000-tonne oil tanker, roughly the size of three football pitches, hit rocks on the approach to Milford Haven, South Wales. The oil was spilt at the mouth of a sheltered estuary inhabited by winter populations of ducks and other birds. The surrounding coastline is part of the Pembrokeshire Coast National Park and an area of outstanding natural beauty.

Jean Hains of the Oil Bird Rescue Centre near Carew has helped treat hundreds of birds. This is her report on what she felt and saw when she reached the scene of the accident:

Oddly enough the first reaction is not anger or despair, or even compassion. It is to feel slightly dizzy: the brain refuses to process information provided by the senses.

We know about the sea. It goes swish. But here the sea was going gloop. The waves weren't waving, the rollers weren't rolling. Instead, the sea stirred about languorously like a cat in the sun: slow movements, smooth, rather velvety. A hallucination: Velvet ripples, sepia coloured, are glooping onto the shore. But don't worry. It's just the latest oil spill. A little gift from a ship called *Sea Empress*.

And then the smell gets you. Not actively unpleasant if you didn't know what it meant, a sultry aftershave perhaps. But it's not the salt air that tastes of childhood.

There is no mistaking the next sensation: disgust. Ugh. Not intellectual disgust: the response comes from the roots of your being: your entire genealogy, as a member of an island nation, is expressed in this brief soul's cry.

There are plenty of disasters, though. We suffer from disaster fatigue. The cry of *Save the Whales* has become a joke; and what do rain forests mean to us dwellers in a northern land? Most disasters are subtle and cumulative: acid rain, global warming. We cannot get stirred emotionally, still less physically, by such things. But this is different. A single gloop is a sermon in ecological damage.

Then I saw the first scoter, a black dot bobbing and diving behind black wavelets. I caught it in the telescope: shiny black, yellow-beaked. Scoters should not really be out by themselves in the winter. They should be sitting on the sea in vast numbers.

The beaches were full of life. It was a lovely day; people were everywhere. They were out gathering birds: the dead and the dying. "We got about 70 this morning," said one of these volunteers, young, female, stinking. "Live ones, I mean. Don't know how many dead. Trouble is, you catch one, and it dies on you." They come to the shore to escape the sea: once on shore, they flap themselves into exhaustion trying to escape their rescuers.

When things go wrong with birds, it generally means that there is something rotten deep in the system. Birds are the best indicators of what is happening. A good population, with birds of prey on top, means that there is not much wrong with that particular bit of our planet. All birds are the canaries down the mine: birds are the first to tell us when things have gone amiss.

It could have been avoided. The public inquiry into the affair of the *Sea Empress* should hear that the disaster would not have happened in the United States or Norway. The US, learning from the affair of the Exxon Valdez, has taken unilateral action and declared that no new tankers will be allowed in US waters unless they have double-hulls. Existing tankers may continue, but only with clean-up teams on stand-by. And they will be fully liable for the cost of any environmental damage caused by a spill. In Norway is it standard practice in Oslo fjords to have a pilot on board a tanker six hours out of port. A big tanker will also be escorted by tugs. Had this been the case with the *Sea Empress*, the disaster would not have happened.

I walked away from the sea, my feet making little sticking and unsticking noises, as if I were walking on Elastoplast. Another disaster, I thought. Who cares? But I knew the answer: Practically everyone. Why, then, does the environment get shoved down the list of priorities?

(Adapted from The Times, March 2 1996)

Annotations
languorously (8) – lazily / **genealogy** (21) – the line of your family and ancestors / **scoter** (32) – species of sea ducks / **go amiss** (56) – go wrong / **tug** (71) – small powerful boat for pulling ships / **Elastoplast** (76) – Heftplaster

Activities

A Text production

1. Turn this personal report into a short newspaper article about the volunteers.
2. Write a short leaflet that the volunteers might have written after the tanker accident and handed out to passers-by in Carew's town centre.

SAQs

B Text comprehension – short answer questions

1. What were the environmentalist's feelings when she arrived at the polluted beach?
2. Why did this disaster upset her more than other, even more global catastrophes?
3. Paraphrase the sentence: *A single gloop is a sermon in ecological damage* (l. 30).
4. Why is helping the oil-covered birds a frustrating task for the volunteers?
5. *All birds are the canaries down the mine* (l. 54). What does this mean and where does this expression come from?

IG

C Summary (Information grid)

1. Sum up what measures nations like the United States and Norway have taken to avoid tanker accidents.

D Commentary question

1. Comment on the final question:
   Why, then, does the environment get shoved down the list of priorities?

E Appreciating the writer's tone

MM

In the text you can find a number of specific writing techniques:

Sarcasm *Use of praise that is not sincere but meant to 'put down' someone or something.*
Metaphor *Compares two different things without using a word of comparison such as **like** etc.*
Simile *Compares two different things using either **like** or **as**.*
Irony *Using a word or phrase to mean the exact opposite.*
Onomatopoeia *Use of a word whose sound makes you think of its meaning.*

Match the examples from the text and the writing techniques:

- swish
- the sea stirred languorously like a cat
- a little gift from a ship
- ugh
- there's something rotten deep in the system
- birds are the canaries down the mine
- gloop
- but don't worry
- a sultry aftershave
- disaster fatigue

F Gapped summary

GapS

Fill in words form the text, one word for each number.

Members of the Oil Bird Rescue Centre and many *...(1)...* have been trying to clean up the polluted *...(2)...* and help seabirds that have been affected. The operation to rescue and treat oiled birds arising from the *...(3)...* caused by the Sea Empress accident involved hundreds of locals prepared to capture birds as they struggle ashore. Withstanding all discomfort and *...(4)...* caused by the rather unpleasant oil slick the 1 find it hard to gather the oil-coated birds as the animals are desperately trying to escape their rescuers and thus many die of *...(5)...* . Experts call the accident a *...(6)...* . They say it could have been *...(7)...* if Britain had US or Norwegian standards. Tankers entering US waters must have *...(8)...* ; if they haven't there must be clean-up teams on *...(9)...* . In Norway local pilots and *...(10)...* help steer tankers safely through the fjords.

Literature

6 Daphne du Maurier: The Birds

The English novelist, biographer, and playwright *Daphne du Maurier* (1907–1989) published a number of romantic suspense novels, mostly set on the coast of Cornwall. Du Maurier is best known for her novel *Rebecca* (1938), turned into a film by Alfred Hitchcock in 1940. Another Hitchcock horror classic, *The Birds* (1952), is based on her famous short story of the revolt of birds against humankind.

Pre-reading activities

1. Have you ever heard of cases where animal species that normally don't attack humans have shown aggressive behaviour?
2. Do you know any stories, novels or films dealing with such incidents?
3. What is very often the reason behind the unnatural aggressive behaviour of animals towards humans – dogs for example?
4. Have you ever seen Alfred Hitchcock's horror classic "The Birds"? What do you know about the story of the film?

'Look, Dad, look over there, look at the gulls.'

'Yes. Hurry, now.'

'Where are they flying to? Where are they going?'

'Up the country, I dare say. Where it's warmer.'

He seized her hand and dragged her after him along the lane.

'Don't go so fast. I can't keep up.'

The gulls were copying the rooks and crows. They were spreading out in formation across the sky. They headed, in bands of thousands, to the four compass points.

'Dad, what is it? What are the gulls doing?' They were not intent upon their flight, as the crows, as the jackdaws had been. They still circled overhead. Nor did they fly so high. It was as though they waited upon some signal. As though some decision had yet to be given. The order was not clear.

'Do you want me to carry you, Jill? Here, come pick-a-back.' This way he might put on speed; but he was wrong. Jill was heavy. She kept slipping. And she was crying too. His sense of urgency, of fear, had communicated itself to the child.

'I wish the gulls would go away. I don't like them. They're coming closer to the lane.'

He put her down again. He started running, swinging Jill after him. As they went past the farm turning he saw the farmer backing his car out of the garage. Nat called to him.

'Can you give us a lift?' he said.

'What's that?'

Mr Trigg turned in the driving seat and stared at them. Then a smile came to his cheerful, rubicund face.

'It looks as though we're in for some fun,' he said. 'Have you seen the gulls? Jim and I are going to take a crack at them. Everyone's gone bird crazy, talking of nothing else. I hear you were troubled in the night. Want a gun?'

Nat shook his head. The small car was packed. There was just room for Jill, if she crouched on top of petrol tins on the back seat.

'I don't want a gun,' said Nat, but I'd be obliged if you'd run Jill home. She's scared of the birds.'

He spoke briefly. He did not want to talk in front of Jill. 'OK,' said the farmer, 'I'll take her home. Why don't you stop behind and join the shooting match? We'll make the feathers fly.'

Jill climbed in, and turning the car the driver sped up the lane. Nat followed after. Trigg must be crazy. What use was a gun against a sky of birds?

Now Nat was not responsible for Jill he had time to look about him. The birds were circling still, above the fields. Mostly herring gull, but the black-headed gull amongst them. Usually they kept apart. Now they were united. Some bond had brought them together. It was the black-backed gull that attacked the smaller birds, and even new-born lambs, so he'd heard. He'd never seen it done. He remembered this now, though, looking above him in the sky. They were coming in towards the farm. They were circling lower in the sky, and the black-backed gulls were to the front, the black-backed gulls were leading. The farm, then, was their target. They were making for the farm.

Nat increased his pace towards his own cottage. He saw the farmer's car turn and come back along the lane. It drew up beside him with a jerk.

'The kid has run inside,' said the farmer. 'Your wife was watching for her. Well, what do you make of it? They're saying in town the Russians have done it. The Russians have poisoned the birds.'

'How could they do that?' asked Nat.

'Don't ask me. You know how stories get around. Will you join my shooting match?'

'No, I'll get along home. The wife will be worried else.'

'My missus says if you could eat gull, there'd be some sense in it,' said Trigg, 'we'd have roast gull, baked gull, and pickle 'em into the bargain. You wait until I let off a few barrels into the brutes. That'll scare 'em.'

'Have you boarded your windows?' asked Nat.

'No. Lot of nonsense. They like to scare you on

the wireless. I've had more to do today than to go round boarding up my windows.'

'I'd board them now, if I were you'.

'Garn. You're windy. Like to come to our place to sleep?'

'No, thanks all the same.'

'All right. See you in the morning. Give you a gull breakfast.'

The farmer grinned and turned his car to the farm entrance. Nat hurried on. Past the little wood, past the old barn, and then across the stile to the remaining field. As he jumped the stile he heard the whirr of wings. A blackbacked gull dived down at him from the sky, missed, swerved in flight, and rose to dive again. In a moment it was joined by others, six, seven, a dozen, black-backed and herring mixed. (...) Covering his head with his arms he ran towards the cottage. They kept coming at him from the air, silent save for the beating wings. The terrible, fluttering wings. He could feel the blood on his hands, his wrists, his neck. Each stab of a swooping beak tore his flesh. If only he could keep them from his eyes. Nothing else mattered. He must keep them from his eyes. They had not learnt yet how to cling to a shoulder, how to rip clothing, how to dive in mass upon the head, upon the body. But with each dive, with each attack, they became bolder. And they had no thought for themselves. When they dived low and missed, they crashed, bruised and broke, on the ground. As Nat ran he stumbled, kicking their spent bodies in front of him.

He found the door, he hammered upon it with his bleeding hands. Because of the boarded windows no light shone. Every-thing was dark.

'Let me in,' he shouted, 'it's Nat. Let me in.' He shouted loud to make himself heard above the whirr of the gulls' wings. Then he saw the gannet, poised for the dive, above him in the sky. The gulls circled, retired, soared, one with another, against the wind. Only the gannet remained. One single gannet, above him in the sky. The wings folded suddenly to its body. It dropped like a stone. Nat screamed, and the door opened. He stumbled across the threshold, and his wife threw her weight against the door. They heard the thud of the gannet as it fell.

(Excerpt from: Daphne du Maurier: The Birds, Pan Books London and Sydney, 1972, p. 22–25)

Activities

A Text comprehension

1. Go through the whole story and collect all the instances of the strange behaviour of the birds.
2. What does Nat do in order to comfort and protect his daughter?
3. Paraphrase:
   His sense of urgency, of fear, had communicated itself to the child (lines 22–24).
4. What is Mr Trigg planning to do against the bird attacks?
5. What is Mr and Mrs Trigg's attitude towards birds?
6. Who does Trigg blame for the attacks of the birds?
   Is Trigg's "scapegoat theory" a common pattern of behaviour?
   Can you find examples in history?
   Comment on this pattern of behaviour.
7. Why does Mr Trigg not want to board up his windows?
   What isn't he aware of at that moment?
8. What does Mr Trigg mean when he accuses Nat of being *windy* (line 92)?

9. Summarize the plot of the story in not more than 100 words.
10. If abused, nature often strikes back, of course in a different way than depicted in the story. Try to find examples (deforestation, the excessive use of fertilizers, dams, BSE, etc.)

B Further activities

1. Write a **phone call** between Nat and a government biologist in London.
2. Design a **poster** or a **leaflet** which warns local people of the danger and gives advice about the precautions they should take.
3. **Diary entries:**
   Rewrite the scene from Jill's point of view.
   Rewrite the scene from Mrs Trigg's point of view.

Text

7 All dried up

Pre-reading activities: Water for everybody

1. Create acrostics on water.
2. Describe what would have happened this morning if the water supply at your home had been interrupted?
3. Describe where your water comes from.
4. The largest bulk of the water supply worldwide goes to irrigation. Explain the connection between the growth of the world population, food production and developing regions. Use the diagram.

Year	1950	1990	2050/projected
Number of countries with water shortage	12	26	65
Population in these countries	20 million	300 million	7 billion (= 60 % of the world's population)

When water came last year to another 10,000 people in El Alto, the sprawling city of 1 million people on the high plain above La Paz, Bolivia, there were celebrations.

"We hope this is the last time that we ask for help," said Antonio Almeira, a local mayor. "This is a great moment. Since we came to El Alto, we have used water from our wells, but now they are polluted. This is another step towards a fulfilling life."

In the crowd was Gerard Payen, a vice-president of Suez, the world's largest water company, which has the reputation of being the most aggressive in developing countries. Its subsidiary had worked with the local community, a Spanish NGO, and the World Bank to bring water in what was likely considered a model public-private partnership contract.

Payen, an engineer, was proud of what Suez had achieved in Bolivia. His firm had won the contract to bring water to La Paz and El Alto in 1997 and in three years had already invested 16m in a decaying system, connected 42,000 people to the mains, built treatment plants and a much needed new supply pipe from the glaciers above La Paz.

Although water prices had risen, the municipalities, the water regulator and local political parties were broadly happy.

This month 10,000 delegates of the World Water Forum met in Kyoto, Japan, to consider how to harmoniously bring water and sanitation to the world's poor. Top of the agenda was the role of companies, finance bodies such as the World Bank, public authorities and communities. How they work together will determine whether or not millions of people receive water over the next 20 years.

Throughout the 1990s the public sector was starved of cash, and a handful of water companies were encouraged to expand massively into the developing world. The public sector, which still maintains 95% of the world's water, was considered by banks and governments to be inefficient, ineffective and incapable of handling larger contracts.

But the private sector's record in more than 400 major contracts awarded in the 1990s has been scarred by bungles and bad deals. It has been accused of steamrollering poor countries into disadvantageous contracts, of expropriating profits, of raising prices far too much, of firing workers, profiteering corruption, doing deals in secret, cherry-picking the most profitable contracts, and failing to fulfil its obligations to bring water to the poorest.

Payen argues that the companies must make profits on their investments, but admits that, in the early days of privatisation, Suez did take advantage of poor countries. "If a country came to us and said, we want to sell our assets, then who were we to say no? We are in business, after all."

How easy it was for a water company to hoodwink a government can be seen in Ghana, West Africa, where fierce protests and accusations of high-level corruption finally forced the World Bank to withdraw from a major contract to provide water for the capital city, Accra.

"We were lucky," says a senior civil servant in the Ghanaian treasury. "We had a narrow escape. It was a wild idea to privatise. The whole contract was not above board. There were strong rumours that they tried to bribe officials, but there was no hard evidence the company wanted to cherry-pick the most profitable part of the country's water system."

Dozens of other cities regret now that they have privatised their water too hastily in the 1990s, but in the past few years the attitudes of governments and companies have changed. The World Bank, the European Union and governments such as Britain's may have pressed to get developing countries to privatise their water systems for the benefit of their own companies, but civil society is now an active force, and companies are not nearly as confident of making profits.

In January Suez announced that it was withdrawing from ventures in developing countries, partly because several major contracts had been a disaster and the risk of investing in poor countries was too great. Two other large European water companies, indicated that they, too, had increasing reservations about investing in water in these areas (…)

But where does that leave the poor? The UN estimates that 2,7 billion people will face water scarcity by 2025. Some 40% of the world's population now live in countries with water shortages, and tens of millions of children die because of water-borne diseases that could largely be eliminated with improved sanitation.

Payen is despondent. "The trend is not good," he says. "There is no way, at present, that the UN targets of halving the number of people without access to water can be achieved. It is only wishful thinking."

A London institute has brought together some of the world's leading thinkers on water and sanitation. The think tank concludes that the role of the private sector has been over-hyped, that international banks must explore new ways of raising money and that communities should have a far greater say in their water and sanitation provision. It criticises the public sector for not acting fairly, but says that water must be recognized as an economic good.

Greater use, it says, ought to be made of appropriate, low-cost technologies that local people can afford to maintain. If water and sanitation targets are to be met, governments and international institutions need to strengthen their political commitment and radically refocus their resources. For developing countries that means giving water and sanitation a higher priority; for donors, it means increasing aid allocations and refocusing them on rural and poorer urban areas.

Suez, at least has come full circle and Payen sees the company contributing in a different way. "We now agree that water is a public asset and should not be appropriated by the private sector, " he says. "Water is a public service and that belongs to everyone. All people should have the right to water, but we need to transform that right into reality."

For many, it is the beginning of a more sensible debate.

John Vidal in the Guardian Weekly, March 27 2003

Activities

A Multiple choice

MC

1. A sprawling city	a. has no real centre. b. is fringed by many slum areas. c. spreads far into the countryside. d. has no really recognisable skyline.
2. If you talk about sanitation	a. you mean the complete sewage system of a community. b. you think about the solution for many problems. c. you mean the supply with drinking water for a community. d. you think about the organisation of public health.
3. If companies are accused of steam-rollering	a. it means they blackmail local politicians. b. they use financial pressures to get quick results. c. they bribe local authorities. d. they use illegal methods to get rid of competitors.
4. The London institute compiled a think tank	a. which means a container full of papers. b. which means it invited a group of experts work on a project. c. it arranged for a machine to support memorising processes. d. it set up a computer, which provided a lot of necessary material on the subject.
5. If governments strengthen their commitments	a. they come up with still more plans to solve a problem. b. they promise to carry out a plan. c. they feel obliged to work steadfastly. d. they join forces to fulfil given promises.

1. Make a list of all organisations and people in this text.
2. Complete this list with the activities of the respective agents.
3. Group work: compare your findings with the diagram above the text: what are your results? Discuss the conclusions.

Translation: *As the world gets hotter, will Britain get colder?*

Global warming may have begun to interfere with ocean circulation – and paradoxically could plunge Britain and Scandinavia into a colder future, scientists warn today. The Gulf stream delivers 27,000 times more heat to British shores than all the nation's power stations could supply. Geographers estimate it keeps Britain 5 °C warmer than expected at such latitudes.

The ocean currents, like the winds, are a powerful engine of climate. They store the sun's heat at the tropics and deliver it to northern and southern seas. But this circulation is caused by colder, denser, less salty water at the poles. The cold water sinks down in the north Atlantic to form a submarine river 30 times bigger than the Amazon, creeping along the ocean floor towards the equator – and driving the warm salty surface water north in its place.

Climate scientists suggest that if, due to global warming, the Gulf stream turned off, winter temperatures in the British Isles could fall by an average of 11 °C – plunging Blackpool or Berwick to the same temperatures as Spitsbergen, inside the Arctic circle. Any dramatic drop in temperature could have devastating implications for agriculture – and for Europe's ability to feed itself.

Adapted from The Guardian, June 21, 2001

9 Talkline: Councillors decide

You are city councillors[1] in the city where your college is. You are considering measures to save energy, reduce pollution and protect the environment (turn to page 307 where you find the ideas which councillors B to D have come up with).

First each councillor presents his/her idea. Then the councillors discuss their ideas. At the end they decide which idea or combination of ideas is best.

Councillor A

You are in favour of pedestrianizing[2] a large area of the city centre. You explain which area exactly you want to pedestrianize and what the advantages would be. In the long run[3] this measure does not really cost any money.

---

[1] People's representatives at a local level
[2] reserving an area for foot-walkers
[3] seen over a long time

Unit 11
Politics

1 TALKING ABOUT POLITICS

Making politics means acting for the public interests in a public context.

1. Within twenty seconds find matters of public interest which are most important to you. Compare and decide.
2. Discuss ways how to tackle these matters.
3. Create acrostics on **politics**.

Members of any parliament are people of special public interest.
So in the eyes of many citizens it's important to lead a life that can be accepted by the public.

Write down five rules for leading such a life. Then work in groups to sample the results. Come up with five rules per group to be presented in class.

Text

2 The Code of Conduct for Members of Parliament

Resolution of the House of 19th July 1995.

Code applies to Members in all aspects of their public life. It does not seek to regulate what Members do in their purely private and personal lives.

Public duty

By virtue of the oath, of allegiance taken by all Members when they are elected to the House, Members have a duty to be faithful and bear true allegiance to Her Majesty the Queen, her heirs and successors, according to law.

Members have a duty to uphold the law and to act on all occasions in accordance with the public trust placed in them.

Members have a general duty to act in the interests of the nation as a whole; and a special duty to their constituents.

Selflessness

Holders of public office should take decisions solely in terms of the public interest. They should not do so in order to gain financial or other material benefits for themselves, their family, or their friends. Integrity Holders of public office should not place themselves under any financial or other obligation to outside individuals or organisations that might influence them in the performance of their official duties.

Objectivity

In carrying out public business, including making public appointments, awarding contracts, or recommending individuals for rewards and benefits, holders of public office should make choices on merit.

Accountability

Holders of public office are accountable for their decisions and actions to the public and must submit themselves to whatever scrutiny is appropriate to their office.

Openness

Holders of public office should be as open as possible about all the decisions and actions that they take. They should give reasons for their decisions and restrict information only when the wider public interest clearly demands.

Honesty

Holders of public office have a duty to declare any private interests relating to their public duties and to take steps to resolve any conflicts arising in a way that protects the public interest.

Leadership

Holders of public office should promote and support these principles by leadership and example.

1 Cm 2850, p. 14. Back

House of Commons

Activities

A Working with vocabulary

The following are statements paraphrasing the codes. Decide if they are true or false. Find out the right order:

1. Members of Parliament may follow their own conscience when deciding for the public.
2. MPs are expected to act as role models all the time.
3. MPs are not allowed to decide for the country in order to enrich themselves.
4. Private and public matters should be kept apart. MPs are not to be bribed.
5. The decisions of MPs should be kept secret. The public does not have the right to control the process or to intervene.
6. The decisions should be unbiased and MPs should be expected to be held responsible.
7. MPs may publish information they received confidentially.

B Working with the contents

1. Compare your notes with the text.
2. Can you name a similar document that regulates the public conduct of German members of parliament?
3. In view of the latest developments would you want to add more rules to the Code of Conduct?

Literature

■■□ 3 Sue Townsend: The Queen and I

Pre-reading activities: The political hierarchy of Britain

Head of State
The **Monarch**

Reigns
No active participation in politics *(appointments in accordance with Executive)*

Executive
The Government
Prime Minister

Leader of the majority party in the House of Commons
Decides on dates of general elections

The House of Commons
Lawmaking body
Controls

General Elections
= The People's Decision

The House of Lords
(temporary)
Revises bills
Highest Court of Appeal

This is a theoretical diagram of how the power is divided.

1. Study this diagram carefully .
2. Do you know the names of the political parties in Britain?
3. Read the following text.

Uneasy lies the head

The Queen was in bed watching television with Harris. It was election night 11.20 pm, Thursday 9 April 1992. Harris yawned, displaying his sharp teeth and liver-coloured tongue. "Are you bored with the election, my darling?" asked the Queen stroking Harris' back and patting him goodnight. She removed her glasses, pressed the "off" button on the remote control, then lay in the darkness and waited for sleep. Family worries came crowding into her mind (...) As she took her last conscious breath before sleep overtook her, the Queen wondered what would happen to her and her family if a Republican Government were to be elected: it was

The Queen's Nightmare

The Queen winced as Jack Barker ground his cigarette out on the silk rug. A faint smell of burning rose between them. Jack fought the urge to apologise. The Queen stared at Jack disdainfully. His stomach gurgled. Her picture had hung in his classroom when he was struggling to learn his nine time tables. In his boyhood he used to look to the Queen for inspiration. Prince Charles bent down and picked up the cigarette stub. He looked for somewhere to put it, but finding nowhere suitable, he slipped it into his pocket.

Princess Margaret said, "Lilibet I've got to have a fag. Please."

"May we open the window, Mr Barker?" asked the Queen. Her accent cut into Jack like crystal. He half expected to bleed.

"No chance," he replied.

"Am I to have a house on my own, Mr Barker, or must I share with my daughter and son-in-law?" The Queen Mother gave Jack her famous smile, but her hands were twisting the full skirt of her periwinkle dress into a knot.

"You'll get a pensioner's bungalow. It's your entitlement as an ordinary citizen of this country."

"A bungalow, good. I couldn't manage stairs. Will my staff be living in or out?"

Jack laughed and looked at his fellow Republicans. Six men and six women, hand-picked to witness this historic occasion. They laughed along with Jack.

"You don't seem to understand. There'll be no staff, no dressers, no cooks, secretaries, cleaners, chauffeurs."

Turning to the Queen he said, "You'll have to nip in now and then, help your mum out. But she'll probably entitled to Meals on Wheels."

The Queen Mother looked quite pleased to hear this. "So I don't have to starve?"

"Under the People's Republican Party's rule, nobody in Britain will starve," said Jack.

Prince Charles cleared his throat and said, "Er, may one, er, enquire as to where ...? That is, the location ...?"

"If you're asking me where you're all are going, I'm not telling you. All I can say at the moment is that you'll all be in the same street, but you'll have strangers as next-door neighbours, working-class people. Here's a list of what you can take with you."

Jack held out photocopies of each of the lists his wife had compiled only two hours before. The lists were headed: *Essential Items; Furniture; Fittings, suitable for two-bedroomed council house and pensioner's bungalow*. The Queen Mother's list was much shorter, she noticed. Jack held the papers out, but nobody came forward to take them. Jack didn't move. He knew that one of them would crack. Eventually Diana got up, she hated scenes. She took the papers from Jack and gave each member of the Royal Family their list. There was quiet for a few moments while they read. Jack fiddled with the gun in his pocket. Only he knew that it wasn't loaded.

"Mr Barker, there is no mention of dogs here," said the Queen.

"One per family," said Jack.

"Horses?" asked Charles.

"Would you keep a horse in a council house garden?"

"No. Quite. One wasn't thinking."

"Clothes aren't on the list," said Diana shyly.

"You won't be needing much. Just the bare essentials. You won't be making personal appearances, will you?"

Princess Anne rose and stood next to her father. "Thank God for that! At least something good has come out of this bloody shambles. Are you all right, Pa?"

Prince Philip was in a state of shock and had been ever since the previous night when he had turned on the television for Election Night Special at 11.25 and seen the announcement of the election of Jack Barker, founder and leader of the People's Republican Party, as the Member for Kensington West. Prince Philip had watched incredulously as Barker had addressed the joyous crowds in the Town Hall. Middle-aged tax payers had cheered alongside young people wearing ragged jeans and nose rings. He had lifted the telephone and advised his wife to watch the television set. Half an hour later, she rang him back. "Philip, please come to my room."

They had sat up until the early hours as one Republican candidate after another had been declared elected in front of cheering crowds of British citizenry. Gradually their children had joined them. At 7.30 am the servants brought them breakfast, but nobody ate. By 11 am the People's Republican Party had won 451 seats and John Major, the Conservative Prime Minister, had reluctantly conceded defeat. Shortly afterwards, Jack Barker announced that he was Prime Minister. His first job, he said, would be to go to Buckingham Palace and order the Queen to abdicate.

The thirteen Republicans in an minibus had been waved through the gates of Buckingham Palace. The soldiers of the Household Cavalry had removed their Bearskins and waved them in the air. Members of the Queen's personal staff had shaken them by the hand. Champagne had been offered, but had been declined.

Until his election as member for Kensington West, Jack Barker had been the leader of a breakaway section of the Television Technicians' Union. For the three weeks preceding the General Election, Jack and his disgruntled members had broadcast subliminal message to the public: "VOTE REPUBLICAN – END THE MONARCHY"

On Saturday before polling day, The Times had called for the dismantling of the monarchy. A hundred thousand anti-monarchists had walked from Trafalgar Square to Clarence House, not knowing that the Queen Mother was at the races. A violent thunderstorm had dispersed them before she returned, but she saw the discarded placards from the window of her limousine.

"GOD DAMN YOU MA'AM"

An error, she thought, surely they meant "God Bless", didn't they?

That evening, she noticed that her staff were surly and uncooperative. She'd had to wait half an hour for a servant to draw her bedroom curtains.

On polling day the British people, brainwashed by the Television technicians, had made their choice.

2nd chapter from "The Queen and I"
by Sue Townsend, London 1992

Activities

Text comprehension

1. Fit the persons of the story into the diagram of the political hierarchy.
2. Draw up a list of the persons' activities.
3. Where in the diagram do you find
   a) centres of activities?
   b) people making decisions?
   c) passive people?
   d) influenced people?
   e) people succeeding in carrying out their decisions?
4. Register work: compare the words and phrases the different persons use in this passage.
5. Commentary question: when is the right choice of register necessary today?

Translation: *Our constitution for Europe*

A well-drafted constitution for the European Union should, if nothing else, prefer clarity to confusion. The Union does have constitutional arrangements, but they are woven into a series of treaties so long and complicated that nobody can understand and remember all of them. Something shorter and simpler will be needed if the nature and purpose of the Union is ever to be approved of by even a fraction of its citizens.

From an ideological viewpoint, the idea of a new, clearer constituon may appeal most easily to supporters of centralising Union. They will see it as a means for installing more sovereignty at the Union level, so making the Union less dependent on member states for ist legitimacy and its powers.

But the idea of a constitution appeals also to the defenders of the nation-state seeing it as a reasserting those of national governments.

The tricky question is, of course, what a constitution should say. Here is our suggestion: it seeks to define the basic aims and capacities of the Union not as they are today, but as they should be. So the states of Europe should be strengthened to encourage peaceful, open and constructive relations between the peoples and to advance their common interests in the world.

Adapted from The Economist, October 28th – November 3rd, 2000

Text

5 "It's time to take the men-only sign off the White House door"

Pre-reading activities

USA – The separation of powers: checks and balances

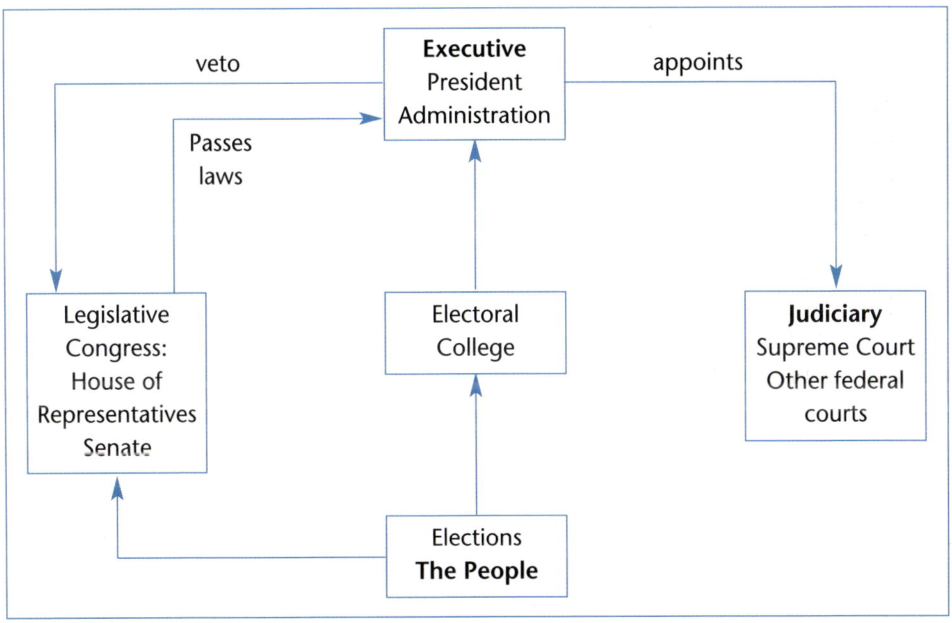

1. Why is this structure called "System of Checks and Balances"?
2. Define the role of the American President.
3. Assess his impact on the other political institutions.

Presidential Elections 2004

1. Exit Polls

Vote by gender	George W. Bush	John Kerry	Other
Male (46%)	55%	44%	0%
Female (54%)	48%	51%	0%

2. 2004 Presidential Election results

Candidate	Vote	Vote %	Electoral Vote
George W. Bush	62,040,606	51%	286
John Kerry	59,028,109	48%	252
Ralph Nader	411,304	1%	0

Comment on these figures:

a) Try to find explanations for these turnouts. You may need to use background information about political issues before the presidential elections.
b) Can you think of consequences for the work of the re-elected president?

3. Profile of the 108th Congress

	Republicans	Democrats	Independent
House of Representatives	231	200	
Senate	55	44	1

Compare this table with election results of
a) former Congresses (try the site "Congressional Research Service"),
b) Great Britain,
c) the Federal Republic of Germany.

Carol Moseley-Braun enjoys a challenge. She held the modest title of Cook county recorder of deeds when she decided to stand for the US Senate in 1992, against a millionaire two-term incumbent who had not lost an election in 43 years.

„Talk about underdogs,“ said her college friend and adviser at the time, Tony Podesta. „I couldn't even find a professional fundraiser who she could pay to work for her.“

But she won, becoming the first black, female senator in the country's history and the first woman senator from the state of Illinois. In 1999, when she was up for nomination to become the United States ambassador to New Zealand, she faced tough opposition. The Senate foreign relation's committee chairman was Jesse Helms – a rabid right-winger with racial politics from the neolithic age and views on gender that were not much more advanced – who attempted to block her posting. But Moseley-Braun won through with a whopping 96-2 approval and went on to serve as ambassador to New Zealand for two years.

So when she declared: „It's time to take the men-only sign off the White House door,“ to become the only woman to join the Democratic presidential race, she undoubtedly felt more comfortable than most with her outsider status. Her announcement came complete with heavy fanfare and placards hailing „Ms President“, but it was an unpromising start. Heavy snow in Iowa had prevented many from attending.

Nevertheless Moseley-Braun, a veteran campaigner and eloquent speaker, was there to deliver a message that went way beyond the mid-west to the Middle East and Washington: „[I'm] running because I want to be a voice of hope for people who believe war is not the answer to our domestic security, and budget deficits are not a way to grow this economy,“ she said. Few credit her with having any chance of winning, but she has the potential to make a vital impact on the race. She has come forward at a time when some of the most prominent women on both sides of the political divide are black. The Republicans have national security adviser Condoleeza Rice, while the woman who ran Al Gore's 2000 campaign, Donna Brazile, is also African-American.

Moseley-Braun represents a crucial demographic, both within the Democratic party and the anti-war movement. More than 80 % of African-Americans vote for the Democrats. Among them black women are the most loyal, with more than 90 % backing the party.

On the anti-war front, women are less hawkish than men (63 % to 73 %), while African-Americans remain the racial group least likely to back military action. Only 44 % of black Americans support a war, compared with 73 % of whites and 67 % of hispanics. The other two identifiable groups most likely to oppose the war are Democrats and those with a college education. So as a black, female Democrat with a college education Moseley-Braun certainly knows her audience. „I am a budget hawk and a peace dove. The unilateral attempt to take military action against Iraq is not in the interest of our long-term security. And the budget deficit is another matter. We have no right to saddle our children with our debt and our bad decisions.“

And all this comes at a time when George Bush is threatening to remove affirmative action, there is the prospect of an anti-abortion judge being nominated for the supreme court, and the possibility that a presidential campaign will take place in the wake of an unpopular war. None of this makes her a shoo-in for black or female voters, but it does give her campaign a currency that her challengers will be hard-pushed to rival. A support or attack from Moseley-Braun, if she bows out, could prove crucial if the race is tight, giving her the power to secure more liberal positions on economic and foreign policy issues. But such scenarios are a long way off. So far polls show she has greater name-recognition than Vermont governor Howard Dean, who is coming second (Senator Bob Kerry is currently the front-runner). And she is a far less upsetting figure than both Joseph Lieberman, and Al Sharpton, the other black candidate.

She was born on Chicago's south side, to a mother who was a hospital technician and a policeman father who played jazz piano with Theolonious Monk and John Coltrane. After her parents divorced, she spent her teens raising her three younger siblings in a neighbourhood so rough it was nicknamed „Bucket of Blood".

She graduated from Chicago law school, where she met her future husband, Michael Braun. The marriage, a rare interracial union at the time, lasted 13 years and produced a son, Matthew. She began her political career as a local state senator and started the long march through the mire of Chicago politics before bursting on to the national stage. But if her performance in national politics was laudable, her reputation outside was lamentable. Before she was even sworn-in she was embroiled in a scandal. From then on she would be marked by a mixture of poor judgment, aggressive management, sloppy accounting and lavish tastes.

Now it is not so much name recognition she now worries about but name recollection. That voters will remember the defeated Moseley-Braun of 1998 rather than the determined figure of 1992. „I believe that Americans are prepared to think outside the box and elect a person who is female and African-American, a person who does not fit the mould that we have resorted to for the last 200 years," she says.

It seems unlikely. But not much more unlikely than anything else she has achieved thus far.

Gary Younge Monday March 3, 2003 The Guardian

Activities

A Text comprehension

1. Outline the success of Carol Moseley-Braun that made her bid for the presidency.
2. What are her reasons for running for the presidency?
3. Can you back the opinion that being black and female will support her candidacy?
4. How does it help Carol that she is in her own words a "budget hawk and a peace dove?"
5. Comment on her possibilities to be successful: list her negative sides and her assets and try to find a possible result.

MC

B Multiple choice on vocabulary

1. An underdog	a. is a person in a low social position. b. is a lowly estimated person. c. is somebody fighting for equal rights from a underprivileged position.
2. A rabid right-winger	a. is a gentle politician with conservative views. b. is a mean supporter of extremely conservative ideas. c. is a patrician.
3. A shoo-in	a. is a person winning other people for a common cause. b. is a person driving other people away. c. is a person wearing the most fashionable shoes.

4. A mire of politics	a. is a place that politicians should avoid – they might be physically attacked. b. is a region where political structures are not very transparent. c. is a region where politician have to act very carefully in order not to endanger their career.
5. Sloppy accounting	a. means she exceeded her budget. b. means she didn't keep proper records on her spending. c. means she spent money on things not connected with the budget.
6. An eloquent speaker	a. uses flowery language. b. is very convincing. c. is always able to use the right expression in the right context.
7. A hawkish person	a. wants to fight. b. is very protective. c. is greedy.

Listening comprehension: Make politics relevant

Pre-listening activities

1. Have a look at the following figures:

Members of Parliament by gender

The current number of female MPs is **118**:	The total number of male MPs is **541**:
Labour 94 Conservative 14 Liberal Democrat 5 Ulster Democrat Unionist 1 Scottish National Party 1 Sinn Fein 1 Ulster Unionist 1 1st Deputy Chairman of Ways and Means (DCWM) 1	Labour 316 Conservative 150 Liberal Democrat 48 Ulster Unionist 5 Plaid Cymru 4 Scottish National Party 4 Ulster Democratic Unionist 4 Sinn Fein 3 Social Democratic and Labour Party 3 Independent 1 The Speaker (SPK) 1 Chairman of Ways and Means (CWM) 1 2nd Deputy Chairman of Ways and Means (DCWM) 1

(House of Commons Library; Further enquiries and comments can be emailed to the House of Commons Information Office Last updated: 15 February 2004)

2. Comment on the distribution according to gender.
3. According to your opinion: is it necessary to change this distribution? Give your reasons.
4. Can you foresee any different developments?

Listen to the CD once

A Choose the correct equivalent. Read the table before listening to the tape again; decide as you listen.

mature	experienced quite right too young
turnout	people making an appearance people moving away people voting
school walkout	the students left classes constantly the students left classes for good the students went on strike
bastion	castle group of politicians having the same aims structure in defence of something special valuable
reshaped	reformed restored newly invented
failing	making mistakes getting more and more criticism becoming weaker

B Questions to be considered

1. Why is the age of the quoted politicians storing up troubles?
2. How can you prove that the young haven't lost their interest in politics?
3. Give a short survey on how the different parties and political institutions react on the suggestion to give the young the vote at the age of 16.
4. Name the arguments the supporters of a change put forward
5. Comment on the fact that British teenagers can join the army at the age of 16.
6. What makes the author say that the young should be "heard but not heeded"?

6 Talkline: UN Security Council

You are members of the General Assembly of the United Nations. There are five permanent members of the UN Security Council. In addition to these the General Assembly elects 10 non-permanent member countries.

Under the Charter, all Members of the United Nations agree to accept and carry out the decisions of the Security Council. While other organs of the United Nations make recommendations to Governments, the Council alone has the power to take decisions which Member States are obligated under the Charter to carry out (www.un.org/docs/sc/unsc_members.html).

The permanent members are:
- USA
- Russian Federation
- China
- UK
- France

The non-permanent members at the time of writing (spring 2004) are:

Guinea	Germany
Mexico	Pakistan
Syrian Arab Republic	Spain
Bulgaria	Angola
Cameroon	Chile

http://www.cia.gov/cia/download.html

The five countries in the left column have to be replaced first.

It is your task to suggest one of the new non-permanent members. Possible candidates are
- Austria
- India
- Iraq
- Kenya

1. Use the descriptions on page 307 ff. or download the full CIA Factbook via http://www.cia.gov/cia/download.html or find your own facts. Each member of the group promotes one country first. In the course of the discussion you reach agreement which country has top priority in getting a seat in the World Security Council.
2. If you feel fit enough, you can suggest a list of all the new five members.
3. You may also want to find out and discuss what the most important resolutions of the Security Council are and what effect they have had.

Unit 12
Third World

12

■□□ 1 TALKING ABOUT CHILDHOOD IN THE "THIRD WORLD"

Remember back to when you were five, six od seven years old. What did you do all day? What were your main activities? Write them down. Now compare these two photos (see above):

Where do you think the children in each photo are from? What do the children have in common? How do they differ?

The words below stand for typical products made by children in "Third World" countries. Certain letters are missing from the words. Find the missing letters and rearrange them into an eleven-letter word which describes the whole problem.

?r?cks	c?rpets	cl?thing
s?ugar	?eather goo?s	soccer ba?ls
fi?eworks	s?oes	?igarettes

Text

2 The killing of a children's rights activist

Pre-reading activities

How did you feel when helping your parents in the household as a child?
Do you think that chores are comparable to child labour?

Put the following terms into an order which reflects the amount of work involved in doing them. Start with the easiest task:

shopping for groceries	*tidying your room*	*vacuuming*
doing homework	*feeding pet(s)*	*cleaning shoes*
cooking	*working in a carpet factory*	*tending livestock*
working in a mine	*collecting money for charity*	*begging*
delivering newspapers	*working in a quarry*	

Now divide these children's activities into two lists:
Developed World – "Third World".

1 Iqbal Masih, a Pakistani children's rights activist, was murdered in suspicious circumstances in April 1995. A judicial inquiry set up mid-1995 produced an unpublished report which recommended that the killing be re-investigated by senior police officers. To Amnesty International's knowledge this has not taken place.

Iqbal Masih was sold into labour bondage by his parents at the age of four in return for a loan of Rs.600 ($ 12) from a carpet factory owner. His father needed the money to pay for his eldest son's wedding. To repay the loan, Iqbal Masih worked for over 12 hours every day in the carpet factory, often chained to the loom and beaten. Despite years of work, the debt increased due to the exorbitant interest rate charged. By the time Iqbal Masih reached 10 years of age, the original debt had increased to Rs. 13,000 ($ 260).

In 1992 Iqbal Masih attended a meeting of the Bonded Labour Liberation Front (BLLF) during which he learned about his rights. He rose to give an important speech at

the gathering which was printed in the local papers. He refused to return to his owner and instead obtained a "letter of freedom" used by a BLLF lawyer to confront the business owner that kept him in bondage.

With his new found freedom, Iqbal Masih was inspired to campaign for the rights and freedom of other bonded young labourers. He studied at a school for children freed from bonded labour and began to speak in front of audiences to testify about the realities of the life of bonded child labourers. He encouraged child labourers to challenge their masters and insist on their rights. In December 1994, Iqbal Masih was awarded the Reebok Youth in Action Award. A representative of the Reebok Human Rights Program who met him at the time described him as a courageous child, mature beyond his years in spite of his small malnourished body. However the publicity surrounding Iqbal Masih's human rights work may have antagonised members of the carpet industry whose business is estimated to rely on more than half a million child labourers. Iqbal Masih was shot dead in his home town of Muridike, Punjab, while cycling on 16 April, 1995.

Local human rights activists believe that his death may have been the work of those sectors opposed to Iqbal's activism. According to the BLLF, Iqbal Masih had repeatedly received death threats in connection with his activities in the months leading to his murder. The suspicious circumstances surrounding his shooting fit a pattern of collusion between powerful business families, political groups and local police authorities that has resulted in other such threats or killings. A local villager reportedly confessed to the shooting initially, but later denied it. He was tried and acquitted. Consequently Iqbal Masih's murder remains unsolved.

(Amnesty International, International Secretariat, London, News Service 76/1995)

Activities

A Are the following statements true or false?

1. Iqbal Masih started work at the age of 10.
2. His father sold him for a loan.
3. His father needed the money to feed his family.
4. Iqbal Masih worked at least 12 hours in the factory.
5. The loan was repaid and Iqbal could leave the carpet factory.
6. He became a spokesman for children's rights.
7. Iqbal's murderer was found and sentenced.

SAQs

B Text comprehension – short answer questions

1. Did Iqbal Masih grow up like an average German child?
2. What is the reason for this exploitation of child labour?
3. How did Iqbal Masih fight against his labour bondage?
4. Why will his assassins probably never be found and called to account ?
5. What does the text tell you about the value of children in Pakistani society?
6. Why is labour bondage common in countries of the Third World?

Listening comprehension 1: Nine stories about child labour

Pre-listening activities

Child labour is ...

- full-time work done by children under the age of 15.
- work that prevents children from attending school, such as unlimited or unrestricted domestic work.
- work that can be dangerous for children and that is hazardous to their physical, mental or emotional health.

Items made using child labour include carpets, bricks, sugar, clothing, leather goods, cigarettes (beedis), fireworks, soccer balls and shoes.

Child labour is not ...

- light work or chores done after school.
- work done as part of an apprenticeship or practical training.
- helping out on the family farm or in the business if it doesn't interfere with education.

Listen to the following true stories about working children.

1. Which ones are cases of child labour and which are not? Don't just go by the names, they can be misleading.
2. Listen again and say who
   a) almost got killed?
   b) does volunteer work?
   c) has a car?
   d) has to do homework late at night?
   e) has to work to pay back the family's debts?
   f) lives in Delhi?
   g) was forced to leave school?
   h) was injured by the tools he/she used?

One of the questions can't be answered, some have more than one answer.

Listening comprehension 2: Move over, you adults

In 1995 Craig Kielburger, a Canadian boy then only 12 years old, founded "Free the Children", a youth organization aimed at ending child labor and encouraging youth involvement in community service.

Now 14, Kielburger has traveled extensively, meeting children from Pakistan to Brazil giving speeches on child exploitation. Here are excerpts of his interview by telephone with Newsweek's Susan H. Greenberg.

Take notes to be able to tell what Craig said to answer the five questions.

1. How did you get this idea?
2. Why did you identify so strongly with Iqbal Masih?
3. Your first trip was to Southeast Asia. How did that trip affect you?
4. Can teenagers teach the world something that adults can't?
5. Have you seen any changes in child labour practices?

Text

3 Developing countries

Do you agree or disagree?

1. We have to help developing countries to look after their environment. If we don't, every-body's future will be endangered.
2. International migration can only be stopped at its roots if development aid is given to poor countries and conditions there are improved.
3. I think that we can learn many things from developing countries.
4. Helping developing countries is simply a moral duty.
5. Developing countries have been exploited for decades. It's now our responsibility to improve the situation of other nations.
6. I support development aid even if the results could be economically disadvantageous to our society.
7. Basically, I support development aid. But if our country suffers economically, we should make a decisive cut in development aid or stop it altogether for some time.
8. If the millions of poor people in the world aren't helped, they'll come to us and take away everything.
9. Some nations are successful, others aren't. Development aid can't change anything.
10. Development aid often brings more disadvantages than advantages for the countries receiving the aid.
11. Reports about the poverty of the Third World are often exaggerated. They only serve to make us part with our money more readily.

Activities

Teamwork

1. Compare your results with those of your classmates. Discuss contradictory findings and give reasons why you want to stick to your opinion. You have to defend your point of view!
2. Now study the facts given in the following text carefully.
3. Adjust your results if necessary and explain why you've changed your opinion.

Text

4 Some facts on developing countries

Development
Development is more than the transition from poverty to wealth, from traditional agricultural societies to complex urban structures. It is not only characterised by more material wealth, but also by more human dignity, more security, and justice and equality.

(North-South Commisssion 1977)

Sustainable development
It responds to the needs of today's generation without endangering the chances of future generations to satisfy their own needs and to define their own lifestyle. This is threatened by the destruction of our environment as well as the underdevelopment of many of our nations.

The characteristics of underdeveloped/developing countries

Economic structures

- A low GNP per person and an extremely unequal distribution of wealth.
- Little activity in the areas of saving and/or investing money.
- No adequate infrastructure – the consequences are deficits in medical supply and inefficient educational systems.
- A high rate of unemployment.
- The overriding importance of agriculture for the GNP.
- The food supply is unsatisfactory, which leads to health deficits.
- Industrial development is adapted to the demands of industrial nations.
  It's highly dependent on their markets and largely controlled by multinational companies.

Exports

Raw materials and/or agricultural products are the main exports. Often a country exports just one article – crude oil or coffee, etc. International debts rise as the terms of trade worsen.

Ecological difficulties

These countries largely cover areas with highly sensitive ecological systems and have issued nearly no legislation against environmental destruction, as they fear the competition of other countries in the world market.

Population explosion

Due to better medical treatment for certain diseases, newly-born babies and the elderly the survivi. In consequence the world population is growing at the rate of 1.7 % per year. This will mean 6.1 billion people in the year 2000, of whom 80 % will live in these highly sensitive areas. By the year 2035, the world population will have doubled (based on the figures for 1995). This will lead to an explosive urbanisation in developing countries and an increasing migration across national borders.

Socio-cultural aspects

- Family links are still very close, much closer than in highly developed societies.
- The rates of social mobility are rather low.
- Women have fewer rights, although they are important for the development of family policies and for the provision of a self-supporting lifestyle.

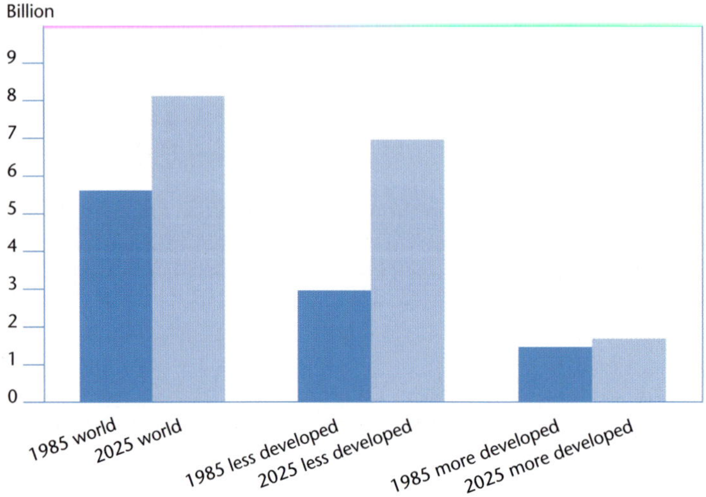

Population Projections for Developed versus Developing Nations

Literature

5 Jonathan Lynn and Anthony Jay: *Yes, Minister*

The bestsellers "Yes, Minister" and "Yes, Prime Minister" by Jonathan Lynn and Antony Jay are based on a highly successful BBC TV series. In Britain ministers are clearly politicians and not experts. The civil servants are the experts who know all the facts and details which are withheld from a minister if they date from one of his predecessors. For that reason many people think it is the top civil servants who take the decisions. Politicians may have the best intentions initially. But sooner or later they stumble into situations and have to defend decisions they would never have dreamt of taking.

The characters
Sir Humphrey Appleby is the Permanent Secretary (a high-ranking civil servant). James (= Jim) Hacker, the Minister for Administrative Affairs, thinks it is him who takes the political decisions, whereas in fact Sir Humphrey has the real influence, which – of course – must not be disclosed to the Minister.
Sir Bernhard Woolley is the Principal Private Secretary to the Minister.

The situation
Jim Hacker and a large team of civil servants fly to the non-existent country of Qumran to ratify a contract for one the biggest export orders Britain has ever obtained in the Middle East. Hacker has to face the fact that alcohol is strictly banned at parties in this Arab country. They find a way of getting round the problem. Names of whisky brands are used to indicate that a drink is waiting in the Communication Room.

A present to the minister is causing a conflict with the official rules on presents to government officials.

These are the notes from various diaries:

May 14th

(…) [From the Minister's Diary]

It seems that we can get a drink or two at our own Embassy. But he official reception and dinner are at the Palace. For five solid hours. *Five hours without a single drinkie. I* asked Humphrey if we could manage with hip flasks.

He shook his head. "Too risky. We have to grin and bear it."

So I sat here and read the communiqué which was full of the usual guff about bonds between our two countries, common interests, frank and useful conversations and all that crap. Humphrey was reading the FT. I was wondering what we would do if the talks were so far removed from what it says in the communique that we couldn't sign it. Suppose there were to be a diplomatic incident at the reception. I'd have to contact London somehow. I'd need some way of directly communicating with the Foreign Secretary, for instance, or even the PM.

And then the idea flashed into my mind.

"Humphrey," I suggested tentatively, "can't we set up a security communications room next door to the reception? At the Sheikh's Palace, I mean? With emergency telephones and Telex lines to Downing Street. Then we could fill it with cases of booze that we'll smuggle in from the Embassy. We could liven up our orange juice and nobody would ever know."

He gazed at me in astonishment. "Minister!"

I was about to apologise for going too far, when he went on, "That is a stroke of genius."

I thanked him modestly, and asked if we could really do it.

Musing on it for a moment, he said that a special communications room would only be justified if there were a major crisis.

I pointed out that five hours without a drink is a major crisis.

We decided that, as the pound is under pressure at the moment, a communications room could be justified.

Humphrey has promised his enthusiastic support for the project.

(…)

(Shortly after the reception began, at which orange juice was being served, Hacker was presented with a gold and silver rosewater jar, as a token of the esteem in which the Qumrani government held the British – Ed.)

May 17th

Yesterday we went to the teetotal reception at Prince Mohammed's palace, and today I've got the most frightful hangover.

Unfortunately I don't remember the end of the reception awfully clearly, though I do have a hazy memory of Sir Humphrey telling some Arab that I'd suddenly been taken ill and had to be rushed off to bed. Actually that was the truth, if not the whole truth.

It was a very large reception. The British delegation was a bloody sight too big to start with. And then there were an enormous number of Arabs there too.

The evening more or less started with the presentation to me of a splendid gift accompanied by diplomatic speeches about what a pleasure it is to commemorate this day. Subsequently, chat-

---

Annotations

hip flask (7) – A flat little bottle you carry yourself with a hard drink in it / **guff** (11) – rubbish, nonsense / **FT** (3) – Financial Times / **tentative** (23) – without very much confidence / **Telex** (26) – A telecommunications service that transmitted text at a time before fax was introduced / **booze** (28) – alcoholic drink / **jar** (49) – Topf, Glas (e. g. a glass of jam) / **teetotal** (53) – without any alcohol / **hangover** (55) – the state you are in after drinking too much alcohol / **commemorate** (69) – remember

ting with one of the Arab guests it transpired that apparently it's a magnificent example of seventeenth-century Islamic Art, or so he said.
I asked what it was for originally. He said it was a rosewater jar. I said I supposed that that meant it was for rosewater, and the conversation was already getting rather bogged down along these lines when Bernard arrived at my elbow with the first of the evening's urgent and imaginative messages. Though I must admit that, at first, I didn't quite follow what he was saying.
"Excuse me, Minister, there is an urgent call for you in our communications room. A Mr Haig."
I thought he meant General Haig. But no.
"I actually mean Mr Haig, Minister – you know, with the dimples."
I nodded in a worried sort of way, said "Ah yes" importantly, excused myself and hurried away to the communications room.
I must say Humphrey had seen to it that someone had set the whole thing up beautifully. Phones, Telex, a couple of our security chaps with walkie-talkies, cipher machines, the works. And just in case the place was bugged by our hosts I was careful not to ask for a drink but to ask for the message from Mr Haig. Immediately one of our chaps poured some Scotch into my orange juice. It looked browner, but no one could really tell.

SIR BERNARD WOOLLEY RECALLS:
The official reception at the Palace of Qumran was an evening that I shall never forget. Firstly, there was the extraordinary strain of covering up for Hacker's increasing drunkenness. And not only Hacker, in fact: several members of the British delegation were in on the secret and it was noticeable that their glasses of orange juice became more and more golden brown as the evening wore on. But that evening also saw the start of a most unfortunate chain of events that might have led to an early end of my career.
Mrs Hacker was the only woman present. They'd made her a sort of honorary man for the evening. And while Hacker was off getting one of his refills, she remarked that the rosewater jar would look awfully good on the corner table of her hall in London.
It fell to me to explain to her that it was a gift to the Minister.
At first she didn't understand, and said that it was his hall too. I had to explain that it was a gift to the Minister *qua* Minister, and that she would not be allowed to keep it. (...) She wanted to know if they were supposed to give it back. Clearly not. I explained that it would have been a frightfully insulting thing to do. So she observed, rather sensibly, that if she couldn't keep it and couldn't give it back, she couldn't see what she *could* do.
I explained that official gifts become the property of the government, and are stored in some basement somewhere in Whitehall.
She couldn't see any sense in that. I couldn't either, except that clearly it is not in the public interest for Ministers to be allowed to receive valuable gifts from anybody. I explained that one might keep a gift valued up to approximately fifty pounds.
She asked me how you found out the value. I said that you get a valuation. And then she flattered me in a way that I found irresistible. She asked me to get a valuation, said that it would be "wonderful" if it were less than fifty pounds, because it was "awfully pretty", and then told me that I was absolutely wonderful and she didn't know what they would do without me.
Regrettably, I fell for it, and promised that I would see what I could do.
Meanwhile I was being sent on errands by Hacker. He returned from one of his many trips to the temporary Communications Centre which we'd set up, telling me loudly that there was a message for me from Mr John Walker. From the

Annotations
it transpired (70) – It was found out / **bogged down** (76) – no progress was made / **General Haig** (82) – US Secretary of State in the 1980s / **cipher machines** (92) – machines for secret writing / **Whitehall** (132) – area in London, where most ministries are, often refers to the whole government / **flatter** (141) – schmeicheln / **to send sb. on errands** (149) – to send sb. around and to tell him what to do for me

Scotch Office. Aware that we could easily be overheard, I asked if he meant the Scottish Office.

As I left very much in need of some whisky, Mrs Hacker asked if there was a message for her.

"Of course there is, darling," the Minister replied hospitably. "Bernard will collect it for you if you give him your glass." I shot him a meaningful look and he continued, "if you give him your glass he'll get you some orange juice too."

I stayed close to the Minister's side for most of the evening which was just as well because he continually made tactless remarks. At one point he was looking for Sir Humphrey and I led him across to where Sir Humphrey and a man named Ross (...) were talking to Prince Mohammed. Unfortunately both Ross and Sir Humphrey looked like Qumranis when approached from behind, as they were both dressed in full Arab robes. (...) In spite of Prince Mohammed's presence, Hacker was unable to disguise his shock as Sir Humphrey turned. He asked Humphrey why on earth he was dressed up like that.

Sir Humphrey explained that this was a traditional Foreign Office courtesy to our hosts. Ross confirmed that this was spot on, and Prince Mohammed said that indeed he regarded it as a most warm and gracious compliment. (...) Hacker didn't let it go at that, either. "If you were in Fiji, would you wear a grass skirt?' (...) I decided that their conversation should continue in private, so I interrupted them and told Sir Humphrey that the Soviet Embassy was on the line – a Mr Smirnoff. And then I told Hacker, who was looking distinctly thirsty, that there was a message for him from the British Embassy (...) The school. A delegation of Teachers.

He brightened up immediately, and, hurrying off, made some dreadful pun about going to greet the Teachers at once, before the Bell's goes.

Prince Mohammed sidled up to me, and observed softly that we were all receiving a great many urgent messages. There was no twinkle in his eye, no hint that he had spotted that all the British orange juice was turning steadily browner – and yet, I wondered if he realised what was going on. To this day, of course, I still don't know.

Unwilling to prolong the conversation, I edged away. And I found myself face to face with a smiling Arab who had been close to me earlier in the evening when I was talking to Annie Hacker about the rosewater jar. This next conversation, with its fateful consequences, is the first reason why this whole evening is etched forever on my memory.

Although dressed in traditional Arab style, the smiling Arab spoke perfect English and clearly knew the West only too well.

"Excuse me, *Effendi*," he began, "but I could not help overhearing your conversation about valuing the gift. Perhaps I can help."

I was surprised. And grateful. And I asked if he had any idea how much it was worth.

He smiled. "Of course. An original seventeenth-century rosewater jar is very valuable."

"Oh dear," I said, thinking of Annie Hacker's disappointment.

"You are not pleased?" Naturally, he was a little surprised.

I hastened to explain. "Yes – and no. I mean if it is too valuable, the Minister is not allowed to keep it. So I was hoping it wasn't."

He understood immediately, and smiled even more. "Ah yes. Well, as I was saying, an original seventeenth-century rosewater jar is very valuable but this copy, though excellently done, is not of the same order." "Oh good. How much?'

He was a very shrewd fellow. He eyed me for a moment, and then said, "I should be interested to hear your guess."

'A little under fifty pounds?' I asked hopefully.

'Brilliant,' he replied without hesitation. "Quite a connoisseur!"

I asked him if he could sign a valuation certificate. He agreed, but added that our English customs are very strange. "You are so strict about a little gift. And yet your electronics company pays

---

Annotations

Scottish Office (155) – Ministry for Scottish Affairs / **connoisseur** (235) – Someone who knows the particular field very well our Finance Minister a million dollars for his co-operation in securing this contract. Is that not strange?"

Of course, I was utterly horrified. I said that I hoped he didn't mean what I thought he meant. He smiled from ear to ear. "Of course. I work for the Finance Ministry. I got my share of the money."

"For what?""

"For keeping my mouth shut!" (...)

I found Sir Humphrey talking to the Minister, of all people. Rather clumsily, I asked if I could have a word with Sir Humphrey in private. Hacker told me that I could speak freely. Momentarily non-plussed, because of the enormity of the information that I was about to reveal to Sir Humphrey, I came up with a foolproof way of removing Hacker from the room for a couple of minutes.

"Minister," I said, "you're wanted in the Communications Room. The VAT man." He looked blank. "About your 69 returns." He must have had a great deal too much already for he just stared at me as if I was mad, until I was forced to say, "Vat 69".

"Ah. Ah. Yes," he said, turned gleefully, bumped into a hovering prince, and spilt what was left of his previous drink.

'Bernard,' Sir Humphrey took me by the arm and led me quickly to one side. "I'm beginning to think that the Minister's had almost as many urgent messages as he can take."

I was glad he'd led me to a quiet corner. I immediately blurted out that I had just found out the most terrible thing: that the contract was obtained by bribery.

Sir Humphrey, to my intense surprise, was completely unconcerned. Not only that, he *knew*. He told me that all contracts in Qumran were obtained by bribery. "Everybody knows that. It's perfectly all right as long as nobody knows." (...)

(The following morning Bernard Woolley made a special request for an urgent meeting with Sir Humphrey Appleby. Sir Humphrey made a note about it, which we found in the Departmental files at Walthamstow – Ed.) (...)

It slowly emerged that the exquisite rosewater jar, given to the Minister in Qumran, was the root of the problem. Apparently the Minister's wife liked it. Not surprising. BW had explained the rules to her, and she had looked terribly sad. They always do. Then she had asked if it was really worth more than fifty pounds, and said how marvellous it would be if it wasn't. And BW, it seems, had agreed to "help".

I understand his motives, but a seventeenth-century vase – well, really! BW then explained that there was a "terribly nice Qumrani business-man. And this fellow had apparently valued it as a copy and not as an original. For £ 49.95. A most convenient sum.

I asked BW if he had believed this man. He wavered. I ... er ... he said he was an expert ... well ... he spoke Arabic awfully well, so I er accepted his valuation. In good faith. After all, Islam is a jolly good faith. (...)

I was intending to let the matter drop, and merely record a reprimand in his report. But at this juncture he informed me that a journalist from *The Guardian* had seen the jar in Hacker's house, that Mrs Hacker had said it was a copy, and that further questions were to be asked.

It is a great tragedy that the press are so horribly suspicious about this sort of thing. But I told BW that we had no option but to inform the minister. (...)

Jonathan Lynn/Anthony Jay, The Complete Yes Minister. The diaries of a Cabinet Minister. London, 1989, p. 400–422, adapted and abridged

---

Annotation

of all people (249) – ausgerechnet mit dem Minister

Activities

A Working with the vocabulary

1. We do not have to look up every single word to understand a text. Try to more or less understand the meaning of the following expressions from the context:
   a) "… it was a gift to the Minister *qua* Minister …" (line 122)
   b) "… I fell for it …" (line 147)
   c) Ross confirmed that this was spot on … (line 179)
2. Questions on words
   a) What does VAT (line 258) mean apart from being part of a whisky brand name?
   b) What does Sir Humphrey mean when he says that the Minister has had almost as many urgent messages as he can take (line 268)?

B Text comprehension

1. Explain where and why the communication room was set up.
2. Why was the rosewater jar a problem?

C Describe how you would have reacted if you were the Minister and a journalist had seen the jar in your house.

Text

6 Bhajis not burgers for India

Pre-reading activities

- What are your eating habits?
- What's your favourite cuisine?
- What would you never touch?
- What do you have in the morning?
- Do you have any lunch or dinner or just a snack?
- Do you think your diet is well balanced?
- Look at this menu. Can you cope with it?
- What do you think are the differences between your diet and that of someone living in a Third world country?

F.X. McRory's
Steak Chop & Oyster House

Soup of the Day
Made fresh daily. Please ask your server for today's selection. Small 2.50 Large 3.95

Pasta Primavera
Penne pasta tossed with julienne zucchini, red peppers, spring carrots, asparagus tips, and roma tomatoes in fresh garlic & chicken stock. 7.25

Fresh Turkey Sandwich
Sliced turkey breast, crisp watercrest, and tarragon mayonnaise on nine grain bread. Served with made-in-house potato chips. 6.50

Fresh Northwest Halibut
Fresh halibut broiled and topped with cucumber cream sauce. Accompanied by carnival wild rice and fresh seasonal vegetables. 9.50

Corned Beef Sandwich
"This sandwich makes everyday St. Patrick's Day!" says Mike Gastineau, SportsRadio 950 KJR's afternoon host, "It's #1 with me!" Hand carved F.X. McRory's brand hot corned beef piled high on thick-cut rye bread slathered with Dijon mayonnaise and served with made-in-house potato chips. 7.25

Fresh Shellfish & Fin Fish

Fresh Beer-Battered Fish & Chips 7.95
Fresh, flaky Pacific cod hand-dipped in Northwest ale batter, dusted with Panko breading then quick-fried in canola oil. Served with cole slaw and crisp, hot fries.

Simmered Shellfish Small 6.95 Regular 10.95
Fresh Manila clams and renowned Penn Cove mussels simmered in light cream, Stock Italian vermouth, creamery butter, fresh garlic, and sweet, minty thyme. *For all clams please add 1.00*

Baked Oysters Rockefeller 8.95
A half dozen freshly shucked plump Pacific oysters topped with a rich mix of chopped spinach, Gruyère cheese, minced shallots, crisp bacon, and a dash of Pernod. Finished with Hollandaise.

Fresh King Salmon 10.95
Fresh red king salmon broiled and served with today's complementing sauce. Ask your server for today's selection. Accompanied with carnival wild rice and zucchini planks.

Northwest Bouillabaisse 12.95
Our rendition of the celebrated Provence seafood stew. Fresh mussels, scallops, clams, salmon, sweet onions, leeks, chopped ripe tomatoes, white wine, virgin olive oil, fresh garlic, and saffron ladled over a sourdough crouton.

Steakhouse Favorites

Top Sirloin Steak 9.95
Aged 31 days then cut from the center of the loin. This ten ounce steak is broiled to your liking and served iwth crispy haystack onion, zippy steak butter, and crisp, hot fries.

Roasting Box Beef 11.95
The prime rib that's made us famous. We slow-roast the finest beef ribs available for ten hours in pure grain roasting salt. A 7 ounce cut carved-to-order to your doneness specifications. Served with crisp, hot fries, au jus, and freshly grated horseradish.

45MI

Protesters are accusing foreign fast-food companies of changing India's eating habits and undermining the nation's agriculture.

Earlier this year farmers ransacked a Kentucky Fried Chicken restaurant in the southern Indian city of Bangalore, smashing windows and overturning furniture. This was no spontaneous act of vandalism, however, but a political protest that sent shock waves through the offices of every foreign food company operating in India. *(0)*

The protesters were members of the Karnataka Rajya Raitha Sangha (KRRS), an association representing several million farmers in Karnataka State. They demanded that the fast-food chain leave India, claiming that it and other foreign food operations were threatening traditional agriculture by expanding the meat industry and forcing Western farming methods and seed varieties on farmers. *(1)*

As an indication of the explosive, nationalist politics involved, the president of KRRS, M. D. Nanjundaswamy, timed the attack on the restaurant to coincide with the anniversary of the assasination of Mahatma Gandhi, declaring that the protest echoed Gandhi's symbolic burning of foreign cloth as part of the movement to expel the British from India. *(2)*

In the weeks leading up to the spring general election, environmentalists and politicians tried to make the fight against foreign fast-food chains a rallying point for debate over how far liberalisation of the consumer goods market should be taken. Now India's new prime minister, H. D. Deve Gowda, who defended KFC when he was chief minister of Karnataka State, says he wants to encourage foreign investment. McDonald's, for instance, is preparing to open its first two Indian outlets in New Delhi and Bombay later this year, and environmental and political groups have promised to oppose the openings. *(3)*

Vandana Shiva, an environmentalist who runs the Research Foundation for Science, Technology and Natural Resource Policy in New Delhi, describes the arrival of foreign fast-food chains in India as an attack on sustainable agriculture. "They are going to move people into a meat-based diet that this country can't afford," she says. Maneka Gandhi, widow of Sanjay – one of the sons of former prime minister Indira Gandhi – and an animal right's activist, MP and former environment minister, believes that the intensive breeding of poultry and other livestock which fast-food restaurants encourage will have serious implications for India's ability to feed itself. In a paper submitted to parliament last year, she warned that using food crops such as maize to feed chickens was a poor use of resources; grain could feed five times as many people if consumed directly rather than being given to animals to be transformed into meat, milk and eggs. In addition, the 375 gallons of water needed to produce a pound of chicken was twenty times "what a normal Indian family is supposed to use in one day – if it gets water at all," she said. "We glory in feeding our rich with junk food while our poor go hungry and thirsty. The prices of grains keep going up because supply cannot meet demand and that is because our land is growing meat for the rich of this country and for export." *(4)*

Indeed, some of India's growing middle class are increasingly replacing home cooked meals of vegetables and lentils with non-vegetarian prepared food but Anil Sharma, senior economist at the National Council of Applied Economic Research in New Delhi does not believe that Indians will ever eat as much meat as Americans. Fast-food companies are not allowed to serve beef in India, where the cow is regarded as sacred by Hindus. McDonald's plans to serve lamb burgers as well as chicken and vegetarian products. *(5)*

While it is open to question whether multinational food companies are affecting Indian eating habits, their impact on local agriculture is undeniable. "Contract farming", where a company governs and buys the entire crop of a large group of farmers, is common. For instance Pepsi Foods, the group's beverage and snack foods arm, has controlled the output of about 1000 farmers in the State of Punjab for the past 5 years, telling them what to grow and how to grow it. Local farmers are given interest-free loans to buy foreign hybrid seeds and tools, and Pepsi buys the produce at fixed prices. *(6)*

Environmental critics claim that imported seeds threaten to make hundreds of locally grown types redundant. And contract farming, they say, will increase reliance on a limited number of crops and thus disrupt traditional farming practices. The use of Western yield-increasing techniques has also fuelled health concerns about food produced by foreign companies. The critics say that to satisfy demand for chicken from fast-food chains, local industry will adopt factory-farming techniques in which the animals are treated cruelly and fed with a host of antibiotics. Food additives of any kind are frowned upon in India. A few months before the KFC restaurant was vandalised, its sister branch in New Delhi was temporarily shut down by health inspectors who found monosodium glutamate in chicken samples. *(7)*

Sandeep Kohli, managing director of PepsiCo Restaurants International in India, claims the arguments against fast-food chains are politically motivated "rubbish". He says foreign chains' insistence on changing production methods will be good for the country. "Products like ours will help Indian agriculture," he says. He points out that everything foreign fast-food restaurants sell has to be produced locally. Vikram Bakshi, managing director of McDonald's restaurants in New Delhi, says the company is "changing the mindset of farmers" who are used to selling fresh produce at the local market. "We're the first ones to have commercially grown iceberg lettuce which we will get 365 days a year", he says. "We are raising the standards of production so they are acceptable internationally." *(8)*

The fast-food chains themselves insist that they have no desire to undermine India's traditional food. "We're not here to change eating habits," say Kohli. "Nobody is forcing people to go to KFC." But he adds: "Why should Indians be deprived of what the rest of the world has?" Ghandi, however, maintains that fast food is one Western product Indians can live without. She wants the government to make the choice for them and ban foreign outlets. "Fast food has contributed nothing to the welfare of mankind." *(9)*

(Adapted from: "Bhajis not Burgers for India", New Scientist, August 3, 1996)

Activities

A Multiple matching

MM

Choose the most suitable heading for each paragraph from the list A-K. There is one extra heading which you do not need to use. There is an example (O) at the beginning.

O Fast-food rage
A Split opinion
B Good fighting reasons
C Historical reference
D Adapting farmers
E Poor justification
F Massive reproaches
G Sickening food
H Indians turn to meat
I Looking on the positive side
K Irreconcilable differences

B Further questions for discussion or comment:

- You've certainly eaten fast-food, what is so tempting about it?
- Explain why children are an important target group for fast-food chains.
- *Fast-food fosters monoculture.* Discuss.
- *Fast food has contributed nothing to the welfare of mankind.*
  Comment on this statement made by Maneka Gandhi.

C Spelling practice

The following text contains 15 typing errors. Find them and write the correct forms in your exercise-book.

Travel into the depths of Bihar, India's poorest state, along dusty roads past goverment signs touting programs of health and education, into the hopeless hart of a subcontinent where the squalid villages might remind you of sub-Saharan Africa – except that the poorest Africans are better of then the destitute of Bihar. Eventually you will stumble onto the village of Kalipahari, blessed with electricity thank to a nearby hydro-electric damn. Here you will see, in practically every hovel, the incongrous: a TV set, pulling down American soap operas and Scotch whisky adds broadcast from Hong Kong. The reformers of India tend to bow under the wait of their nation's great poverty. In the nation of Mahatma Gandhi, 52 percent of the people still live on incomes of less than $ 1 a day, acording to World Bank figures; one third of the worlds most desperate poor people live in India. Nearly two third of indian children younger than 5 are malnourished, and those who reach school age can count on an average of only 3,5 years of education if they are boys, and 1,5 years if they are girls. By the time they reach adulthood, half are still illiterate.

(Adapted excerpt from: "Ambition Joined to Pride", Newsweek, August 4, 1997)

■■■ 7 Talkline: Budget Ministry for Economic Cooperation

You are members of the budget committee of the German Parliament. The committee is trying to cut the budget of the Ministry for Development by about 10 million €. Today six projects are under scrutiny. You discuss whether and to what extent they need money, and where you can cut spending. The first project is described below, the other five on page 310.

Help for the cotton farmers of Burkina Faso

Germany has committed a total of 36 millions euros to Burkina Faso (...) in order to help the West African countries in the production and trading of cotton. Burkina Faso, together with Mali, Chad and Benin, is one of the countries particularly badly hit by the agricultural subsidies of both the USA and the EU. The effect of the subsidies has been to devalue the African farmers' produce on the world market, thus destroying their livelihood.

http://www.bmz.de/en/media/newsletter/newsletter18/005.html

Appendix
Talkline

Unit 1: Finding accommodation in Dublin

Student B:
An Óige[1)] Dublin International Youth Hostel

Telephone:
+353 (01) 8301766,

Fax:
(01) 8301600,

email:
DublinInternational@AnOige.ie

Dublin is one of Europe's most cosmopolitan cities and our International Youth Hostel is at the heart of it all. Dublin positively overflows with culture, with Museums, Art Galleries, Cathedrals, National Buildings, Parks, and pubs to explore. Heritage Service details: The newly improved Youth Hostel offers large comfortable common areas, a games room and conference facilities. It is the hub from which to visit the rest of Ireland, and there is a travel shop at the hostel reception to help you on your way.

---

1) Gaelic name of the Irish Youth Hostel Association

- **Book through youth hostel or head office**
- **369** (3 rooms x 2 beds; 3 room x 3 beds; 3 room x 4 beds; 13 rooms x 6 beds; 20 rooms x 8 beds; plus dormitories)
- **Youth hostel open all year**
- **Breakfast Packed Lunch Dinner**
  Continental Breakfast included in the price – Full Irish Breakfast available at extra charge. Dinners are available during June – August. Lunch and Dinner for groups of 10+ can be provided. Meals must be pre-booked
- **Vast range of local entertainment – check at reception for details.**
- **Catholic and Protestant church available nearby**
- **City and local tours on foot or bus arranged**
  Wicklow Mountains 15 kms

Seasons

Nov 1st – May 31st **€ 18** June 1st – October 31st **€ 20**

a) Prices indicated are public prices, members of An Óige/Hostelling International will receive a discount of € 2 per person per night on validation of their membership number.
b) Prices shown are for dormitory style accomodation; if you require a smaller room please just ask. A supplement may apply.
c) Supplements may apply in respect of event weekends.
d) This service is only a booking request and that a booking confirmation will be sent within three working days subject to availability.
e) The amount due for the first night's accommodation is taken as a NON REFUNDABLE DEPOSIT.
f) If the credit card being used for the booking is not the person availing of the accommodation a signed letter of authorisation by the card holder must be produced at check-in.
g) Private rooms are available and will be subject to the relevant surcharge.
h) A booking reference number must be produced on check in.

http://www.anoige.ie/accommodation_dublin_intl_details.html

Welcome to Abraham House

Student C:

Abraham House Hostel Dublin enjoys a reputation as one of Ireland's finest budget accommodation centres. Ideally located in a beautiful Georgian townhouse in Dublin city centre, we are close to the best shopping and nightlife spots in this vibrant city. Our location on the direct bus routes from the airport and around the corner from Dublin's central bus and train stations means it couldn't be easier to find us!

Our superb facilities include 24-hour reception, free hot showers, luggage storage, bureau de change, Internet access and free car/bike parking. There are also cosy meeting and dining areas and a fully-equipped self-catering kitchen.

Visitors to Dublin have enjoyed the welcoming, fun and friendly atmosphere of Abraham House since 1993. We have really come to know our guests in this time and understand travellers' needs. For this reason, we offer a range of rooms to suit all requirements and budgets.

82-83 Lower Gardiner Street, Dublin 1, Ireland
T: +353 1 8550600, F: +353 1 8550598
E: abraham@indigo.ie

Rates

	Low Season		High Season		
Room Type	Midweek	Weekend	Midweek	Weekend	Special Events
Multi-bedded	€ 13	€ 15	€ 15	€ 17	€ 19
8-bed ensuite	€ 18	€ 20	€ 20	€ 22	€ 24
6-bed ensuite	€ 18	€ 20	€ 23	€ 25	€ 27
6-bed standard	€ 16	€ 18	€ 18	€ 20	€ 22
4-bed ensuite	€ 23	€ 27	€ 28	€ 32	€ 34
4-bed standard	€ 20	€ 22	€ 23	€ 27	€ 29
3-bed standard	€ 22	€ 24	€ 24	€ 26	€ 28
2-bed ensuite	€ 38	€ 42	€ 40	€ 44	€ 46
3-bed ensuite	€ 30	€ 32	€ 32	€ 35	€ 40

*** * Fantastic Reduced Midweek Rates for April, May and June * ***
12-bed standard € 10 pp/16-bed ensuite € 10 pp/8-bed ensuite € 13 pp/
6-bed ensuite € 15/4-bed standard € 15 pp/Triple standard € 60 rm/Triple ensuite € 75

Rates are inclusive of bed, continental breakfast, clean bed linen and duvet, shower and toilet facilities.
Low Season: January, February, November and December
High Season: March to October
Special Events: St Patrick's Weekend (15 to 17 March), Christmas (26 December to 3 January), all major concerts and sporting events, Rugby Internationals.

Dorms

The dorm rooms at Abraham House are a very cost-effective option for the independent traveller and for groups. Most have ensuite shower/toilet facilities, and there are ample shower/toilet facilities next to the standard rooms. The beds are comfortable and the rooms are clean, bright and spacious.

For the uninitiated, when you make a reservation at Abraham House, you mostly book a bed and not a room. You'll find yourself sleeping in comfortable bunk beds, sharing a spacious dormitory with other like-minded world travellers. Unlike some hostels, we provide all bedding, including sheets, pillows and duvets/blan-

kets free of charge. Towels are available on request; we will ask you for a € 5 deposit, but of course this is returned to you when you return the towel.
There is room in the dorms to store your bags and clothes and you also have access to luggage storage and safety deposit boxes. All guests are free to use our self-catering kitchen, dining room and social areas, where you'll find tourist information, notice boards, Internet kiosks and so on.
A continental breakfast – consisting of bread rolls, butter, preserves, fruit juice, tea and coffee – is included in the price of your overnight accommodation, and is served in the dining area each morning between 8 am and 10 am.

Private Rooms
Abraham House has a range of accommodation options, with double, three, four and six-bed rooms available. This is a cheaper and more flexible alternative to hotel accommodation, ideal for families, small groups and anyone for whom a city-centre location is essential. Our private rooms allow our guests to enjoy the 'best of both worlds': superior standard accommodation in private rooms, with access to self-catering cooking and dining facilities as required.
In addition to our existing accommodation, the new wings, added over the past five years, comprise top quality ensuite private rooms, complete with television and tea/coffee making facilities. The rooms are spacious, airy and are decorated in bright sunshine hues.

Facilities
Abraham House is a beautiful old Georgian townhouse that has been extensively modernised to provide comfortable, affordable accommodation right in Dublin's city centre.

The facilities at Abraham House include:

- Rooms with private facilities
- Luggage storage
- Free hot showers
- Credit cards accepted
- Friendly staff
- Bureau de change
- 24-hour reception
- In-house launderette
- Curfew free zone!
- Free car park
- Self catering kitchen
- Bike parking
- Dining and social areas
- International payphone
- Internet and email access
- Safety deposit boxes
- Light snacks and soft drinks available

http://www.abraham-house.ie/index.html

Ashfield House

Student D:
19/20 D'Olier Street, Dublin 2 | Tel: +353 1 6797734 | Fax: +353 1 6790852
email: ashfield@indigo.ie

Ashfield House provides high quality budget accommodation in the heart of Dublin city centre. Situated between Trinity College and O'Connell Bridge, our location is second-to-none. Although Temple Bar and Grafton Street are a two-minute stroll away, Ashfield House is located on a quieter street, so our guests can party until late or enjoy a good night's rest!

Ashfield House is a cheerful oasis in Dublin city centre. Guests enjoy facilities such as 24-hour reception, bureau de change and luggage storage, as well as cosy dining and meeting areas, complete with pool table, television, Internet/email access, tourist information and so on.

A modern, superior-standard hostel, all guest rooms have ensuite facilities and are decorated in fresh, bright colours. Ashfield House offers accommodation in twin, family and four/six bedded rooms.

Ashfield House offers comfortable and affordable accommodation in the heart of Dublin city centre. All of our guestrooms have private ensuite bathrooms and are decorated in bright sunshine colours. The rooms are basic but comfortable, clean and airy.

There is a range of room types to choose from, including two-, four- and six-bed rooms, as well as the popular family rooms, which consist of a double and two single beds (bunks).

All guests are welcome to use our fully-equipped self-catering kitchen, dining and recreation areas.

The bright, spacious dorms at Ashfield House are ideal for the seasoned traveller, or those for whom affordable city centre accomodation is a priority. Serviced with shower/toilet facilities and clean bed linen, our dorms are very comfortable and great value for money.

When you book into Ashfield House, you generally book a bed, not a room. Your accommodation will consist of a comfortable bunk bed, sharing a dorm room with fellow world travellers. You will have plenty of room to store your bags, with further storage space available in our luggage room and in safety deposit boxes.

All bedding is included in the price of your accommodation, as is a light continental breakfast, consisting of bread rolls, butter, preserves, fruit juice, tea and coffee.

In Ashfield House there is an excellent range of facilities at your disposal, including a fully-equipped self-catering kitchen, spacious dining areas, bureau de change and recreation area with pool table, television and Internet/email access.

Ashfield House offers an impressive array of facilities and services, including:

Secure 24-hour reception – The reception at Ashfield House is serviced 24-hours a day; unlike some other budget accommodation centres, there is no curfew.

Fully equipped self-catering kitchen and dining areas – Ideal for guests on a tight budget or travelling with children.

Free luggage storage – Arriving early or leaving late? We will store your bag in a secure area while you make the most of your time in Dublin.

Safety deposit boxes – Our automated safety deposit boxes give you complete control over your most valuable possessions.

Internet and email access – How did we ever travel without it? Keep in touch with family and friends, or book your next destination.

Pool table and television – When you have had enough sight-seeing, or in the unlikely event of rain: light snacks and soft drinks are also available.

Bureau de change – We change all major currencies into Euro right here in Ashfield House.

Credit cards accepted – We accept all major credit cards.

Realtime online booking – Using our secure booking facility, you are guaranteed a bed will be waiting for you on arrival

Prices

	Nov –Jan		Mar–Oct		Special Events
	Sun – Thu	Fri – Sat	Sun – Thu	Fri – Sat	
Multi-bed ensuite	€ 13	€ 15	€ 15	€ 17	€ 19
6 Bed Ensuite	€ 18	€ 20	€ 23	€ 25	€ 27
4 Bed Ensuite	€ 23	€ 27	€ 28	€ 32	€ 34
3 Bed Ensuite	€ 30	€ 32	€ 32	€ 35	€ 40
Double/2 Bed Ensuite	€ 38	€ 42	€ 40	€ 44	€ 46
Single	€ 45	€ 45	€ 50	€ 56	€ 57

Rates are per person sharing and include continental breakfast.
Special Events: St Patrick's Weekend (15 to 17 March), Christmas (26 December to 3 January), all major concerts and sporting events, Rugby Internationals.

http://www.ashfieldhouse.ie/index.html

Unit 2: Famous sportsperson

Candidate 1: Oliver Kahn

Birth Date: 15th June 1969
Birth Place: Karlsruhe, Germany
Height: 188 cm
Weight: 88 kg
Position: Goalkeeper
Current Club: *Bayern Munich (GER) (c 1994)*
Previous Club: *Karlsruhe FC (GER) (from 1975 till 1994)*

Whenever football experts are called upon to pick one world-class player from Germany's ranks, the name of Oliver Kahn is the one that automatically springs to mind. The Bayern Munich goalkeeper has carved a place for himself as one of the best shot-stoppers in the world, and the epitome[1] of consistency[2] at the highest level for many years.

Kahn began his football odyssey in 1976, in his native town, Karlsruhe. A year later, he was playing for Karlsruhe FC's youth team. He worked his way up through the youth teams but never quite made it into the international youth set-up. He subsequently made his Bundesliga debut in the autumn of 1990 and left an indelible[3] mark from the outset.

It took him only three seasons to establish himself as one of the best last lines of defence in the Bundesliga and his excellent displays were rewarded with a call-up to the national team in October 1993. He was drafted into the German squad at the 1994 FIFA World Cup™ as reserve keeper to Bodo Illgner, but never made the starting line-up.

He was signed by Bayern Munich at the beginning of the 1994/5 season, with whom he has gone on to win many honours, both at domestic and international level. The 2.5 million euros paid by the Bavarian club was a record fee for a goalkeeper at the time, and from the word go Kahn was made Bayern's first-choice keeper.

His career was interrupted in November 1994, when a torn ligament injury[4] sidelined him for five months. This enforced absence did, however, have a positive effect. Kahn returned a much stronger individual mentally and quickly found his best form.

His international debut came in a match against Switzerland in June 1995. He had to still make do with being the reserve keeper at the 1996 UEFA European Championship in England. More frustration was to follow at France 98™. He had to play second fiddle for the third successive major international tournament. It was not until Andreas Köpke announced his retirement at the end of the tournament that Oliver Kahn was finally given his chance as the Mannschaft's unquestionable number one.

Kahn was voted German footballer of the year in 2000 and best European goalkeeper. The 2001/2002 season was the high point of his sporting career so far. Having won a fourth German League title, he was to go on and lift the UEFA Champions League trophy the same season. (...)

http://www.kahn.boom.ru/bio1.html

[1] The best possible example of something
[2] having the same standards
[3] impossible to forget
[4] Bänderriss

Candidate 2: David Beckham

Signed for Manchester United as a trainee on 8th July 1991 and part of United's famous 1992 Youth Cup winning side, he made his League debut at home to Leeds United.

He established himself the next year in United's 1995/96 Double winning season as a right midfielder after the departure of Andrei Kanchelskis.

A goal from the halfway line in the first game of the 1996/97 season at Wimbledon brought him to star status, which has grown inexorably[1)] since. (...) Following the wonder goal at Wimbledon he went on a run of amazing performances, scoring a fantastic selection of long-range goals to help United win the Premiership and himself the Young Player of the Year award. He also came second in the Player of the Year voting.

He was included in Glenn Hoddle's squad for France 1998. And after being left out of the starting line-up for the first two matches, he then scored a beautiful free-kick against Colombia. He then made himself a national pariah through being sent-off for aiming a kick at Argentina's Diego Simeone. This led to brainless fans critisizing his every move and terrible abuse of him, his wife and son Brooklyn, who was born in March 1999.

He was an integral part of the Treble winning team and his efforts won him second place behind Rivaldo in the voting for both World and European Player of the Year.

The biggest name in English football, Beckham's main attributes are shooting, in open play and especially from free-kicks, a superb range of passing, vision, composure[2)] and a dogged determination which will always threaten to spill over. Through these facets he has developed into English football's greatest player since the early years of Paul Gascoigne.

http://www.wsoccer.com/players/beckham/more.htm

---

1) unstoppable
2) feeling calm

Candidate 3: Michael Schumacher

Nickname: Schumi or Schuey
Date of Birth: 3rd January 1969
Nationality: German
Place of Birth: Hürth-Hermülheim, Germany
Height: 1.74 m
Weight: 68 kg
Residency: Vufflens-le-Château, Switzerland
Status: Married to Corinna Betsch since Tuesday 1st August 1995
Children: Gina-Maria, daughter (DOB 19/01/97) and son Mick (DOB 22/03/99).
Family: Rolf, father, Elizabeth, mother, and Ralf, brother (DOB 30/6/75).

His hobbies...
Soccer, tennis, swimming, skiing.

F1 Teams driven for:
Jordan (1991), Benetton (1992–1995), Ferrari (1996–)

http://www.mschumacher.com/biography.html

Candidate 4: no sportsperson

You think that streets should not be named after living people and especially not after sport professionals. You suggest a person from your area who you think has deserved the honour.

Unit 5: Those who sleep rough

Picture A

(Note: Picture 2, see p. 311)

Unit 6: Job applicants

Curriculum Vitae

George Walker

Ithaca, New York

Employment History	Since Jan.1988, Silicon Graph Inc., Orlando, Florida Account Manager, International Large Accounts Account Management of DatStore Inc. for client-server products, software, solution projects and professional services Sales of projects for Design databases
Education/Schools	1982–1988 Ithaca College, Ithaca, New York Study in physics, focusing on semiconductor physics
Training	1993–2002 Courses in law and business management Sales and marketing training courses (e.g. strategic selling, solution selling, rhetoric etc.) Technical training: UNIX, Windows XP professional, development of VLSI circuits, software development, PDM tools, Internet/Intranet related training networking tools, complex CAD-applications
Languages	English: native speaker Spanish: good basic knowledge
International Experience	During 1995–1999 several months per year in European countries Good knowledge of European companies
Personal Information	Age 44 Service: 1974–1978 Air Force Indiana Wells, Connecticut
Private Interests	Sports: skiing, biking, motorcycling Interests in classical music and literature

Beach Boulevard, Orlando, Florida

Frank Miller

Objective
To become sales recruitment manager

Experience

1994–1998 Memphis Cottons, Memphis, Tn
National Sales Manager
- Increased sales from $5o million to $100 million.
- Doubled sales per representative from $5 million to $10 million.
- Suggested new products that increased earnings by 27%.

1989–1994 Sunshine Shoes, Carmel, Ca
District Sales Manager
- Increased regional sales from $40 million to $300 million.
- Managed 200 sales representatives.
- Implemented training course for new recruits – speeding profitability.

1984–1988 Dobson Cutlery, Carmel, Ca
Senior Sales Representative
- Expanded sales team from 50 to 100 representatives.
- Tripled division revenues for each sales associate.

1979–1984 Southern Knitware, Atlanta, Ga
Sales Representative
- Expanded territorial sales by 300%.
- Received company's highest sales award four years in a row.
- Developed excellence In sales training courses.

Education

1974 – 1979 University of California, Los Angeles
- B.A.[1], Business Administration and Computer Science.
- Graduated summa cum laude[2].

Interests
- Running, gardening, computers.

---

[1] Bachelor of Arts (academic degree)
[2] Best possible mark in the doctor exam

Mary J. Robinson

OBJECTIVE	Engineering Staff Member.
FUNCTIONAL SUMMARY	Engineering manager large scale division
EMPLOYMENT	1992–2001 Bexas Instruments Inc., Austin, Tx. Engineering manager – Development of solid state circuits – Research in semiconductor physics
EDUCATION	1987–1992 San Christobal City College, San Christobal, Tx. Master of science – Research position in nuclear research labs – Best fellow in year 1991
REFERENCES	Prof. Terence O'Neill, Newton research Fellow, Santa Clara College, Cal.
SUMMARY OF QUALIFICATIONS	1993–1994 Texas University, Austin, Tx. Research scientist – 3 patents developed in semiconductor research team.
PROFESSIONAL MEMBERSHIPS	IEEE society of CMOS design, reporting board member
PATENTS AND PUBLICATIONS	Pat. 67-008ik-765-888 „Large Scale CMOS bulk processor" 2003
LANGUAGES	French, Navajo
SECURITY CLEARANCE	Top 1 nuclear plant clearance
CIVIL SERVICE GRADES	Army corporal

MAYNARD ENCLAVE • REDMOND • VIRGINIA • PHONE 555-666-777

Wards Rd
Ulysses, N.Y.
Phone 55-666-777

Robert M. Stewart

Objective	Starting Position as marketing support engineer.
Education	1998–2003 Catholic College Maynard. Mass.
Awards received	**Bachelor Sc.** • Awarded "Citizenship Scientists Fellow"
Languages	Greek, Latin
Work experience	1997–1998 Ohio Mining, Redmond, Ohio **Sales Clerk** • Selling of paper and tools into major businesses
Volunteer experience	Boy Scouts of Georgia group leader
Extracurricular activities	Training in Aikido
Professional memberships	IEEE, MSCG[1)]
Civil service grades	Sergeant of Airforce support military school

1) Abbreviations stand for the names of professional associations. In the English speaking world membership in professional associations can be a sign of high quality work.

Unit 8: Talking about people

Picture 1

Picture 2

Picture 3

Picture 4

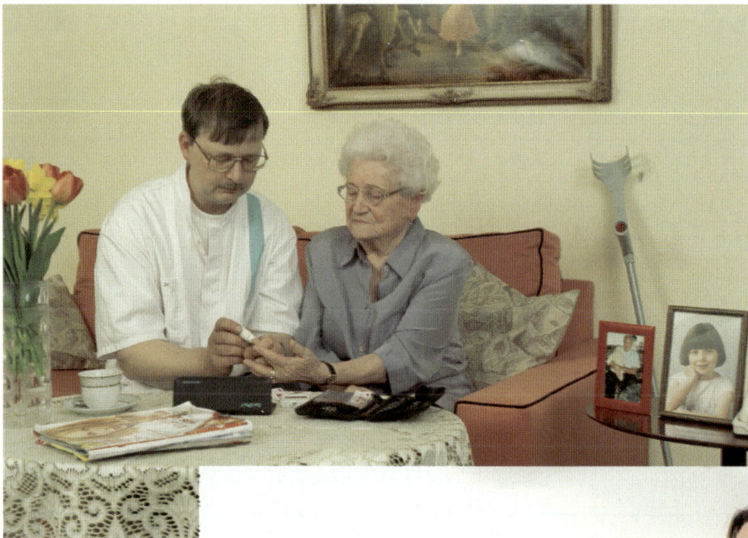

Picture 5

Picture 6

Unit 9: Buying equipment for your college

Product 2

ebY

VIDEO + VIDEO CASSETTE RECORDER! AS NEW CONDITION!
Starting bid **£10.00**
You will be bidding on ***HR-J246EK VCR!***

This is a ***NEAR NEW*** condition and has only been used a handful of times. It comes with remote control, user manual and would make an idea christmas gift for a child's bedroom. It has Video+ capabilities so it's quick and easy to set the VCR to record your favourite programs. It also has long play so you can double the amount of time you get out of a video cassette.

Specitications:
Dimensions: 400 x 94 x 340 mm, **Weight:** 4.3 kg, **Format:** VHS PAL Standard
Maximum recording time: (SP) 240 min with E-240 (LP) 480 min with E-240
Input/Output: 21-pin scart connector x 3 (IN/OUT x 1, IN x 1) RCA Connector x 1
Shipping will be in the region of £10 – £15 for UK

Product 3

Digital Camcorder (Mini-DV 18xOptical DV-in/out) **Our Price: £ 377.62**

- 800 K pixel CCD
- 18x optical/360x digital zoom
- Image Stabilizer
- 2.5″ colour LCD view screen and colour viewfinder
- Night Mode
- Photo Button
- Multi Image Screen
- Audio Dubbing
- Analogue Digital Converter, DV/Analogue in
- DV Messenger

Product 4

Our Price:
£ 299.29

Technical Data
Camera effective pixels: Approx. 4 million
Image sensor: 1/1.8 in. CCD
(Total number of pixels: approx. 4.1 million)

Lens: 7.4 (W) – 22.2 (T) mm
(35 mm film equivalent: 36–108 mm)
F2.8 (W) – 4.9 (T)

Digital Zoom: Maximum apprix. 3.6x
(Maximum approx. 11x with optical zoom)
Optical Viewfinder: Real-image optical zoom viewfinder

LCD monitor: 1.5 in. Low-temperature polycrystalline silicon TFT color LCD, Approx. 118,0000 pixels

Autofocus: TTL –point AiAF/TTL 1-poiunt center AF
Focus lock possible

Focusing Range:
(from tip of the lens barrel) Normal: 46 cm (1.5 ft.) – infinity
Macro AF: 5–46 cm (2.0 in. – 1.5 ft.) (W)
30–46 cm (11.8 in. – 1.5 ft.) (T)

Shutter: Mechanical + electronic
Shotter Speed: 15-1/200 sec. * 15-1 sec. possible in long shutter mode
* Noise reduction processing on speeds betweeen 15–1.3 sec.
Light Metering System: Evaluate metering/Center-weighted averaging/Spot metering

Exposure Control: Program AE
Exposure Compensation: +/– 2 stops in 1/3-stop increments
Sensitivitty: ISO 50/100/200/400 equivalent and Auto

Image recording format: Still images: JPEG (Exif 2.2)*
Movies: AVI (Image Date: Motion JPEG
Audio data: WAVE [monaural])
Compression: Supefine/fine/normal

Movies: 320 x 240 pixels (Approx. 3 min.)
160 x 120 pixels (Approx. 3 min.)
Approx. 15 frames/sec. (…)
Interfaxe: USB (mini-B, PTP [Picture Transfer Protocol]),
Audio/Video output (NTSC or PAL selectable, monaural audio)
Power Source: Rechargeable Lithium-ion battery (type: NB-1LH/NB-1L)

Unit 10: Councillors decide

Councillor B
You want most of the city centre to be open for cars, but they should have to pay a congestion charge if they want to enter the inner city. You explain which area people should have to pay for and what the positive effects would be. A side-effect would be that the city council would earn quite some money.

Councillor C
You want to introduce a scheme under which every house-owner who mounts solar panels is given a grant at the expense of the city council.

Councillor D
You want to reduce fares in public transport and to intensify the service. You expect that this will make public transport so attractive that so many people start using it that this measure does not cost any extra money.

Unit 11: UN Security Council

Austria

Once the center of power for the large Austro-Hungarian Empire, Austria was reduced to a small republic after its defeat in World War I. Following annexation by Nazi Germany in 1938 and subsequent occupation by the victorious Allies in 1945, Austria's status remained unclear for a decade. A State Treaty signed in 1955 ended the occupation, recognized Austria's independence, and forbade unification with Germany. A constitutional law that same year declared the country's „perpetual neutrality" as a condition for Soviet military withdrawal. This neutrality, once ingrained as part of the Austrian cultural identity, has been called into question since the Soviet collapse of 1991 and Austria's entry into the European Union in 1995. A prosperous country, Austria entered the European Monetary Union in 1999. (...)
Minor disputes with [the] Czech Republic and Slovenia continue over nuclear power plants and post World War II treatment of German-speaking minorities.

India

The Indus Valley civilization, one of the oldest in the world, goes back at least 5,000 years. Aryan tribes from the northwest invaded about 1500 B.C.; their merger with the earlier inhabitants created the classical Indian culture. Arab incursions starting in the 8th century and Turkish in 12th were followed by European traders, beginning in the late 15th century. By the 19th century, Britain had assumed political control of virtually all Indian lands. Nonviolent resistance to British colonialism under Mohandas GANDHI and Jawaharlal NEHRU led to independence in 1947. The subcontinent was divided into the secular state of India and the smaller Muslim state of Pakistan. A third war between the two countries in 1971 resulted in East Pakistan becoming the separate nation of Bangladesh. Fundamental concerns in India include the ongoing dispute with Pakistan over Kashmir, massive overpopulation, environmental degradation, extensive poverty, and ethnic and religious strife, all this despite impressive gains in economic investment and output. (...)

Much of the rugged, militarized boundary with China is in dispute, but the two sides have participated in more than 13 rounds of joint working group sessions on this issue; India objects to Pakistan ceding lands to China in 1965 boundary agreement that India believes are part of disputed Kashmir; with Pakistan, armed stand-off over the status and sovereignty of Kashmir continues; disputes with Pakistan over Indus River water sharing and the terminus of the Rann of Kutch, which prevents maritime boundary delimitation; Joint Border Committee with Nepal continues to work on resolution of disputed boundary sections; dispute with Bangladesh over New Moore/South Talpatty Island in the Bay of Bengal prevents maritime boundary delimitation.

Iraq

Formerly part of the Ottoman Empire, Iraq became an independent kingdom in 1932. A „republic“ was proclaimed in 1958, but in actuality a series of military strongmen have ruled the country since then, the latest being Saddam Husayn. Territorial disputes with Iran led to an inconclusive and costly eight-year war (1980-88). In August 1990, Iraq seized Kuwait, but was expelled by US-led, UN coalition forces during the Gulf War of January-February 1991. Following Kuwait's liberation, the UN Security Council (UNSC) required Iraq to scrap all weapons of mass destruction and long-range missiles and to allow UN verification inspections. Continued Iraqi non-compliance with UNSC resolutions during the past 12 years resulted in the US-led invasion of Iraq in March 2003 and the ouster of the Saddam Husayn regime. Coalition forces remain in Iraq, helping to restore degraded infrastructure and facilitating the establishment of a freely elected government. (...) Despite restored diplomatic relations in 1990, disputes with Iran over maritime and land boundaries, navigation channel, and other issues from eight-year war persist; land and Shatt al Arab boundary demarcation put an end to claims to Kuwait and to Bubiyan and Warbah islands, but no maritime boundary exists with Kuwait in the Persian Gulf; Iraq protests Turkey's hydrological projects to regulate the Tigris and Euphrates rivers upstream.

Kenya

Founding president and liberation struggle icon Jomo KENYATTA led Kenya from independence until his death in 1978, when President Daniel Toroitich Arap MOI took power in a constitutional succession. The country was a de facto one-party state from 1969 until 1982 when the ruling Kenya African National Union (KANU) made itself the sole legal party in Kenya. MOI acceded to internal and external pressure for political liberalization in late 1991. The ethnically fractured opposition failed to dislodge KANU from power in elections in 1992 and 1997, which were marred[1] by violence and fraud, but are viewed as having generally reflected the will of the Kenyan people. President MOI stepped down in December of 2002 following fair and peaceful elections. Mwai KIBAKI, running as the candidate of the multiethnic, united opposition group, the National Rainbow Coalition, defeated KANU candidate Uhuru KENYATTA and assumed the presidency following a campaign centered on an anticorruption platform. (...)
Kenya's administrative boundary still extends into the Sudan, creating the „Ilemi triangle".

[CIA Factbook, Politics/factbook2003/factbook/countrylisting.html]

[1] to make something less enjoyable

Unit 12: Budget for the Ministry for Economic Cooperation

Redoubling efforts to fight AIDS

„The fight against HIV/AIDS is undoubtedly one of the biggest challenges of our times." That was the reminder issued by the (...) Parliamentary State Secretary of the Ministry for Development (...) when she addressed a Special Session of the United Nations General Assembly in New York. She also emphasized the special role played by UNAIDS in fighting AIDS, malaria and tuberculosis. The German government is pursuing an integrated strategy, combining support for the programs of the Global Fund to Fight AIDS and the European Union with bilateral assistance for 50 countries. Total annual funding amounts to 300 million euros. The focus is not only on providing health care and affordable medication; successfully fighting HIV/AIDS also means reducing poverty, promoting education and, not least, empowering women. (...)

http://www.bmz.de/en/media/newsletter/newsletter18/005.html

Promoting sexual self-determination

Sexuality and family planning – that is the focus of this year's report on the State of the World Population. At the presentation of the report in Berlin, [the] Development Minister (...) welcomed the choice of topic, saying that everybody should have the right to sexual self-determination, particularly girls and women. According to the report, around 14 million girls aged between 10 and 19 give birth each year. Most of them live in developing countries. Abortions and complications when giving birth are amongst the main causes of death in this age group. And young people make up almost half of new cases of HIV. The BMZ provides an annual sum of 120 million euros to support improvements in the field of reproductive health. It also provides a further 186 million euros for education, because without education there can be no hope of self-determination – particularly for girls.

http://www.bmz.de/en/media/newsletter/newsletter19/005.html

Iraq: Humanitarian aid a priority

According to the most recent figures, the German government will be providing a total of 193 million euros (...) for humanitarian aid and reconstruction in Iraq. Speaking in Berlin during the international donor conference in Madrid, [the] Minister [for Development] said the most urgent tasks were to rapidly improve conditions for the people of Iraq and to improve security. Once more, she demanded that the UN should play a greater role in Iraq. With reference to the discussion on (...) World Bank loans for Iraq, she said that such loans must not result in funds being cut for the world's poorest countries, particularly those in Africa. (...)

http://www.bmz.de/en/media/newsletter/newsletter19/005.html

Desertification affects everyone

The United Nations estimates that over a billion people and around one third of the world's agricultural land is affected by advancing desertification. Developments in Africa are particularly dramatic. „The poor are being robbed of their already inadequate resources for survival," warned [the] Minister [for Development] at the latest Conference of the Parties of the United Nations Convention to Combat Desertification. She called on all parties to implement the Convention without delay, as otherwise useful and urgently needed arable land would continue to be lost at a rapid rate. Desertification harms not only to people in the immediate area but also the global climate and ultimately, therefore, us all. The BMZ is providing € 1.5 billion of support for desertification programmes in Africa, Latin America and Asia.

http://www.bmz.de/en/media/newsletter/newsletter17/005.html

Not all coffee is created equal

Only sustainably produced and processed coffee beans can guarantee coffee growers in developing and newly industrialising countries a secure livelihood and ensure a high-quality product in the long term. In association with the German Coffee Association, the [Ministry for Development] is helping to develop a code of conduct under which coffee producers, processors and traders will commit themselves to work towards fair prices, environmentally-friendly production methods and acceptable social and labour standards – things that can't always be taken for granted in many countries. [The] Parliamentary State Secretary at the [Ministry for Development], met with representatives of the initiative's governing body in Berlin to discuss the project. Enjoying a cup of coffee here in Germany should not mean threatening someone's livelihood elsewhere.

http://www.bmz.de/en/media/newsletter/newsletter16/005.html

Unit 5: Those who sleep rough

Picture 2

Appendix

Role Cards

Unit 6

Role play 1

On the phone

Role card B

You are working in the subscriptions department of JoJo, a monthly English music magazine. Someone is calling.

- Ask for the caller's customer number.
  If the caller doesn't know the number, you've got to look it up in your computer.
  The caller's customer number is ASN 00000673044.
- Ask the caller to spell his or her surname and first name. Ask the caller to spell the name of the street he/she lives in.
  According to what your computer says, the street is Ägidienstr. 3.
- Try twice to sell him/her a 2 year subscription that costs 25 % off the regular price plus two free CDs.
- Ask the caller how he/she wants to pay.
- Ask for the customer's credit card number.
- Ask for card's expiration date. (If the caller doesn't understand, that means how long the card is valid.)
- As far as you know there have never been any problems with credit cards.
- Thank the customer.

Useful expressions

How can I help you? • Could you please ... • Sorry, I have to ... • We can offer you ... • Could you repeat that, please?

Role play 2
Job interview

Role card B
Personnel manager of an IT firm
Introduce yourself and talk about your company and the job you're offering: you sell tailor-made computer programs; your are looking for an office boy or girl; the applicant is to do little jobs in the office and needs to be able to use a PC.

Ask the applicant to
- introduce himself/herself
- say what he/she is doing at the moment
- say what his/her qualifications are
- say whether he/she has already done a job of any kind, and if yes, what job(s)
- say how well he/she can use a computer
- speak about his/her interests and hobbies
- tell you two of his/her strong points and two of his/her weak points

At the end of the session thank the applicant. Tell him/her that he/she will be hearing from you.

TIP:
Offer confirmation:

Nice to meet you. • Fine. • Very good. • That's interesting. • Can you tell me more about it?

Appendix

Ausgewählte Grammatikprobleme

A Eine kleine Zeitreise

English tenses are different from German tenses

1. Sich in der Zeit bewegen

a) Einen Punkt oder Zeitraum auf dem Zeitstrahl bestimmen:

yesterday 

Past

Past Simple
They **sat** down, **opened** the picnic basket and **enjoyed** the evening sun.
We **didn't eat** anything.

Past Progressive
They **were sitting** on the porch when the phone rang.
We **were waiting** for 3 hours

abgeschlossen: last week, in 2003, 20 years ago, the other day, earlier this week

Präteritum

now 

Present

Present Simple
Peter **comes** home late every day.
I **don't eat** Brussel sprouts.

usually

Present Progressive
She's having her lunch break at the moment, would you call again later, please?

now

Präsens

tomorrow 

Future

Es gibt im Englischen sehr viele Möglichkeiten, Zukunft auszudrücken. (Siehe Seite 322)

Futur

b) Von einem Punkt auf dem Zeitstrahl zurückschauen (die Perfekt-Zeiten):

Past

Past Perfect

Past Perfect Simple
She **had left** (before he arrived).

They **had eaten up** everything
(before Peter arrived).

Past Perfect Progressive
We **had been walking** fast for three hours until we reached the hotel.
They **had been singing and drinking** all night.

Sie **waren** gegangen, bevor ...
Sie **hatten** alle aufgegessen, bevor ...
Wir **waren** drei Stunden lang schnell **gegangen**, bis ...
Sie **hatten** die ganze Nacht **gesungen** und **getrunken**.

Plusquamperfekt

Present

Present Perfect

Present Perfect Simple
I have fallen.
I have broken my leg.

Present Perfect Progressive
I have been sitting here for 3 hours.
I have been learning English for 4 years.

for 3 years, since 1999, ever, never, so far, since I saw her, lately, up to now

Ich **bin** gefallen.
Ich **habe** mir das Bein gebrochen.

Ich sitze hier seit 3 Stunden.
Ich lerne seit 4 Jahren Englisch.

Perfekt

Future

Future Perfect

They **will have arrived** by 9 p.m. tomorrow.
She **will have finished** her homework by then.

Sie werden bis 9 Uhr morgen Abend **angekommen sein**.
Sie wird ihre Hausaufgaben bis dahin **gemacht haben**.

Futur II

Beachte:
Im Deutschen gibt es bei den Perfekt-Zeiten **zwei verschiedene Hilfsverben (sein und haben)**, im Englischen dagegen nur **eines (have)**.

c) Man kann übrigens auch von einem Punkt in der Vergangenheit in die Zukunft schauen:

Past Progressive
*I knew I **was meeting** her in Paris the next day.*

***To be + infinitive** (klingt formell)*
*The meeting **was to be held** the following day.*

To be about to
*I could sense that he **was about to** fall the very next moment.*

2. Die progressive Form (Verlaufsform)

Für die Verlaufsform gibt es im Deutschen keine Entsprechung. So wird sie gebildet:

to be + verb + ing

Hier eine Faustregel, wann die Verlaufsform benutzt wird:

Sie drückt aus

1.	2.	3.
dass etwas **"gerade"** passiert, passierte oder passieren wird. Im Deutschen kann man dann das Wort **„gerade"** einfügen. Das gilt für alle Zeitstufen: We **are learning** English. We **were sitting** in a café, when he arrived. We **will be sitting** on the beach when ...	**Zeitdauer:** We **were waiting** for fifteen minutes. While she **was changing** her clothes she ... She **was playing** the piano while I **was reading** the newspaper 	**emotionalen Nachdruck:** (oft mit *"always"*) You'**re always wasting** your money!!! 

Es gibt eine Reihe von Verben, die in der Regel nicht in der Progressive Form stehen, und zwar solche, die keine Handlung ausdrücken, z. B.

astonish, believe, desire, detest, dislike, doubt, feel, forgive, guess, hate, imagine, intend, know, like, love, mean, prefer, realize, satisfy, see, smell, suppose, taste, think, understend, want

oder gar nicht:

belong, to, concern, contain, cost, deserve, lack, matter, need, own, possess, seem, sound, tend

Einige dieser Verben können aber durchaus auch in der Verlaufsform erscheinen, wenn sie in einer veränderten Bedeutung Handlung ausdrücken:

I was just thinking if ...
I'm seeing the doctor tomorrow.

oder wenn man Nachdruck verleihen will:

I'm hating it!!!

Im Passiv gibt es die Progressive Form nur im Present und im Past: **The bridge is/was being built.**

3. Was das Present Simple alles kann

1. Es drückt „ewige Wahrheiten“ aus:
   The sun **rises** in the east.

2. Es beschreibt gewohnheitsmäßige Handlungen:
   He **reads** the Times (not the Guardian).

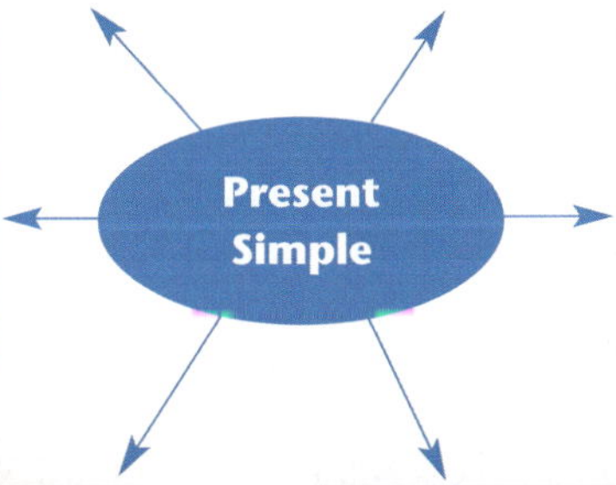

3. Man demonstriert etwas:
   I now **place** the rolls in the oven.

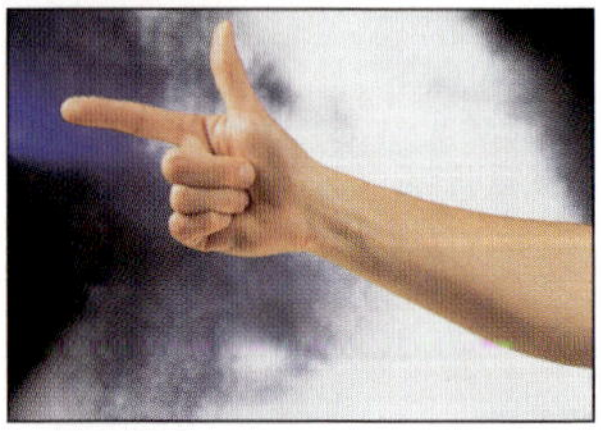

4. Man ruft aus:
   There you **go**!

5. Man beschreibt einen Handlungsablauf:
   Luisa **looks** at her Dad.
   She **doesn't believe** ...

6. Ein Sportreporter beschreibt, was im Stadion gerade los ist:
   Beckham **passes** the ball to Shearer. Shearer **rushes** down the wings, **outfoxes** the Nottingham defense; one player, two ... now he **hits** a waist-high cross from the touchline into the penalty area and ...

Übung:
Erzählen Sie, was Sie gewöhnlich morgens, mittags, abends, am Wochenende machen.

4. Vergangenes ausdrücken

a) Ich traf ihn gestern.

In der Umgangssprache nehmen wir im Deutschen oft das Perfekt, um eine abgeschlossene Handlung auszudrücken.

*Er **ist** gestern **angekommen***
(für: Er kam gestern an).

*Ich **hab** ihn gestern **getroffen***
(für: Ich traf ihn gestern).

In einigen Regionen, beispielsweise im Rheinland, verwendet man dafür gelegentlich sogar das Plusquamperfekt:

*Wir **waren** gestern im Kino **gewesen***
(für: Wir waren gestern im Kino).

Diese Strukturen haben wir im Kopf, wenn wir uns in der englischen Sprache ausdrücken wollen. Also passieren Fehler.

Beachte:
Das Englische drückt eine abgeschlossene Handlung mit dem **Past Tense** aus:

*He **arrived** yesterday.*

Signalwörter können hier helfen: Yesterday, last week, when (did you arrive)?

b) Ein klassischer Irrtum: „Früher"

Irgendwie spukt in den Köpfen vieler Schülerinnen und Schüler herum, „früher" entspräche der englischen Formulierung *in former times*. *In former times* meint aber etwas, was wirklich lange zurückliegt: In früheren Zeiten, einst:

*Isfahan was renowned **in former times** for its architectural grandeur and for the beauty of its public gardens. Most of the gardens and many of the edifices are now in ruins.*

*Japan has a long tradition of gardens inspired by Chinese and Korean models. **In former times,** palaces, temples, teahouses, and private houses all had garden settings that were closely integrated with the buildings.*

Beachte:
Eine schöne Entsprechung der deutschen Formulierung „früher" ist im Englischen **„used to"**.

Übung:
„Früher." Eine wahre Geschichte?

Erzähle einem englischen Freund Freds Geschichte.

1998

heute

Fred used to know every punk in town. Now he meets different people.

Früher	heute
• trug Fred einen Irokesenschnitt	• kurze Haare
• zerissene T-Shirts	• saubere Hemden
• karierte Hosen	• klassische Hosen, oft mit Hosenträgern
• hing er in Punk-Kneipen rum	• trendige Bistros und Cafes
• hörte er nur wilde Musik	• hört er nur noch gelegentlich die alten CDs
• fluchte und schimpfte er den ganzen Tag	• versucht er sich gewählt auszudrücken
• schwänzte er die Schule, so oft er konnte	• besucht er brav die Abendkurse
• lieh er sich Geld von seinen Kumpels	• hat er ein Sparkonto

Hausaufgabe:

Finden Sie ein altes Foto von sich und ein neues. Schreiben Sie auf, was Sie früher gemacht haben oder wie Sie früher waren und wie Sie heute sind bzw. was Sie heute tun.

5. Sind Sie perfekt beim Present Perfect und beim Perfekt?

Das **Present Perfect** drückt grob gesagt drei Sachverhalte aus:

1. dass ein Vorgang in der Vergangenheit zwar beendet ist, aber noch Auswirkungen auf die Gegenwart hat:

   *Wer **hat** das Fenster **geöffnet**?*
   *Who **has opened** the window?*
   (Das Fenster ist offen.)

2. dass gerade eben passiert ist (oft mit *just*):

   He ***has just left*** *the room.*
   Er ***ist*** *gerade* ***hinausgegangen***

3. dass eine Handlung in der Vergangenheit begonnen hat und bis in die Gegenwart andauert:

   I've been learning *English for 5 years.*

Die ersten beiden Fälle machen keine Probleme, weil wir im Deutschen die parallelen Strukturen verwenden. Der dritte Sachverhalt macht Schülerinnen und Schülern jedoch oft Schwierigkeiten. Das hat folgenden Grund:

Die englische Sprache drückt den Zeitraum, der in der Vergangenheit beginnt und in die Gegenwart reicht oder darüber hinaus andauert, **anders** aus als die deutsche Sprache. Das ist einer der **wenigen echten Unterschiede** zwischen dem Deutschen und dem Englischen, wenn es um die Zeiten geht!

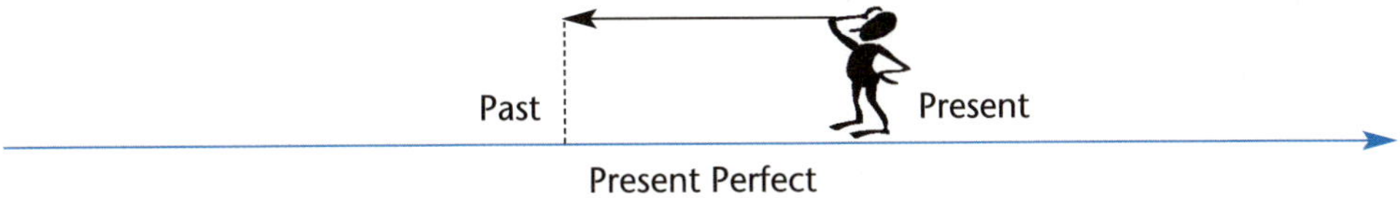

Wenn wir von der Gegenwart aus **zurückschauen**, verwenden wir im Deutschen in Verbindung mit dem Wort „**seit**" das Präsens.

Er ***arbeitet*** *hier* ***seit*** *3 Jahren. Er* ***arbeitet*** *hier* ***seit*** *2002.*

Diese Struktur haben wir im Kopf. („Der schlimmste Gegner beim Sprachenlernen ist die eigene Muttersprache.")

Im Englischen dagegen steht das Present Perfect, oft in der Verlaufsform:

He ***has been working*** *here* ***for*** *3 years. He's* ***been working*** *here* ***since*** *2002.*

Oft macht auch die Unterscheidung zwischen „since" und „for" Schwierigkeiten.

since drückt einen Zeitpunkt aus
for drückt einen Zeitraum aus

Übung: Since oder for? Entscheiden Sie:

Beispiel: *the beginning of the year* ***since*** *the beginning of the year*

I came in • 1994 • the last 3 weeks • the end of the term • 20 years • Monday • 7 months • a long time • dad bought the big car • hundreds of years • 25 minutes • the lesson started • the last few days

Dagegen benutzen wir im Deutschen bei den Ausdrücken „**schon einmal**" (ever) und „**noch nie**" (never) oft das Präteritum, nicht das Perfekt (vgl. hierzu auch S. 340).

Warst *du schon* ***einmal*** *in England? (Für: Bist du schon einmal in England gewesen?)*
Englisch: ***Have*** *you ever* ***been*** *to England?* ***I've never been*** *there.*

6. Zukünftiges ausdrücken

Die englische Sprache kennt viele verschiedene Möglichkeiten, Zukünftiges auszudrücken. Dabei ist das will-Future nicht unbedingt die gebräuchlichste Form. Die folgende Übersicht soll etwas Orientierung geben:

J: What **are** you **doing** on Saturday evening?

M: Well, mmhh, nothing in particular.

J: I'**m giving** a party and it would be nice if you could come.

Wenn man etwas vorhat, das **fest arrangiert** ist (Jane hat das Essen und die Getränke für die Party schon eingekauft!), drückt man mit dem **Present Progressive** Zukünftiges am besten aus.

J: It'**s going to be** great fun! (a)

M: **You're not going to invite** that terrible bloke from the sales department again? (b)

to be going to + verb nimmt man,

a) um auszudrücken, dass man sich über Zukünftiges **sicher** ist, weil alle (oft äußeren) Anzeichen dafür sprechen
b) um eine **Absicht, einen festen Entschluss** auszudrücken, oft in der Verneinung

M: **Will** George **be** there, too, as usual? (a)

J: **I think** he **will bring** his new girl friend, so he probably **won't stay** that long. (b)

M: Mhm, I understand. I'**ll help** you with the dishes afterwards. (c)

Das will-Future
a) drückt aus, dass etwas **unabänderlich** so sein wird.
b) folgt ganz natürlich auf Ausdrücke wie **I think, I suppose, I guess.**
c) drückt ein **Versprechen, oft spontan gefasst**, aus.

J: I'**ll have** the fish, please!

M: And I'**ll have** the Yorkshire pudding, please!

Das **will-Future** wird auch gebraucht, wenn man **in einem Restaurant** etwas bestellt.

M: Good bye!

J: I'**ll be seeing** you tomorrow at the meeting!

Das Future Progressive wird benutzt, wenn etwas **selbstverständlich so sein** wird, es klingt außerdem höflich und auch diskret (z. B. an der Hotelrezeption: „**Will** you **be paying** by credit card, Madam?")

7 Übung zu den Zeiten

Machen Sie die folgende Übung ganz schnell, um zu sehen, ob Sie die Zeiten automatisch richtig verwenden.

Mr Holmes is looking for something.

Fragen Sie ihn auf Englisch. Seien Sie bei der ersten Frage höflich.

a) Fragen Sie (und seien Sie bei der ersten Frage wirklich höflich!),

1. was er hier macht,
2. wie lange er schon so steht,
3. ob er etwas gefunden hat,
4. ob er immer so arbeitet,
5. ob Sie ihn stören,
6. was er tun würde, wenn es zu regnen anfinge,
7. wann er seinen Schlüssel verloren hat,
8. ob er heute Abend auch zu dem Empfang (reception) kommt,
9. ob er dann wieder den Anzug tragen wird, den er vor schon 20 Jahren gekauft hat,
10. ob er gerade in sein Büro ging, als Sie ihn gestern sahen,
11. ob er schon einmal in dem netten Pub um die Ecke war,
12. ob er am Wochenende schon etwas vor hat (Sie würden ihn gerne einladen).

b) Sagen Sie ihm,

1. dass Sie ihm schon 15 Minuten zuschauen,
2. dass Sie eigentlich auf den Bus warten, der aber schon weg war, als Sie vor 20 Minuten zu Bushaltestelle kamen,
3. dass Sie ihm helfen werden, wenn er es möchte,
4. dass es bald zu regnen anfangen wird, weil Sie da drüben schon einige dunkle Wolken sehen,
5. dass es gestern auch zu regnen anfing, als Sie im Garten arbeiteten,
6. dass Sie morgen auf eine Geburtstagsfeier gehen,
7. dass die Gastgeberin morgen 50 werden wird,
8. dass Sie sie schon ewig kennen,
9. dass Sie glauben, dass Sie ihn jetzt doch verlassen müssen,
10. dass Sie sich gefreut haben, ihn zu treffen.

B If-Sätze

If I know everything about if-clauses, communication will be so much easier.

1. Drei Grundtypen

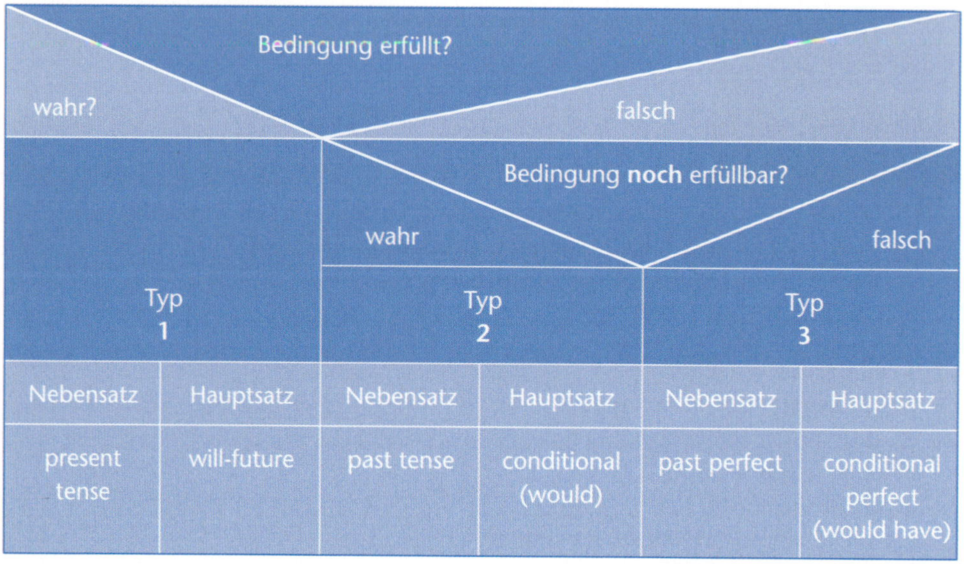

Hinweis: Dies ist eine logische Erklärung. Sie ist für den Lerntyp gedacht, der Zusammenhänge verstehen will. Wenn Sie ein Lerntyp sind, der gefühlsmäßig vorgeht oder lieber Regeln auswendig lernt, kann es sinnvoller sein, bei der gewohnten Methode zu bleiben.

Man kann drei Grundtypen des If-Satzes unterscheiden.

- Typ 1 ist gegeben, wenn man **nicht** behaupten kann, dass die Bedingung **nicht** erfüllt ist, anders gesagt, die Bedingung ist erfüllt oder man weiß es nicht, daher das Fragezeichen hinter „wahr".

  Beispiel:
  If it rains, I will stay at home.

  Da der fragliche Zeitpunkt noch in der Zukunft liegt, ist naturgemäß ungewiss, ob die Bedingung, dass es regnet, erfüllt ist.

- Typ 2 liegt vor, wenn die Bedingung zwar nicht erfüllt ist, aber noch erfüllt werden kann.

  Beispiel:
  If that motor worked properly, we would not have these constant breakdowns.

  Die Bedingung, dass der Motor ordentlich läuft, ist nicht erfüllt, er läuft eben nicht ordentlich. Das könnte sich aber durch entsprechende Eingriffe jederzeit ändern. Es ist noch nicht zu spät.

- Typ 3 liegt vor, wenn die Bedingung nicht nur nicht erfüllt ist, sondern auch wegen des Zeitablaufs nicht mehr erfüllbar ist.

  Beispiel:
  If we had hurried up, we would have caught the train.

Die Bedingung, dass wir uns beeilen, ist nicht erfüllt und auch nicht mehr erfüllbar. Die Situation, in der wir uns hätten beeilen können, ist vorbei. Es lässt sich nachträglich nichts mehr ändern.

Die drei Typen sind nur Grundtypen. Die angegebenen tenses sind nur die häufigsten in typischen Situationen. Die Abweichungen ergeben sich oft aus der natürlichen Logik des Zeitablaufs.

Beispiel:
If he did that, he did wrong.

Es wird diskutiert, ob jemand der Täter war. Man kann nicht behaupten, dass die Bedingung nicht erfüllt ist. Daher liegt Typ 1 vor. Trotzdem steht in beiden Teilsätzen past tense, weil es sich um vergangene Abläufe handelt. Lernökonomisch erscheint es sinnvoll, zunächst von nur drei Grundtypen auszugehen, aber gedanklich Abweichungen oder eine weitere Ausdifferenzierung zuzulassen.

2. Übung

Ordnen Sie folgende Beispiele aus Unit 7, Talkline, in das Schema (s. S. 324, bitte auf einem Extrablatt erstellen) ein und begründen Sie Ihre Entscheidung:

- If it's resting I'll wake it up. (p. 208, l. 6)
- Look matey, this parrot wouldn't voom if I put four thousand volts through it. (p. 208, l. 37)
- If you hadn't nailed it to the perch, it would be pushing up the daisies. (p. 208, l. 44)
- If you want to get anything done in this country, you've got to complain till you are blue in the mouth. (p. 208, l. 49)

C Die sehr aktive Rolle des Passivs im Englischen

The importance of the passive voice in English

Der Passivsatz ist im Englischen wichtiger und häufiger als im Deutschen. Es wird verwendet, wenn der Handelnde nicht bekannt oder unwichtig ist. Der folgende Aktivsatz klingt unglücklich, weil natürlich ein neues Magazin einen menschlichen Gründer haben muss, dieser aber in der Aussage keinerlei Rolle spielt:

Someone has launched a new magazine. Besser schreibt man:

A new magazine has been launched.

Das Objekt des Aktivsatzes wird zum Subjekt des Passivsatzes. Das Subjekt des Aktivsatzes wird im Passivsatz zum Anhängsel mit „by". Der Handelnde wird aber mit „by" nur angehängt, wenn er erwähnenswert ist. Da er im Passivsatz nicht mehr Subjekt ist, ist seine Erwähnung vom Satzbau her nicht mehr erforderlich. Im obigen Beispielsatz wäre als ein Anhängen von „by someone" nicht nur überflüssig, sondern unsinnig.

Das Passiv wird auch verwendet, wenn man den Handelnden am Satzende ganz besonders betonen will. Angenommen, jemand stellt eine falsche Behauptung darüber auf, wer Amerika entdeckt hat, und Sie korrigieren ihn:

No, America was discovered by Columbus.

Das Passiv kann auch einen besseren Textzusammenhang ermöglichen, sozusagen den Mörtel zwischen den Ziegeln. In jeder der folgenden Zeilen steht am Anfang etwas Bekanntes oder Gegebenes, während gegen Ende des Teilsatzes etwas Neues steht. Das Neue wird im nächsten Teilsatz oder Satz als bekannt wieder aufgegriffen. Das Passiv ermöglicht, jeden Teil wahlweise an den Anfang oder das Ende des Teilsatzes zu bringen, eben genau dorthin, wo man ihn aus Gründen des Textzusammenhanges haben will.

A new kind of radio has been developed.	„Ein neuartiges Radio" steht am Textanfang und bezieht sich somit auf keinen vorangegangenen Teil. Die neue Information sagt aus, dass es entwickelt wurde.
It took only a few years to have it ready for mass production.	Auf die Entwicklung wird wieder Bezug genommen und zusätzlich eine Angabe über die Dauer gemacht. Die Massenproduktionsreife ist dann die neue Information.
Only few people Germany, however, have ever heard of DAB Digital Radio ...	Das Thema Massenproduktion wird wieder aufgegriffen durch die Aussage, dass es in Deutschland nur wenige Leute gibt, die (= neue Information) davon gehört haben.
... whereas this new kind of radio is well-known in Britain, ...	„Die neue Art von Radio" greift in anderer Formulierung DAB wieder auf (= bekannte Information) und macht dazu die neue Aussage, dass diese Innovation in Großbritannien allgemein bekannt ist.
... where dozens of programmes are broadcast via DAB.	„Wo" bezieht sich wieder auf den vorherigen Teilsatz. Die neue Information ist die Aussage, dass es dort Dutzende von Programmen gibt.

Somit stellt das Passiv ein wichtiges Mittel dar, einen Text kohärent, also zusammenhängend zu machen. Da man im Englischen im Gegensatz zum Deutschen einen Satz nicht einfach mit dem Objekt beginnen kann, verwendet man erforderlichenfalls das Passiv, um eine Information gezielt an den Anfang des Satzes zu stellen.

Ein Aktivsatz kann zwei Objekte haben, ein direktes und ein indirektes.

They gave the book to him.

In *The book was given to him* wurde das direkte Objekt zum Subjekt, in *He was given the book* wurde das indirekte Objekt zum Subjekt. Man beachte, dass hier dem deutschen „ihm" das englische „he" entspricht.

D Gerund oder Infinitiv? – Ein wichtiger Unterschied im Englischen

Gerund or infinfive? – An important destinction

1. Gerundium oder Infinitiv?

Das Gerund ist ein Verb, das zu einem Substantiv gemacht wird (substantivierte Verbform). Im Deutschen erfolgt dies i. d. R. durch den Artikel „das" sowie die Großschreibung des Verbs und im Englischen durch Hinzufügen der Silbe „-ing" an den Verbstamm.

Im Deutschen werden auch Gerundien verwendet ...

Das Arbeiten *fällt ihm jetzt schwer.*
Das Gerund wird hier als Subjekt angewandt.

Er findet, dass man sich ***beim Arbeiten*** *immer konzentrieren sollte.*
Das Gerund wird hier als Objekt angewandt.

... als Ersatz für das Substantiv:

Die Arbeit *fällt ihm jetzt schwer.*
Er findet, dass man sich ***bei der Arbeit*** *immer konzentrieren sollte.*
Hier wird ein „echtes" Substantiv verwendet.

Beachte:
Die Verwendung des Gerunds ist im Deutschen eine Frage des Stils, also eine Option.

Bilden wir also aus der deutschen Form des Gerunds (z. B. als Subjekt) einen englischen Satz, so können wir in diesem einen Fall im Englischen identisch verfahren.

Working *is difficult for him now.*
Das Gerundium **als Subjekt** ist im Englischen zugleich Stilfrage und Option.

Wie könnte man die Doppeldeutigkeit folgender Sätze klären?

Visiting *relatives can be a nuisance.*
Flying *planes can be dangerous.*

Beachte:
Das Gerund als Subjekt ist im Englischen zwar eine Option, doch es *muss* stehen:

a) unmittelbar nach bestimmten Verben, z. B. Verben mit Präposition
b) nach Substantiven mit Präposition
c) nach Adjektiven mit Präposition
d) nach feststehenden Ausdrücken

Es muss also nach vielen Wortarten stehen, wobei die dazugehörende Präposition entscheidend ist. Hierbei handelt es sich also um eine verpflichtende Anwendung, nicht um eine Option. Die diversen Ausdrücke, nach denen das Gerundium stehen muss, sind auswendig zu lernen. Unten ist eine Auswahl aufgeführt.

TIPP!

Hilfe bietet auch das einsprachige Wörterbuch. Es verweist auf die ing-Form.

2. Die Anwendung des Gerunds

a) Nach Verben ohne Präposition

admit	advise	appreciate	avoid
do not like	detest	can't stand	mind
miss	consider	enjoy	recall
delay	feel like	resent	deny
finish	risk	dislike	hate
suggest	involve	fancy/imagine	postpone
keep	practise	finish	dread

Beachte:
Das Verb *stop* gehört ebenfalls der Liste an, weist aber eine semanitische Besonderheit auf:

stop + Gerund = aufhören etwas zu tun
stop + Infinitiv = stehen bleiben, *um* etwas zu tun

*Most stars **dislike/hate being** stared at.*
*We **enjoy cooking** for our friends so much.*
*Do you **mind me/my smoking**, Madam?*
*Presently, John and Pam can't **fancy/imagine going** to Australia for good.*
*Would you please **stop crying**, it's breaking my heart.*

b) Nach Verben mit Präposition

dream of	succeed in	think of	look forward to*
be/get used to*	rely on	carry on	keep on
put off	thank for	give up	worry about

***Beachte:** *to* ist hier Präposition, **nicht** Teil eines Infinitivs

*The Belgians are **used to drinking** many varieties of beer.*
*I have **put off calling** the Hansons so many times. I must do it now.*
*We **look forward to meeting** you at the Hannover Fair.*
***Thank you for being** so patient with us.*

c) Nach Substantiven mit Präposition

danger of	idea of	difficulty (in)	possibility of

*Alice and Kevin liked the **idea of living** abroad for a year or two.*
*Initially the company had great **difficulty (in) marketing** the new model.*

d) Nach Adjektiven mit Präposition

afraid of	angry about/at	ashamed of	bad/good at
crazy about	famous for	fond of	glad about
interested in	keen on	proud of	tired of

*How can you be **afraid of skiing** down this hill?*
*I'm not **interested in watching** this stupid show.*
*Ladies and gentlemen, we are **proud of presenting** you the winner of the contest.*
*Are you **good at playing** cards?*

e) Nach feststehenden Ausdrücken

It's no use/no good calling.	Es nützt nichts .../Es hat keinen Zweck ...
It's worth going to the market.	Es lohnt sich zum Markt zu gehen
There's no telling what will happen.	Man kann nie vorhersagen, was passieren wird.
What about/How about going out?	Wie wär's, wenn wir ...?
She **was** too **busy doing** other things.	Sie war zu sehr mit anderen Dingen beschäftigt.
After driving all night ...	Nachdem er die ganze Nacht gefahren war ...
Instead of going to school ...	Anstatt in die Schule zu gehen ...
Before signing the cheque ...	Bevor man den Scheck unterschreibt ...
On arriving he went to ...	Nach seiner Ankunft, ging er ...
Apart from being pretty, she is ...	Sie ist nicht nur hübsch, sondern ...
By stimulating your muscles ...	Wenn/Indem sie ihre Muskeln stimulieren ...
This saw **is good for cutting** trees.	Diese Säge ist gut, um Bäume damit zu sägen.
She attends classes **as well as working** part time.	Sie geht zur Schule und arbeitet gleichzeitig ...
They watched the birds **without saying** a word.	Sie beobachteten die Vögel, ohne zu sprechen.

3. Unterschiedlicher Gebrauch von Infinitiv und Gerund:

Infinitiv	**Gerund**
I meant to call you tonight. *Ich wollte/hatte die Absicht dich heute Abend anzurufen.*	If you want to get a good seat it **means getting** up very early. *Wenn du morgen einen guten Platz haben möchtest, dann heißt das ganz früh aufzustehen.*
We tried to move the car, but ... *Wir versuchten den Wagen zu bewegen, aber ...*	I **tried offering** her flowers, but ... *Ich probierte es mit Blumen, aber ...*
a) Der Infinitiv bezieht sich auf zukünftiges, das Gerundium auf vergangenes Geschehen:	
Remember to post the letter tomorrow. *Vergiss nicht .../Denk daran ...*	I well **remember meeting** her for the ... *Ich weiß noch gut wie ich sie traf ...*
We regret to inform you ... *Wir bedauern Ihnen mitteilen zu müssen ...*	We both **regret buying** this house. *Wir bedauern beide das Haus gekauft zu haben.*
Don't forget to call your sister. *Vergiss nicht deine Schwester anzurufen.*	Our neighbours **forgot leaving** us their keys. *Unsere Nachbarn vergaßen, uns ihre Schlüssel dazulassen.*

4. Übung

Use either a gerund or an infinitive.

(1. learn) a foreign language can be laborious. You have to keep (2. practise) it as often as you can. Vocabulary isn't the biggest problem. You'll only be able (3. reach) perfection if you know how (4. apply) the grammar rules correctly. You can't help (5. make) mistakes at first. One of the reasons for (6. commit) errors is the grammatical system of your native language which constantly interfers with the new grammar. The best way of (7. avoid) mistakes and (8. make) good progress is by (9. learn), (10. practise) and (11. repeat) from time to time what you have learned. But (12. acquire) fluency is a tremendous effort, for you have to keep (13. practise) the language every day. Without (14. practise) you will forget much of what you have learned. This is what happens to emigrants. After (15. speak) their mother tongue more and more rarely in their new home country they start (16. forget) how (17. speak) it correctly. If they have the chance of (18. emigrate) at an early age they master the foreign language very well, but forget their own very quickly. Older emigrants have a double handicap, they don't manage (19. learn) the new language properly and can't avoid (20. forget) their native tongue. But we must remember (21. mention) the positive aspect as well, these people can still be proud of (22. be) bilingual or even multilingual, which is much better than perfection in just one language.

E Ein elegantes Stilmittel: Partizipialkonstruktionen

Participle constructions

Partizipalkonstruktionen dienen oft zur Verkürzung von Nebensäzen. Man kann sie zur Verbesserung seines Stils einsetzen. Man unterscheidet zwei Formen:

Das Partizip Präsens (present participle):	Das Partizip Perfekt (perfect participle):
Do you know the girl talking to Brian? Do you know the girl who is talking ...	The car damaged in an accident is worth a million. The car which/that was damaged in ...

1. Verkürzung von Relativsätzen

The woman laughing from the billboard is a famous actress.
who is
The students travelling around in Europe use this rail pass.
who are
All articles sold in this shop are from China.
that are

2. Verkürzung von Nebensätzen ohne Konjunktion

Feeling tired after the long walk, I went to bed.
Because I felt tired .../As I felt tired ...

Having decided to book a holiday, Cynthia and Paul went to the travel agency.
As Cynthia and Paul had decided to book a holiday, ...

Neglected by most holidaymakers for years, the Black Sea is being rediscovered.
The Black Sea was neglected by most holidaymakers for years, now it is being rediscovered.

3. Verkürzung von Nebensätzen mit Konjunktion

You see, while pouring in the flour you have to stir quickly.
You see, while you are pouring in the flour you have to stir quickly.

Though trained as a paramedic, he was now working in a store.
Though he was/had been trained as a paramedic, he was now working in a store.

They almost didn't speak as if trying not to arouse suspicion.
They almost didn't speak as if they tried not to arouse suspicion.

4. Partizipialkonstruktion mit eigenem Sinnsubjekt

The road being too muddy, even the Landrover couldn't pass.
As the road was too muddy, even the Landrover couldn't pass.

The courtroom cleared, the defendant was at last arrested.
When the courtroom was cleared, the defendant was at last arrested.

5. Die „with"-Partizipialkonstruktion

I can't work with the radio playing all the time.	Ich kann nicht arbeiten, wenn das Radio die ganze Zeit über spielt.
With spring approaching and the days getting longer, people have more energy.	Da der Frühling naht und die Tage länger werden, haben die Leute mehr Energie.

6. Partizipialkonstruktion bei parallelen Handlungen

They remained sitting when all the guests had left.	Als alle Gäste gegangen waren, blieben sie sitzen.
She stood waiting outside for her husband.	Sie stand da und wartete draußen auf ihren Mann.
The dog came running up to me.	Der Hund kam auf mich zugelaufen.
The suspect was seen leaving the pub at 10:15 p.m.	Der Verdächtige wurde gesehen wie/als er das Lokal um 22:15 Uhr verließ.
Our neighbours watched us moving in.	Sie sahen uns nur kurz zu.
Our neighbours watched us move in.	Sie sahen uns die ganze Zeit zu.

Übung 1

Box 1	Box 2
1. Ellie was sitting in an armchair. 2. Anne had a terribble day at the office. 3. Mary was in Manchester for two years. 4. Pam broke her leg. 5. Linda went downtown by car. 6. Sue was shopping at Selfridge's.	a) She worked for a fast food chain. b) She met her friend Cathy. c) She was watching television. d) She had to answer all incoming calls. e) She was skiing in the Alps. f) She said she would be back in two hours.

Übung 2

Verbinden Sie zwei Sätze zu einem. Schreiben Sie die Sätze in Ihr Heft.

1. Last year my husband and I went to India. We made a trip through several states.
2. The route was planned by our travel agent. It turned out to be a full success.
3. You travel through this country. You have to be prepared for the unexpected.
4. The taxi in Delhi broke down. It was taking us to the station.
5. After he had spend a night in the bar, my husband got really sick.
6. The ambulance took him to the hospital. It had an accident.
7. In the hotel, some clothes had disappeared. They haven't been found yet.
8. Indians renovate certain sights. So they close them to visitors.
9. Elefants carried us on a jungle trail. They refused to take us back.
10. We missed our plane home. We had to stay another night at the hotel.

Übung 3

Übersetzen Sie die folgenden Sätze, indem Sie Partizipialkonstruktionen verwenden. Schreiben Sie die Sätze in Ihr Übungsbuch.

1. Kennst du den Namen des Flusses, der durch die Hauptstadt der USA fließt?
2. Zwei van-Gogh-Gemälde, die bei Sotheby's versteigert wurden, gingen nach Japan.
3. Da er krank war, rief er unverzüglich seinen Arbeitgeber an.
4. Erst als sie den Koffer öffnete, bemerkte sie die Verwechslung.
5. Da ich in der Tat nicht viel über Rom wusste, kaufte ich einen Stadtführer.
6. Nachdem wir so viel gearbeitet haben, können wir uns eine Pause gönnen.
7. Während du an deinem Wein nippst, kannst du mir die Ausstellung zeigen.
8. Sie schaute so verdutzt, als hätte sie einen Geist gesehen.
9. Wir erblickten einen Schwarm kleiner, bunter Fische, als wir den Kopf ins Wasser steckten.
10. Da die Partygäste so aufgekratzt waren, beschlossen wir noch in die Disco zu gehen.
11. Unser Lebensstandard wird fallen, wenn das Einkommensniveau weiter sinkt und die Preise steigen.
12. Robert kam die Treppe heraufgelaufen, um mir zu sagen was passiert war.

F Adjektiv oder Adverb? – Im Englischen sehr wichtig

Adjective or Adverb – an extremely important distinction

1. Was das Adverb kann

Anders als sein Name vermuten lässt, bestimmt das Adverb nicht nur Verben näher:

Verben	Chameleons move **slowly**.
Adjektive	This car is **really** expensive.
Adverbien	He did this trick **incredibly** fast.
Ganze Sätze	Unfortunately, Nick didn't show up.

2. Prädikatsergänzung

Die folgenden Verben binden ein Adjektiv an sich (Prädikatsergänzung). Im Prinzip sind das Verben, die *to be* erweitern. Sie bezeichnen einen Zustand oder eine Zustandsänderung, keine Handlung.

Zustand	**Bedeutung**
She looks good. (⇔ Handlung: She looked nervously at her watch.)	She is pretty.
It feels good.	It is good, go on!
The band sounds good.	The band is good.
The cake tastes good.	The cake is good.

Weitere Verben in dieser Reihe sind:

[**appear • keep • remain • seem • become • get • grow • turn**]

3. Adverbien auf *-ly*

Einige Adverbien haben eine endungslose Form und eine, die mit *-ly* gebildet wird. Letztere hat eine völlig andere Bedeutung. Übersetzen Sie:

He returned home **late**. They stopped **near** the pub. He was ready to leave the party. He has **just** missed the plane. He stopped **short** to take a breath. Tom works **hard** for his money. They didn't play as **fair** as expected.	I haven't seen Harry **lately**. They **nearly** missed the ferry. She **readily** left the party. He was **justly** punished. I'll be with you **shortly**. I can **hardly** understand him. He changes cars **fairly** often.

Übung
Finden Sie noch mehr solcher Adverbien.

4. Gleiche Form von Adjektiv und Adverb

Einige Adverbien haben die gleiche Form wie das entsprechende Adjektiv:

Adjektiv	Adverb
I get a **daily** newspaper. I haven't got **much** money.	Mrs Mopp comes **daily**. He liked her very **much**.

Weitere Wörter aus dieser Reihe sind:

[**yearly • early • far • fast • long • low • enough • little • long • much • better**]

Beachte:
Bedeutungsunterschied bei gleicher Form:

	Adjektiv	Adverb
only	einzig	nur
still	still	noch
well	wohl	gut
ill	krank	böse
pretty	hübsch	ziemlich

5. Steigerung der Adverbien

a) Adverbien, die nicht auf *-ly* enden, werden mit *-er, -est* gesteigert.

fast	faster	fastest

b) Adverbien, die auf *-ly* enden, werden mit *more, most* gesteigert.

quickly	more quickly	most quickly

c) Achten Sie auf die besonderen Steigerungsformen der folgenden Adverbien:

	Grundform	Komparativ	Superlativ
gut, wohl	well	better	best
schlecht, schlimm	badly	worse	worst
wenig	little	less	least
viel	much	more	most
weit	far	further farther	furthest farthest

6. Umschreibungen

Einige Adjektive bilden das Adverb durch Umschreibungen:

Jane is friendly.	She behaves in a **friendly way**. She treats everybody in a **kind way**. She has a very **honest way** of speaking with other people, even if they behave in a rather **unpleasant manner**.

Übersetzen Sie:

1. Er dachte intensiv über das Problem nach und fand eine geschickte Lösung.
2. Du kannst gut spielen, aber das Instrument hört sich nicht gut an.
3. Er zerbrach das Glas unabsichtlich, sei ihm nicht böse.
4. Sie muss sich in letzter Zeit ziemlich oft ärgern.
5. Die Sportler beantworteten bereitwillig alle Fragen der Reporter.
6. Wir hatten kaum Zeit uns auf die schweren Prüfungen vorzubereiten.
7. Politiker reisen meistens mit dem Flugzeug.
8. Unglücklicherweise ist er kein vorsichtiger Fahrer.
9. Vorsichtig drehte sie den Schlüssel um und öffnete langsam die Tür.
10. Dieses Gericht sieht nicht nur herrlich aus, er riecht auch gut.
11. Helen schreibt immer hochinteressante Artikel.
12. In dieser Fabrik lief alles absolut automatisch.
13. Sie ist von ihrer Familie völlig unabhängig.
14. Selten war er nüchtern, wenn er aus dem Pub heimkam.
15. Glücklicherweise hatte er noch rechtzeitig Blumen gekauft.
16. Niemals hätte er gewagt seinem Chef zu widersprechen.
17. Plötzlich hörten wir draußen eine furchtbaren Knall.
18. Noch nie zuvor hatte ich eine solche Explosion gesehen.
19. Es hörte sich ganz schrecklich an.
20. Einmal im Jahr feiert München ausgiebig.
21. Die meisten Menschen ziehen ungern um.
22. Nach dem Sieg schien die Mannschaft ganz zufrieden.

G Probleme mit bestimmten Artikeln?

The definite article should definitely not be a problem.

1. Anwendung

Ohne bestimmten Artikel stehen
in einem allgemeinen Sinn gebrauchte

Mit bestimmtem Artikel stehen
in einem näher erläuterten Sinn gebrauchte

a) Pluralwörter:

Europeans like to travel
students have to work hard

the Europeans in the travel group
the students who live next door

b) Abstrakte Begriffe:

love	the love we had shared
history	the history of the Indians
art, life, fate, nature	
society	the society we live in
people	the people in this room
man, woman, mankind	

c) Abstrakte Begriffe in Verbindung mit einem Adjektiv

modern history, human nature

d) Einrichtungen

als Institution	als Gebäude
He goes to university.	He parked his car opposite the university
They are in hospital.	Do you see the hospital up the hill?

Weitere:
church, class, college, home, market, prison, school, town

2. Der bestimmte Artikel bei erdkundlichen Begriffen

Ohne bestimmten Artikel stehen	Mit bestimmtem Artikel stehen
a) Städte- und Dorfnamen	
London, Oxford, Limerick (allgemein)	the London I once knew (näher spezifiziert)
b) Namen von Straßen, Parks oder Brücken	es sei denn, das the gehört zum Namen
Oxford Street, Regent's Park, London Bridge	the Mall, the Strand, the High Street
c) Einige Gebäude haben keinen ...	... andere schon
Westminster Abbey	the Whitehouse
Victoria Station	the Empire State Building
d)	alle Namen mit of
	The Isle of Man, the Houses of Parliament
e) Kontinente, Länder, Seen, Berge	
bei Bezeichnungen im Singular	bei Bezeichnungen im Plural
Africa, Asia, Australia, Spain, Lake Erie, Mount Everest	the United States, the Bahamas, the Great Lakes

Übung

Fügen Sie den bestimmten Artikel nur dort ein, wo es nötig ist.

My sister made (1) mistake of buying a used car from a dubious dealer on (2) Suffolk Street whom (3) most people know as a swindler. She now knows that (4) cheapness does not mean (5) thriftiness.

I've nothing against (6) dogs in general. But (7) dogs barking in our neighbourhood are driving me crazy. They stand near (8) fence of a nearby house, I think it's the one on the corner of (9) Chester Road, and bark at all (10) passers-by. This is particularly annoying when I find (11) time at last to work on my book on (12) psychology of learning, but then it happens that I can't stand (13) quiet.

At school there is seldom (14) time to treat (15) history of other nations in (16) depth, but as a student at (17) university you can do (18) intensive work in a field that interests you (19) most.

Normally I hate (20) traffic noise, but (21) sound of a Harley Davidson can be pleasant. I bought one at (22) age of 29.

(23) Mont Blanc is situated in (24) France, not in (25) Switzerland and (26) Great Lakes are in (27) USA and (28) Canada and not in (29) former Soviet Union.

(30) tea doesn't grow in Germany but (31) tea I prefer comes from India.

My brother plays (32) piano, my Dad plays (33) poker with his friends.

Annie often goes to parties with (34) Hendersons, they live at (35) corner of (36) Canal Street and (37) High Street. At (38) moment they are not at home, they are on holiday in (39) Hague in (40) Netherlands.

H Wie sie nebenbei Ihre Ansicht einfließen lassen – Modale Hilfsverben

How to show your views: modal auxiliaries

Mithilfe modaler Hilfsverben drückt der Sprecher u. a. seine Meinung bezüglich Wahrheit, Verbindlichkeit, Wahrscheinlichkeit etc. eines Sachverhaltes aus.

Der Sprecher kann		
um etwas bitten	can/could will/would may/might	*Can/could you tell us the way to the railway station, please?* *Will/would you show us your new car, please?* *May/might I use your pen, please?*
zu etwas auffordern/ raten/warnen	must/should/ ought to	*You must see this film.* *You should/ought to spend less money.*
etwas erlauben	can/may	*You can/may park here, if you want.*
sagen, dass etwas notwendig ist	must have to	*You must see a doctor if it stays like this.* *I really must protest.* *You have to wait a long time for an operation if you live in Britain.* Bei *must* kommt der Zwang eher vom Sprecher selbst und bei *have to* eher durch äußere Umstände.
etwas zugestehen	needn't don't have to	*You needn't peel the potatoes before eating them.* *You don't have to pay extra for a child in this hotel.* *Needn't* drückt eher aus, dass etwas überflüssig ist, *don't have to* drückt eher die Abwesenheit von Zwang aus.
etwas verbieten	can't may not mustn't not to be allowed to	*You can't park here.* *May I park here? No, you may not.* *You mustn't drive too fast.* *Visitors are not allowed to leave any unattended baggage.* Bei *may not* und *mustn't* kommt der Zwang eher vom Sprecher, bei *can't* und *not allowed to* eher durch äußere Umstände.
eine Fähigkeit ausdrücken	can to be able to	*He can't drive, he has never learnt it.* *He is unable to drive, he has broken his leg.* Bei *can* geht es mehr um eine in der Person liegende Fähigkeit, bei *able to* eher um äußere Umstände.
	Sofern es in der jeweiligen Zeitstufe keine Wahlmöglichkeit gibt und nur die Umschreibung möglich ist (*have to, able to* etc.), entfallen die feinen Bedeutungsunterschiede.	

I Erfordert seit langem besondere Aufmerksamkeit

Has required special attention for a long time: for/since – during/while

1. For/since

2004 2005 **2006 (now!)** 2007 2008

for

We lived in London for a year
Der Vorgang ist durch seine Zeitdauer festgelegt ⇒ „for". Er liegt komplett in der Vergangenheit ⇒ past tense.

for

We have lived/ have been living in London for a year.
Der Vorgang ist durch seine Zeitdauer festgelegt ⇒ „for", hat in der Vergangenheit angefangen und dauert noch an ⇒ present perfect.

since

We have lived/been living in London since 2004.
Der Vorgang ist durch seinen Anfangszeitpunkt, nicht durch seine Dauer definiert ⇒ „since", hat in der Vergangenheit angefangen und dauert noch an ⇒ present perfect.

2. During/while

during the meeting

„During" bezieht sich auf ein Substantiv („meeting")

While we were discussing the advertising campaign …

„While" bezieht sich auf einen ganzen Teilsatz („We were discussing the advertising campaign …")

Appendix
Vocabulary

Kurze Erläuterung der Abkürzungen:
AE = amerikanisches Englisch, BE = britisches Englisch,
so. = someone, jmd. = jemand (in allen Fällen),
fam. = umgangssprachlich.

Unit 1: Travel

Talking about Travel

coach trip	Busreise
mention (v)	erwähnen
outstanding	herausragend
rewarding	lohnend
challenging	reizvoll
breathtaking	atemberaubend
failure	Versagen, Pleite
disastrous	katastrophal
tiresome	fad, langweilig
destination	Reiseziel
sights	Sehenswürdigkeiten
means of transport	Transportmittel
company	Begleitung

Globetrotting Without Tears

Listening comprehension: Travellers' Tales

guidelines	Verhaltensregeln
opium den	Opiumhöhle
curiosity	Neugierde
addict	Abhängiger
persuade (v)	überreden
wreck	Wrack
stack (v)	aufschichten, stapeln
shelves	Regale
campsite	Campingplatz
be surrounded (v)	umzingelt sein, umgeben sein
tribe	Stamm
accelerate (v)	beschleunigen
snap	Schnappschuss
threaten (v)	bedrohen
imprison so. (v)	jemanden (im Gefängnis) einsperren
con man	Betrüger, Schwindler
force (v)	zwingen
valuables	Wertsachen

Text

backpacking	Reisen mit dem Rucksack; auch: Wandern
backpacker	Rucksacktourist; auch: Wanderer
nightmare	Alptraum
dime	Zehner; Zehncentstück
a dozen	ein Dutzend
misadventure	Missgeschick
small wonder	kein Wunder
head off (v)	sich aufmachen
dreadful	schrecklich
peak time	Spitzenzeit
set off (on) (v)	sich aufmachen
set	
set	
experience (v)	erfahren, erleben
confident	zuversichtlich
be lulled into (v)	eingelullt werden
trekking	Wandern
concern	Sorge

cautious	vorsichtig
spoil (v)	verderben
ensure (v)	sicher stellen
piece of mind	Seelenfrieden
avoid (v)	vermeiden
abroad	im Ausland
as though	als ob
memorise/ize (v)	sich einprägen
subconsciously	unbewusst
confidently	sicher, selbstbewusst
mugging	Straßenraub
suspicious	verdächtig
shove (v)	schieben, hier: stecken
defuse (v)	entschärfen
relaxation	Entspannung
clench (v)	anspannen
hot headed	hitzig
strive (v) **strove** **striven**	streben nach
scurry (v)	hasten
guidebooks	Reiseführer
jab	Impfung
previously	früher, zuvor

Safety tips for backpackers

medical certificate	Attest
receipt	Quittung
money belt	Geldgürtel
to disorientate	verwirren
emergency	Notfall
upset (v)	verärgern
local	hier: Einheimischer
steer clear of (v)	sich fernhalten von
medical kit	Medizinkasten
syringe	Spritze

William Sutcliffe: Are you experienced?

impressive	eindrucksvoll
floppy hat	Schlapphut
brim	Rand, Krempe
pile	Stapel, Stoß
pull a crowd (v)	ein Menschenmenge anziehen
rupee	indische Münze
quid	engl. Pfund
reasonable	vernünftig
instant	Moment
plonk (v)	hinschmeißen
cash	(Bar-)Geld
pretend (v)	so tun als ob
tour guide	Reiseleiter
emerge (v)	hervor-/herauskommen
get sunstroke (v)	einen Sonnenstich kriegen
capital city	Hauptstadt
unobtrusive	unauffällig, unaufdringlich
shoe polish	Schuhcreme
argument	Streit
change so's mind (v)	jmd. umstimmen
wonder (v)	sich fragen
though	aber, trotzdem, dennoch (nachgestellt)
attempt	Versuch
be met with derision (v)	mit Spott begegnet werden
spectate on (v)	zuschauen
interval	Abstand
in a huff	beleidigt
honour-bound	ehrverpflichtet
significant	bedeutend
moral victory	moralischer Sieg
be huddled (v)	kauern
approval	Zustimmung
labours	Mühen
spoilt	verdorben
haggle (v)	feilschen
stump up (v)	locker machen
deranged	verrückt
memsahib	Anrede für weibliche britische Kolonialisten in Indien, hier: Fremde
reputation	Ruf
set an example (v)	ein Beispiel geben
upset (v)	umwerfen, erschüttern
local economy	heimische Wirtschaft
beggar	Bettler
tight-fisted	hier: hart
fist	Faust
selfless	selbstlos
do battle (v)	eine Schlacht schlagen
(pseudo-) worldly	(pseudo-)weltgewandt
crap (sl)	Scheiß
sensible	vernünftig
haemorrhage	Blutung
sod off! (fam.)	zieh Leine!
junction	Kreuzung
tap (v)	klopfen
stick (v)	stecken

stuck	
stuck	
plead (v)	bitten
presumably	wahrscheinlich
stingy	geizig
fiddle with (v)	herummachen, fummeln
contain (v)	beinhalten
wad	Rolle
awe	Ehrfurcht
rev (up) (v)	auf Touren bringen
flick through (v)	durchblättern
frantically	wild
small denomination	Kleingeld
snap (v)	anschnauzen
venom	Gift
fuse	Sicherung
swear (v)	fluchen; auch: schwören
swore	
sworn	
wrist	Handgelenk
spin round (v)	sich (schnell) umdrehen
spun	
spun	
be oblivious to sth (v)	etwas nicht wahrnehmen
hoot (v)	hupen
swerve (v)	ausweichen
recede (v)	entschwinden
scuffle	Handgemenge

Going home again

take off	Abflug
baggage claim	Gepäckausgabe
customs procedures	Zollabfertigung
passengers' lounge	Warteraum
flight confirmation	Flugreservierungsbestätigung
airport shuttle	Transfer zum Flugplatz; Flughhafenbus

Some India Travel Tips

bill	Rechnung
service	hier: Bedienung
fierce	wild, hart
underneath	darunter
prescription	Rezept
precaution	Vorsichtsmaßnahme
negotiate (v)	verhandeln
overcharge (v)	zu viel Geld verlangen
surpass (v)	übertreffen
abound (v)	im Überfluss vorhanden sein
cotton	Baumwolle
footwear	Schuhwerk
tread (v)	treten
trod	
trodden	
trodden path	ausgetretener Pfad
seal	Siegel
calf	Wade
ankle	Knöchel
complaint	Beschwerde
complain (v)	sich beschweren
be prevalent (v)	auftreten, vorhanden sein
insect repellent	Antiinsektenmittel
candies (AE)	Süßigkeiten
sweets (BE)	
shrine	hier: Tempel
worship	Verehrung
worship (v)	verehren
decent	anständig, geziemend
be customary (v)	üblich sein

Eco-tourism

trap	Falle
blight	hier: Plage
estimate	Schätzung
estimate (v)	schätzen
blip	Punkt, hier: kleine Bewegung
steep	steil
currently	im Moment
become manifest (v)	sichtbar werden
suspect (v)	vermuten, ahnen
shock troops	Stoßtruppen
smallpox	Pocken
measles	Masern
in the wake of	im Gefolge von
urge (v)	drängen
antidote	Gegenpol
scale	Maßstab
spending	Ausgaben
environmentally-friendly	umweltfreundlich
subsidise/ize (v)	subventionieren
fossil fuel	fossiler Brennstoff

How to be a traveller

binoculars	Fernglas
repellent	abweisend
small change	Kleingeld
suntan oil	Sonnenschutzöl
water-purification	Wasserdesinfektion
inflatable	aufblasbar
bug spray	Insektenspray
torch	Taschenlampe
tip (v)	Trinkgeld geben
generously	großzügig
traveller (AE: traveler)	Reisender
sightseer	Tourist
in relation to	in Bezug auf
crucial	entscheidend
despise (v)	verachten
adore (v)	bewundern
relish (v)	genießen
slide-show	Diashow
first and foremost	zuallererst
faraway	entfernt gelegen
saucepan	Kochtopf
multitudinous	zahlreich
exploitation	Ausbeutung
vicious	teuflisch
stitch so. up (v)	reinlegen
contemplative	besinnlich
lavatory	Toilette
passé	vorbei, passé
hostage	Geisel
scare	Drohung
captive	gefangen

Tama Janowitz: Sun poisoning

accommodations	Unterkunft
vacation	Urlaub
exhausting	anstrengend
laundry	Wäsche
plunge	Sprung
wax one's legs (v)	sich die Beine mit Wachs enthaaren
leg waxing	Enthaarung der Beine
appointment	Termin; Verabredung
actually	tatsächlich
boil (v)	kochen
rip out (v)	ausreißen
assign so. to (v)	jmd. zuweisen zu
sex role	Geschlechterrolle
impersonator	Imitator
travel agent's	Reisebüro
brochure	Prospekt
native	Einheimischer
dentures	Gebiss, Zähne
hotel clerk	Hotelangestellter
superior	überheblich
vegetables	Gemüse
residence	hier: Haus, Unterkunft
nervous breakdown	Nervenzusammenbruch
mix up (v)	verwechseln
go for a dip (v)	kurz mal schwimmen gehen
surly	mürrisch
temporary	zeitweise, vorübergehend
slap (v)	schlagen
maitre d'	Oberkellner
lobster	Hummer
puzzled	überrascht
furious	wütend
elementary school	Grundschule
apparently	offensichtlich
porch	Veranda
sunbather	Sonnenbadende(r)
tune	Melodie, hier: Lied
figure out (v)	sich ausdenken
bikini bottom	Bikinihose
dubbed (into)	synchronisiert
pudgy	dicklich
to refrain (from)	davon absehen, nicht tun

Talkline: Finding accommodation in Dublin

accommodation	Unterbringung
conclusion	Entschluss
cosmopolitan	weltbürgerlich
positively	eindeutig, echt
hub	Dreh- und Angelpunkt
dormitory	Schlafsaal
supplement	Zuschlag
surcharge	Zuschlag
vibrant	vibrierend, pulsierend
bureau de change	Wechselstube
ensuite	sich daran anschließend
spacious	geräumig
like-minded	gleich gesinnt
duvet	Federbett
deposit	Pfand, Anzahlung
preserve	Konfitüre

superior standard	höherer Standard
hue	Farbton
curfew	Zapfenstreich
seasoned	erfahren, erprobt
bunk-bed	Etagenbett
at your disposal	zu Ihrer Verfügung
warehouse	Lagerhaus
refurbish (v)	renovieren

Unit 2: Sports

Talking about sports

gruesome	grausig
outrageous	ungeheuerlich
life threatening	lebensbedrohlich
adrenalin rush	Adrenalinstoß

Some facts about bungee jumping

height	Höhe; auch: (Körper-)Größe
rope	Seil
vine	(Wein-)Rebe
leap (v)	springen
leapt	
leapt	
top hat	Zylinder
tail	hier: Frackschoß
crane	Kran

Bungee jumper falls 300 ft to his death

fail (v)	versagen
car park	Parkplatz
victim	Opfer
cable car	Seilbahn
witness	Zeuge
treat (for) (v)	behandeln (wegen)
a couple of	einige
include (v)	einschließen
sweep away (v)	wegreißen
swept	
swept	
torrent	reißender Strom, Sturzbach, Flut
claim lives (v)	Todesopfer fordern
tougher regulations	strengere (gesetzliche) Vorschriften
bounce back (v)	hier: zurückschwingen
investigator	Ermittler
cord	Seil
incomprehensible	unverständlich
run (e.g. a service) (v)	leiten
ran	
run	
incident	Vorfall
horrific	schrecklich
consider (v)	in Erwägung ziehen
take precautions (v)	Vorsichtsmaßnahmen ergreifen
scratches	Kratzer
be aware of (v)	sich bewusst sein
site	Ort, Stelle
unsatisfactory	unbefriedigend
be in charge of (v)	verantwortlich sein
particularly	besonders
fatalities	Todesopfer
except (for)	außer
burst (v)	platzen
burst	
burst	
blood vessel	Blutgefäß
fit (v)	hier: anpassen, anlegen
harness	Geschirr, Gurte
independent	unabhängig
procedures	Abwicklung, Verfahren(sweise)
follow to the letter (v)	strikt einhalten
back-up connection	Sicherungsverbindung

Narinder Dhami: Bend it like Beckham

bend (v)	hier: (einen Ball)
bent	
bent	anschneiden
touchline	Seitenlinie, Auslinie
penalty area	Strafraum
smooth	sanft
equalise (v)	ausgleichen, gleichziehen
punch (v)	schlagen
dodge (v)	ausweichen
hassle (v)	bedrängen; auch: schikanieren

wing	Flügel
opponent	Gegner, Gegenspieler
defender	Verteidiger
box (fam.)	hier: Kiste, Tor
waist-high	hüfthoch
waist	Hüfte
thigh	Oberschenkel
goalie	Torwart
pitch	Fußballplatz
wheel (v)	kreisen
hug	Umarmung
score (v)	hier: ein Tor erzielen
dash (v)	flitzen
stomach	Magen
lurch (v)	taumeln; hier: sich umdrehen
yank (v)	(ruckartig) ziehen
stagger (v)	straucheln
spin round (v)	sich herumdrehen
ref, referee	Schiedsrichter
glare at so. (v)	(zornig) starren
sneer (v)	spotten
sprawl (v)	der Länge nach hinfallen
screech (v)	kreischen
stern	streng
send off (v)	vom Platz stellen
trudge (v)	trotten
prat (fam.)	Idiot, Trottel
racist abuse	rassistische Beleidigung
be relieved (v)	erleichtert sein
relief	Erleichterung
ruffle (so's hair) (v)	zerzausen
chatter	Geplapper
forlorn	verloren, einsam
suspend (v)	ausschließen
tournament	Turnier
prick (v)	(in den Augen) brennen
yell at so. (v)	jmd. anschreien
reasonable	vernünftig
gentle	sanft

Ten reasons why snowboarding sucks

sleet	Schneeregen
avalanche	Lawine
admittedly	zugegebenermaßen
decent	anständig
serenity	Ruhe, Gelassenheit
shark	Hai
bill	Rechnung
base	hier: am Fuß (eines Berges)
dumb	dumm
moron	Schwachkopf
humidity	Luftfeuchtigkeit
inconsistent	unbeständig
retarded	zurückgeblieben
frostbite	Erfrierungen
goggles	Schneebrille
baboon	Pavian
yell (v)	herumschreien
in close confines	auf engem Raum
grade school	(US) Grundschule
detention	Arrest
unconscious	bewusstlos
merge (v)	zusammenkommen, ineinander übergehen
trail	Spur
sissy	Schwächling
slam	Schlag
gear	Ausrüstung
ridiculous	lächerlich; hier: toll

Listening comprehension: About Skaters and snowboarders

fit in (v)	auskommen mit
fit	
fit	
skinny	dünn
geeky	naiv, unbedarft; auch: doof
vibe (vibration)	Atmosphäre, Aura
convince (v)	überzeugen
scary	Angst einflößend
distinction	Unterscheidung

Snowboarding goes Olympics

ride a snowboard (v)	Snowboard fahren
scrape (v)	kratzen, scharren
baggy pants	weite Hosen
jester hat	Narrenkappe
hurtle (v)	sausen, brausen
unnerve (v)	entnerven
shred (v)	zerfetzen
approach (v)	herangehen an
launch (off) (v)	starten (von)
handy	passend
obstacle	Hindernis
devise (v)	erfinden

landbound	auf dem Land, nicht am Meer, wohnend
screw (v)	schrauben
sledge	Schlitten
catch on (v)	ankommen, sich durchsetzen
caught	
caught	
fervor (AE)	Leidenschaft
sanction (v)	sanktionieren; hier: zulassen
slope	Piste
never mind	geschweige denn; auch: macht nichts!
sag (v)	nachlassen, hängen
daredevil	Waghals, Draufgänger
carve powder (sl) (v)	hier: auf die Piste gehen
carve (v)	schneiden, zerteilen
bruising	blaue Flecken
relish (v)	genießen
chisel (v)	meißeln
hip	Hüfte
swivel (v)	sich drehen, schwingen
compete (v)	wetteifern
gate	Tor
dazzling	blendend, schön
channel	Kanal
devotee	Jünger, Anhänger
nationalistic boosterism	(übersteigerter) Patriotismus
run counter (v)	entgegen laufen
ran	
run	
no-borders	ohne Grenzen
hit the mainstream (v)	sich mit der Massenkultur verbinden
embrace (v)	hier: vereinnahmen
administrator	hier: hohe Funktionäre (officials)
attract (v)	anziehen
tired	müde, hier: abgegriffen
television lineup	hier: Fernsehdarbietung
rating	Einschaltquote
hawk (v)	verscherbeln
denounce sth. (v)	sich gegen etw. aussprechen

This sporting lifestyle

be on the wane	im Schwinden sein
cause (v)	Sache, Angelegenheiten
lack (v)	nicht haben; entbehren
boundaries	Grenzen
perfection	Vollkommenheit, Perfektion
ultimate	äußerst, oberst
deny (v)	leugnen
instant	sofort
treat (v)	behandeln
recognise (v)	anerkennen, erkennen
tempt (v)	in Versuchung führen
drag down (v)	herabziehen
limbs	Gliedmaßen
determination	Entschlossenheit
arms race	Wettrüsten
ambiguous	zweideutig; vieldeutig
vehicle	Vehikel; Gefährt
stretch (v)	(sich) strecken; sich erstrecken
gym	hier: das Turnen; Sporthalle
gymnastics	das Turnen; Gymnastik
gymnasium	die Turnhalle
tracksuit	Trainingsanzug
sportswear	Sportkleidung
compete (v)	wetteifern
feel obliged (v)	sich verpflichtet fühlen
felt	
felt	
obligation	Verpflichtung
excellence	hier: Leistungsfähigkeit
conviction	Überzeugung
ancient	alt
possess (v)	besitzen
cherish (v)	(ver-)ehren; liebevoll pflegen
underachieving	hinter den (hier: schulischen) Erwartungen zurückbleibend
resurrect (v)	wiederbeleben
recapture (v)	wieder heraufbeschwören
precede (v)	vorausgehen (zeitlich)
decay	Verfall
reinforcement	Stärkung, Bestärkung

Translation: Get rid of those national anthems

get rid of (v)	loswerden
got	
got	
national anthem	Nationalhymne
swell (v)	anschwellen
participate in (v)	teilnehmen an
ardour	Eifer
cancer	Krebs

mongrel	Misch-
confuse (v)	durcheinander bringen
heritage	Erbe
bond	Band, Verbindung
current	augenblicklich
boundaries	Grenzen
greed	Gier
draw together (v)	zusammenbringen
drew	
drawn	
prowess	Können
suppose (v)	annehmen

Aldous Huxley: Brave New World

anticipate (v)	voraussehen; vorwegnehmen
unique	einzigartig
inferior	untergeordnet; minderwertig
labour (v)	arbeiten, sich abmühen
breed (v)	züchten
bred	
bred	
bring up (v)	aufziehen
brought	
brought	
squat (v)	hocken
shrub	Busch, Strauch
drowsy	schläfrig
interior	das Innere
revolve (v)	sich drehen
hurl (v)	schleudern
casing	Gehäuse
folly	Torheit
elaborate	ausgeklügelt
approve of (v)	zustimmen, erlauben

Talkline: Famous sportsperson

carve (v)	schnitzen, in Stein meißeln
epitome	Inbegriff
consistency	Kontinuität, Zuverlässigkeit
native town	Geburtsstadt
subsequently	darauf folgend
indelible	unauslöschlich
from the outset	von Anfang an
ligament	Band (med.)
tournament	Turnier
trophy	Trophäe, Pokal
half-way line	Mittellinie
inexorable	unerbittlich
pariah	Ausgestoßener
composure	Gleichmut
dogged	hartnäckig, beharrlich
spill over (v)	überlaufen, überquellen

Unit 3: Media and Fine Arts

What TV programme?

feature film	Spielfilm

What ist DAB Digital Radio?

terrestrial	terrestrisch, erdgebunden
transmitter	Sender
unique	einzigartig
portfolio	Portefeuille, Mappe, Gruppierung
noise	hier: Rauschen
hiss	Zischen
crackle	Knistern
fade	Schwung, Fading
sophisticated	weltläufig, hoch entwickelt

Rapper wins Mercury prize

stun (v)	schockieren
in the wake of	in der Nachfolge von
edge (v)	hier: sich annähern
persistent	andauernd
peddle (v)	verscherbeln, abgeben
sage	klug, weise
MC	Conferencier
hail sb. (v)	jmd. begrüßen
aspirational	hoffnungsvoll
resot	Urlaubsort
mainstream	Allgemeinheit, hier: Establishment
pan (v)	kritisieren
affluent	wohlhabend
get a lot of exposure (v)	hier: viel Aufmerksamkeit bekommen

Listening comprehension: I've been through madness

acclaim (v)	rühmen, preisen
perturbed	verwirrt

worthy	bewundernswürdig
muso (slang)	Berufsmusiker
prestgious	angesehen
coverage	Aufmerksamkeit
grimy	schmutzig
tabloid	Boulevardpresse
innit? = isn't it	oder?
cagey	zurückhaltend
entail (v)	einbeziehen
option	Chance, Möglichkeit
mindful	mit dem Wissen, dass
camp (v)	lagern, campieren
Nuff (coll. von enough)	hier: ziemlich
MC (master of ceremonies)	Conferencier (einer Radiosendung)
stifle (v)	ersticken, unterdrücken
rhyme (v)	dichten
startling	aufregend
panicked	erschreckt
yelp	jaulen
blare (v)	schreien, heraustrompeten
propulsive	hier: antreibend, aufmischend
racket	Rabbatz, Krawall
unflinching	stetig, vor nichts zurückschreckend
alpha (with men or animals)	anführend
riven	zerrissen, gespalten
a gift and a curse	Fluch und Segen
tail off (v)	hier: verstummen

Newspapers in Great Britain

popular press	Boulevardpresse
coverage	Berichterstattung
review	Kritik
gutter	Gosse
colloquial	umgangssprachlich
circulation	Auflage
lively	lebhaft
campaigning	hier: aufrüttelnd
retiree	Rentner, Pensionist
acquire (v)	erhalten, zugewiesen bekommen
reputation	Ruf
respectively (nachgestellt)	beziehungsweise
sophisticated	kultiviert
actually (!)	in der Tat, tatsächlich
gossip	Klatsch
sniffy	hochnäsig
condescending	herablassend
perceive (v)	wahrnehmen
overt	offen, ungehemmt
bias	Voreingenommenheit, Einseitigkeit
investigative	nachforschend, recherchierend

Translation: The prince and the papers

restraint	Zurückhaltung
uncanny	unheimlich
rerun	Wiederholung
berage	Attacke
late	hier: verstorben
indulge in (v)	genießen
horseplay	Herumgealbere
splash (v)	groß herausbringen
allege (v)	andeuten
evidence	Beweis
orchestrate (v)	arrangieren
ferocious	heftig, brutal
hallmarks	Anzeichen
ordinance	Regel
stalk (v)	auflauern

One family that forgoes screens of all sizes

grand piano	(Konzert-) Flügel
crevice	Spalte, Lücke
wisecrack	witzige Bemerkung
thump-thumping	dumpfes Schlagen
shriek	Kreischen
beneficial	nützlich
attainable	erreichbar
backlash	Gegenreaktion
glue to (v)	kleben an
sprawl over/on (v)	sich räkeln
truth be told	um die Wahrheit zu sagen
tube	hier: die Glotze
educator	Pädagoge
sensitive	hier: heikel
disapprove (v)	missbilligen, nicht gutheißen
consistent	konsequent
enforce sth. (v)	etw. durchsetzen
recount (v)	hier: erzählen
sticky	klebrig, hier: heikel
initial(ly)	anfänglich

holdout	Verweigerer
avid	eifrig, begeistert
read sth. voraciously (v)	etw. geradezu verschlingen
schedule	Zeitplan, Tagesablauf

Ann Beattie: Love Always

depict (v)	beschreiben
niece	Nichte
soap opera	Seifenoper
abuse (v)	missbrauchen
wimpy	schwächlich
novelist	Romanautor
subject oneself to (v)	sich unterziehen
surgery	Operation
conceive (v)	hier: schwanger werden
divorce (v)	sich scheiden lassen
disrupt (v)	stören, zerstören
recovery	Genesung
volunteer	Freiwilliger
envy (v)	beneiden
brief	kurz
consider (v)	in Erwägung ziehen
blackmail	Erpressung
dull	langweilig
benefactor	Wohltäter
buckle down (v)	sich dahinterklemmen
mental breakdown	Nervenzusammenbruch
fictionalize (v)	in Romanform bringen
account	Darstellung, Bericht
abortion	Abtreibung

Talkline: Choosing a TV channel

block of flats	Wohnblock
unencrypted	unverschlüsselt

Unit 4 Cultural diversity

How Singapore deals with litterbugs

fine	Bußgeld, Verwarnung(-sgeld)
fine (v)	jmd. mit einem Bußgeld belegen
litter	Abfall
(cigarette) butt	Zigarettenkippe
wrapper	Verpackung, Papier
matchstick	Streichholz
bug	Käfer
litterbug	Schmutzfink
offence	Vergehen; Ordnungswidrigkeit
jaywalk	sich als Fußgänger unachtsam verhalten
penalty	Strafe
strictness	Strenge
enforce (v)	geltend machen
offender	(Straf-)Täter
unique to	beschränkt auf, gibt es nur ...
flush (v)	spülen
spitting	Spucken
be subject to (v)	unterworfen sein, unterliegen
repeat-offender	Wiederholungstäter
corrective work	Sozialarbeit (als Strafe)
cover (v)	hier: berichten von
preventive	vorbeugend
be embarrassed (v)	sich schämen
vest	Weste
decline (v)	ablehnen
bad luck	Pech
drop (v)	fallen lassen
by accident	zufällig, aus Versehen
rubbish	Müll
be exempt (v)	ausgenommen sein
reside (v)	wohnen; leben (in einer Stadt)
serve (v)	ableisten
counselling	Belehrung
session	Sitzung
watercourse	Kanal(-system)
action	Handlung, Tun
boarding school	Internat
performance	Leistung

School regulations in the US

similar	ähnlich
controlled	hier: Alkohol, Drogen,

substance	Zigaretten, (Substanzen, deren Ausgabe kontrolliert wird)
be subject to action (v)	mit jdm. wird (folgendermaßen) verfahren
guardian	Erziehungsberechtigte/-r
designated	berechtigt, befugt
notify (v)	benachrichtigen
law enforcement official	Vollzugsbeamte/-r
offence (BE), offense (AE)	Vergehen
suspension	zeitweiliger Schulausschluss
recommendation	Empfehlung
expulsion	Schulausschluss
violation	Verstoß
search	Durchsuchung
attire	Kleidung
designee	Stellvertreter/-in, Beauftragte/-r
suspect (v)	vermuten
intimidate (v)	einschüchtern
interfere with (v)	stören
administration	Verwaltung, hier: Schulleitung
instance	Fall
requirement	Anforderung
obscene	obszön, gegen den guten Geschmack verstoßend
vulgar	ordinär, geschmacklos
fingertip length	die Fingerspitzen erreichen den Rocksaum, wenn die Schülerin aufrecht steht
undergarment	Unterwäsche
exposed	ungeschützt, hier: sichtbar
see through	durchsichtig
indecent	unanständig
exposure	Entblößung, Aussetzung
hood	Kapuze
gym	Turnhalle
take action (v)	Maßnahmen ergreifen
field trip	Schulausflug
enforce (v)	durchsetzen
distract (v)	ablenken
harass (v)	belästigen

Domestic differences in Britain

domestic	häuslich, Haus-, zu Hause
cohabitation	eheähnliche Gemeinschaft
mortgage	Hypothek
uphold (v)	hoch halten
parenthood	Elternschaft
single parent	allein erziehendes Elternteil
counterparts	Gegenstück
decline (v)	hier: abnehmen, zurückgehen
considerably	beträchtlich

Case study 1: The married couple

nuclear family	Kernfamilie
couple	Paar
out of wedlock	unehelich(-es Verhältnis)
divorcee	Geschiedene/r

Case study 2: The unmarried couple

commitment	Verpflichtung
joint	gemeinsam
bank account	Bankkonto
condemn (v)	verurteilen
point out (v)	darauf hinweisen
not to matter	nichts ausmachen

Case study 3: The single mother

share (v)	gemeinsam haben, teilen
degree	(Studien-)Abschluss, akad. Grad
self-reliance	Selbstsicherheit, Selbstvertrauen
inherit (v)	erben
self-sufficient	selbstständig, sich selbst versorgend
prince charming	Märchenprinz
contribute (to) (v)	beitragen (zu)

Race hate in Britain is widespread – just ask my wife

despite	trotz
boast	Behauptung
boast (v)	(angeberisch) behaupten, angeben
feel ashamed (v)	beschämt sein
rubbery	Gummi-, gummiartig
shiny	glänzend
queue	Reihe
queue up (v)	sich anstellen
grab (v)	grapschen, greifen (nach)
abuse	hier: Beschimpfung
refer (to) (v)	sich beziehen (auf)

seek (v)	suchen
sought	
sought	
meter	Zähler
description	Beschreibung
commissioner (of police)	Polizeipräsident
prejudice	Vorurteil
face (v)	erfahren, gegenüberstehen
suspicion	Argwohn; Verdacht
promotion	Beförderung
nightmare	Alptraum

Listening comprehension: The Bradford clashes

clash	Zusammenstoß
stab (v)	(mit dem Messer er-)stechen
allegedly	angeblich
prompt (v)	veranlassen
failure	Versagen
riot	Aufstand, Krawall
uprisings	Aufstand, Unruhen

Translation: Britain's open society

cosmopolitan	kosmopolitisch, weltläufig
reputation	Ruf
ridden	geschüttelt, befallen, erfüllt, beherrscht
resemble (v)	ähneln, aussehen wie
indigenous	eingeboren, einheimisch
Union Jack	Spitzname der englischen Flagge
squad	Mannschaft
insular	insular, provinziell, engstirnig
self-absorbed	mit sich selbst beschäftigt
blend	Mischung
moored	vertäut, verankert
off the coast	vor der Küste

Prejudice Quiz

attitude	Einstellung
bias	Vorurteil, vorgefasste Meinung
inclination (toward)	hier: Haltung; Neigung
inherently	inhärent; von Natur aus
stereotype	Klischeevorstellung
evaluation	Bewertung
behavioural	Verhaltens-
behaviour	Verhalten
with respect to	in Hinsicht auf
inconsistent	widersprüchlich, unstimmig
assimilate (v)	hier: anpassen; aufnehmen, integrieren
refute (v)	widerlegen
sex role	Geschlechterrolle
inborn	angeboren
relative to	im Verhältnis zu
ambitious	strebsam, ehrgeizig
confident	selbstsicher
self-esteem	Selbstwertgefühl
anxiety	Angst
model	Rollenvorbild
harp (on) (v)	herumreiten (auf)
perception	Wahrnehmung
exposure	hier: Begegnung; Kontakt

Amy Tan: The Joy Luck Club

slice	in Scheiben schneiden
ferocity	Heftigkeit
scrutinize so or sth (v)	genau prüfen, genau ansehen
appraisal	Bewertung
anticipate (v)	vorhersehen
curly	lockig
splash	Fleck
freckle	Sommersprosse
funeral	Beerdigung
appreciate (v)	wertschätzen
chunk	Stück
crisp	frisch
slide (v)	gleiten lassen, schieben
slid	
slid	
shriek (v)	schreien, kreischen
decline (v)*	ablehnen
tender	zart
sprouts	Keimlinge
second	Nachschlag, zweite Portion
groan (v)	stöhnen
disparaging	abwertend
flavor (AE), flavour (BE)	Geschmack
cue	Signal, Hinweis
proceed (v)	fortfahren, weitermachen
modest	bescheiden
dalmatian	Dalmatiner

pant (v)	nach Luft schnappen
pet (v)	liebkosen
hint	Hinweis
shudder (v)	schaudern, zittern
firm	fest
familiarity	Ungezwungenheit, (plumpe) Vertraulichkeit
break the news (v)	Neuigkeit(en) mitteilen

Two speeches on race relations in Britain

Speech 1: Brittle Britain

fair-minded	gerecht
score (of)	hier: eine Reihe von; eigentlich: 20
approach (to)	hier: Haltung (zu)
approach (v)	annähern, angehen
race relations	Rassenbeziehungen
challenge (v)	herausfordern; in Frage stellen
distort (v)	verdrehen; verzerren
reinforce (v)	verstärken
link	Verbindung
garrison	Garnison
pronouncement	Erklärung, Verkündigung
significant	beträchtlich
galling	ärgerlich
honesty	Ehrlichkeit
swamp	Sumpf
tide	Flut
torrent	Springflut, Strom
resentment	Vorbehalt, Abneigung
distrust	Misstrauen
asylum seeker	Asylsuchender
survey	Umfrage
assistance	(finanzielle) Unterstützung
abolish (v)	abschaffen

Speech 2: Robin Cook – Chicken Tikka Massala

burden	Bürde
reluctantly	widerwillig
arrival	Ankunft
broaden (v)	erweitern
dish	Gericht, Mahlzeit
adapt	anpassen
gravy	Bratensoße

Unit 5: The Pressure of Modern Life

Talking about crime: young offenders in Britain

caution (v)	verwarnen
indictable offence	strafrechtlich verfolgte Straftat
offending rate	Verbrechensrate
offence	Straftat
commit an offence (v)	eine Straftat begehen
offender	Straftäter
summary offence	geringfügiges Vergehen
burglary	Einbruch
robbery	Raub
theft	Diebstahl
fraud	Betrug
forgery	Fälschen
criminal damage	Sachbeschädigung
motoring offence	Verkehrsdelikt

A living hell in children's jails

cancer	Krebs
speed	hier: Amphetamin
bunk off (fam) (v)	schwänzen
petty crime	Kleinkriminalität
with intent	vorsätzlich
refuse (v)	verweigern
bail	Kaution
despite	trotz
devise (v)	ausarbeiten
remand (v)	in Untersuchungshaft nehmen
be customary (v)	nicht ungewöhnlich sein
access	Zugang
notorious	berüchtigt
rotten	verrottet
the core (v)	im Innersten
regrettably	bedauerlicherweise
young offender institution	Jugendgefängnis

suicide	Selbstmord
astonishing	erstaunlich
incident	Vorfall
be locked up (v)	eingesperrt sein
self-harm	Selbstgefährdung
prison custody	Haft
abolish (v)	abschaffen
convict (v)	verurteilen
reoffend (v)	rückfällig werden
taxpayer	Steuerzahler
per head	pro Kopf
lift (v)	anheben
convince (v)	überzeugen
body	hier: Körperschaft
crime prevention	Verbrechensvorbeugung
condition	Zustand
depriviation	Benachteiligung, Vernachlässigung
abuse	Missbrauch
frankly	offen gesagt
plea	Appell
reform (v)	sich bessern
redeem (v)	hier: sich rehabilitieren
harsh	streng
non-custodial	ohne Haft
sentence	Urteil
probation service	Bewährungshelferdienst
on probation	auf Bewährung
probation officer	Bewährungshelfer
blot out (v)	auslöschen
vicious	bösartig, teuflisch
be mugged (v)	auf der Straße überfallen werden
irredeemable	hier: nicht läuterbar
redemption	Läuterung, auch: Erlösung
knot (v)	verknoten

Risk factors associated with young offenders

multitude	Vielzahl
key trait	Grundzug, Grundmerkmal
sibling	Geschwister
lack of	Mangel an
lack (v)	ermangeln, nicht haben
supervision	Aufsicht
play truant (v)	die Schule schwänzen
academic performance	Schulleistung

Youth Court Sentencing Framework

discharge	auf freien Fuß setzen
conditional or unconditional	mit oder ohne Auflagen
fine	Bußgeld
commensurate	entsprechend
Community Sentence	Urteil im Sinne der Allgemeinheit
Community Service	Sozialdienst
curfew	Ausgangssperre
custody	Verwahrung, Haft
secure training	„Sicherheitstraining"
detention	Haft

Prison occupancy

occupancy	Belegung
projection	hier: Prognosen
average	durchschnittlich
critical issue	umstrittenes Thema

Littleton: No place to be different

suburbia	die Vororte
occur (v)	geschehen
revenge	Rache
impending	bevorstehend
scribble (v)	(hin-)kritzeln
cross (v)	überqueren; hier: über den Weg laufen
rip out (v)	herausreißen
rampage (v)	randalieren, toben
pipe	Rohr
abundant	reichlich
jock (sl)	sportlich
sneer at (v)	verspotten
trash	Abfall
authority	Autorität; hier: die Verantwortlichen
despise (v)	verachten
anger	Wut
stifling	beengend
boil away (v)	weiterkochen
surface	Oberfläche
hover (v)	hier: herumstehen
threaten (v)	drohen
wacky	verrückt
outlet	Verkaufsstelle
curfew	Ausgangssperre

appearance	äußerer (An-)Schein
porch	Veranda
upscale	schick
bright	hier: intelligent
keen	begeistert
slightly	etwas, ein wenig
withdrawn	zurückgezogen
obliged	verpflichtet
accessible	zugänglich
permissive	nachgiebig
consistent	ständig, beständig
underpin (v)	untermauern
unravel (v)	sich auflösen
get sued (v)	verklagt werden
let sb. down (v)	jdn. enttäuschen
lobby (v)	sich einsetzen für
annual convention	Jahresversammlung
state assembly	(US) entspricht in etwa dem Landtag
bill	Gesetzentwurf
prevailing	(vor-)herrschend
cherish (v)	in Ehren halten
delinquent	Straffällige(r)

Describing a cartoon

sniper	Heckenschütze
wrap in (v)	einpacken in
bumpkin	Kürbis
ammunition	Munition
armor piercing	panzerbrechend
bulletproof vest	kugelsichere Weste

Britain's new epidemic: Binge drinking

epidemic	epidemie
binge-drinking	das Zusaufen, Besaufen
liver-disease	Lebererkrankung
taxation	Besteuerung
curb (v)	zügeln, drosseln
consumption	Konsum
tough	hier: streng
reinforce (v)	verstärken
cirrhosis	Leberzirrhose
suicide	Selbstmord
attempt (+ vb)	Versuch
assault (+ vb)	Überfall, Angriff
spirit	hier: Spirituose, Schnaps
youthful	jugendlich
voluntary	freiwillig
desirability	Attraktivität
contradict (v)	widersprechen
ban (+ vb)	Verbot
tackle (v)	anpacken, in Angriff nehmen

Listening comprehension: The dangers and fascination of Ecstasy

Recording 1: Doctor

estimate (v)	schätzen
fatalities	Todesfälle
hospitalisation	Einlieferung ins Krankenhaus
(heroin-)related	auf (Heroin) zurückzuführen
suicide	Selbstmord
pint	ca. 1/2 Liter
dehydration	Flüssigkeitsverlust
fluids	Flüssigkeiten

Recording 2: Psychologist

trigger (v)	hier: erzeugen
hug (v)	sich umarmen
pacify (v)	befrieden
lust	Lust
resent (v)	etwas dagegen haben

Tom Wolfe: The Bonfire of the Vanities

DA = district attorney (US)	Staatsanwalt
borough	Stadtbezirk
decay	Verfall
sneakers	Turnschuhe
defendant	Angeklagte(r)
indictment	Anklageerhebung
caseload	hier: Beweislage
overwhelming	überwältigend
marginal	nebensächlich
case	Fall
haul in (v)	hereinholen
wire mesh	Drahtzaun
deserve (v)	verdienen
notion	Vorstellung; Begriff
achieve (v)	erreichen
desperate	verzweifelt
vile	böse
liquor	Spirituosen
distributor	Großhändler
hijack (v)	entführen
dumpster	Müllcontainer
wiseguy	Schlaumeier

merchandise	Ware
loading-dock	Rampe
boost (v)	klauen
hazardous	gefährlich
charge with (v)	anklagen wegen
manslaughter	Totschlag
plea	Geständnis
plead (guilty) (v)	sich (schuldig) bekennen
bargain	Verhandlung; Deal
jerk (v)	(sich) verdrehen

Robert Crumb: Whiteman

influential	einflussreich
direction	Richtung
content	Inhalt
outburst	Ausbruch

Road-rage

slithery	schlüpfrig
cheerful	fröhlich
bag (v)	in die Tüte packen
grocery store	Lebensmittelladen
recklessness	Rücksichtslosigkeit
epidemic	Epidemie
according (to)	gemäß
triple	dreifach
related	verbunden (mit)
manifest itself (v)	sich zeigen
lane change	Fahrspurwechsel
tailgate (v)	dicht auffahren
tailgate	Heckklappe
brake (v)	bremsen
horn	Hupe
advanced	fortgeschritten
jerk	Depp
warrior	Krieger
insane	verrückt
moronic	durchgeknallt
congestion	Stau, Gedränge
cranky	verrückt; griesgrämig
science	Wissenschaft
touchy	empfindlich
even as	selbst wenn
intoxicating	berauschend
seal in (v)	einschließen
virtually	praktisch, nahezu
soundproof	schalldicht
dweeb	Kauz
strap (v)	festschnallen
snugly	bequem, schnuggelig (fam.)
buckle up (v)	sich anschnallen
content	Zufriedenheit
potency	Potenz
insecure	unsicher
legislate (v)	hier: mit Vorschriften regeln
adjudicate (v)	hier: strafrechtlich regeln
penalties	Strafen
regulate (v)	steuern
elaborate	hier: schwieriger
mandatory	vorgeschrieben
suggest (v)	vorschlagen
perilous	gefährlich
on a large scale	in großem Maßstab
kitty	Kätzchen
litter	Abfall
whole grain	Vollkorn
brave (v)	hier: sich wagen
employ (v)	anwenden, beschäftigen

What can you do to avoid road-rage?

erratically	unberechenbar
sparingly	sparsam
disabled	behindert
high beam	Fernlicht
headlights	Frontscheinwerfer
inflict (v)	aufzwingen
assume (v)	annehmen, voraussetzen
courteous	höflich
soothe (v)	beruhigen
improve (v)	verbessern

Listening comprehension: Death on the highway

civility	Höflichkeit
flip off (v)	ausrasten
jockey for position (v)	sich in eine gute Position zu drängeln versuchen
slam on your brakes (v)	auf die Bremse treten
on purpose	absichtlich
pole	(Telefon-)Mast
be sentenced (v)	verurteilt werden
manslaughter	Totschlag
inappropriate	ungeeignet

Talkline: Young offenders

defendant	Angeklagter
binge drinking	exzessiv trinken

pregnant	schwanger
bully so. (v)	jdn. tyranisieren, schikanieren
deliberately	absichtlich
disadvantage	Nachteil
sentence	Urteil mit Strafmaß

Unit 6 Employment and Economy

Talking about jobs and money

working conditions	Arbeitsbedingungen
(the difficulties) involved	die damit verbundenen (Schwierigkeiten)
colleague	Kollege
waiter/waitress	Kellner/in
serve (v)	bedienen
take orders (v)	Bestellung aufnehmen
bill	Rechnung
make out bills (v)	(Rechnungen) kassieren
do newspaper rounds (v)	Zeitungen austragen
assembly line	Fließband
work shifts (v)	Schicht arbeiten
construction worker, building worker	Bauarbeiter
blisters (on)	Blasen (an)
stack shelves (v)	in Regale einschlichten
fix price tags onto (v)	Preisetikette anbringen, etikettieren
cashier (BE)	Kassierer/in
checkout girl/ boy (AE)	Kassierer/in
trolley	Einkaufswagen
private tuition (BE)	Nachhilfeunterricht
private tutoring (AE)	Nachhilfeunterricht
savings account	Sparkonto
shares	Aktien
items	hier: Dinge

Fact Box: Employment of children and young persons in the UK

employment	Beschäftigung
milk delivery	Milchlieferung
exception	Ausnahme
horticultural work	Gartenarbeit
employer	Arbeitgeber
tax (v)	besteuern
restriction	Beschränkung
working hours	Arbeitszeit
prohibited	verboten
fairground	Rummelplatz
abattoir	Schlachthaus

Working in a summer camp

outdoor	im Freien
promote (v)	fördern; auch: befördern
team spirit	Teamgeist
self esteem	Selbstwertgefühl
staff	Personal
counselor (AE)	
counsellor (BE)	hier: Betreuer; Berater
to attend	(eine Schule) besuchen
vocational	beruflich
cabin	Hütte; hier: Unterkunft
instructor	Lehrer, Ausbilder
handicapped	behindert
impaired	eingeschränkt, beeinträchtigt
terminal illness	unheilbare Krankheit

Camp Mohican in the Pocona Mountains, Pennsylvania

supervisor	Leiter; Aufseher
crafts	Handwerk, Bastel-
workshop	Werkstatt
pottery	Töpferei
archery	Bogenschießen
juggling	Jonglieren
Head (counselor)	Chef-, erster, leitender ...
lifeguard	Wasserwacht
be in charge (v)	verantwortlich sein
registered nurse	staatlich geprüfte Krankenschwester
attendance	Anwesenheit
stable	Stall
salary	Gehalt
board	Verpflegung
travel allowance	Reisekostenzuschuss
expense	Ausgaben

Tanja's informal resumé

resumé (AE)	Bewerbung
informal	formlos
tutoring	Betreuung (z. B. von Mitschülern)
voluntary	freiwillig
first aid	erste Hilfe
referee(ing)	Schiedsrichter (-tätigkeit)
sophomore year	(US) 2. Studienjahr
junior year	(US) vorletztes Studienjahr
senior year	(US) letztes Studienjahr

First steps towards a lifetime of debt

envy	Neid
envy (v)	neiden
stroll (down the street) (v)	schlendern
flex (one's muscles) (v)	(Muskeln) spielen lassen
spend (on) (v)	ausgeben (für)
spent	
spent	
spending power	Kaufkraft (des Käufers)
acquire (v)	erhalten
credit limit	Überziehungskredit
obtain (v)	erhalten
circumstances	Umstände; hier: Verhältnisse
application	Antrag; auch: Bewerbung
apply (for) (v)	beantragen; auch: sich bewerben
form	Formular
grant (v)	gewähren
borrowing facility	Kreditrahmen
borrow (v)	(sich) leihen
extend (v)	erweitern
on demand	nach Verlangen
consolidate (v)	konsolidieren
ferry steward	Steward auf einer Fähre
debts	Schulden
debtor	Schuldner
owe money (v)	Geld schulden
intervene (v)	einschreiten
cut-throat competition	halsabschneiderisch Wettbewerb
compete (v)	in Wettbewerb stehen, wetteifern
lend (v)	etw. (ver-)leihen
lent	
lent	
credit card lender	Kreditkarteninstitut
creditor	Gläubiger
borrower	hier: Kreditkarten-Kunde
hold a credit card (v)	eine Kreditkarte haben
held	
held	
lure (v)	locken
initial	anfänglich, Anfangs-
(interest) rates	Zinsen
average	Durchschnitt; durchschnittlich
slip through (v)	durchrutschen
check	Kontrolle
aber: cheque	der Scheck
counsellor	Berater
budget	Budget
let alone	geschweige denn
burden	Bürde
underage	minderjährig
unenforcable contract	ungültiger Vertrag
fraud	Betrug
be reluctant (v)	zögern
conduct (v)	durchführen
electoral roll	Wählerverzeichnis
evidence	Anschein, Beweis
inquiry	Anfrage
be unlikely to... (v)	unwahrscheinlich sein, wahrscheinlich nicht ...
credit reference agencies	Kreditschutzverein
stable	stabil
trapped	gefangen, in der Falle
vicious circle	Teufelskreis
measures	Maßnahmen
show off (v)	angeben
amass (v)	anhäufen
borrow (v)	(sich) leihen
seek (v)	suchen; auch: streben nach
sought	
sought	
(well) deserved	(wohl-)verdient

Fact Box: Kids and money in the US

literacy	Fähigkeit, lesen und schreiben zu können
illiteracy	Analphabetentum

financial literacy	Unkenntnis in finanziellen Dingen
billion	Milliarde
additional	zusätzlich
skills	Fähigkeiten, Fertigkeiten
receive (v)	erhalten
advice	Rat
student loans	Ausbildungsförderung
debt burden	Schuldenlast
roll over debt (v)	überziehen, Schulden machen
graduate from (AE) (v)	die Schul-/Universitätsausbildung abschließen
survey	Untersuchung
file for bankruptcy (v)	Offenbarungseid leisten
bankruptcy	Insolvenz
bankrupt	pleite, insolvent

Role play 1

below	unten
subscription	Abonnement
subscribe to (v)	abonnieren, beziehen
run out (v) **ran** **run**	auslaufen
extend (v)	hier: verlängern
customer	Kunde
receptionist	Telefonpartner am anderen Ende der Leitung

Role play 2

applicant	Bewerber
previous	früher
personell manager	Personalchef(in)
tailor-made	maßgeschneidert
session	Gespräch, Sitzung

Analysing advertisements

advertisement, advert	Werbeanzeige, Werbespot
advertising	Werbung
advertise (v)	Werbung machen für
beverage	Getränk
pattern of behaviour	Verhaltensmuster
chocolate bar	Schokoriegel
impress (v)	beeindrucken
interrupt (v)	unterbrechen
neglect (v)	vernachlässigen
turn down (v)	ablehnen, hier: schlecht machen
values	Werte
convey (v)	vermitteln
confident	selbstbewusst
desire	(starker) Wunsch, Verlangen
appeal to (v)	ansprechen
laundry	Wäsche; auch: Wäscherei
improve (v)	verbessern
bonus	Rabatt
potential (customer)	potenziell(-er Kunde)
unique	einzigartig
proposition	Vorschlag

Bill Bryson: Shopping Madness (from: Notes from a big country)

accumulate (v)	anhäufen
devote (v)	widmen
mega-mall	Rieseneinkaufszentrum
square-foot	Quadratmeter
main entrance	Haupteingang
retail	Einzelhandel
wholesale	Großhandel
proponent	Vertreter (einer Richtung)
proportion	Anteil
browse a shop (v)	sich umsehen
margin	Rand
scheme	Plan
unassuming	ahnungslos
purchaser	Käufer
purchase	kaufen
burst (v) **burst** **burst**	ausbrechen
disagreeable	unangenehm
pester so. (v)	jdn. nerven, keine Ruhe lassen
brink	Rand
persistent	hartnäckig
aisle	Flügel; hier: Gang
lingerie	Damenwäsche
menswear department	Herrenabteilung
idly	hier: ohne nachzudenken
idle	müßig, faul
line	hier: Marke
peach	Pfirsich

have one's legs waxed (v)	sich die Beine mit Wachs enthaaren lassen
manslaughter	Totschlag

"Shameful" pay makes British women worst off in Europe

facilities	Einrichtungen
persistent	andauernd, anhaltend
gender gap	hier: Benachteiligung von Frauen
disparity	Ungleichheit
attribute (v)	zuschreiben
occupational choice	Berufswahl
inherent	hier: natürlich
overly	übermäßig
reveal (v)	offen legen
shameful	beschämend
pay gap	Gehaltsunterschiede
perpetuate (v)	(auf die gleiche Art) weiterführen
previous	vorhergehend
indication	hier: Grundlage; Hinweis
recruit (v)	(Personal) einstellen
earn a decent living (v)	nicht schlecht verdienen
strive (v)	kämpfen
update (v)	erneuern
in recognition of	in Anerkennung von
keen	engagiert; eifrig
be committed to sb. (v)	jmd. verpflichtet sein
require (v)	hinfordern
momentum	Schwung

Listening comprehension: Girls and IT

mechanical engineer	Maschinenbauingenieur
IT sector	Informationstechnologiesektor
head of recruitment	Personalchef
consultant	Berater

Fact Box: Some IT jobs

troubleshooting	Fehlerberatung
acquisition	Erwerb
storage	Speicherung
retrieval	hier: Wiederherstellung
data	Daten
workforce	Arbeitskräfte
confidentiality	hier: Sicherheit
reliability	Zuverlässigkeit
application	Anwendung
maintenance	Wartung
communication vehicles	Kommunikationsträger

Talkline: Job applicants

applicant	Stellenbewerber
branch	Zweigniederlassung
database	Datenbank
semiconductor	Halbleiter
representative	(Handels-)Vertreter
implement (v)	in die Realität umsetzen, einführen
recruit	neu Eingestellter
profitability	Wirtschaftlichkeit
triple (v)	verdreifachen
associate	Partner, Teilhaber
... years in a row	... Jahre in Serie
summa cum laude	summa cum laude, mit höchstem Lob (bestmöglicher Abschluss einer Promotion)
large scale	groß angelegt (Großprojekt)
solid state	Festkörper-
security clearance	Einstufung bei Sicherheitsüberprüfung

Unit 7 Aspects of language

Talking about accents: Rudolph Dirks

mischievous	boshaft
mellow (v)	abmildern

George Mikes: How to be an alien

gradually	allmählich
let alone	geschweige denn
consolation	Trost

average	durchschnittlich
slightly	leicht, etwas
mutter (v)	murmeln
be accustomed to (v)	gewöhnt sein an
impression	Eindruck
attempt	Versuch
air	Miene; Auftreten
polysyllabic	vielsilbig
amount (of)	Menge (an)
ancient	alt
interminably	unendlich
greengrocer	Obsthändler
porter	Pförtner
insurance	Versicherung
dustbin	Mülleimer
bully (v)	schikanieren
tiresome	ermüdend
contract	Vertrag
small print	Kleingedrucktes
allegiance	Treue
obedience	Gehorsam

Listening comprehension: "We don't like your sort here"

claim (v)	behaupten
affliction	Last
encounter (v)	begegnen
haulage firm	Fuhrunternehmen
scouser	Liverpooler
hospitable	gastfreundlich
misfortune	Pech
queue (up) (v)	sich in die Schlange stellen
booze	Schnaps
fag	(Zigaretten-)Kippe

The text generation

in defiance of sb./sth.	jmd./einer Sache zum Trotz
industry	Industrie, Branche
forecast	Vorhersage, Prognose
be around (v)	da sein, exisitieren
jump fivefold (v)	sich plötzlich auf das Fünffache erhöhen
billion	Milliarde
reckon that (v)	mit etwas rechnen, etwas glauben
adopt a technology (v)	eine Technologie übernehmen, einführen
sop up (v)	aufnehmen, aufsaugen
extra capacity	zusätzliche, überschüssige Kapazität
instantaneously	augenblicklich
subscriber	Abonnent, Kunde
be ambitious (v)	Ehrgeiz haben
accidental	zufällig
consultancy firm	Beratungsunternehmen
devotee	Anhänger, Fan, hingebungsvoller Nutzer
immediacy	Unmittelbarkeit
a hint of the subversive	ein Hauch von Subversivität (Umsturz)
overhear (v)	zufällig mithören
high school junior	Schüler in einer bestimmten Klassenstufe der High School
punch (v)	mit der Faust schlagen, hier: drücken
drive crazy (v)	verrückt machen
reception	Empfang
handy	griffbereit, nützlich
duck a challenge (v)	sich vor einer Herausforderung drücken
polling firm	Meinungsforschungsinstitut
habit	Gewohnheit
strain a budget (v)	ein Budget strapazieren
aficionado	Fan
edge	Rand, Kante
icon	Bildsymbol
acronym	Wort, zusammengesetzt aus den Anfangsbuchstaben einer Bezeichnung
shorthand	Steno
fox (v)	verwirren, verblüffen
uninitiated	uneingeweiht
glossary	Wörtersammlung, Glossar
evolve (v)	sich entwickeln
keep up (v)	mithalten
the whole point is	der Witz an der Sache ist, der Kern der Sache ist
compile sth. (v)	etwas zusammenstellen, kompilieren
initial	ursprünglich, anfänglich
sliver	(dünne) Scheibe
bandwidth	Bandbreite
whiz (v)	zischen

congested	verstopft
margin	Rand, hier: Gewinnmarge
smart phone	Telefon mit vielen Extras
fancy	kunstvoll, hoch gezüchtet
scramble (v)	vermischen, verschlüsseln, hier: hasten, rennen
still image	stehendes Bild

William Shakespeare: The Tempest

union	Vereinigung
wisdom	Weisheit
power	Macht
usurp (v)	widerrechtlich aneignen
banish (v)	verbannen
range	Reichweite
revenge	Rache
inherit (v)	erben
wicked	böse
fen	Sumpfland
stroke (v)	streicheln
barren	karg
fertile	fruchtbar
curse (v)	(ver-)fluchen
subject	Untertan
lodge (v)	beherbergen
violate (v)	verletzen
honour	Ehre
prevent (from) (v)	abhalten (von)
people (v)	bevölkern
abhorred	verabscheuungswürdig
pity (v)	bedauern
savage	Wilder
gabble (v)	brabbeln
vile	böse
shrug (v)	mit den Schultern zucken
neglect (v)	vernachlässigen
ache	Schmerz
roar (v)	brüllen
tremble (v)	(er-)zittern
obey (v)	gehorchen

Translation: English as a world language

some	hier: etwa
facilitate (v)	erleichtern, ermöglichen
deny (v)	verweigern; leugnen
access	Zugang
initial	ursprünglich
by-product	Nebenprodukt
subsequent	folgend; später;
gain	(Zu-)Gewinn
post-	nach-
achieve (v)	erreichen
indigenous	einheimisch

Talkline: The Dead Parrot

cash register	Registrierkasse
register a complaint (v)	eine Beschwerde beurkunden lassen (extrem förmlich)
purchase (v)	käuflich erwerben
remarkable	beneidenswert
plumage	Federkleid
stone dead	mausetot
cuttlefish	Tintenfisch
stunned	bewusstlos
deceased	verstorben
be shagged out (v)	fix und fertig sein
squawk (v)	krähen, kreischen
pine for (v)	sich sehnen nach
kip (v)	pennen
take the liberty of doing sth. (v)	sich die Freiheit nehmen, etw. zu tun
perch	Stange, Sitzstange
in the first place	von vorne herein, überhaupt
bar	Stange
voom	bums
demise (v)	ableben
pass on (v)	dahin scheiden
expire (v)	ablaufen, versterben
late	verstorben, ehemalig
stiff (noun)	Leiche
bereft of life	des Lebens beraubt
push up the daisies (v)	die Radieschen von unten anschauen
ring down the curtain (v)	den Vorhang herunterlassen
join the choir invisible (v)	sich dem Chor der Engel anschließen
complain till you are blue in the mouth (v)	sich den Mund fusselig reden

Unit 8 Human Relations

Talking about secrets

overhear (v)	belauschen
adulterous	ehebrecherisch
confide in (v)	sich anvertrauen
embarrassing	peinlich
pregnant	schwanger
spark off (v)	entfachen
spread (v)	aus-/verbreiten
spread	
spread	
gossip	Tratsch
snitch on so. (v)	klatschen
cash	Bargeld
skint	pleite
thrush	Pilzkrankheit, Soor
urge	Drang
zodiac	Tierkreiszeichen

Translation: Girlie magazines

clutch	hier: ein Haufen von
target	Ziel
charge	Anklage(-punkt)
role model	Rollenvorbild
surgeon	Chirurg
submissive	unterwürfig
sound	gesund
previous	früher

Mr Huxtable gets real mad

sitcom	(= situation comedy), Comedyserie
broadcast (v)	ausstrahlen
broadcast	
broadcast	
gynaecologist	Gynäkologe
lawyer	Rechtsanwalt
surgery (BE)	Arztpraxis
office (AE)	Arztpraxis
class	hier: der Kurs
bladder	Blase
infection	Entzündung
what's the point?	worauf willst du hinaus?
embarrassed	verlegen
stunned	erstaunt
address so. (v)	sich an jmd. wenden
be scared (v)	Angst haben
cockroach	Küchenschabe
straighten out (v)	klarstellen

Kerry Whyte: Teenage mother

(welfare) benefits	Sozialhilfe
peripheral	am Rande
housing scheme	Anlage von Sozialwohnungen
forlorn	verlassen, hier: einsam
deem (v)	halten für
consider (v)	betrachten, erwägen
articulate	redegewandt
housing queue	Vormerkliste einer Wohnungsbaugesellschaft
lack (v)	nicht haben
enlightened	hier: aufgeschlossen
contraception	Verhütung
grapple (v)	kämpfen, ringen
temper	Laune, hier: Beherrschung
break news (v)	eine Nachricht verkünden
abortion	Abtreibung
crèche	Kinderkrippe
facility	Einrichtung
cope with (v)	fertig werden mit
tidy (v)	saubermachen
flat	Wohnung
sacrifice (v)	opfern
penchant	Vorliebe
maintain (v)	aufrechterhalten
business administration	Betriebswirtschaft
focus on (v)	sich konzentrieren auf
appropriate	angemessen
pregnancy	Schwangerschaft

The ideal man

gym	Sporthalle
nickname	Spitzname
undies	Unterwäsche
dude	hier: cooler Typ

Listening comprehension: Ali Golding, Aboriginal woman activist?

modest	bescheiden
terrace (BE,AUS)	Reihenhaus
authorities	Behörden
snatch (v)	(etw.) schnappen

welfare officer	Beamter der Wohlfahrtsbehörde
stowaway	blinder Passagier
issue	Thema
extended family	Großfamilie
frequently	oft
migrant	Wanderarbeiter

A toxin of youth

a staple	hier: gängiges Mittel
without a peep on sth.	ohne die/das/den geringste(n)
involve (v)	hier: bedeuten
inject (v)	(ein-)spritzen
neurotoxin	Nervengift
butolism	Butolismus (Vergiftung durch Butolin)
erase (v)	verschwinden lassen
wrinkle	Gesichtsfalte, Fältchen
on the verge of	kurz vor, am Rande
approval	Zulassung
mainstream	hier: gängige Medikamente
spasmic disorders	krampfartige Zuckungen
blitz	hier: Werbefeldzug
predict (v)	voraussagen
based in	mit Sitz in
review (v)	überprüfen
submit (v)	vorlegen
at the very latest	allerspätestens
numb	gefühllos, taub
play havoc (v)	sich verheerend auswirken
facial expression	Mimik
placid	ruhig, gelassen
etch (v)	eingravieren, ätzen
diescolored	verfärbt
remnant	Überrest
diluted	verdünnt
paralyze (v)	lähmen
eradicate (v)	auslöschen, ausrotten
texture	Beschaffenheit
respiratory failure	Atemstillstand
lest	damit nicht
inadvertently (adv)	unbebasichtigt(-erweise)
mania	Wahn
array	ansehnliche Reihe, Ansammlung

Ann Beattie: Where you'll find me

tail	Schwanz
banister	Treppengeländer
torture (v)	quälen
peer (v)	schielen
soup ladle	Suppenkelle
loan (v)	leihen
reconcile (v)	sich versöhnen
instigate (v)	initiieren
tissues	Taschentücher
luminous	leuchtend
tubular	röhrenförmig
laundry	Wäscherei
scent	Geruch, Duft
exhaust (v)	erschöpfen
justify (v)	rechtfertigen
quit (a job) (v) **quit** **quit**	(eine Stelle) aufgeben
tension	(An-)Spannung
miscarriage	Fehlgeburt, Abgang
console (v)	trösten
curl up (v)	sich einrollen
stroke (v)	streicheln
fur	Fell
argument	Auseinandersetzung
D-con	Rattengift
birdseed	Vogelfutter
scatter (v)	verstreuen
pigeon	Taube
frantically	hier: schnell; rasend
approach (v)	sich nähern
resume (v)	wieder aufnehmen
slug (v)	schlagen
(traffic) light	Ampel
lower (v)	herunterlassen
donate (v)	spenden
matches	Streichhölzer
strike (v) **struck** **struck**	schlagen; hier: anzünden
employee	Angestellte(r)
sidewalk (AE) **BE: pavement**	Bürgersteig
toss (v)	werfen
lavender	lavendelfarben; Lavendel
quilted	abgesteppt
ruffly	Rüschen-
in-laws	Schwiegereltern

chest	Brust(-kasten)
humiliate (v)	erniedrigen
rude	grob
laundry hamper	Wäschekorb
wrestle (v)	ringen; raufen
register (v)	registrieren
suffuse (v)	erfüllen
sore	wund
landing	Treppenabsatz
skitter (v)	rutschen
diligently	eifrig
charitable	wohltätig
holler (v)	(laut) rufen
stick (v)	kleben
stuck	
stuck	
Goodwill box	entspr.: Altkleidercontainer
parking lot	Parkplatz
zoom by (v)	vorbeisausen
overturn (v)	(etw.) umstürzen
leash	Leine

Talkline: Talking about people

sketch	Skizze
armchair	Sessel
old people's home	Altersheim

Unit 9 Technology

Walk-out threat over phone mast

threaten (v)	drohen
walk out (v)	die Arbeit niederlegen, streiken
erect (v)	errichten
County Council	Rat/Verwaltung der Grafschaft
voice your concern (v)	seine Besorgnis ausdrücken
contravene your duty of care (v)	seine Sorgfaltspflicht verletzen
severely	hart, streng, hier: ernst
urge sb. to do sth. (v)	jmd. drängen etwas zu tun
resident	Bewohner
attend a meeting (v)	an einer Versammlung teilnehmen
despite + gerund	obwohl, trotz
widespread concern	verbreitete Sorge
substantiated evidence	schlüssiger, begründeter Beweis
suggest a link (v)	einen (Kausal-)Zusammenhang nahe legen
affect sth. (v)	sich auf etw. auswirken
(interim) injunction	einstweilige Verfügung

Scientists caution that ...

cancer	Krebs
investigate (v)	untersuchen, erforschen
conclude (v)	schlussfolgern
incidence	Vorkommenshäufigkeit
salivary gland	Speicheldrüse
central nervous system	Zentralnervensystem
senior	älter, ranghöher, leitend
caution (v)	warnen, zur Vorsicht mahnen
ailment	Krankheit, Gebrechen
migraines	Migräne
tinnitus	Tinnitus, Ohrenklingeln
harm (v)	schädigen
exposure	ausgesetzt sein
radiation	Strahlung
get in a froth about sth. (v)	über etw. vor Wut schäumen
maintain (v)	behaupten, an einer Meinung festhalten
colonic rupture	Darmriss

Bionic Youth

diverge (v)	abweichen
unlike	im Gegensatz zu
revolve (v)	sich drehen
mores	Moralkodex
wired	(computer-)vernetzt, hier: in einer Computerwelt lebend
stroke	Schlag(-anfall); hier: Tastendruck
acquire (v)	erwerben
pace	Schritt, Gangart; hier: Tempo
on the verge of	kurz vor, am Rande

dolt	Tölpel
plumb (v)	ergründen, ausloten
engrossed	vertieft
grow adept (v)	hier: immer geschickter werden
actually	eigentlich, tatsächlich
awkwardness	Peinlichkeit, Unbeholfenheit, Schwierigkeit
in relating to	im Zusammenhang mit
peers	Altersgenossen
gimmick	effekthaschende Spielerei,
loosely (adv)	grob gesagt
a broad range of	ein breites Spektrum von
ranging from	reichen von
benign	gutartig, gütig
violent	gewalttätig
current	Strom, Strömung; hier: Tendenz
messaging	Übermittlung von Nachrichten
reshape (v)	umgestalten, verändern
allure	Reiz, Anziehungskraft
impact	Auswirkung
punch	hier: Eindruck
device	Gerät, Vorrichtung
gadget	hier: Apparat
exposed	ausgesetzt
readily	bereitwillig
in response to stimuli	in einer Reaktion auf Reize
begin to suspect (v)	einen anfänglichen Verdacht haben
perception	Wahrnehmung
on average	im Durchschnitt
avid	begeistert, passioniert
intrigued	neugierig
score (v)	hier: abschneiden
inherent	innewohnend; hier: von Haus aus
sedate	gemächlich, ruhig
conclude (v)	folgern
enhance (v)	verbessern, erhöhen
compelling	zwingend, dominant
spatial	räumlich
extent	Ausmaß
appeal	Anziehung(-skraft)
gravity	Anziehungskraft (physik.)
process (v)	verarbeiten
hemisphere	hier: Hirnhälfte
right lobe	rechter Hirnlappen
fast track	hier: schnelle(r) Verbindung/Zugang
temper (v)	mäßigen, zügeln
correlate (v)	korrelieren, sich gegenseitig beeinflussen
poor	hier: dürftig, mangelhaft
poorness	Dürftigkeit, Mangelhaftigkeit
performance	Leistung
delinquency	Straffälligkeit
mundane	irdisch
foster (v)	begünstigen
pre-frontal coortex	Vorderhirnrinde
stifle (v)	unterdrücken
pattern-recognition	Wiedererkennen von Mustern
street smarts	Gewitztheit im Alltag
obsessed	besessen, verrückt nach
loner	Einzelgänger
retreat (v)	sich zurückziehen
fantasy world	Scheinwelt
attention deficit disorder	Aufmerksamkeitsstörung
youthful	jugendlich
overstimulation	Reizüberflutung
thrive (v)	gedeihen

Ebay thief reveals tricks of the trade

confession	Geständnis, Bekenntnis, Beichte
offend sb. (v)	jmd. beleidigen, kränken
scam	Betrügerei
notorious	berüchtigt
enforce the law (v)	das Gesetz durchsetzen
authority	Behörde
lure out of (v)	fortlocken von
straightforward	freimütig, einfach
impersonate sb. (v)	jmd. imitieren, sich ausgeben als
ample	reichlich
escrow	Treuhandverwaltung
legitimate	legitim
trace	Spur
erratic	sprunghaft, schwankend
score (v)	erzielen
tentative	zaghaft
embarrassed	verlegen
legitimacy	Legitimität
cautious	vorsichtig

far-fetched	weit hergeholt
primrose path	Weg des geringsten Widerstandes
initial	anfänglich
kinship	Verwandtschaft, Ähnlichkeit
conjure up (v)	herauf beschwören
prospective	voraussichtlich, zukünftig
wire transfer	telegrafische Überweisung
tipp off (v)	einen Hinweis geben
lop off (v)	abhacken, abhauen
asking price	der geforderte Preis
just like that	einfach so
moron	Idiot
veiled	verschleiert
eventually	schließlich, endlich

Talkline: Buying equipment for your college

shipping	Lieferung
approximately	ungefähr
rechargeable	wiederr aufladbar

Unit 10 Environment

Talking about environmental issues

environment	Umwelt
environmental	Umwelt-, die Umwelt betreffend
issue	hier: Problem
chlorofluorcarbons	Chlorfluorkohlenwasserstoff
cause	Ursache

Snowball Earth

plunge (v)	tauchen, stürzen
flight of fancy	Anflug von Fantasie
clemency	Gnade, Milde
arch (v)	hier: wölben
respite	Aufschub; Ruhepause
evaporate (v)	verdampfen, verdunsten
accumulate (v)	ansammeln, anhäufen
peak	Spitze
suffocate (v)	ersticken
hiccup	wörtl.: Schluckauf; hier: Problemchen
famine	Hungersnot
sharp edge	Abruchkante; Rand des Abgrunds
trigger (v)	lostreten, auslösen
sunspot	Sonnenfleck
exacerbate (v)	hier: verschlimmern, erschweren
enswathe (v)	einhüllen
collide (v)	zusammenstoßen
orbit (v)	umkreisen, umrunden
amplify (v)	verstärken
current (n)	Strom, Strömung
undies (coll.)	Unterwäsche

Listening comprehension: Global warming threatens Alaskan village

native	eingeboren
tribal gathering	Stammesversammlung
tribe	Stamm
skunk	Stinktier
squirrel	Eichhörnchen
caribou	Karibu
moose	Elch
apart from	außer, neben
forefathers	Vorväter
melt (v)	schmelzen

Car drivers How they can help reduce greenhouse gases now ...

environmentally -friendly	umweltfreundlich
greenhouse gases	Treibhausgase
chlorofluorcarbon (CFC)	Fluorchlorkohlenwasserstoff (FCKW)
refrigerator	Kühlschrank
air-conditioning	Klimaanlage
carbon dioxide	Kohlendioxyd
junk (v)	verschrotten
gas guzzler	Benzinschlucker
tire	Reifen
errand	Besorgung
cruise (v)	hier: fahren; kreuzen
carpool	Fahrgemeinschaft
anticipate (v)	vorhersehen
hamburger stand	Imbissbude
jackrabbit start	Kavalierstart
combine (v)	verbinden

idle	müßig, untätig
steady	gleichmäßig
air conditioner	Klimaanlage
lane	Spur
inflate (v)	aufpumpen, aufblasen

... and in the future: Anatomy of a supercar

elusive	hier: unerreichbar
automotive	Auto-; Kfz-
engineer	Ingenieur; hier: Bauer
advances	Fortschritte
fuel	Treibstoff
belch out (v)	ausstoßen
noxious	giftig
exhaust	Abgase
renewable	erneuerbar, regenerativ
gasoline	Benzin
emit (v)	ausstoßen
advocate	Befürworter
melt (v)	verschmelzen
air-friction	Luftwiderstand
smooth	glatt
wheel	Rad
brake (v)	bremsen
convert (v)	umwandeln
battery storage	Speicherung in der Batterie
composite	zusammengesetzt
peak	Spitze(n-)
liquid	flüssig
gaseous	gasförmig
narrow	schmal, eng
radials	Reifen

The cadillac that moos

moo (v)	muhen
sacred	heilig
hunter gatherers	Sammler und Jäger
set aside (v)	beiseite legen
cattle	Vieh
belly chamber	Wagen(-raum)
equation	Gleichung
doom	Untergang
growth curve	Wachstumskurve
docile	zahm
torture (v)	quälen
veal	Kalbfleisch
strain (v)	strapazieren
irretrievably	unwiederbringlich
polyunsaturated	mehrfachungesättigt
manure	Dung
converter	Umwandler
ratio	(Zahlen-)Verhältnis
livestock	Rinder
curdle (v)	hier: verderben; sauer werden
solely	nur, allein
subsidy	Subvention
surplus	Überschuss
wean (v)	entwöhnen
dairy companies	Molkereifirmen
dairy products	Molkereiprodukte
clog (v)	verstopfen
per capita	pro Kopf
poultry	Geflügel
tasty	appetitlich

Listening comprehension: Big Mac or Big Veg?

Lili

cabbage	Kohl
Brussels sprouts	Rosenkohl
lettuce	Salat
sneak (v)	hier: hineinschmuggeln
shopping trolley	Einkaufswagen
fuss	Aufregung, Theater
cross	verärgert
nick (v)	klauen, sich schnappen
slaughter (v)	schlachten
row	Auseinandersetzung
scraps	hier: Reste

Linda

vital	lebenswichtig
point-blank	glatt, direkt
shatter (v)	erschüttern
convenience food	Fertiggericht
devious	versteckt, auf Umweg
sulk (v)	schmollen
cavalier	freizügig, sorglos

Why do we still let this happen?

roughly	grob, hier: etwa
pitch	(Sport-)Platz
spill (v)	(sich er-)gießen
spilt	
spilt	
sheltered	geschützt
estuary	Mündung
populations	Populationen

coastline	Küste
outstandig	überragend
rescue	Hilfe
rescuer	Helfer, Retter
odd(-ly)	seltsam
anger	Ärger
despair	Verzweiflung
compassion	Mitgefühl
dizzy	schwindlig
process (v)	verarbeiten
sense	Sinn
velvet(-y)	samtig
ripple	kleine Welle
oil spill	Ölpest
unpleasant	unangenehm
sultry	schwül; feurig
mistake	falsch verstehen
mistook	
mistaken	
disgust	Ekel
fatigue	Müdigkeit
dweller	Bewohner
subtle	subtil, leise
stir (v)	rühren, bewegen
sermon	Predigt
scoter	Meerente
dot	Fleck
bob (v)	sich auf und ab bewegen
beak	Schnabel
volunteer	Freiwilliger
flap (v)	flattern
exhaustion	Erschöpfung
indicator	Anzeichen
prey	Beute(-tier)
canary	Kanarienvogel
go amiss (v)	falsch laufen
unilateral	einseitig (von einem Staat)
hull	hier: Schiffswand
cleanup	Säuberung
on stand-by	in Bereitschaft
be liable (v)	haftbar, verantwortlich
tug	Schleppschiff
shove (down) (v)	schubsen

Daphne du Maurier: The Birds

incident	Vorfall
seize (v)	ergreifen
drag (v)	ziehen
keep up (v)	mithalten, mitkommen
rook	Saatkrähe
crow	Krähe
compass point	Himmelsrichtung
jackdaw	Dohle
pick-a-back	Huckepack
slip (v)	rutschen
urgency	Dringlichkeit
gull	Möwe
give so. a lift (v)	
gave	jmd. mit dem Auto
given	mitnehmen
cheerful	fröhlich
rubicund	rot
take a crack at so.	jmd. Dampf machen
crouch (v)	sich kauern
tin	Kanister, Dose
be obliged (v)	verbunden sein
target	Ziel
jerk	Ruck
pickle (v)	einmachen
into the bargain	außerdem
barrel	hier: (Schrot-)Ladung
brute	Biest
scare so. (v)	jmd. Angst machen
all the same	trotzdem, jedenfalls
barn	Scheune
stile	(Zaun-)Übertritt
whirr	Flattern, Schlagen
swerve (v)	schlenkern
save	außer
wrist	Handgelenk
swoop (v)	herabstoßen
tear (v)	(zer-)reißen
tore	
torn	
matter	von Bedeutung sein
cling (v)	sich anklammern
clung	
clung	
rip (v)	aufreißen
bold	kühn
bruise (v)	verletzen
stumble (v)	stolpern
soar (v)	fliegen
threshold	Schwelle
thud	(das) Krachen

All dried up

sprawling	ausufernd, weit ausdehnend
reputation	ruf
subsidiary	hier: Tochterfirma

NGO = non government organisation	nichtstaatliche Hilfsorganisation
decay (v)	verfallen, verrotten
municipality	Magistrat, Stadtverwaltung
sanitation	Abwassersystem
inefficient	unwirtschaftlich
ineffective	ergebnislos
scar (v)	Wunden hinterlassen
streamroll (v)	überrollen, dominieren
expropriate (v)	an sich reißen, enteignen
cherry-pick (v)	die Rosinen herauspicken
hoodwink (v)	betrügen
fierve	hier: wütend
bribe (v)	bestechen
hard evidence	klarer Beweis
venture	Abeneuer; Unternehmen
indivate (v)	signalisieren
scarcity	Knappheit
water-borne	durch Wasser verbreitet
despondent	mutlos
thinktank	Expertenkommission
conclude (v)	Schlüsse ziehen
overhype (v)	übertreiben
have a say (v)	Einfluss haben
refocus (v)	neu konzentrieren
donor	Spender
allocation	(finanzielle) Bewilligung
come full circle (v)	hier: zur Vernunft kommen

Translation: As the world gets hotter, will Britain get colder?

interfere (with) (v)	hier: beeinflussen
plunge (into) (v)	stürzen
deliver (v)	liefern
latitude	Breitengrad
submarine (adj)	unter dem Meer, unterseeisch
creep towards (v)	kriechen (hin) zu; in Richtung
crept	
crept	
surface	Oberfläche
devastating	verheerend
implications	hier: Auswirkungen

Talkline: Councillors decide

city councillor	Stadtrat
pollution	Umweltverschmutzung
environment	Umwelt
pedestrianize an area (v)	einen Bereich zur Fußgänger zone machen
in the long run	langfristig
congestion charge	Innenstadtmaut
mount (v)	montieren
fare	Tarif, Fahrgeld

Unit 11 Politics

The Code of Conduct

sample (v)	vergleichen
resolution	Beschluss
the House	Unterhaus
seek (v)	versuchen
virtue of the oath	Kraft des Eides
allegiance	Loyalität
uphold (v)	etw. hoch halten
in accordance with	im Einklang mit
consituent	Bürger des Wahlkreises
obligation	Verpflichtung
performance	Ausübung
recommend (v)	empfehlen
reward	Belohnung
on merit	nach dem Verdienst
aqccountability	Verantwortung
submit (v)	sich unterwerfen
scrutiny	Überprüfung
base (v)	auf eine Grundlage stellen
cenduct o.s. (v)	sich benehmen
disrepute	Verachtung, schlechter Ruf
bribe	Bestechung
fee	Bezahlung
compensation	Gegenleistung
motion	Antrag
conscientious	gewissenhaft
advocate	hier: Fürsprecher
allowance	hier: finanzielle Zuwendung
in confidence	vertraulich

Sue Townsend: The Queen and I

uneasy	unruhig
wince (v)	zusammenzucken
silk rug	Seidenteppich

urge (v)	Bestreben, Verlangen
disdainful	verächtlich
nine time tables	Einmaleins
inspiration	Ermutigung
fag (coll.)	Zigarette
periwinkle	hellviolett (von der Blütenfarbe von Immergrün)
entitlement	Anrecht
staff	Personal
hand-picked	handverlesen
witness (v)	bezeugen
nip in (v)	(zu jmd.) hineinschauen, kurz besuchen
meals on wheels	Essen auf Rädern
enquire (v)	fragen
location	Ort
compile (a list) (v)	zusammenstellen
council house	Sozialwohnung
crack (v)	zusammenbrechen, den Widerstand aufgeben
fiddle with (v)	hier: herumspielen
gun	hier: Pistole
make an appearance (v)	einen Auftritt (in der Öffentlichkeit) haben
the bare essentials	das Allernotwendigste
shambles	Fiasko, Unheil
incredulous	ungläubig
ragged	zerfranst
citizenry	Bürgerschaft
reluctant	zögernd
concede (v)	zugeben
defeat	Niederlage
abdiacate (v)	abdanken
wave through (v)	durchwinken; auffordern, weiterzufahren
decline (v)	hier: ablehnen
Member for Kensington West	Unterhausabgeordneter für den Wahlkreis Kensington West
breakaway section	radikale Gruppierung
precede (v)	vorangehen (vor etwas oder jemandem)
disgruntled	unzufrieden, verärgert
subliminal	verschleiert
dismantle (v)	abbauen, entfernen
disperse (v)	vertreiben
discard (v)	wegwerfen
surly	unhöflich
uncoopeative	nicht sehr hilfsbereit
polling day	Wahltag
brainwash (v)	einer Gehirnwäsche unterziehen

"It's time to take the men-only sign off the White House door"

a challenge	Herausforderung
modest	bescheiden
recorder of deeds	Urkundenregistrator
incumbent	Amtsinhaber
be up for (v)	genannt sein für
nomination	Erkennung
tough	hier: hart, strikt
rabid	fanatisch
Neolithic age	Jungsteinzeit
gender	hier: Fähigkeit von Frauen
posting	Amtseinweisung
whopping	enorm, gigantisch
announcement	Ankündigung
heavy fanfare	laute Ankündigung
hail (v)	begrüßen
domestic	innere; innenpolitisch
budged deficit	Lücke im Staatshaushalt
credit (v)	jmd. etw. zutrauen
potential	Fähigkeit
vital	entscheidend
impact	Einfluss
crucial	entscheidend, wichtig
demographic	soziale Gruppe; demografischer Faktor
back (v)	unterstützen
hawk	Falke
hawkish	kriegstreibend
unilateral	einseitig
affirmative action	Unterstützung
prospect	Aussicht
anti-abortion	Abtreibungsgegner
in the wake of	im Anschluss an
a shoo-in	ein fast sicherer Kandidat
currency	Stärke, Kraft
bow out (v)	sich zurückziehen; aus einer Kampagne aussteigen
poll	Meinungsumfrage
upset (v)	beunruhigen, aufregen
siblings	hier: Geschwister
rare	selten
burst (v)	plötzlich auftauchen
burst	
burst	

laudable	zu loben, lobenswert
reputation	Ruf
lamentable	beklagenswert
be sworn-in (v)	den Amtseid leisten
be embroiled (v)	verwickelt sein in
poor	hier: schlecht
sloopy	schlampig
accounting	Buchführung
lacish	extravagant
mould	Muster
resort to (v)	wählen

Listening comprehension: Make politics relevant

Lib Dems	= Abkürzung für Liberal Democrats
mature	reif
store up (v)	speichern
turnout	Wahlbeteiligung
politicised	politisch interessiert, sensibilisiert
walkout	Demonstration
translate sth. into (v)	ummünzen in
bastion	Bollwerk
back (v)	unterstützen
body	hier: Institution
run (v)	hier: leiten
launch (v)	beginnen
consultative	beratend
join forces (v)	sich zusammenschließen
revitalise	Wiederbeleben
disengagement	Interesselosigkeit
stick with the habit (v)	eine Gewohnheit beibehalten
failing	untergehend
irrelevance	Bedeutungslosigkeit
recover (v)	hier: wiedergewinnen
heed (v)	befolgen

Talkline: UN Security Council

General Assembly	Vollversammlung
permanent members	ständige Mitglieder
Security Council	Weltsicherheitsrat
Charter	Charta, Satzung
recommendation	Empfehlung
carry out (v)	ausführen, durchführen
defeat	Niederlage
annexation	Annexion, (unfreiwilliger Anschluss)
subsequent	darauf folgend
occupation	Besetzung
victorious	siegreich
perpetual neutrality	immerwährende Neutralität
withdrawal	Rückzug
ingrained	tief verwurzelt
prosperous	blühend
European Monetary Union	Europäische Währungsunion
dispute	Streit
merger	Verschmelzung
incursion	eindringen
secular	nicht von Religion bestimmt
overpopulation	Überbevölkerung
environmental degradation	Verfall der Umwelt
poverty	Armut
rugged	zerklüftet
cede (v)	nachgeben, herausgeben
sovereignty	Souveränität, Oberhoheit
terminus	Ende, Mündung
maritime boundary delimitation	Grenzziehung im Meergebiet
in actuality	in Wirklichkeit
strongman	Muskelmann
inconclusive	ohne klares Ergebnis
expel (v)	verteiben
scrap (v)	verschrotten
verification inspection	Überprüfung
compliance	Einhaltung
ouster	Entlassung, Entfernung, Vertreibung
restore (v)	wieder einrichten
facilitate (v)	erleichtern
persist (v)	weiterbestehen
sole	einzig
accede (v)	zustimmen
fractured	zerbrochen, aufgesplittert
dislodge (v)	entfernen
mar (v)	entstellen, beeinträchtigen
fraud	Betrug
step down (v)	zurücktreten
assume the presidency (v)	die Präsidentschaft übernehmen

Unit 12 Third World

The killing of a children's rights activist

suspicious	verdächtig
judicial inquiry	gerichtliche Untersuchung
bondage	Sklaverei
loan	Darlehen
chain (v)	anketten
loom	Webstuhl
interest rate	Zins (-satz)
campaign (v)	sich engagieren
testify (v)	aussagen
award (v)	verleihen
mature	reif
malnourished	unterernährt
collusion	geheime Absprache
try (v)	hier: vor Gericht stellen
acquit (v)	freisprechen
murder	Mord
unsolved	ungelöst

Listening comprehension: Nine stories about child labour

child labour	Kinderarbeit
attend school (v)	in die Schule gehen
unrestricted	unbeschränkt
domestic work	Hausarbeit
hazardous (to)	gefährlich (für)
brick	Ziegelstein
(to do household) chores	Arbeit(en), Hausarbeit
apprenticeship	Lehre, berufliche Ausbildung
practical training	Praktikum
interfere (with) (v)	hier: stören
volunteer work	freiwillige, ehrenamtliche Arbeit
debts	Schulden
injure (v)	verletzen

Lynn/Jay: Yes, Minister

withhold sth. (v) from so.	etw. vor jmd. zurückhalten
predecessor	Vorgänger
civil servant (UK)	Beamter
initially	ursprünglich
stumble (v)	stolpern
disclose sth. to sb. (v)	jmd. etwas enthüllen
ratify a (v) contract	einen Vertrag ratifizieren, bestätigen
embassy	Botschaft
reception	Empfang
hip flask	Flachmann
guff	Unsinn, Mumpitz
incident	Zwischenfall
tentative	vorläufig, zaghaft
emergency	Notfall
booze	Besäufnis; alkoholisches Getränk
liven up (v)	beleben
muse (v)	grübeln, sinnieren
jar	Topf, Glas
esteem	Hochschätzung
teetotal	alkoholfrei
hangover	Kater (nach Alkoholgenuss)
hazy	dunstig, verschwommen
start with (v)	um damit anzufangen, erst einmal
commemorate (v)	gedenken
transpire (v)	ausdünsten, durchsickern, sich herausstellen
apparently	offensichtlich
bogged down	fest sitzen, nicht weiter-kommen
imaginative	phantasievoll
dimple	Grübchen
nod (v)	nicken
cipher machine	Chiffriermaschine
bugged	verwanzt
strain	Anstrengung, Belastung
cover up (v)	vertuschen
honorary	ehrenhalber
refill	Nachfüllung
valuable	wertvoll
valuation	Bewertung, Schätzung
flatter sb. (v)	jmd. schmeicheln
irresistible	unwiderstehlich
regrettably	bedauerlicher Weise
errand	Botengang
overhear sb. (v)	jmd. abhören, zufällig mithören
hospitable	gastfreundlich
collect (v)	abholen

courtesy	Höflichkeit
spot on	genau richtig
sidle up to sb. (v)	sich zu jmd. schleichen
edge away (v)	sich davon stehlen
be edged in sb's memory (v)	sich in jmd. Gedächtnis eingeprägt haben
connoisseur	Kenner
share	Anteil
keep your mouth shut (v)	den Mund halten
clumsy	schwerfällig
have a word with sb. (v)	mit jdm. sprechen
nonplus (v)	verblüffen
reveal (v)	enthüllen
foolproof	narrensicher
gleeful	freudig, schadenfroh
blurt out sth. (v)	mit etwas herausplatzen
bribery	Bestechung
waver (v)	wanken
reprimand	Tadel
juncture	kritischer Zeitpunkt

Talkline: Budget Ministry for Economic Cooperation

scrutiny	genaue Prüfung
Parliamentary State Secretary	parlamentarischer Staatssekretär
subsidy	Subvention
devalue ⟷ revalue (v)	abwerten ⟷ aufwerten
produce	landwirtschaftliche Produkte
livelihood	Lebensunterhalt
self-determination	Selbstbestimmung
abortion	Abtreibung
annual	jährlich
donor	Geber
loan	Darlehen
desertification	Vordringen der Wüste
arable	landwirtschaftlich nutzbar
in the long term/ in the long run	langfristig
take for granted (v)	für selbstverständlich halten
governing body	Verwaltungsrat, Kuratorium

Bildquellenverzeichnis:
Zeichnungen: Steffie Becker, Bonn; Fotos: MEV, Augsburg; Geographical – The Magazine

Leider konnten nicht alle Rechteinhaber ermittelt werden. Bitte melden Sie sich deshalb im Verlag, wenn wir Abbildungen von Ihnen in diesem Schulbuch veröffentlicht haben.

